THE WAY OF THE WORLD

The *Bildungsroman* in European Culture

New Edition

FRANCO MORETTI

Translated by Albert Sbragia

VERSO

London • New York

First published in English by Verso 1987
© Franco Moretti 1987
This new edition first published by Verso 2000
© Franco Moretti 2000

Verso
UK: 6 Meard Street, London W1V 3HR
USA: 180 Varick Street, New York, NY 10014–4606

Verso is the imprint of New Left Books

ISBN: 978-1-85984-298-0

British Library Cataloguing in Publication Data
A catalogue record for this book is available from the British Library

Library of Congress Cataloging-in-Publication Data
A catalog record for this book is available from the Library of Congress

Typeset by M Rules
Printed by Biddles Ltd, Guildford and King's Lynn

Contents

Preface

Twenty Years Later

The idea for this book arose in the summer of 1979; the research
was done from 1979 to 1984, and the writing between 1981 and
1985. Since then, the cultural atmosphere has significantly
changed, as has literary history, and also, more modestly, my own
work. The pages that follow address some of these novelties,
mixing retrospective reflection, bibliographic updating, and a few
new ideas. Take them as so many notes written on the margin of
The Way of the World; as a sort of bridge between the book I
wrote then, and the one I would perhaps write today.

The novel as a calm passion. In the fourth chapter of the second
book of *Wilhelm Meister's Apprenticeship Years* — the archetype
of the European *Bildungsroman*, written in the final years of
the nineteenth century — Wilhelm has just arrived in a small
provincial town, where he decides to stop for a few days. He
walks into the courtyard of his inn, looks at some workers erecting
a platform, and buys a bunch of flowers from a girl. A woman
opens a window on the other side of the street; she seems to be
looking at Wilhelm, and after a while sends a boy to ask for the
flowers. Wilhelm gives him the flowers and begins to walk up the
stairs, where he crosses paths with 'a young creature running
down in a hurry'. He asks who she is, but she looks askance and
runs away without saying a word. A floor up, two men are
fencing; Wilhelm stops to look, one of them gives him a foil, they
fence. Then they begin to talk, but are soon interrupted by the
acrobats announcing their show for the evening.

In the Italian paperback where I first read *Wilhelm Meister*, these two pages have remained completely blank: no marks, no notes, nothing. I must have glided by absent-minded, waiting for those legendary scenes — the *Hamlet* discussion, the letter on the aristocrat and the bourgeois, Mignon's death — where I expected to discover the novel's true meaning. The rest was background, interlude: a grey universe, where Wilhelm's projects were being constantly deflected, and the sense of the narrative seemed always on the brink of disappearing. 'Prose of the world', said Hegel: exactly. As in Edgar Reisz's great collective *Bildungs-film* (*Die zweite Heimat*, The second homeland), with its daily life always filmed in a strangely opaque black and white.

It was only later, while writing *The Way of the World*, that my perspective shifted, and I realized that the many episodes like the one I have just described, far from being obstacles to the establishment of the novel's meaning, were rather the *specific medium* of its manifestation. The theatre, Mignon, the Beautiful Soul, the masonic society — all great ideas, of course. But Goethe's unique contribution to the 'bourgeois half millennium' (Thomas Mann) lies elsewhere: in having 'activated' — made narratively interesting — the bland rhythm of everyday reality. Like the hundred encounters that unfold without hurry in the twenty-six hours of *Heimat*, Goethe's narrative 'fillers' are always more than that: they are chances, opportunities that begin to take shape. On that first day at the inn, Wilhelm does not 'recognize' Mignon (nor Philine, nor Laertes), but he has met them nonetheless. *Something* has happened.

Not much? Maybe; but it reminds me of Weber's capitalist, who prefers the limited (but certain) profit of regular trade over the unpredictable seductions of economic adventure. The same happens in *Wilhelm Meister*: whose countless down-to-earth episodes usually have a limited interest, but are never without *some* interest. And so, to paraphrase another great historian of the bourgeois temperament, the reading of novels becomes — for the first time in history — a 'calm passion'.

I lost my subjectivity but found a world, said Goethe of his Italian journey, and he could be speaking of Austen, Balzac, Keller, Eliot: life has offered less than expected, true, but in another sense it has also offered more — all the unforeseeable chances that have opened along the way. It's the symbolic miracle, or mirage perhaps, of the *Bildungsroman* between 1789 and 1848: a beautiful balance between the constraints of modern socialization, and its benefits: between the meaning which will be lost in the prose of the world, and the meaning which will be found. Then, after the mid-century earthquake, the atmosphere darkens, and a gloomy downward trajectory begins.[1] It will end — let us say: around 1914 — in the painful traumas of *Törless*, *America*, and the young Stephen Dedalus.

'*Mastering of historical time.*' The everyday that becomes interesting. Strange idea. 'Horses, servants, old women, peasants blowing smoke from cutty pipes' — writes Hegel about Dutch painting in the *Aesthetics* — 'the glitter of wine in a transparent glass, chaps in dirty jackets playing with old cards: these and hundred of other things... that we scarcely bother about in our daily lives'.[2] But why on earth should one paint things about which we scarcely bother? With words that seem stolen from the ageing Faust, here is Hegel's response:

> If we look at it more closely, the proper subject-matter of these paintings is not so common [*gemein*] as is usually supposed... The Dutch have themselves made the greatest part of the land on which they dwell and live, and have to continually defend and maintain it against the storms of the sea. By resolution, endurance, and courage, burghers and peasants threw off the Spanish dominion of Philip II... This citizenship, this love of enterprise, in small things as in great, in their own land as on the high seas, this painstaking as well as clean and neat well-being, this joy and exuberance in their own sense that, for all this, they have their own activity to thank — all this is what constitutes the general content of their pictures. But this is not a common content...[3]

What a page. 'If we look at it more closely', the Dutch everyday transforms itself, loses its everydayness, and turns into a milestone of World History — the beginning of Modernity, in fact. It's the same 'elevation' of the everyday that we encounter in Bakhtin's view of the *Bildungsroman* as a 'mastering of historical time': in these novels, he writes, 'man emerges along with the world and he reflects the historical emergence of the world itself... the image of the emerging man begins to surmount its private nature (within certain limits, of course) and enters into a completely new, spatial sphere of historical existence...'[4]

The new sphere of historical existence; the mastering of historical time... True, but only if those words mean: knowing how to keep history *at a safe distance*, separating the destiny of the individual from the great collective waves of the nineteenth century. The French revolution, the Napoleonic wars, the industrial take-off, 1830, Chartism, 1848: in the *Bildungsroman* (and indeed in the novel as a whole), European history is hardly the 'sphere' of the action, but merely its horizon (usually, quite a distant one). Even in decades when public life has become explosive and passionate, I mean, novels opt resolutely for the *private* sphere (which is also, of course, the scene of their reading), with its stubborn, 'realistic' capacity to survive the tempests of social conflict. For this characteristic withdrawal from political life, the novel is really an aspect of the *liberté des modernes*, as Constant memorably defined it: nothing less than that — but also nothing more.

Between two classes. 'On the border between two epochs, and at the transition point from one to the other', as Bakhtin puts it, the *Bildungsroman* is also situated on the border between two social classes, and at the transition point between them: between bourgeoisie and aristocracy. It's the story of the young merchant Wilhelm Meister, adopted by a small group of enlightened landowners, and of Elizabeth Bennet's journey from Cheapside to Pemberley; of Stendhal's Julien (from the provincial *notables* to the Marquis de la Mole), and Balzac's Lucien (Lucien Chardon... or Lucien de Rubempré?); of *Jane Eyre* (the governess and the landowner), and in a slightly more oblique way of several characters in Dickens and Eliot. It's only with *Sentimental Education* that this 'doubling' of the ruling class disappears — and it may be a coincidence, but Flaubert's novel also marks the end of the great European *Bildungsroman*.

How should one account for such double presence, then? The thesis presented in the first chapter of this book still strikes me as plausible: the encounter, and in fact the 'marriage' of the two classes is a way to heal the rupture that had generated (or so it seemed) the French revolution, and to imagine a continuity between the old and the new regime. It is the 'attempt at compromise' which Lukács's *Theory of the Novel* sees as the core of novelistic structure. And indeed, around 1800, the compromise makes perfect sense: the bourgeois who wants to ennoble himself — this typical target of seventeenth- and eighteenth-century comedy — finally has a chance to realize his ambitions. But that the compromise should still hold even after the take-off of capitalism makes less sense. And yet, in novel after novel, the protagonist of the *Bildungsroman*, whose social origin is often in what German historians call *Bildungsbürgertum*, or bourgeoisie of culture, does not direct his steps towards the *Besitzbürgertum*, or bourgeoisie of property, but rather — think of the frequent episode of the hero's 'farewell to his bourgeois friend' — towards an aristocratic universe with which it feels a far deeper kinship.[5]

Back then, I was very surprised by this abandonment of the bourgeois universe, which so clearly contradicted the idea of the *Bildungsroman* as the great bourgeois form. Today, I would try to explain it as follows. From Weber's puritan to Hirschmann's merchant, we have wonderful studies of the bourgeois work ethic, and of the anthropological revolution it entailed. Outside of work, however, things are not equally clear, and many bourgeois groups (especially the young bourgeois) seem to have entrusted their identity to forms of socialization — journeys, conversation, music, dance, humanistic culture — *which had been already developed within the aristocratic universe*. And which, as a consequence, rather than emphasizing the novelty of the bourgeois figure, largely assimilated him to the aristocratic type.[6]

Revolutionary conjuncture aside, then, the encounter of bourgeois and aristocrat in these novels has a long-term explanation: the nineteenth-century bourgeoisie refunctionalized some aspects of the aristocratic way of life for its own cultural formation — and the *Bildungsroman*, for its part, was the symbolic form which most thoroughly reflected on this state of affairs. One senses in these novels a recurring question — outside of work, what is the bourgeois? what does he do? how does he live? — and an answer that returns again and again: it's a strange mix of the old and the new, with a shifting, piecemeal identity. Between question and answer unfolds the brief trajectory of modern youth: this experimental season of bourgeois existence, which explores the possible compromises between the two social models.

'The modern vice of unrest'. Bourgeoisie, aristocracy. And the *Bildungsroman* of the others — women, workers, African-Americans...? The simplest reply to this frequently posed objection would point out how the spatio-temporal coordinates of my study (European culture between the French revolution and the triumph of capitalism) inevitably excluded later texts. But a deeper reason for those exclusions lies in the very elements that characterize the *Bildungsroman* as a form: wide cultural formation, professional mobility, full social freedom — for a long time, the west European middle-class man held a virtual monopoly on these, which made him a sort of structural *sine qua non* of the genre. Without him, and without the social privileges he

enjoyed, the *Bildungsroman* was difficult to write, because it was difficult to imagine.[7]

The mistake of my book, then, is not that of having 'denied' the *Bildungsroman* to this or that human group, as if it were health coverage (which indeed should never be denied anybody); it consists rather in never fully explaining why this form was so deeply entwined with one social class, one region of the world, one sex. Just think of how social mobility, which is such an essential trait of the *Bildungsroman*, literally vanishes in the presence of manual labourers: it worked within the bourgeois sphere, or between the new and the old ruling class, but below the middle class — in *Jude the Obscure*, or *Martin Eden*, or *Sons and Lovers* — it seems to defy narrative imagination.

Let me be clear, this is not just a matter of imagination, but of reality. 'Unlike their bourgeois counterparts, young workers don't enjoy that period of ease and self-formation that makes individual sociability and autonomous forms of expression possible', writes Michelle Perrot in an interesting comparative essay: 'the early entry in the workplace drains all of their energies, while depriving them of the rights enjoyed by adults.'[8] A short, oppressive youth — and even more so for the heroes of these novels, who are all struggling against the curse of manual labour. In workers' autobiographies 'discipline is mentioned much more often than revolt', writes Perrot,[9] and one remembers the relentless repression of pleasure that poverty forces on to Jude and the others: the nights at their desks, studying, fighting off sleep; the erotic frustrations; hunger, loneliness, cold...

A youth *without the right to dream*: this is what makes the working-class *Bildungsroman* incomparable to *Wilhelm Meister* or *Père Goriot*. In a sense, Hardy's cruel sentence says it best: Goethe's 'aspirations', Stendhal's 'ambition', Balzac's 'illusions', Dickens's 'expectations', Eliot's 'yearnings' — all these emotions are here rewritten as the stark double negative of the 'modern vice of unrest'. And even when sublimated in culture and art, self-repression only ends in another, truly definitive exclusion: no longer at home among his old fellow workers, but never accepted by the new bourgeois milieu, the hero suddenly sees the impossibility of his position ('And at the instant he knew, he ceased to know', reads the last sentence of Jack London's novel) — and drowns.

Encounter with Julien Sorel. And politics? Not much, in the *Bildungsroman*. The only true exception is *The Red and the Black*;

who knows, perhaps because Julien's social leap is so extreme that the regular rhythm of bourgeois prose would never accomplish it, and Stendhal needs politics as a special channel for social mobility (and after all, for his generation the archetypal 'career open to talent' had been the politico-military venture of the *Grande Armée*).

Stendhal's politics, of course, is far from linear: Julien's Jacobin 'sense of duty' is often silly, and just as often subordinated to his own private interest, or pleasure. And yet, around 1980 it was precisely this mix of radicalism and ambiguity that made me see *The Red and the Black* as the centre of *The Way of the World*; perhaps not the best chapter, I really can't say, but certainly the one which had most inspired both me and my students in Salerno (and the only one to be published by itself, in *Quaderni Piacentini*, which was the theoretical journal of the Italian new left). But today, it's always the most difficult book to teach; I do it out of a vague sense of duty, and am always uneasy about it. Perhaps because, at fifty, the idea of going to the guillotine to avoid a couple of compromises rings very strange; but then again, those who are Julien's age don't like the book any better. In ten years in New York, only one of them was really struck by it — an African-American student named Paul Young, who launched into a splendid analogy between the European Restoration and the American Reconstruction (and proceeded to compare Julien to the Black Panthers).

To fully evoke the atmosphere of *The Red and the Black*, Paul was the most intelligent student in the class — and had no money. He stayed in school by working in the kitchen of a nearby church, he told me at the end of the course, and couldn't write the second paper by the appointed date, but really needed the grade. Feeling very much like the Marquis de la Mole, I told him I'd give him his A anyway, and he could turn the paper in at the end of summer. OK? OK. And he vanished. And I wonder if that name — Paul *Young*, for heaven's sake — was really his own... Anyway, bravo.

Bricolage, compromise. Looking back at the writing of *The Way of the World*, the relationship between form and ideology is probably where the final product is most distant from my initial intentions. In the late seventies, my ideas on the matter — drawn from Della Volpe's aesthetics, the Frankfurt school, and early structuralism — were rather straightforward. First, the specific objects of literary criticism are the techniques, the devices, the forms of literature (you want to understand Balzac? begin by figuring out how the plot of the *Comédie* works). But those forms are in their turn historical constructs, that fully participate in social and cultural conflict (Balzac's narrative logic transforms the reality of modern capitalism into a fascinating scenario).

The most profoundly social aspect of literature is its form, as the young Lukács once insolently put it (before he grew up, and forgot). Fine. But as I went on with my work, I kept running into a kind of evidence that I didn't know how to explain. To begin with, these novels' morphology was a very composite one: the various formal elements 'disagreed' among themselves all the time (Balzac's plot, for instance, flatly contradicted his narrative style), so that texts seemed to hold themselves together only by a tortuous process of *bricolage*. On the ideological plane, another oddity: the *Bildungsroman* seemed to have its own private ideology, that had almost nothing in common with what one knew from the history of ideas or of political theories. There was always something strange, something 'messy', in these novels, and finally I understood why: they were not trying to shape consistent worldviews, but rather *compromises among distinct worldviews* — like Balzac's conservative-progressive hybrid, or the absurd blend of intolerance and justice of the English novel.[10]

Morphological *bricolage* and ideological compromise, of course, have a lot in common: they are both adjustments: pragmatic, contingent, imperfect (although usually well-functioning). But... how was I to conceptualize imperfection? 'Recognizing' it is already hard (one tends to glide over it, or pretend that texts work much better than they actually do); even more difficult is acknowledging its frequency in the history of culture; and as for explaining theoretically why things should function this way — the introduction to *The Way of the World* addresses the question, sure, but offers only the beginning of an answer. Then, fortunately, I encountered a very elegant explanation of morphological *bricolage* in evolutionary theory (to which I devoted the only article I wrote in the five years after *The Way of the World*.)[11]

Once I found the conceptual model, the morphology of *bricolage* became the backbone of my next book (*Modern Epic*, finished in 1994). But the other half of the problem, the ideological one, remained largely unresolved: partly because of the metaphysical backlash brought about by deconstruction, and partly because intellectual history had never produced a theory of ideological compromise comparable to the Darwinian account of morphological *bricolage*. There were some splendid case studies — Bakhtin's Rabelais, Ginzburg's Menocchio, Blumenberg's *Legitimacy of the Modern Age*, French *histoire des mentalités...* — but no genuine *conceptualization* of the issue. Francesco Orlando had constructed a very persuasive theory of literature as a 'compromise formation', true, but it was a strictly literary theory, which could not be applied *tel quel* to the history of culture. And so, for one reason or another, the problematic of the ideological compromise, which seemed designed to bring together intellectual historians and literary historians, was lost along the way.

And then, around 1980, a new type of political criticism began to develop, fuelled by the archival findings of new historicism, and the enlargement of the literary field induced by post-colonial studies. So fresh and exciting were these new objects of study, that a whole generation began to concentrate directly on historical materials, shifting the critical focus from the analysis of form to that of content (to use those venerable, but still useful terms). Whether the shift constituted a genuine methodological advance over the 'formalist' version of political criticism, of course, remains to be seen. I personally doubt it: formal patterns are what literature uses in order to master historical reality, and to reshape its materials in the chosen ideological key: if form is disregarded, not only do we lose the complexity (and therefore the interest) of the whole process — we miss its strictly *political* significance too. Or so it seems.

This, however, is not the right place to settle the dispute. I mentioned the transformations of political criticism because they certainly identify this book, for better or worse, with a different intellectual moment: closer in time, and even more in spirit, to the 1960s than to the 1990s.

So be it. After all, this was my youth.

Acknowledgements

I would like to thank the many people who have discussed with me the pages that follow, and especially Perry Anderson, Pierluigi Battista, Paola Colaiacomo, D.A. Miller, and Niccolò Zapponi who have all been generous enough to read and criticize the entire manuscript. Thanks also to the students of the University of Salerno who between 1979 and 1983 were the patient, interested and stimulating witnesses to the genesis of this study. And thanks finally (however strange it may sound, in a text that so often applauds separation from the family) to my parents, my brother and my sister for the affection and happiness of all these years.

As for more bureaucratic matters, the novels examined here are generally cited as follows: title (at times abbreviated) in italics, roman numeral to indicate part or volume (when there is one), arabic numeral or title within quotation marks to indicate chapter or strophe. Translations from other languages are generally from current English-language editions, but have often been modified for reasons of fidelity to the original. (One more thanks, to Antonella d'Amelia, without whom I never would have been able to verify the Russian texts.) A more or less definitive version of the second chapter appeared (in Italian) in *Quaderni Piacentini*, 10, 1983; and part of the first chapter appeared under the title of 'The Comfort of Civilization' in *Representations*, 12, 1985. The Appendix was first published, in only slightly modified form, in *Studies in Historical Change*, Ralph Cohen, ed., University Press of Virginia 1992. Finally, research funds granted from the Italian Ministry for Public Education have contributed to the publication of this volume.

1

The *Bildungsroman* as Symbolic Form

Nothing I had, and yet profusion:
The lust for truth, the pleasure in illusion.
Give back the passions unabated,
That deepest joy, alive with pain,
Love's power and the strength of hatred,
Give back my youth to me again. (Goethe, *Faust*.)

Achilles, Hector, Ulysses: the hero of the classical epic is a mature man, an adult. Aeneas, carrying away a father by now too old, and a son still too young, is the perfect embodiment of the symbolic relevance of the 'middle' stage of life. This paradigm will last a long time (*'Nel mezzo del cammin di nostra vita...'*), but with the first enigmatic hero of modern times, it falls apart. According to the text, Hamlet is thirty years old: far from young by Renaissance standards. But *our* culture, in choosing Hamlet as its first symbolic hero, has 'forgotten' his age, or rather has had to alter it, and picture the Prince of Denmark as a young man.

The decisive thrust in this sense was made by Goethe; and it takes shape, symptomatically, precisely in the work that codifies the new paradigm and sees *youth* as the most meaningful part of life: *Wilhelm Meister*. This novel marks simultaneously the birth of the *Bildungsroman* (the form which will dominate or, more precisely, make possible the Golden Century of Western narrative)[1], and of a new hero: Wilhelm Meister, followed by Elizabeth Bennet and Julien Sorel, Rastignac and Frédéric Moreau and Bel-Ami, Waverley and David Copperfield, Renzo Tramaglino, Eugene Onegin, Bazarov, Dorothea Brooke ...

3

Youth is both a necessary and sufficient definition of these heroes. Aeschylus's Orestes was also young, but his youth was incidental and subordinate to other much more meaningful characteristics — such as being the son of Agamemnon, for instance. But at the end of the eighteenth century the priorities are reversed, and what makes Wilhelm Meister and his successors representative and interesting is, to a large extent, youth as such. Youth, or rather the European novel's numerous versions of youth, becomes for our modern culture the age which holds the 'meaning of life': it is the first gift Mephisto offers Faust. In this study I hope to illuminate the causes, features and consequences of this symbolic shift.

I

In 'stable communities', that is in status or 'traditional' societies, writes Karl Mannheim, ' "Being Young" is a question of biological differentiation'.[2] Here, to be young simply means not yet being an adult. Each individual's youth faithfully repeats that of his forebears, introducing him to a role that lives on unchanged: it is a 'pre-scribed' youth, which, to quote Mannheim again, knows no 'entelechy'. It has no culture that distinguishes it and emphasizes its worth. It is, we might say, an 'invisible' and 'insignificant' youth.

But when status society starts to collapse, the countryside is abandoned for the city, and the world of work changes at an incredible and incessant pace, the colourless and uneventful socialization of 'old' youth becomes increasingly implausible: it becomes a *problem*, one that makes youth itself problematic. Already in Meister's case, 'apprenticeship' is no longer the slow and predictable progress towards one's father's work, but rather an uncertain exploration of social space, which the nineteenth century — through travel and adventure, wandering and getting lost, 'Bohême' and 'parvenir' — will underline countless times. It is a necessary exploration: in dismantling the continuity between generations, as is well known, the new and destabilizing forces of capitalism impose a hitherto unknown *mobility*. But it is also a yearned for exploration, since the selfsame process gives rise to unexpected hopes, thereby generating an *interiority* not only fuller than before, but also — as Hegel clearly saw, even though he deplored it — perennially dissatisfied and restless.

Mobility and interiority. Modern youth, to be sure, is many

other things as well: the growing influence of education, the strengthening of bonds within generations, a new relationship with nature, youth's 'spiritualization' — these features are just as important in its 'real' development. Yet the *Bildungsroman* discards them as irrelevant, abstracting from 'real' youth a 'symbolic' one, epitomized, we have said, in mobility and interiority.[3] Why this choice?

Because, I think, at the turn of the eighteenth century much more than just a rethinking of youth was at stake. Virtually without notice, in the dreams and nightmares of the so called 'double revolution', Europe plunges into modernity, but without possessing a *culture* of modernity. If youth, therefore, achieves its symbolic centrality, and the 'great narrative' of the *Bildungsroman* comes into being, this is because Europe has to attach a meaning, not so much to youth, as to *modernity*.

The *Bildungsroman* as the 'symbolic form' of modernity: for Cassirer, and Panofsky, through such a form 'a particular spiritual content [here, a specific image of modernity] is connected to a specific material sign [here, youth] and intimately identified with it'.[4] 'A specific image of modernity': the image conveyed precisely by the 'youthful' attributes of mobility and inner restlessness. Modernity as a bewitching and risky process full of 'great expectations' and 'lost illusions'. Modernity as — in Marx's words — a 'permanent revolution' that perceives the experience piled up in tradition as a useless dead-weight, and therefore can no longer feel represented by maturity, and still less by old age.

In this first respect youth is 'chosen' as the new epoch's 'specific material sign', and it is chosen over the multitude of other possible signs, because of its ability to *accentuate* modernity's dynamism and instability.[5] Youth is, so to speak, modernity's 'essence', the sign of a world that seeks its meaning in the *future* rather than in the past. And, to be sure, it was impossible to cope with the times without acknowledging their revolutionary impetus: a symbolic form incapable of doing so would have been perfectly *useless*. But if it had been able to do *only this*, on the other hand, it would have run the risk of *destroying itself as form* — precisely what happened, according to a long-standing critical tradition, to Goethe's other great attempt at representing modernity: *Faust*. If, in other words, inner dissatisfaction and mobility make novelistic youth 'symbolic' of modernity, they also force it to share in the 'formlessness' of the new epoch, in its protean elusiveness. To become a 'form', youth must be endowed with a very different, almost opposite feature to those already mentioned: the very simple and slightly philistine notion that youth 'does not last forever'. Youth is brief, or at any rate circumscribed, and this enables, or rather *forces* the *a priori* establishment of a formal constraint on the portrayal of modernity. Only by curbing its intrinsically boundless dynamism, only by agreeing to betray to a certain extent its very essence, only thus, it seems, can modernity be *represented*. Only thus, we may add, can it be 'made human'; can it become an integral part of our emotional and intellectual system, instead of the hostile force bombarding it from without with that 'excess of stimuli' which — from Simmel to Freud to Benjamin — has always been seen as modernity's most typical threat.[6]

And yet — dynamism and limits, restlessness and the 'sense of an ending': built as it is on such sharp contrasts, the structure of the *Bildungsroman* will of necessity be *intrinsically contradictory*. A fact which poses extremely interesting problems for aesthetics — the novel as the form 'most open to dangers' of the young Lukács — and even more interesting ones for the history of culture. But before discussing these, let us try to retrace the internal logic of this formal contradiction.

II

'Youth does not last forever.' What constitutes it as symbolic form is no longer a 'spatial' determination, as in the case of Renaissance perspective, but rather a *temporal* one. This is not surprising, since the nineteenth century, under the pressure of modernity, had first of all to reorganize its conception of *change* — which too often, from the time of the French Revolution, had appeared as a meaningless and thus threatening reality ('Je n'y comprends rien,' wrote De Maistre in 1796, 'c'est le grand mot du jour'). This accounts for the centrality of *history* in nineteenth-century culture and, with Darwin, science as well; and for the centrality of *narrative* within the domain of literature. Narrative and history, in fact, do not retreat before the onslaught of events, but demonstrate the possibility of giving them order and meaning. Furthermore, they suggest that reality's meaning is now to be grasped solely in its historico-diachronic dimension. Not only are there no 'meaningless' events; there can now be meaning only *through* events.

Thus, although there exist countless differences (starting with 'stylistic' ones) among the various kinds of *Bildungsroman*, I shall organize this study around *plot differences*: the most pertinent, in my opinion, for capturing the rhetorical and ideological essence of a historico-narrative culture. Plot differences or, more exactly, differences in the ways in which plot generates meaning. Following basically Lotman's conceptualization, we can express this difference as a variation in the weight of two principles of textual organization: the 'classification' principle and the 'transformation' principle. While both are always present in a narrative work, these two principles usually carry an uneven weight, and are actually inversely proportional: as we shall see, the prevalence of one rhetorical strategy over the other, especially in an extreme form, implies very different value choices and even opposite attitudes to modernity.

When classification is strongest — as in the English 'family romance' and in the classical *Bildungsroman* — narrative transformations have meaning in so far as they lead to a particularly marked ending: one that establishes a classification different from the initial one but nonetheless perfectly clear and stable — definitive, in both senses this term has in English. This teleological rhetoric — the meaning of events lies in their *finality* — is the narrative equivalent of Hegelian thought, with which it shares a strong *normative* vocation: events acquire meaning when they led to *one* ending, and one only.

Under the classification principle, in other words, a story is more meaningful the more truly it manages to *suppress itself as story*. Under the transformation principle — as in the trend represented by Stendhal and Pushkin, or in that from Balzac to Flaubert — the opposite is true: what makes a story meaningful is its narrativity, its being an open-ended process. Meaning is the result not of a fulfilled teleology, but rather, as for Darwin, of the total rejection of such a solution. The ending, the privileged narrative moment of taxonomic mentality, becomes the most *meaningless* one here: *Onegin*'s destroyed last chapter, Stendhal's insolently arbitrary closures, or the *Comédie Humaine*'s perennially postponed endings are instances of a narrative logic according to which a story's meaning resides precisely in the impossibility of 'fixing' it.

The oppositions between the two models can obviously go on *ad infinitum*. Thus, on the side of classification we have the novel of marriage, seen as the definitive and classifying act par excellence: at the end of the *Bildungsroman*'s development, marriage will even be disembodied into an abstract principle by Eliot's Daniel Deronda who marries not so much a woman, as a rigidly normative culture. On the side of transformations, we have the novel of adultery: a relationship inconceivable within the Anglo-Germanic traditions (where it is either totally absent, or appears as the sinister and merely destructive force of *Elective Affinities* or *Wuthering Heights*), it becomes here, by contrast, the natural habitat of an existence devoted to instability. And in the end adultery too becomes a disembodied abstraction with Flaubert's Frédéric Moreau who, in perfect parallelism with Daniel Deronda, no longer commits adultery with a woman, but with the immaterial principle of indetermination.

An equally sharp contrast appears when we view these differing narrative rhetorics in terms of the history of ideas. Here, the classical *Bildungsroman* plot posits 'happiness' as the highest value, but only to the detriment and eventual annulment of 'freedom' — while Stendhal, for his part, follows just as radically the opposite course. Similarly, Balzac's fascination with mobility and metamorphoses ends up dismantling the very notion of personal identity — whereas in England, the centrality of the latter value generates an equally inevitable repugnance to change.

Moreover, it is clear that the two models express opposite attitudes towards modernity: caged and exorcised by the principle of classification, it is exasperated and made hypnotic by that of transformation. And it is especially clear that the full development of the antithesis implies a split in the image of youth itself. Where the classification principle prevails — where it is emphasized, as in Goethe and in the English novelists, that youth 'must come to an end' — youth is subordinated to the idea of 'maturity': like the story, it has meaning only *in so far as* it leads to a stable and 'final' identity. Where the transformation principle prevails and youthful dynamism is emphasized, as in the French novelists, youth cannot or does not want to give way to maturity: the young hero senses in fact in such a 'conclusion' a sort of betrayal, which would *deprive* his youth of its meaning rather than enrich it.

Maturity and youth are therefore inversely proportional: the culture that emphasizes the first devalues the second, and vice versa. At the opposite poles of this split lie Eliot's *Felix Holt* and *Daniel Deronda*, and Flaubert's *Sentimental Education*. In Eliot's novels, the hero is so mature from the very start as to dissociate himself suspiciously from anything connected with youthful restlessness: the 'sense of an ending' has suffocated any appeal youth may have had. In Flaubert, on the other hand, Frédéric Moreau is so mesmerized by the potentialities inherent in his youth that he abhors any determination as an intolerable loss of meaning: his prophetic and narcissistic youth, which would like to go on without end, will abolish maturity and collapse overnight into a benumbed old age.

With perfect symmetry, the excessive development of one principle eliminates the opposite one: but in so doing, *it is the Bildungsroman itself that disappears* — Eliot's and Flaubert's being the last masterpieces of the genre. However paradoxical it may seem, this symbolic form could indeed exist, not despite but *by virtue of its contradictory nature*. It could exist because within it — within each single work and within the genre as a whole — *both* principles were simultaneously active, however unbalanced and uneven their strength. It could exist: better still, it *had* to exist. For the contradiction between conflicting evaluations of modernity and youth, or between opposing values and symbolic relationships, is not a flaw — or perhaps it is *also* a flaw — but it is above all the paradoxical *functional principle* of a large part of modern culture. Let us recall the values mentioned above — freedom and happiness, identity and change, security and metamorphoses: although antagonistic, they are *all equally important* for modern Western mentality. Our world calls for their *coexistence*, however difficult; and it therefore also calls for a cultural mechanism capable of representing, exploring and testing that coexistence.

A particularly 'strong' attempt to control this contradictory coexistence and to 'make it work' is to be found, once again, in *Faust*. Here, amidst the many souls of modern culture — amidst the desire for happiness ('Stop, thou art so beautiful ...') and the freedom of *streben* that 'sweeps us ever onward'; amidst the irrepressible identity of the protagonist and his countless historical transformations — here Goethe suggests the possibility of an all-embracing *synthesis*. Yet this synthesis has never managed to dispel our doubts — the doubt that Gretchen's tragedy, and that of Philemon and Baucis, can never be erased; that the bet has been lost; that Faust's salvation is a sham: that synthesis, in other words, is an ideal no longer attainable. And so, in the same decades as *Faust*, the enormous and unconscious collective enterprise of the *Bildungsroman* bears witness to a different solution to modern culture's contradictory nature. Far less ambitious than synthesis, this other solution is *compromise*: which is also, not surprisingly, the novel's most celebrated theme.

An extraordinary symbolic stalemate thereby develops, in which Goethe does not cancel Stendhal, nor Balzac Dickens, nor Flaubert Eliot. Each culture and each individual will have their preferences, as is obvious: but they will never be considered *exclusive*. In this purgatorial world we do not find — to refer to Lukács' early essay on Kierkegaard — the tragic logic of the 'either/or', but rather the more compromising one of the 'as well as'. And in all likelihood it was *precisely this predisposition to compromise* that allowed the *Bildungsroman* to emerge victorious from that veritable 'struggle for existence' between various narrative forms that took place at the turn of the eighteenth century: historical novel and epistolary novel, lyric, allegorical, satirical, 'romantic' novel, *Künstlerroman* ... As in Darwin, the fate of these forms hung on their respective 'purity': that is to say, the more they remained bound to a rigid, original structure, the more difficult their survival. And vice versa: the more a form was capable of flexibility and compromise, the better it could prosper in the maelstrom without synthesis of modern history. And the most bastard of these forms became — the dominant genre of Western narrative: for the gods of modernity, unlike those of *King Lear*, do indeed stand up for bastards.

All this compels us to re-examine the current notion of 'modern ideology' or 'bourgeois culture', or as you like it. The success of the *Bildungsroman* suggests in fact that the truly central ideologies of our world are not in the least — contrary to widespread certainties; more widespread still, incidentally, in deconstructionist thought — intolerant, normative, monologic, to be wholly submitted to or rejected. Quite the opposite: they are pliant and precarious, 'weak' and 'impure'. When we remember that the *Bildungsroman* — the symbolic form that more than any other has portrayed and promoted modern socialization — is also the *most contradictory* of modern symbolic forms, we realize that in our world socialization itself consists first of all in the *interiorization of contradiction*. The next step being not to 'solve' the contradiction, but rather to learn to live with it, and even transform it into a tool for survival.

III

Let us begin with a question: how is it that we have Freudian interpretations of tragedy and myth, of fairy-tale and comedy — yet nothing comparable for the novel? For the same reason, I believe, that we have no solid Freudian analysis of youth: because the *raison d'être* of psychoanalysis lies in *breaking up* the psyche into its opposing 'forces' — whereas youth and the novel have the opposite task of fusing, or at least bringing together, the conflicting features of individual personality. Because, in other words, psychoanalysis always looks *beyond* the Ego — whereas the *Bildungsroman* attempts to *build* the Ego, and make it the indisputable centre of its own structure.[7]

The Ego's centrality is connected, of course, to the theme of socialization — this being, to a large extent, the 'proper functioning' of the Ego thanks to that particularly effective compromise, the Freudian 'reality principle'. But this then compels us to question the *Bildungsroman*'s attitude towards an idea very embarrassing for modern culture — the idea of 'normality'. Once again, we may begin with a contrast. As is well known, a large part of twentieth-century thought — from Freud, let us say, to Foucault — has defined normality against *its opposite*: against pathology, emargination, repression. Normality is seen not as a meaning-ful, but rather as an unmarked entity. The self-defensive result of a 'negation' process, normality's meaning is to be found *outside itself*: in what it excludes, not in what it includes.

Leaving aside the most elementary form of the *Bildungsroman* (the English tradition of the 'insipid' hero — a term which is the culinary equivalent of 'unmarked', and was used by Richardson for *Tom Jones* and by Scott for *Waverley*, and which also applies to *Jane Eyre* and *David Copperfield*), it is quite clear that the novel has followed a strategy opposed to the one we have described. It has accustomed us to looking at normality *from within* rather than from the stance of its exceptions; and it has produced a phenomenology that makes normality interesting and meaningful *as* normality. If the *Bildungsroman*'s initial option is always explicitly anti-heroic and prosaic — the hero is Wilhelm Meister, not Faust; Julien Sorel and Dorothea Brooke, not Napoleon or Saint Theresa (and so on to Flaubert, and then to Joyce) — these characters are still, though certainly all 'normal' in their own ways, far from unmarked or meaningless in themselves.

An internally articulated, interesting and lively normality — normality as the expulsion of all marked features, as a true semantic void. Theoretically, the two concepts are irreconcilable: if one is true, the other is false, and vice versa. Historically, however, this opposition becomes a sort of division of labour: a division of space and time. Normality as 'negation', as Foucault has shown, is the product of a double threat: the crisis of a socio-cultural order, and the violent reorganization of power. Its time is that of crisis and genesis. Its space, surrounded by peculiarly strong social institutions, is the purely negative area of the 'unenclosed'. Its desire is to be like everyone else and thus to go by unnoticed.

Its literary expression, we may add, is nineteenth-century mass narrative: the literature of states of exception, of extreme ills and extreme remedies. But precisely: mass narrative (which, not by chance, has received ample treatment from Freudian criticism) — not the novel. Only rarely does the novel explore the spatio-temporal confines of the given world: it usually stays 'in the middle', where it discovers, or perhaps creates, the typically modern feeling and enjoyment of 'everyday life' and 'ordinary administration'. Everyday life: an anthropocentric space where all social activities lose their exacting objectivity and converge in the domain of 'personality'. Ordinary administration: a time of 'lived experience' and individual growth — a time filled with 'opportunities', but which excludes by definition both the crisis and genesis of a culture.[8]

Just think of the historical course of the *Bildungsroman*: it originates with Goethe and Jane Austen who, as we shall see, write as if to show that the double revolution of the eighteenth century could have been avoided. It continues with Stendhal's heroes, who are born 'too late' to take part in the revolutionary-Napoleonic epic. It withers away with 1848 in Flaubert's *Sentimental Education* (the revolution that was not a revolution) and with the English thirties in Eliot's *Felix Holt* and *Middlemarch* (the 'Reforms' that did not keep their promises). It is a constant elusion of historical turning points and breaks: an elusion of tragedy and hence, as Lukács wrote in *Soul and Forms*, of the very idea that societies and individuals acquire their full meaning in a 'moment of truth'.[9]

An elusion, we may conclude, of whatever may endanger the Ego's equilibrium, making its compromises impossible — and a gravitation, in contrast, to those modes of existence that allow the Ego to manifest itself fully.[10] In this sense — and all the more so if we continue to believe that moments and occasions of truth, despite everything, do still exist — the novel must strike us as a *weak* form. This is indeed the case, and this weakness — which, of course, is ours as well — goes together with the other features we have noted: its contradictory, hybrid and compromising nature. But the point is that such features are also intrinsic to that way of existence — everyday, normal, half-unaware and decidedly unheroic — that Western culture has tried incessantly to protect and expand, and has endowed with an ever-growing significance: till it has entrusted to it what we keep calling, for lack of anything better, the 'meaning of life'. And as few things have helped shape this value as much as our novelistic tradition, then the novel's weakness should strike us perhaps as being far from innocent.

1

The Comfort of Civilization

Bildungsroman. A certain magnetism hovers around the term. It stands out as the most obvious of the (few) reference points available in that irregular expanse we call the 'novel'. It occupies a central role in the philosophical investigations of the novel, from Hegel's *Aesthetics* to Dilthey to Lukács's *Theory of the Novel.* Found in the broad historical frameworks of Mikhail Bakhtin and Erich Auerbach, it is even discernible in the models of narrative plot constructed by Yuri Lotman. It reappears under various headings ('novel of formation,' 'of initiation,' 'of education') in all of the major literary traditions. Even those novels that clearly are *not Bildungsroman* or novels of formation are perceived by us against this conceptual horizon; so we speak of a 'failed initiation' or of a 'problematic formation'. Expressions of dubious usefulness, as are all negative definitions; nonetheless they bear witness to the hold of this image on our modes of analysis.

Such semantic hypertrophy is not accidental. Even though the concept of the *Bildungsroman* has become ever more approximate, it is still clear that we seek to indicate with it one of the most harmonious solutions ever offered to a dilemma conterminous with modern bourgeois civilization: the conflict between the ideal of *self-determination* and the equally imperious demands of *socialization.* For two centuries now, Western societies have recognized the individual's right to choose one's own ethics and idea of 'happiness', to imagine freely and construct one's personal destiny — rights declared in proclamations and set down in constitutions but that are not, as a result, universally realizable, since they obviously give rise to contrasting aspirations. And if a liberal-democratic and capitalist society is without a doubt one that can best 'live with' conflict, it is equally true that, as a *system* of social and political relationships, it too tends to settle itself into an operational mode that is predictable, regular, 'normal'. Like all systems, it demands agreement, homogeneity, consensus.

How can the tendency towards *individuality*, which is the necessary fruit of a culture of self-determination, be made to coexist with the opposing tendency to *normality*, the offspring, equally inevitable, of the mechanism of socialization? This is the first aspect of the problem, complicated and made more fascinating still by another characteristic of our civilization, which, having always been pervaded by the doctrines of natural rights, cannot concede that socialization is based on a mere compliance with authority. It is not enough that the social order is 'legal'; it must also appear *symbolically legitimate*. It must draw its inspiration from values recognized by society as fundamental, reflect them and encourage them. Or it must at least seem to do so.

Thus it is not sufficient for modern bourgeois society simply to subdue the drives that oppose the standards of 'normality'. It is also necessary that, as a 'free individual', not as a fearful subject but as a convinced citizen, one perceives the social norms as *one's own*. One must *internalize* them and fuse external compulsion and internal impulses into a new unity until the former is no longer distinguishable from the latter. This fusion is what we usually call 'consent' or 'legitimation'. If the *Bildungsroman* appears to us still today as an essential, pivotal point of our history, this is because it has succeeded in representing this fusion with a force of conviction and optimistic clarity that will never be equalled again. We will see in fact that here there is no conflict between individuality and socialization, autonomy and normality, interiority and objectification. One's formation as an individual in and for oneself coincides without rifts with one's social integration as a simple *part of a whole*. These are two trajectories that nourish one another and in which the painful perception of socialization as *Entsagung*, 'renunciation' (from which will emerge the immense psychological and narrative problematics of the nineteenth and twentieth centuries) is still inconceivable. The 'comfort of civilization': perhaps the *Bildungsroman*'s historical meaning can best be summarized in these words.

The classical *Bildungsroman* as the synthesis that nullifies the previous opposition of *Entwicklungsroman* (novel of 'development', of the subjective unfolding of an individuality) and

Erziehungsroman (novel of 'education', of an objective process, observed from the standpoint of the educator). The classical *Bildungsroman* as a synthetic form: and yet, as I progressed in my work, I realized that this definition accounts for one aspect only of the works under examination. To use an analogy, it is as if the structure of the classical *Bildungsroman* consisted of two large planes partially superimposed. The common area is the domain of synthesis: it occupies the centre of the figure, but not the whole, and neither, perhaps, is it meant to. More than depicting the two opposing tensions of modern existence as coextensive and isomorphous, the synthetic vocation of the classical *Bildungsroman* presents them as complementary. In organic balance, certainly, but also — or better yet, precisely because — they are profoundly different and distant.

If the area of synthesis is then the starting-point of our analysis, the second and third sections of this chapter will be devoted to quite different phenomena. In the second I will deal with those aspects of narrative structure that emphasize individual 'happiness': the space of 'aesthetic' harmony, of the free and open construction of personality, of narrative *sjuzhet*. In the third section, the other side of all this: the world of social vigilance, of 'organic' inequalities, of necessity, of the *fabula*.

Different values, ascribed to different areas of existence, and governed by different perceptional modes and narrative mechanisms. Different, and distributed with a masterful asymmetry: so captivating as to seem almost deceitful. Because the values and experiences that gratify our sense of individuality are always in the forefront; flaunted, bright, full, they constitute the main part of the narration: the *sjuzhet*. But there is no *sjuzhet* without a *fabula*, and even though the former may be a thousand times more fascinating, appearing to be the 'dominant' aspect of the work, the latter — essential, logical, wholly self-contained — remains in any case its 'determinant' element: less visible, but far more solid.*

Beyond organicistic synthesis, what appears here is that indelible image of bourgeois thought — exchange. You would like such and such values to be realized? — fine, but then you must also accept these others, for without them the former cannot exist. An exchange, and one in which something is gained and something is lost. Precisely what we shall try to establish.

---

* See page 70 for further definitions of these terms.

I

The Ring of Life

> I lost myself in deep meditation and after this discovery I was more
> restful and more restless than before. After I had learnt something,
> it seemed to me as though I knew nothing, and I was right: for I did
> not see the connection of things [*Zusammenhang*], and yet
> everything is a question of that. (*Wilhelm Meister*, I, 4.)

> The presence of the ancient well-known works of art attracted and
> repelled him. He could grasp nothing of what surrounded him, nor
> leave it alone; everything reminded him of everything. He
> overlooked the whole ring of his life; only, alas, it lay broken in
> pieces in front of him, and seemed never to want to unite again.
> (*Wilhelm Meister*, VIII, 7.)

Both at the beginning and the end of his novel, Wilhelm's problem
is the same: he cannot make a 'connection', give his life the shape
of a ring, and seal it. And if this does not take place, his life risks
remaining unfinished — worse yet: *meaningless*. For 'meaning'
and 'connection' are one and the same in *Meister*: Dilthey,
'Goethe's Poetical Imagination':

> By making the casual links of events and actions obvious, [the
> poetical work] revives the values which belong to an event and to its
> individual parts in the plot [*Zusammenhang*] of all life. In this way,
> the event is raised to its significance ... The brilliance of the greatest
> poets consists precisely in portraying the event in such a way that it
> illuminates the relationship between life and its meaning. Poetry
> thus opens the intelligence of life to us. Through the eyes of a great
> poet, we discover the value and the link [*Zusammenhang*] of human
> things.[1]

Zusammenhang: the double meaning of this term is an excellent
introduction to the narrative logic of the classical *Bildungsroman*.
It tells us that a life is meaningful if the *internal* interconnections of
individual temporality ('the plot of all life') imply at the same time
an opening up to the *outside*, an ever wider and thicker network of
external relationships with 'human things'. In this vision —
Dilthey observes further along — man is truly 'himself' only in as
much as he exists 'für das Ganze', for the Whole.[2] The idea that
socialization may provoke crises, or impose sacrifices on
individual formation, is unthinkable here. Self-development and

integration are complementary and convergent trajectories, and at their point of encounter and equilibrium lies that full and double epiphany of meaning that is 'maturity'. When this has been reached, the narration has fulfilled its aim and can peacefully end.

To reach the conclusive synthesis of maturity, therefore, it is not enough to achieve 'objective' results, whatever they may be — learning a trade, establishing a family. One must learn first and foremost, like Wilhelm, to direct 'the plot of [his own] life' so that each moment strengthens one's *sense of belonging* to a wider community. Time must be used to find a homeland. If this is not done, or one does not succeed, the result is a wasted life: aimless, meaningless. The proof of this, in the final books, is the fate of Aurelie, the Harpist — Mignon: ' "Naughty child ... , are you not forbidden all violent exercise? Look how your heart is beating."

"Let it break ... It beats already too long." ' (*Wilhelm Meister*, VIII, 5.)

These are Mignon's final words. For her, the passing of time — plot as a chronological sequence — has not been transfigured into plot as a system of relationships, as a 'ring': her nostalgia — *Kennst du das Land, wo die Zitronen blühn ...* — is the symptom of a life in which no homeland has replaced the original one. Time is here an unchanging beat, a mechanical and exhausting effort which the organicist teleology of the classical *Bildungsroman* banishes as if it were the pounding of death. Outside the Whole, outside the world-as-homeland there is no life whatsoever.

Within it, dubious compensation, there is something more than life: or perhaps just rosier. Wilhelm's final words: 'I do not know the value of a kingdom ... , but I know that I have attained a happiness which I do not deserve, and that I would exchange for nothing in the world.' (*Wilhelm Meister*, VIII, 10.)

These are also the final words of the novel. The 'ring' is complete, life has found its meaning: having reached its goal, time continues to flow, in a circle, free from jerks and changes. The ring, the circle — images of the *abolition* of time: Wilhelm — 'a happiness which I do not deserve and that I would exchange for nothing in the world' — hopes for its disappearance with childish ingenuousness. Perplexing conclusion: that maturity speaks the language of fairy-tales.

The plot as a 'ring', or a 'network', is the most significant of the many novelties introduced by Goethe in the second draft of *Wilhelm Meister*, the *Lehrjahre*. In the first draft — the *Theatralische Sendung* — the progression of plot was much more 'dramatic' and unpredictable, and the character of Wilhelm enjoyed an undisputed prominence over all else. In the *Years of Apprenticeship* the flow of time slows down in a thick continuum of prophecies, memories and anticipations; while with the growing relevance of secondary characters, the 'centrality' of the protagonist acquires a different meaning. It is the antithesis of drama and novel, discussed at length in the fifth book:

> In the novel it is feelings and events that are chiefly represented; in the drama characters and deeds. The novel must proceed slowly and the feelings of the hero must, in some way or other, restrain the tendency of the whole to its development. The drama should hurry on, and the character of the hero must press forward to the end and only be restrained. The hero of the novel must be suffering, or at least he must not be in a high degree active. Grandison, Clarissa, Pamela, the Vicar of Wakefield, Tom Jones himself, are, if not suffering, yet retarding personalities and all the events are modelled to some extent according to their feelings. In the drama the hero models nothing after himself; everything withstands him; he clears and removes the hindrances out of his way, or sinks beneath them (*Wilhelm Meister*, V, 7).

In drama, we may paraphrase, the protagonist exhausts within himself a universe of values, a paradigmatic field: it is the 'loneliness' of the tragic hero, to whom the meaning of life is entrusted, to be achieved through *conflict*. But in the classical *Bildungsroman* this is impossible: as later in Hegel, the certainty of meaning lies here not in conflict, but in a *participation* in the Whole. A 'dramatic' classical *Bildungsroman* is a contradiction in terms — and it was not by chance that Goethe never managed to 'conclude' the *Theatralische Sendung*, which is simply interrupted and abandoned without the first Wilhelm having completed his formation.[3] When, nearly ten years later, Goethe takes up the project again, he does not even try to finish the first draft: he begins totally anew and, in addition to modifying the structure of the plot, clearly opts for a different type of novelistic hero. The type described by Schiller in a letter to Goethe of 28 November, 1796:

> Wilhelm Meister is the most necessary character, but not the most important; one of the peculiarities of your novel is that it neither has nor needs a hero. Everything takes place around him, but not *because of him*: precisely because the things which surround him represent and express energies, and he instead pliability, his relationships with the other characters had to be different from those of the heroes of other novels.

The transition from drama to novel — the representation of a successful *Bildung* — requires then a *pliant* character: no longer 'alone', and still less at odds with the world, he is the well-cut prism in which the countless nuances of the social context blend together in a harmonious 'personality'. 'The most necessary character, but not the most important', as Schiller rightly observes. Important — as a potential cause of plot — Wilhelm certainly is not. But he is necessary, if, as it does, the classical *Bildungsroman* seeks to put forward as exemplary the trajectory of a hero who — 'suffering, or at least ... not ... in a high degree active' — leaves to others the task of shaping his life. '... It appears to you impossible to decide,' Wilhelm reasons midway through the text, 'you wish that some kind of preponderance from outside may determine your choice' (*Wilhelm Meister*, IV, 19). And at the end: 'I have attained a happiness which I *do not deserve*' or, in other words, I exist, and I exist happily, only because I have been allowed access to the plot patiently weaved 'around me' by the Society of the Tower. I have acquired 'form', I exist 'for myself', because I have willingly agreed to be determined from without. It is indeed the ideal paradigm of modern socialization: I *desire* to do what I in any case *should* have done. The final marriage, when Wilhelm *is forced to be happy* in spite of his intentions, is the perfect miniature and conclusion of the entire process.

If Wilhelm can become an individual only by accepting the guardianship of the Tower, the reverse is true as well: 'strong' social institutions like the Society of the Tower have the right to devise and weave plots only in order to satisfy their novice. It is not an exaggeration to say that, in *Wilhelm Meister*, the Tower exists solely to permit Wilhelm's 'happiness'. Lothario has been to America — but he very quickly returns: ' "Here or nowhere is America!" ' (*Wilhelm Meister*, VII, 3.) The characters so insistently entangled with one another will have to be scattered throughout the world, in America, in Russia. But all this lies beyond Goethe's novel: what interests us about Lothario and the others is not their autonomous existence, but only the effects they have had on Wilhelm. Werner's sudden reappearance towards the end of the novel has the sole purpose of attesting, through the words of a somewhat envious outsider, the effectiveness of the Tower's pedagogical system: 'No, no ... such a thing has never come before me, and yet I know I am not mistaken. Your eyes are deeper, your forehead broader, your nose has become fine and your mouth more loving. Look at him, how he stands! How it all suits and fits together! ... I, on the other hand, poor devil ... if I had not during this time gained a good deal of money, there would be nothing about me at all.' (*Wilhelm Meister*, VIII, 1.)

The Tower exists then 'for' Wilhelm because it shapes him (even improving, as Werner says, his physical features): but also in a more fundamental sense. In the last page of the seventh book, Wilhelm discovers that *The Years of Apprenticeship of Wilhelm Meister* is a parchment preserved in the Hall of the Past, the most secret apartment of the Tower, to which he has finally been admitted. In other words, the novel we are reading has been written by the Tower *for* Wilhelm, and only by coming into its possession does he assume full possession and control of his life. In the parchment, all ambiguity disappears, the confusing succession of events acquires a logic and a direction, the 'sense of the whole' is finally visible. And as for the Tower, this episode confers upon it a double legitimation: it has succeeded in generating an exemplary *Bildung* like Wilhelm's — and also in writing a paradigmatic text like *The Years of Apprenticeship of Wilhelm Meister*.

The Rhetoric of Happiness

A perfect circle: Wilhelm's formation is achieved only by subordinating himself to the Tower — the Tower's legitimation only by making Wilhelm happy.[4] It is a beautiful symmetry, a perfect match: 'to the advantage of both,' to use the words of Elizabeth Bennet. A perfect marriage: like those that conclude *Wilhelm Meister* and *Pride and Prejudice*.

Let us recall our initial question: how is it possible to convince the modern — 'free' — individual to willingly limit his freedom? Precisely, first of all, through marriage — *in* marriage: when two people ascribe to one another such value as to accept being 'bound' by it. It has been observed that from the late eighteenth century on, marriage becomes the model for a new type of *social contract*: one no longer sealed by forces located outside of the individual (such as status), but founded on a sense of 'individual obligation'.[5] A very plausible thesis, and one that helps us understand why the classical *Bildungsroman* 'must' always conclude with marriages. It is not only the foundation of the family that is at stake, but that 'pact' between the individual and the world,[6] that reciprocal 'consent' which finds in the double 'I do' of the wedding ritual an unsurpassed symbolic condensation.

Marriage as a metaphor for the social contract: this is so true that the classical *Bildungsroman* does not contrast marriage with celibacy, as would after all be logical, but with death (Goethe) or 'disgrace' (Austen). One either marries or, in one way or another, must leave social life: and for more than a century European consciousness will perceive the crisis of marriage as a rupture that not only divides a couple, but destroys the very roots — Anna Karenina, Emma Bovary, Effi Briest — of those sentiments that keep the individual 'alive'. For this world view a crisis, a divorce, can never be a plausible 'ending': the impossible yet real *A Doll's House - Part II* — which forced Nora Helmer to either go back, or else bring death and misery to everybody — were to be the swan song of this nineteenth-century 'truth'.

Here, then, lies the reason for the centrality of the classical *Bildungsroman*, not only in the history of the novel, but in our entire cultural legacy. This genre depicts, and re-enacts as we read it, a relationship with the social totality permeated with that 'intimate and sweet well-being', with that serene and trustful feeling-at-home that Schiller mentioned to Goethe during the composition of *Wilhelm Meister*: 'I explain this feeling of well-being [continues his letter of 7 January, 1795] with the clarity, peace, concreteness and transparency that dominate everywhere in the novel, even in those minor details that could leave the soul unsatisfied and restless, never forcing its emotions more than is necessary to rekindle and preserve in man the joy of life...'

The joy of life. The happiness superior to the merit of Wilhelm and Elizabeth. It sounds like an echo of famous words: 'life, liberty, the pursuit of happiness ...'; 'happiness, this new idea for Europe ...' But the 'happiness' of Schiller and Goethe is the very opposite of that imagined by Jefferson and Saint-Just. For the latter, happiness is the accompaniment of war and revolution: it is dynamic, de-stabilizing. It is still linked — a problematic link, which will continue till Stendhal, and then dissolve — to the idea of 'liberty'. This happiness must be 'pursued' without rest or compromise: at the cost, if necessary, of war and revolution. For revolution represents 'the opening of a society to all its possibilities': the 'promise of such magnitude' that 'has a birth but no end'.[7]

For Schiller and Goethe, instead, happiness is the *opposite* of freedom, the *end* of becoming. Its appearance marks the end of all tension between the individual and his world; all desire for further metamorphosis is extinguished. As is indicated by the German term *Glück* — which synthesizes 'happiness' and 'luck', *bonheur* and *fortune, felicità* and *fortuna*[8] — and which not by chance appears in the last sentence of *Meister*, the happiness of the classical *Bildungsroman* is the subjective symptom of an objectively completed socialization: there is no reason to bring into question such dialectical homogeneity.

We have already seen that the classical *Bildungsroman* typically seals this happiness with marriage. But the family is here still a metaphor for a possible *social* pact: it is not that 'haven in a heartless world' that Christopher Lasch has constructed for the following century. The family is not, in other words, the *only* domain in which the subjective-objective complementarity of happiness can exist, but simply the most probable and typical.[9] As a consequence, it is not a question of retreating within the family to pursue there those ends which the public sphere seems to frustrate, but of irradiating *outside* the family that notion of inner harmony and trustful acceptance of bonds that are its most salient features.[10] It is a question, in other words, of instituting — midway between the intimate and the public sphere — the reassuring atmosphere of 'familiarity'. An enterprise that demands a redrawing of modern everyday life, and first and foremost of the role and symbolic value of *work* in human existence.

Anti-Robinson

One of the most celebrated episodes of *Wilhelm Meister* is the discussion in which Werner — Wilhelm's alter ego — illustrates to his close friend the merits of trade:

> Now visit first a couple of large commercial towns, a couple of harbours, and you will certainly be carried away with the idea. When you see how many people are occupied, when you see how much is transmitted, and where it goes, you will certainly see it with pleasure pass through your hands. The smallest goods you will see in connection with the whole trade, and therefore you will regard nothing as small, because everything increases the circulation from which your life derives its nourishment. (*Wilhelm Meister*, I, 10.)

Werner's speech is generally considered an epoch-making exposition of the new 'bourgeois' principles, and specifically of the Weberian rationality implict in double-entry book-keeping, of which he speaks a few lines later. The passage just quoted, however, can be read in a wholly different sense. The market mechanism is not praised for its *economic* merits, but as the system best adapted to discover the 'connection' that links the most disparate human activities; to assign a meaning to even the most negligible and insignificant things. Precisely when Wilhelm is about to leave his father's home, and must therefore decide on the meaning of his future life, Werner suggests to him a possible meaning, a plot, a network that would make social relationships visible, and show the individual how to place himself within them: 'Cast a glance on the natural and artificial products of all quarters of the earth, consider how they have become in turn necessities! What a pleasant and intellectual task it is to know ... everything which at the moment is most sought for ...' (*Wilhelm Meister*, I, 10.)

But Wilhelm rejects this possible plot, this viewpoint on human affairs. What is much more important, Goethe himself rejects them: the *Bildung* hero will not be Werner, but Wilhelm. The most classical *Bildungsroman*, in other words, conspicuously places the process of formation-socialization *outside* the world of work.

The process of formation-socialization placed outside work: a surprising and somewhat disturbing development, given our automatic tendency to juxtapose 'modern ethics' and 'capitalism'. I am not, naturally, trying to deny here that capitalist production has generated a set of values wholly functional to its logic. It *has* generated them, and this is evident: but we must nevertheless ask ourselves whether these values have ever taken hold outside of the strictly economic domain, and if it is to them — or to other values, and which — that Western modernity turns in order to make existence 'meaningful'.

Let us begin then by observing that the representation of the economic domain, and of its symbolic universe, has had in the great narratives of the last two centuries almost no importance whatsoever. Never having been in love with the theory of art as reflection, I do not perceive this lack as a catastrophe. But a few problems it definitely does pose: if anything, it may make us wonder why the novel does not speak of work, and why *Bildung* must take place outside its orbit. The beginning of an answer lies perhaps in another passage of Werner's speech:

> What advantages does the double entry afford to the merchant. It is one of the most beautiful inventions of the human mind, and every good housekeeper ought to introduce it into his business. ... form and matter are here made one; one without the other cannot exist. Order and clarity increase the pleasure in sparing and earning. A man who keeps house badly, easily finds himself in the dark; he may not like to reckon up the accounts he is owing. On the other hand,

26

for a good manager nothing can be more pleasant than drawing to
himself every day the sum of his increasing good fortune. (*Wilhelm
Meister*, I, 10.)

Werner's very last words explain why capitalist rationality
cannot generate *Bildung*. Capital, due to its purely quantitative
nature, and the competition it is subject to, can be a fortune only in
so far as *it keeps growing*. It must grow, and change form, and
never stop: as Adam Smith observed in *The Wealth of Nations*, the
merchant is a citizen of no country in particular. Quite true, and
this is precisely the point: the merchant's journey can never come
to a conclusion in those ideal places — the holdings of the Tower,
the Pemberley estate of *Pride and Prejudice* — where everything is
'well-being, transparency and concreteness'. He will never know
the quiet happiness of 'belonging' to a fixed place.

And just as he can never stop in space, his adventure can never
come to an end in time, as Defoe discovered when writing the last
pages of *Robinson Crusoe*. Last, not conclusive: he will
immediately have to start writing a second *Robinson*. Yet the
problem of how to end the novel is still unsolved: and so a third
Robinson. Where Defoe does finally find a solution, but only
because he transforms the novel into an allegory: thereby
abolishing the problematic of temporality instead of confronting it
on its own territory.

Not so in the classical *Bildungsroman*. Here, just as in space it is
essential to build a 'homeland' for the individual, it is also
indispensable for time to stop at a privileged moment. A *Bildung* is
truly such only if, at a certain point, it can be seen as *concluded*:
only if youth passes into maturity, and comes there to a stop there.
And with it, time stops — narrative time at least. Lotman:

> Once the agent has crossed a border [here: after having begun his
> youthful 'journey'], he enters another semantic field, an 'anti-field'
> *vis-à-vis* the initial one. If movement is to cease, he has to merge
> with the field, to be transformed from a mobile into an immobile
> persona. If this does not happen, the plot sequence is not concluded
> and movement continues.[11]

For the plot sequence to stop, therefore, a 'merging' of the
protagonist with his new world is necessary. It is a further variant
of the metaphorical field of 'closure': the happy acceptance of
bonds; 'meaningful' life as a tightly-closed ring; the stability of
social connections as the foundation of the text's meaning. And

Lotman is right: when the 'merging' has occurred the journey can end, and the classical *Bildungsroman* is over — it has achieved its function. But the 'semantic anti-field' to which all these metaphors belong — and which therefore presides over the full realization of *Bildung* — is certainly not symbolically neutral, or untouched. It is not 'the' world, as the structuralist credo would have it — it is *a* possible world: with rather special historico-cultural features. And its own problematic relationship with modernity. Agnes Heller:

> Appropriation of the system of objects, habits and institutions is never simultaneous, nor is it something that is concluded when the child becomes an adult. To be precise — the more highly developed, the more intricate the patterns, the less speedy and efficient the acquisition process. In static societies, or static circles within these societies, the stage of minimum capability in everyday life is reached on becoming an adult. ... that he can now successfully reproduce himself as a person, upon attaining maturity, is no longer in doubt.
>
> The more dynamic the society, the more fortuitous the relationship between the person and the society into which he is born (and this is particularly true of capitalist society from the eighteenth century onwards), the more sustained is the effort which the person is required to make *throughout his life* to substantiate his claim to viability, and the less true is it that appropriation of the given world is completed on attaining maturity.[12]

The definitive stabilization of the individual, and of his relationship with the world — 'maturity' as the story's final stage — is therefore fully possible *only in the precapitalist world*. Only in the world of 'closed social forms' — as Heller often repeats, echoing a famous page of the *Grundrisse* — can 'happiness' be the highest value: the ideal that *valorizes* borders rather than seeing them as intolerable limitations. Only far from the metropolis, as in the conclusive places of *Wilhelm Meister* and *Pride and Prejudice,* can the restless impermanence of youth be appeased: only there does the 'journey' reveal itself to have a clear and insuperable goal.[13]

Yes — 'maturity' is hardly compatible with 'modernity'. And contrariwise. Modern Western society has 'invented' youth, mirrored itself in it, chosen it as its most emblematic value — and for these very reasons has become less and less able to form a clear notion of 'maturity'. The richer the image of youth grew, the more inexorably that of adulthood was drained. The more engaging, we may add, the 'novel' of life promised to be — the harder it became to accept its conclusion; to write, with a firm and lasting conviction, the words: 'The End'.

But all this will become clearer in the following chapters. The classical *Bildungsroman* — with its perfect, and perfectly meaningful conclusion — is still on this side of the great symbolic divide. Better yet, it acts like a hinge between the two worlds: here youth is already full, and maturity not yet drained; the young hero already 'modern', but the world not yet. The attempt was bold and ambitious, but also ephemeral: just ten years later, with *Elective Affinities,* Goethe will show that marriage is no happy ending, no lasting conclusion to modern life; while in *Faust,* the connection between happiness and the acceptance of limits will be more problematic still.

But in the fairy-tale-like closed world of the classical *Bildungsroman* these problems are not yet present, and the merchant Werner, who would like to break its closed form with his endless columns of figures, and his visions of distant ports, will occupy a very secondary role, from which to contemplate with bitter envy the human fullness of his indolent friend.

II

So far we have seen the domain of 'synthesis': some of the essential junctures of the *Bildungsideal.* Essential, but also 'extreme': we have only discussed what happens at the beginning and, especially, at the end of the novel. Beginning and end are, certainly, decisive moments of any narration: they frame it, give it perspective, circumscribe its field of possibility. But they circumscribe that field — they do not populate it. If the ultimate assumptions of a work are generally found at its margins — its fascination, as with any true journey, seems instead to lie 'in the middle'. And here the harmonious picture we have been sketching does not fall apart, but it certainly becomes more dense and complex. The two tensions — autonomy and socialization — are less predetermined in their development; their reconciliation is less evident and straightforward. The attempt to join modernity and tradition remains: but these two historical and cultural poles acquire a more unusual and interesting appearance. And the same is true for the rhetorical strategy of the novel as a genre: which becomes more articulate and rich, and not without its surprises.

Let us then resume our analysis where we left off: with the image of work proposed by *Wilhelm Meister.*

Aesthetic Education

The characters in *Wilhelm Meister* are not idlers. If they make this impression on Werner it is because, as a proper merchant, he cannot conceive of work that does not bring with it renunciation, ascesis, sacrifice. But the immense wager of the Society of the Tower, previously announced by Wilhelm in the letter to Werner on the differences between the noble and the bourgeois (*Wilhelm Meister*, V, 3), is that a kind of work can be created that would enhance not 'having' but rather 'being'. A work that produces not commodities (objects that have value only in the market exchange that distances them forever from their producer) but, as Wilhelm hints, 'harmonious objects'[14]: objects that 'return' to their creator, thereby permitting the entire 'reappropriation' of one's own activity.

In this second sense, work is fundamental in *Meister*: as *non*capitalistic work, as reproduction of a 'closed circle'. It is an unequalled instrument of social cohesion, producing not commodities but 'harmonious objects', 'connections'. It gives a homeland to the individual. It reinforces the links between man and nature, man and other men, man and himself.[15] It is always *concrete* work. It does not require a producer who is 'average,' 'abstract', denatured, but is addressed to a specific individual, and to the end of emphasizing his peculiarities.

In both its 'harmonious' results, and in its relationship with man, work seems to have as its end the *formation of the individual*. It is, in its essence, *pedagogy*. This is the true occupation, much more so than its landed enterprises, of the Society of the Tower, which, after all, owes its origin to a pedagogical experiment. Producing men — this is the true vocation of the masons in *Meister*:

> Free your mind, where it is possible, from all suspicion and all anxiety! There comes the Abbé. Be friendly towards him until you learn still more how much gratitude you owe him. The rogue! there he goes between Natalia and Theresa. I would bet he is thinking something out. As he above all likes to play a little the part of Destiny, so he does not often let a marriage be made from lovemaking. (*Wilhelm Meister*, VIII, 5.)

The Abbé and Jarno (who pronounces these words) are precisely those who have worked at educating Wilhelm. They have written his *Years of Apprenticeship* and will also decide, overcoming his resistance, which woman he should marry. These are all double-edged particulars. On the one hand, they are reminiscent of what Schiller envisaged in his *Letters on the Aesthetic Education of Man:* a situation in which the 'goal' of society is man. On the other hand, the premises and consequences of this utopia cannot but appear disturbing. If the end of society is man, then it goes without saying that those who hold social power have the right and duty to chart the progress of their 'product' even in its minimal details; while he, in his turn ('be friendly towards him'), is also required to show gratitude. Here organicism and liberty, organicism and critical intelligence, are antithetical — for an organic system is without a doubt an inviting homeland, but in every organism, as will gradually become more clear, there is room for only one brain.

The 'harmony' that characterizes work in *Meister* is due to the fact that work does not follow a strictly economic logic, necessarily indifferent to the subjective aspirations of the individual worker. Instead of forcibly sundering an 'alienated' objectification and an interiority incapable of being expressed, work in the *Bildungsroman* creates a continuity between external and internal, between the 'best and most intimate' part of the soul and the 'public' aspect of existence. Once again we have the congruence of formation and socialization, but there is more. For a work defined in this way is in fact indistinguishable from what a large part of the German culture of the time called 'art'. Humboldt:

> Everything towards which man directs his attention, whether it is limited to the direct or indirect satisfaction of his merely physical wants, or to the accomplishment of external objects in general, presents itself in a closely interwoven relation with his internal sensations. Sometimes, moreover, there co-exists with this external purpose, some impulse proceeding more immediately from his inner being; and often, even, this last is the sole spring of his activity, the former being only implied in it, necessarily or incidentally. ... A man, therefore, whose character peculiarly interests, although his life does not lose this charm in any circumstances or however engaged, only attains the most matured and graceful consummation of his activity, when his way of life is in harmonious keeping with his character.
>
> In view of this consideration, it seems as if all peasants and craftsmen might be elevated into artists; that is, into men who love their labour for its own sake, improve it by their own plastic genius and inventive skill, and thereby cultivate their intellect, ennoble their character, and exalt and refine their enjoyments. And so humanity would be ennobled by the very things which now, though beautiful in themselves, so often go to degrade it.[16]

According to this current of thought, which will continue up to Ferdinand Tönnies's *Community and Society,* work can assume two opposing forms. The first — capitalistic work — 'degrades' humanity. It serves not man but rather (say Schiller and the Abbé in *Meister*) the god of 'profit'; in so doing it betrays the very essence of work, what it is 'in and for itself'. Beautiful. Ennobling. Formative. If only this second type of work can be substituted for the first ...

Indeed. What would happen then? Or to put it in other words, *from what standpoint* is this 'aesthetic' and humanizing work superior to one that is instrumental and alienated? Certainly not for its productive capacities. Schiller, in fact, in his *On the Aesthetic Education of Man,* postulates an inversely proportional relationship between the 'wealth of nations' and the 'aesthetic education of man'. To the 'superiority of the species' that characterizes the modern period from classical Greece must be opposed the 'inferiority of the individual' (letter 6). This is what the harmony of work as art (or as 'play') must remedy — cost what it may:

> Partiality in the exercise of powers, it is true, inevitably leads the individual into error, but the species to truth. Only by concentrating the whole energy of our spirit in one single focus, and drawing together our whole being into one single power, do we attach wings, so to say, to this individual power and lead it artificially beyond the bounds which Nature seems to have imposed upon it....
> Thus, however much may be gained for the world as a whole by this fragmentary cultivation of human powers, it is undeniable that the individuals whom it affects suffer under the curse of this universal aim.... The exertion of individual talents certainly produces extraordinary men, but only their even tempering makes full and happy men.[17]

The reversal undertaken by Schiller in the second of these paragraphs is one of the keys for understanding the universe of values of the classical *Bildungsroman.* This genre does not bother with 'extraordinary men', 'universal aims', or what 'may be gained for the world as a whole'. Its purpose is to create 'full and happy men' — full and happy because 'tempered', not 'partial' or unilateral. Free from that disharmonious specialization that, in the eyes of Wilhelm, constitutes the specific curse of the 'bourgeois':

He is to cultivate individual capabilities so as to become useful, and it is already presupposed that there is no harmony in his manner of existence nor can there be, because he is obliged to make himself useful in one direction and must, therefore, neglect everything else. *(Wilhelm Meister,* V, 3).

Only if the individual renounces the bourgeois who dwells within him will he be able to become an harmonious entity: to be 'full and happy'. Only then will he feel that he again 'belongs' to his world, and only then will the strife that pervades the modern age be at an end. For the aesthetic utopia is a *social* utopia:

Though need may drive Man into society, and Reason implant social principles in him, Beauty alone can confer on him a social character. Taste alone brings harmony into society, because it establishes harmony in the individual. All other forms of perception divide a man, because they are exclusively based either on the sensuous or on the intellectual part of his being; only the perception of the Beautiful makes something whole of him, because both his natures must accord with it.[18]

Schiller is wishing here for the advent of a 'social' society, spontaneously cohesive, devoid of lacerations and strife. It is for this end that 'beauty', 'play', and 'art' are necessary. And yet, it is clear, these cannot really modify the functioning of the great, alienated social mechanisms: the 'mechanical' state, production for profit. To bring harmony 'to the individual and to society', aesthetic education follows a more indirect and elusive strategy. Instead of directly confronting the great powers of social life, it creates a new realm of existence in which those abstract and deforming forces penetrate less violently, and can be reconstituted in syntony with the individual aspiration toward harmony. This realm is organized according to the dictates of 'beauty' and 'play'; it is pervaded with the 'happiness' of the individual; and the *Bildungsroman* is its narrative explication. Fine. As always, however, when one is dealing with utopias, the question arises: *where* exactly is the realm of aesthetic harmony to be located? Furthermore, *which* aspects of modern life has it effectively involved and organized?

The Art of Living

A fairly simple and reasonable answer can be offered for these questions. Schiller's aesthetic 'sociableness', like Humboldt's artistic 'work', represent in fact the precapitalist community and its craftsmanship; just as typically prebourgeois is the idea — dealt with at length by Werner Sombart — that man is 'the measure of all things'.[19] The notorious 'Deutsche misère' corroborates this hypothesis, which contains without a doubt much of the truth. The allure of *On the Aesthetic Education of Man* or of *Wilhelm Meister* would therefore stem, in large measure, from regret for a lost harmony. Although this seems very likely, I would like to propose here a different type of historical interpretation, according to which aesthetic organicity, and the happiness that comes with it, belong not only to a *past* that precedes capitalist production and the 'mechanical' state, but endure in modern times as well. Except that now they are shifted 'to the side of' the great collective institutions, which they engage in a silent and unending border war.

Following the lead of various recent studies, I will call this parallel world the sphere of 'everyday life'. Henri Lefebvre:

> Everyday life is defined as totality. Considered in their specialization and technicalization, the higher activities leave among themselves a 'technical void' filled in by everyday life. The latter engages *all* activities in an extensive relationship and encompasses them together with their differences and their conflicts; it constitutes their meeting ground and their common link.[20]

Lefebvre is *half* right. That there are no limits to what can be incorporated by everyday life seems, to me, to be true. But it is also true that, if we must define a sphere of life, and declare it limitless, then we have not come very far. A new element must be inserted; we must specify that what characterizes everyday life (as well as Schiller's aesthetic education, for that matter) is not the nature or the number of its pursuits but their 'treatment'. That is to say, the direction that they assume, the end to which they are subordinated. Karel Kosik:

> The everyday appears ... as the world of familiarity... . The everyday is a world whose dimensions and potentialities an individual can control and calculate with his abilities and resources. In the everyday, everything is 'at hand' and an individual can realize his intentions... . In the everyday, the individual develops relations on [the] basis of *his own* experience, *his own* possibilities, *his own* activity, and therefore considers the everyday reality to be his own world.[21]

We may thus speak of everyday life whenever the individual subordinates any activity whatsoever to the construction of 'his own world'. We are at the antipodes of Protestant ethics, of the ascetic and imperious Weberian vocation. In everyday life, it is activity — *any* activity, at least potentially — that must be submitted to the service of the individual. It must become proportional to 'his abilities and resources'. If the enterprise succeeds, 'an individual can realize his intentions', and the world acquires the comforting dimensions of familiarity. It is no longer the world of hardship and duty. It is a world where man truly is the measure of all things.

We have more or less retraced the picture hypothesized in *On the Aesthetic Education of Man*. Further proof of this affinity between aesthetic education and everyday life is to be found in Agnes Heller's work, who, following Lukács, defines Kosik's 'individual' as a 'particularity' that 'tends towards self-preservation, and subordinates everything to this self-preservation.'[22] Heller, reappropriating Hegel's notion of the 'world-historical individual,' thus opposes 'particularity' to what she defines as 'individuality': 'It is the individualities — particularly those most developed individualities ... to whom we shall refer as "representative individuals" — who individually incorporate the evolutionary generic maxima of a given society.'[23]

'These great men,' Hegel had written, 'seem to follow only their passions, their free will, but what they want is the universal, and this is their pathos.'[24] Consequently:

> It was not happiness they chose but exertion, conflict, and labour in the service of their end. And even when they reached their goal, peaceful enjoyment and happiness was not their lot. Their actions are their entire being... . When their end is attained, they fall aside like empty husks. They may have undergone great difficulties in order to accomplish their purpose, but as soon as they have done so, they die early like Alexander, are murdered like Caesar, or deported like Napoleon... . The fearful consolation [is] that the great men of history did not enjoy what is called happiness.[25]

To use once again Schiller's terminology: these individuals may be 'advantageous to the species' but they are not 'full and happy' men. They are 'representatives', for Heller, 'of the evolutionary generic maxima of a given society', of its major historical crises and acquisitions. But precisely for this reason they are *not* representatives of those times 'of ordinary administration' that, we will see, constitute the privileged historical context of the novel, especially of the *Bildungsroman*.[26] Here the 'representative individual' does not want 'exertion, conflict, and labour in the service of his end': these struggles will take place (and in an extremely problematic way) only in Stendhal, whose heroes, bewitched by the 'world-historical' model of Napoleon, give life to a narrative plot whose typical event is a clash with the existing order. But the hero of the classical *Bildungsroman,* like Heller's 'particularity', '... wants to find his place in the world, his own place, and seeks after a life which is reasonable for him ... .'[27] His compass is personal happiness, and the plot that will permit him to realize it will follow the model of *organic integration:* the polar opposite of the conflictual plot.

Although they are different in many ways, the studies of Lefebvre, Kosik, and Heller nevertheless all converge on a single goal, the formulation of a *critique* of everyday life. They want to 'disalienate' it, reveal its wretchedness or transience, unmask the 'happiness' it promises as something mean or imaginary. In doing this, all three contrast it, more or less echoing Hegel, with the great crises of universal history, and there can be no doubt that, against such a backdrop, this happiness seems a truly poor and fragile entity.

Further along, in discussing the attitude of the classical *Bildungsroman* to the French revolution, we too will find a particularly lucid example of the polar relationship between the two spheres of life. A difficulty remains, however: the viewpoint of universal history, on which the critique of everyday life rests, is certainly not the only one possible, and above all *it is not the one assumed by novelistic form.* Not blind to the progress of universal history, novelistic form nevertheless 'reshapes' it as it is perceived from the viewpoint of everyday life. Furthermore, the novel 'funnels' universal history into this mode of existence in order to amplify and enrich the life of the 'particularity'.

In other words, in the classical *Bildungsroman* the significance of history does not lie in the 'future of the species', but must be revealed within the more narrow confines of a circumscribed and relatively common individual life. What is involved here is an *a priori* condition of this 'symbolic form'; whether we like it or not, this is how things stand. It thereby follows that the novel exists not as a critique, but as a *culture of everyday life.* Far from devaluing it, the novel organizes and 'refines' this form of existence, making it ever more alive and interesting — or, with Balzac, even fascinating.

Given the affinity between aesthetic education and everyday life, one of the tasks of the *Bildungsroman* will be to show how pleasing life can be in what Goethe called 'the small world'. Once again, Agnes Heller:

> Satisfaction in everyday life is an amalgam of two main components — pleasure and usefulness. ... Of the two, it is pleasure which is exclusively relevant to everyday life. It might be defined as that feeling of affirmation which accompanies and permeates our physical and mental state ... [28].

Pleasure: the comfort or ease of being in the world. And it is precisely this satisfied equilibrium that renders such comfort deaf — in the same way as Schiller's 'aesthetic education' — to the proud harshness of modern, 'autonomous' art. Heller continues, 'The emotion felt in major achievement, the successful conclusion of a non-everyday enterprise, is either not pleasure or more than pleasure.'[29] In both cases it is art itself that makes impossible the 'full and happy' temperance of Schiller's project. Is there no way then to fuse art with life? Not exactly, there is a solution that appeared precisely in the Goethean decades: kitsch.

> Kitsch is linked to an art of living, and it is due to this world that it has found its authenticity, for it is difficult to live intimately with artistic masterpieces *tout court*, whether those of woman's fashion or those of Michelangelo's vault. Kitsch, instead, is of *human* proportions....
>
> Kitsch is acceptable art, that which does not transform our spirit via a transcendence beyond the bounds of everyday life, via a force superior to ourselves — especially if it must make us overcome ourselves. *Kitsch* has human porportions, whereas art is beyond these....
>
> In the adaptation of the tonality of the environment to that of the individual we find a *recipe of happiness*. Kitsch is the art of happiness, and each exaltation of the messages of happiness is at the same time an exaltation of Kitsch. Hence its universality... Kitsch coincides with the material environment of everyday life. It is difficult to conceive of it without some concrete prop.[30]

From 'happiness' as an insertion into an organic whole to its miniaturization in the aesthetic harmony of the individual — and from here to kitsch and to everday life. Kitsch literally 'domesticates' aesthetic experience. It brings it into the *home*, where most of everyday life takes place. Moreover, it raids all sorts of aesthetic material to construct what will be the typical household of modern times. In *Meister* the 'harmonious objects' *par excellence*, those that make the world an inviting 'homeland', are precisely homes, and this is even more true for *Pride and Prejudice*. The crucial episode, here, is Elizabeth Bennet's visit to Pemberley, Darcy's country residence. Pemberley is open to the public: it is a monument of 'beauty' for the admiration of outsiders. But there is nothing museum-like about it, and the reaction it arouses in Elizabeth certainly is not 'aesthetic'. On seeing Pemberley, she instead thinks of Darcy for the first time as a possible husband: not because of ambition or avarice, but because Pemberley reveals that the everyday — domestic — life of a man like Darcy can precisely be something very beautiful.

Beautiful? Not exactly. Jane Austen, who chose her words with legendary precision, attributes the adjective *beautiful* only to the 'natural' beauty of the estate. The house, the rooms, and the furniture are not 'beautiful' — they are 'handsome'. A term that indicates a 'decorous' and 'balanced' beauty, 'without harshness', 'comfortable' (as the etymology itself suggests). A beauty, in a word, of human proportions. Repeated three times in a page to indicate objects, *handsome* reappears a page later — four times in ten lines! — to designate Darcy.

'Handsome': a beauty that is not in the least threatening or disconcerting, not in the least autonomous. It envelops the ideal of a golden mean, of a clear and reciprocal translatability between the individual and his context. It is the miracle of eighteenth-century 'taste' — of the 'artistic period' that literary historiography sees as ending with Goethe's death. An 'artistic' period not because marked by a matchless aesthetic production, but because art still seems within it to form a whole with 'life'. With the life of the social elite, of course, which becomes ever broader and richer, while artistic production (especially architecture and painting, but also music), which has not yet installed itself in the marketplace, remains in good part within the bounds and rhythms of that existence, with which it achieves a 'natural' fusion, without suffering any disgrace or deformation.

It is the miracle, we have said, of eighteenth-century taste. To associate such a fusion with *bad* taste might seem a gratuitous slap in the face: in the end, when a musical cigarette case plays Mozart's serenade, something has changed. Granted — but the point is that the kitsch that will engulf the following century — and which is already leering in the castle episode in *Wilhelm Meister*, or in the Rosing chapters of *Pride and Prejudice* — is not different from neoclassical taste because it has betrayed its aspirations, but because it has remained faithful to them in a historical context that has changed too radically. And what has especially changed is the position and self-knowledge of the aesthetic sphere: 'My dear Fräulein,' observes the musician Klesmer in George Eliot's *Daniel Deronda*, 'you have developed your qualities from the *Standpunkt* of the salon.' This *Standpunkt* could still be relevant to Darcy and Elizabeth, whose path Gwendolen Harleth would in fact like to follow. Halfway through the nineteenth century, however, art leaves the salons. Thus, Klesmer coldly concludes, 'You must unlearn all that.'

Aesthetic education must be *un*learned because it has no more worth. It is neither true aesthetics nor true education. In the lives of Eliot's heroes, we witness its replacement with a much more demanding 'vocation': a much more rigid and 'depersonalizing', and also, as we will see, more painful or self-damaging ideal. And this explains why it has been so difficult, for Western culture, to find a true substitute for the harmonious 'dilettantism' celebrated in *Wilhelm Meister* (Eliot herself will pay tribute to it with *Middlemarch*'s Will Ladislaw). The aesthetic fullness of everyday life in fact ensured a 'humanization' of the social universe that will be, in the future, difficult to imagine. We should not therefore be surprised if it has continued for a long time, in countless metamorphoses, to enhance the existence of the modern individual.[31]

Personality

The balanced harmony that strikes Elizabeth at Pemberley is not only an architectural style but also the visible manifestation of a pedagogical ideal. An ideal of the greatest importance, in an age in which the formation of the individual had become charged with new problems. Philippe Ariès:

> Our modern minds are puzzled because they refuse to accept the mixing of ways of life which are nowadays carefully separated: the intimate way of life (family and friends), the private way of life (leisure and amusement), the religious way of life (devotional activities), or the corporate way of life (meetings of those who share the same profession with the object of learning it or exploiting it or defending it). Modern man is divided by a professional life and a family life which are often in competition with each other ... The modern way of life is the result of the divorce between elements which had formerly been united ... [32]

If by 'individual' we mean something fundamentally unitary, then the human being described in these lines is no longer so — or not yet so. The variety of his fields of activity has certainly enriched him, but it has also deprived him of all cohesion. The modern individual is marked from birth by this heterogeneity of occupations, by a perennial disequilibrium of his symbolic and emotive investments. To become an individual in the full sense of the word, he will have to learn how to master this multiplicity, and how to keep it from turning into a wearisome disharmony.

How can this be done? Richard Sennett's *The Fall of Public Man* is one of the most intelligent reconstructions of this effort.[33] For Sennett, the conflict can be reduced to the two extreme poles of 'public' and 'intimate' life. During the last two centuries, the meaning of existence, for the Western individual, has moved ever more decisively into the intimate sphere, resulting, therefore, in 'the fall of public man'. When faced with each situation or collective institution, this individual has turned more and more to a magical and almost obsessive phrase — 'What does this mean *for me?*' — which reflects the transfer of the 'meaning of life' and celebrates the triumph of the sociopsychological attitude known as 'narcissism'.

Richly intuitive in the most divergent fields, Sennett's reconstruction has perhaps only one weak point. It is not necessarily true that the narcissistic 'for me' has always resided in the sphere of *intimate* life. Heedless of the 'objective' significance of what surrounds him, the narcissistic 'I' is in fact basically irresponsible, whereas the intimate life of the last two centuries — the realm of marital and familial relationships in the narrow sense — has in fact been dominated even too much by ideals of responsibility, self-sacrifice, and consideration of the other. The origin of narcissism should not be looked for here: the intimate realm is too 'strong' emotionally, too full of symbolic and legal obligations to allow for the evasion of responsibilities. We must look for a world of less rigid and demanding relationships; such as to leave the individual a wider range for the centripetal and narcissistic manipulation of external reality.

This more pliable realm is in fact the sphere of everyday life. Agnes Heller has called it the sphere of the 'fattening of the particularity'. Here all relationships, intimate as well as public, are only worthwhile in their contribution to the development and consolidation of the individual personality. 'Personality': elusive keyword of our times, its semantic content changes precisely in the decades between the eighteenth and nineteenth centuries, as it fixes on two intertwined meanings.

First of all, personality is a distinctive trait. It designates what renders an individual unique and different from others. But this distinction — and here the second aspect of the term comes into play — never applies to a single activity or to a single characteristic. The modern individual feels that no occupation, be it work or family life or whatever, ever permits one to 'express fully' one's personality. Multilateral and prismatic, personality remains a consistently unsatisfied idol. It would prefer never to have to bend for anything, never to be the means toward an end, whatever that end might be. It would instead prefer that each activity lose its autonomy and objective consistency in order to become a mere instrument of its own development.

For all these reasons, modern personality lodges at the centre of everyday life, which it connects with the culture of *Bildung* and with the theory of the novel itself. Georg Simmel:

> Here we see the source of the concept of culture, which, however, at this point follows only our linguistic feeling. We are not yet cultivated by having developed this or that individual bit of knowledge or skill; we become cultivated only when all of them serve a psychic unity which depends on but does not coincide with them. Our conscious endeavours aim towards particular interests and potentialities. The development of every human being, when it is examined in terms of identifiable items, appears as a bundle of developmental lines which expand in different directions and quite different lengths. But man does not cultivate himself through their isolated perfections, but only insofar as they help to develop his indefinable personal unity. In other words: culture is the way that leads from the closed unity through the unfolded multiplicity to the unfolded unity.
>
> This can refer only to a development towards something prearranged in the germinating forces of personality, sketched out within itself, as a kind of ideal plan.[34]

During the same years in which Simmel was recapitulating this ideal of individual culture — aware, likewise, that the development of capitalism and of the metropolis had made it by then unattainable (and it is not by chance that neither play a relevant role in the classical *Bildungsroman*) — György Lukács was following an analogous path. *The Theory of the Novel*:

> The content of such maturity is an ideal of free humanity which comprehends and affirms the structures of social life as necessary

forms of human community, yet, at the same time, only sees them as an occasion for the active expression of the essential life substance — in other words, which takes possession of these structures, not in their rigid political and legal being-for-themselves, but as the necessary instruments of aims which go far beyond them... .

The social world must therefore be shown as a world of convention, which is partially open to penetration by living meaning.

A new principle of heterogeneity is thereby introduced into the outside world: a hierarchy of the various structures and layers of structures according to their penetrability by meaning. This hierarchy is irrational and incapable of being rationalised: and the meaning, in this particular case, is not objective but is tantamount to the possibility of a personality fulfilling itself in action.[35]

There is one point on which Lukács and Simmel seem particularly to agree: that it is fairly difficult for modern 'personality' to reach its goal in a professional occupation alone, that is to say, in work. Work has become too fragmented in its nature and also too 'objective', too impervious to 'living meaning'. Those who devote themselves to a modern profession must give up their own personality: thus Max Weber, writing in the same years as Simmel and Lukács. And in his letter on the antithesis between the nobility and the bourgeoisie, thus *Wilhelm Meister*: 'A bourgeois may acquire merit and with great trouble cultivate his mind, but his personality is lost, whatever he may do.' (*Wilhelm Meister*, V, 3.)

That this not happen, *Wilhelm Meister* suggests that one turn to occupations at the same time more pliable and more integral: the 'pedagogic' vocation, 'aesthetic' enjoyment — we will see other examples shortly. But the crucial suggestion is that we will find the key to modern personality not so much in specific activities, but in a peculiar *disposition of the soul*. This infiltrates little by little into each activity, ruminates on it, appraises it, and assails it if it must, in its efforts to render it consonant with the development of the individual as an 'unfolded unity'. If we can say, with Jean Baudrillard, that everday life is a *system of interpretation*, the same holds true for personality: both are ways of 'reshaping' the world, of perceiving and evaluating it according to human proportions. In the words of Lukács quoted above, external reality acquires value according to the 'possibility of a personality fulfilling itself in [it]'. Whatever lies beyond this circle and cannot be translated into 'experience' becomes, conversely, 'insignificant': it does not attract the eye, the novel has no desire to tell it. It is, to paraphrase

Sennett, 'the fall of public perception': an ethical-intellectual nearsightedness that blurs our image of the modern individual. Without it, however, that individual himself would be difficult to imagine.

Trial, Opportunity, Episode

If we read *Wilhelm Meister*, or even better *Pride and Prejudice*, with a dose of healthy critical ingenuity, sooner or later arises the inevitable question of what precisely the main characters are 'doing'. Werner gives a response upon seeing Wilhelm anew: 'Look at him, how he stands! How it all suits and fits together! How idling makes one flourish!" *(Wilhelm Meister,* VIII, 1.) Yes, in the end Wilhelm and Elizabeth engage in 'idling'. But this, we have seen, does not mean doing *nothing*, but rather not entrusting the definition of one's personality to any *one* activity.

We have here a further convergence between the particularities of everday life and the categories of the theory of the novel. By not defining himself in a single sphere of life, the novelistic protagonist ceases to be definable as a 'role' — the 'merchant' Werner, the 'minister' Collins, the 'mother' of the Bennet sisters. He becomes instead, to echo Philippe Hamon, a 'polyparadigmatic character.' This is to say, he becomes an entity defined by various, heterogeneous traits that may even contradict one another.[36]

To explain the genesis of this 'polyparadigmaticity', narrative theory usually makes use of some conception of 'realism'. Somewhere along the line we learned to represent existence in a more 'faithful' way. If this is true, however, how do we explain why such a multiplicity of traits always applies to a very small number of characters in a novel? Another explanation is needed, and it may be that, by putting a polyparadigmatic character at the center of a story, every event becomes automatically attracted *into the orbit of 'personality'.* Each event draws its meaning from its relationship with the other levels of Wilhelm and Elizabeth's existence: from the internal harmony that it helps to bind or crack.

It is therefore not a question of representing things or people in a more *truthful* way, but of deciding that a certain aspect of existence is more *meaningful* than others and can consequently have a special function in the story's organization — a 'central' function, that puts the narration into perspective: and the 'network' plot discussed in the first section of this chapter has its center, in fact, in the multilateral development of the protagonist.

This 'focused' perception of a structure, in its turn, is precisely the image of social relationships most consonant with the *anthropocentrism* that is the point of departure and arrival of everyday life.

A 'focused' plot, a 'network' plot: but plot is still, nevertheless, a *diachronic* succession of events. How do we reconcile our spatial metaphors of 'centrality' and 'focus,' which convey an idea of equilibrium and harmony, with a temporal dimension that implies change and instability? In other words: how do we reconcile a *novelistic* plot, which is uncertain and gripping, with the familiar and pleasing rhythm of everyday life? With the rhythm of 'ordinary administration'?

Perhaps we can start by observing that the 'ordinary' course of modern everyday life does not coincide, as at first sight would appear inevitable, with banality, inertia, and repetition. Lefebvre, who initially held this position, had later to write a few hundred pages to refute it.[37] More concisely, Karel Kosik:

> The everyday has its experience and wisdom, its sophistication, its forecasting. It has its replicability but also its special occasions, its routine but also its festivity. The everyday is thus not meant as a contrast to the unusual, the festive, the special, or to History: hypostatizing the everyday as a routine over History, as the exceptional, is itself the *result* of a certain mystification.[38]

Kosik is right. Modern everday life is no longer reducible to a mere repetition of prescribed, 'uneventful', narratively *in-significant* events that do not deserve being related. The presence of personality has broken down the rigid barrier between 'workday' monotony and 'holiday' exception:

> One day in winter, as I came home, my mother, seeing that I was cold, offered me some tea, a thing I did not ordinarily take. I declined at first, and then, for no particular reason, changed my mind. She sent out for one of those short, plump little cakes called "petites madeleines"...

In this all too familiar example, the grayness of modern everyday life is seen to preserve within itself the 'Sunday mornings' of chiidhood ('and all the flowers in our garden and in M. Swann's park, and the water-lilies on the Vivonne and the good folk of the village and their little dwellings and the parish church and the whole of Combray'), only to return them to us at the most insignificant moments, from the depths 'of my cup of tea'. And the spark of the entire process is precisely the work, voluntary or not, of personality, which the novel uses to bring to life a sort of temporal third dimension, with ever-expanding confines, in which nothing can be declared *a priori* as entirely without significance, and nothing as absolutely significant. Nothing is mere repetition; nothing is sheer novelty. The typical novelistic 'episode', as we shall shortly see, always contains within itself something of Proust's *madeleine*: it is an experiment with time.

The two views of time that dominate *The Theory of the Novel* — hope and, above all, memory — are only superficially connected to the past or to the future. In fact, they confer on novelistic time a particular focusing, a curvature that continually has past and future converge *on the present*. On a present that is 'individualized', and is the constant work of reorganization of what has taken place, as well as a projection of what is to come. It is an elastic, elusive present, the exact opposite of the definitive 'here and now' of tragedy. Not only of tragedy, however, for it is in such a representation of temporality that one perceives the absolute incompatibility between the *Bildungsroman*, and modern formation-socialization, and that 'initiation' with which it is so often confused. Not just the initiation of primitive ritual but, even more so, that of a work which preceded *Wilhelm Meister* by only a few years, and which Goethe admired enough to sketch a continuation of it: Mozart and Schickaneder's *The Magic Flute*.

The 'trial', in *The Magic Flute*, is the typical exceptional event. It breaks Tamino's life into two parts that have nothing in common. Before, Tamino is a boy, 'ein Jüngling' — after, he is a man, 'ein Mann'. Before, he is a prince in exile — after, the true heir of his father the king. Before, a wandering and solitary individual — after, the member of a powerful community. Before, the tortured admirer of Pamina — after, her legitimate spouse.

Before, after ... and *during* the trial? During the trial, and this is the point, Tamino is nothing. He is pure potentiality. He can be what he ends up being, or he can be knocked back down to what he was. But in the course of the *Prüfungszeit* he is on hold, at zero degree, just as time in fact is on hold. The 'trial' of initiation consists precisely in accepting that time stop and that one's own identity vanish. It consists in being willing *to die* in order to have the possibility *to be reborn*. The only virtue put on trial is courage in the sense of 'patience', the virtue of exceptional circumstances, virtue in the face of death. The test does not measure the capacity to *live*, which does not seem to concern it at all, but only the ability to endure the stark alternative (there is no gray area between the Night Realm and the Court of Sarastro) of death and rebirth.

The opposite is true in *Wilhelm Meister*. Just like Tamino, Wilhelm is accepted into a secret society, but without ever submitting to a recognizable 'trial'. Just as in space there is no line that separates the world of the initiates from the one outside (there is no symbolic door on which to 'knock three times' as in *The Magic Flute*, where this sound is heard from the very 'Overture'),[39] so in time there is no irreversible moment in which everything, in one fell swoop, is decided. Wilhelm's *Bildung* consists also in his becoming aware of such a state of affairs, and in his no longer searching for the decisive act, the event from which his destiny shines forth. The Wilhelm of *Theatrical Mission*, still a prisoner of this vision,[40] will never finish his quest. The Wilhelm of the *Years of Apprenticeship*, vice versa, will succeed precisely because he has adopted a flexible attitude toward the passage of time. There is a warning of the Society of the Tower that accompanies him constantly — it almost torments him: 'Remember to live!' Not to live in one way or another, but simply to live. What is important is not to establish a goal and concentrate all of one's forces for the moment in which it draws close, the moment of the trial. What is important is to be able to dispose of one's energies *at every moment* and to employ them for the countless occasions or opportunities that life, little by little, takes upon itself to offer.

'Seize the opportunities.' If we project this notion on to the diachronic axis of plot we get the contours of the novelistic 'episode'. Unlike what occurs in the short story or in tragedy, the novelistic episode does not refer back to an objective necessity, but to a subjective possibility. It is that event which *could also not have taken place*. Every novel is in effect a great system of events that are potentially crucial but frustrated, and of others that, apparently of little consequence, acquire instead an unexpected importance. The 'meetings' in *Wilhelm Meister*, the 'conversations' in *Pride and Prejudice*: they are on every page, but not all become equally meaningful.

They *become* meaningful: that is the point. The novelistic episode is almost never meaningful *in itself*. It becomes so because someone — in the *Bildungsroman* usually the protagonist — *gives it meaning*. He prolongs the encounter, he probes into the conversation, he recalls it, he puts his hopes in it... The novelistic plot is marked by this curvature toward interiority, which dispenses meaning and thereby creates events. 'Remember to live': remember that all you run into can be used for the building of your life; it can all be made meaningful.

It is the uneven glimmer of 'experience': another keyword of the culture we are examining, experience too changes in meaning in the second half of the eighteenth century. Contrary to that famous aphorism ('Experience consists in experiencing something that we would have preferred not to experience') this word no longer indicates something that is essentially displeasing: the experience of pain, baroque desengaño, the loss of an original innocence. It now refers to an acquisitive tendency. It implies growth, the expansion of self, and even a sort of 'experiment' performed with one's self. An experiment, and thus provisional: the episode becomes an experience if the individual manages to give it a meaning that expands and strengthens his personality....

... but also manages to put an end to it before personality becomes unilaterally and irrevocably modified. This is the other side of the novelistic event. It demands — again: unlike what occurs in the short story or in tragedy — that one does not get in too 'deep', for if no episode in itself is immune to meaning, no episode, on the other hand, can contain the *entire* meaning of existence. No character will ever reveal his essence in a single gesture or encounter: Elizabeth Bennet, by forcing in this way her interpretation of Darcy, thereby risks destroying her 'novel'.[41]

The 'trial' that the protagonist of the *Bildungsroman* must overcome consists thus in accepting the deferment of the ultimate meaning of his existence. It is the new pedagogical ideal of the eighteenth century, which substitutes admiration for precocity with the image of a gradual growth, a few steps at a time.[42] For this to happen — and Rousseau returns constantly to this point in *Emile* — one must first of all learn to control the imagination, which is the source of the two errors that can throw us off the path towards 'maturity'. Restlessness, first of all, the 'rambling thoughts' of Robinson Crusoe, that make man too much of a wanderer, too detached from his environment, and thereby prevent him from extracting all the potential meaning it contains. But even more than restlessness, *intensity*: which compels him to see an *excess* of meaning in what surrounds him, and to bind himself too thoroughly and too quickly. Prematurely: in ways that are not those of an 'adult'.

The middle road of the hero of the *Bildungsroman* is lined with characters who err in the opposite directions. Restless characters, such as Lydia Bennet, who are prey to futility; and intense characters, their pathetic innocence driving them to a tragic end: Mariane, Aurelie, the Harpist. And, of course, Mignon. The episode that decides her death — one of the most disagreeably cruel in all world literature — embodies without half-tones the eighteenth-century repudiation of premature and passionate desire. Mignon, one night, secretly enters into Wilhelm's bedroom spurred on by a desire that she cannot yet well define. She hides and waits for Wilhelm to arrive, but Philine arrives instead, slips into bed, as does Wilhelm, half drunk, moments later. From her hiding place, Mignon will be the silent witness to their encounter.

Not much can be said about the meaning of this scene: it is such a very clear and banal 'everything has its time and place'. But it is a cruel banality: when Goethe shows us his philistine side, he does absolutely nothing to appear affable. In an episode like this we see the convex side of everyday life: the part of it that faces not the elect individual but rather the outside world. Its conventions seem so flexible and inoffensive, almost without confines — but only as long as one remains within them, and within a spiritual disposition consonant with them. If one gives in to the flight of imagination, however, one then discovers that those confines do indeed exist, and with a cutting edge: but then it is too late. The limbs that are severed from the organism, in *Wilhelm Meister,* can never be rejoined. An interiority which is fervid and alive because not yet objectified, and perhaps not objectifiable, that new and closed dimension of the spirit marked by strife which will dominate the great nineteenth-century novels is, in the relentlessly 'industrious' and 'objectified' environment of the *Bildungsroman,* a symptom of illness. It is a betrayal of life, its opposite. This explains the frequency, most uncommon for novels of the period, with which Goethe kills off his characters or drives them mad. Beyond the organism there is not loneliness but — as already in *Werther,* and later in *Elective Affinities* — nightmares, insanity, or death.

A death, it is understood, by which the imminent and radiant conclusion must not be upset. Thus the repugnant *mise en scène* of Mignon's burial — embalmings and choirs of angels to conceal the reality of the corpse and transform even the funeral into an 'episode' worthy of being lived. The gaze must be removed at the first opportunity from the spot that will remain empty: one must immediately move on to new tales, to new connections. It is that 'immediately' that makes one shudder, cruel as only Goethe, in his well-known abhorrence of death, managed to be. Every void must be filled, every void *can* be filled without real losses. There is no room for doubt: we can easily reformulate 'Remember to live!' as 'Forget the dead!'. Mourning does not become Wilhelm Meister.

Conversation

Trial, in *The Magic Flute,* is an obstacle. To enter into one's own role as an adult an external barrier must be overcome — the four elements in revolt of the final test. It is an archaic mechanism that makes one think of Vladimir Propp's models of narrative plot; linear sequences of thrusts and counterthrusts, with corresponding allies and opponents. Trial, in the *Bildungsroman,* is instead an opportunity: not an obstacle to be overcome while remaining 'intact', but something that must be *incorporated,* for only by stringing together 'experiences' does one build a personality. If Tamino ceases to exist during his *Prüfungszeit,* Wilhelm exists *only* in the course of his 'years of apprenticeship'.

This antithesis between initiation and formation can be seen with exemplary clarity in the different functions that language is called upon to perform in these works. In *The Magic Flute* Tamino must above all remain *silent.* That maturity is confirmed with silence illuminates how terrible, how essentially violent, the ritual of initiation can be: to be silent means, first of all, not to scream from pain (or, in the less bloody world of *The Magic Flute,* from fear). It also means that, in the climactic moment of his existence, the individual agrees to deprive himself of his most elementary right: the right to talk, to reason, to 'have his say'. It is a logical privation, in any case, since he is introduced to a role that has existed before him, in which his arguments must remain mute.

There is more, however. In the course of the final test Tamino is permitted — a detail that does not really fit in with the logic of the plot, and is for this reason all the more interesting — to use the flute given to him by the Queen of the Night. Uneasy surrogates for words, more 'potent' than them but tremendously more enigmatic, the notes of the flute tell us that the crucial point, in Tamino's trial, rests not so much on not emitting any sound, but on not emitting any sound *endowed with meaning.* Either language is renounced, or a language is used that is by definition asemantic. No 'meaning' is given, or can be given, to the trial, which lies beyond the verbal sphere and wishes to remain outside it. Conversely, language becomes 'twaddle': it suits Papageno, not

Tamino, and it will never be an essential stage in the process of formation.[43]

Those who are familiar with *Wilhelm Meister* and *Pride and Prejudice* know well that, in these works, the paradigm is reversed. Here, if anything, characters talk too much. They talk too much: the formation of the individual, once located within everyday life, involves language primarily as *conversation*. A decisive turning point in Wilhelm's *Bildung* is when he abandons the 'theatrical' rhetoric of impassioned monologue for the much more prosaic art of dialogue. Elizabeth and Darcy, for their part, must literally learn to talk to one another: only thus will they be able to overcome those 'embarrassing moments of silence' that mark and frustrate their every encounter.

'To learn to talk to one another', to talk to one another 'sincerely'. These are circumlocutions to say that one must *trust* in language. In the magic circle of everyday life language in fact appears — as does work — as a *sociable* social institution. If one abandons oneself to it without reserve, the double operation of 'expressing oneself' and of 'understanding others' then becomes possible. One will be able, in other words, to reach an agreement: as every conversation beyond a mere exchange of civilities (or of insults) presupposes the willingness of the participants to abandon their own viewpoint in order to embrace that of the other.[44] It is a secret inclination — just as strong in Goethe as in Jane Austen — to separate conversation from that violent, noisy, and partisan *discussion* that had accompanied the formation of eighteenth-century public opinion. Discussion took place in strictly public places — cafés, inns, post stations — and excluded on principle all interest in and reference to the private condition of the participants: each individual spoke only as an abstract member of the public.[45] In comparison with this historical precedent, conversation brings the linguistic exchange back to a more domestic and 'familiar' space. It is reserved for persons who know each other well, and are not only aware of the personal import of their words, but actually strive to understand and emphasize that element. Conversation seems then to lead back, not to the 'rational public debate' that Jürgen Habermas sees at the foundation of public opinion, but to the less demanding language of 'worldliness' — 'se rendre agréable dans la société' — examined by Peter Brooks in *The Novel of Worldliness*.[46] It is as if the term *conversation* were still faithful to its etymology, thereby indicating — beyond and more than a verbal relationship — an everyday familiarity, a concrete habitat, a serene and varied way of occupying one's place in the world.

Conversation, just like everyday life, is born of the attempt to assimilate every sort of experience. It presents itself as that rhetorical form which allows one to talk 'about everything'. To talk about everything, however, is not easy; or, more exactly, it too is a type of rhetoric, a system of rules that must be observed. But conversation has become by now so habitual, having read so many novels and engaged in so many conversations, that it is hard for us to see it as something artificial, as only one of many possible modes of discourse — with its advantages and its limits, its words and its silences. Limits and silences that do not refer to the *subjects* of conversation (obviously enough, every era has permissible and forbidden topics) but to its *form,* which consists of avoiding in a systematic way the *purity* of reasoning. For in the modern world one can truly talk 'about everything' only if one 'forgets' a break, and a truly irreversible one, in the history of thought. Agnes Heller:

> In antiquity any type of scientific thought could refer more or less to the experience of everyday life... . In the Platonic dialogues Socrates always begins with an everyday occurrence, with everyday thought... He 'raises' to philosophical theory experience present in everyday thinking, whether he is dealing with theories relating to 'natural sciences', to metaphysics, to gnoseology, ethics, aesthetics, or politics.[47]

From the Renaissance on, however, this continuity is broken: knowledge progressively loses its anthropomorphic traits and becomes incommensurate with everyday experience. Moreover, it as a rule begins to challenge common sense, to demonstrate that from it no cognitive 'growth' is any longer possible. 'Familiarity,' Kosik succinctly summarizes, 'is an obstacle to knowledge.'[48]

Yet, in the *Bildungsroman,* the exact opposite takes place. Here thought's greatest risk is to become *abstract.* 'Ideas' must never drift too far from 'life'. Goethe:

> Wilhelm saw himself free at the moment when he could not be at unity with himself... . He had sufficient opportunity for noticing that he was lacking in experience and therefore he laid an excessive value on the experience of others and the results which with conviction they deduced from it, and thereby he came still more deeply into error. What he lacked he thought he could acquire if he

undertook to collect and keep all the memorable things which he should come across in books and in conversation. He therefore wrote down his own and other people's opinions and ideas, indeed whole conversations which interested him. In this way, unfortunately, he kept the false as well as the true, stayed much too long on one idea — one might say on a simple maxim... . No one had been more dangerous to him than Jarno. This man had a clear intellect which could form a correct and severe decision about present things, but with this he had the mistake of expressing these individual decisions with a kind of universality, whereas the verdicts of the intellect have force only once and would be incorrect if one applied them to others. (*Wilhelm Meister,* V, 1.)

Here it is, the anthropocentric vocation of everyday life: that, with the *art* of conversation, subjugates the manifestations of thought and draws from them a plastic and pliable language, a refined and unedited rhetoric of the 'concrete'. The language and rhetoric, if one thinks about it, of the *novel*: the first and only literary genre that firstly has chosen not to accentuate its irreducibility to what we call 'ordinary language', but has even contributed, as little else has, to the diffusion and dignifying of the idea of linguistic 'normality' itself, and to making significant that mode of discourse which aims at continually converting the concrete into the abstract and vice versa. Once again, it is the eighteenth-century taste for inclusion and harmonizing: the comfort of civilization.

If all this is contained in the form of conversation, what remains outside it? Or to put the problem in historical terms, 'against' what form of the manifestation of thought do Goethe and Austen conjure up their magnificent dialogues?

The beginnings of an answer can be found in a memorable chapter of *L'Ancien Régime et la Révolution:* 'How, towards the middle of the Eighteenth century, men of letters have become the most important political men in the country, and of the consequences which have resulted.' In these pages, Tocqueville reflects on the peculiarities of the Enlightenment intellectual in France: neither 'mixed up in everyday affairs or administration, as in England', nor 'as in Germany, totally extraneous to politics, confined to the world of pure philosophy or of the *belles lettres.*' The fact is that there emerges in France a new and explosive form of thought, at once fundamentally and stubbornly *political* ('French intellectuals continually are concerned with problems connected with the activities of government'), and dangerously *abstract* ('All believe that it is good to substitute with simple and elementary rules, based on reason and natural law, those complex customs sanctioned by tradition which govern our society').

Given this, I would not exclude the notion that the relaxed and pliant language of novelistic conversation has its counterpart, not in silence, but in the revolutionary pamphlet or oration. It is an antithesis that brings with it many others: the 'curbing' earthiness of concreteness against the cold and daring universalism of principles; the dialogic convertibility of the 'I' in 'you' against the rigid demarcation between orator and audience; the attention toward the patient weaving of a 'plot' against the urge to tear, the passion for 'beginning anew'. Irreconcilable contrasts that tell us a common truth — everyday life and revolution are incompatible — and a little less common truth: that this incompatilibity also exists between revolutionary epochs and the narrative structures of the novel.

Yes, the novel, even though born declaring that it can and wants to talk about everything, chooses as a rule to pass over revolutionary fractures in silence.[49] Because they are fractures, upheavals in the narrative continuum that are too abrupt and radical, of course. But also because they affect that particular sphere of action — the centralized power of the state — in relation to which the culture of the novel, in contrast to that of tragedy, is the victim of an unmistakable and very real taboo.

'Inevitable evils'

Hostility towards the State — or at least indifference — is a further meeting point between the novel and the *Bildungsideal.* The original title of Humboldt's essay cited earlier is *On the Limits of the Action of Government,* and there runs throughout it, as throughout Schiller's *Letters,* the conviction that the State must confine itself to punishing crimes and conducting wars: any other intervention would be hostile to the free and harmonious formation of the individual.

One can evoke, especially for Humboldt, the tradition of liberal thought; or observe that, in Germany, the State is still an absolutist State; or hold to Reinhardt Koselleck's historical reconstruction,[50] according to which bourgeois public opinion could develop only by claiming an increasing freedom *from* the State. All true. But, in the culture I am describing, the antithesis between civil society and the State in no way coincides with the one between freedom and coercion. Even though the apologia for civil society is constructed precisely on such an antithesis, once we move beyond the assertion of principles we discover, obviously enough, that civil society must also have its own form of *authority*: and what makes civil society preferable to the State, paradoxically, is precisely the greater *solidity* of its forms of authority.

Solidity, not force. The State embodies a 'mechanical' and 'abstract' form of social cohesion, intrinsically remote and foreign to the countless articulations of everyday life: this is why its exercise of power appears of necessity to be an *outside* coercion, a force inclined by its very nature to be arbitrary, violent. Civil society appears instead to be the sphere of 'spontaneous' and 'concrete' bonds. Its authority merges with everyday activities and relationships, exercising itself in ways that are natural and unnoticeable: strictly speaking, within civil society it is improper to speak of the 'exercise of authority' as something distinct from the normal course of things.

The pliancy of this second form of power nevertheless has a price, or more precisely, a concrete foundation: the capillary and preventive surveillance of any potential infractions. Only where the causes of conflict have already been removed from the start is there no need for repression. It is the aristocratic utopia of Tocqueville: 'A powerful aristocracy not merely shapes the course of public affairs, it also guides opinion, sets the tone for writers, and lends authority to new ideas.'[51]

This aristocracy is the persuasive and versatile Society of the Tower; the impeccable intelligence of Fitzwilliam Darcy. Not so bad, one may say, and yet, had this really been the ruling class of the age, Europe would have never known the Enlightenment, the criticism of all that rests solely on tradition, the 14th of July...

The question cannot be solved however by evoking crystal-clear class distinctions. The eighteenth century also generates a 'bourgeois' model of the self-regulation of civil society — the Masonic lodges — which inculcates the very same message. According to data gathered by Koselleck, the lodges were literally obsessed with the idea of *visibility:* each disciple had to provide the Masters (who kept themselves invisible to him) with extremely detailed *curricula,* to be kept and updated — even, if necessary, through delations. The episode in which *The Years of Apprenticeship of Wilhelm Meister* is discovered in the Library of the Tower is the barely softened echo of this incredibly impalpable and efficient supervision.

The aim of masonry, wrote Lessing in *Ernst and Falk: A Dialogue for Freemasons* (1778), is 'to render as harmless as possible the consequences of the inevitable evils of the State'. This sentence also reveals the hidden logic of the everyday life of the classical *Bildungsroman*. It is a form of life which comes into being, and acquires its symbolic value, by specializing in activities — filtering, mixing, harmonizing; and later, as we shall see, consuming — all on the side of the consequences, of the effects of the great social mechanisms. It can never be a *causa sui:* it is inherently hetero-directed. And its chosen genre, the novel, retreats when confronted with those moments of truth — political or military — which were the substance of tragedy and epic, and which in *Wilhelm Meister* and *Pride and Prejudice* are 'strangely' distant or absent.

A remarkable sieve against the passing of time, everyday life requires, in making its benefits felt, an unchallenged stability of social relationships. But if this stability comes undone, and history starts to run, farewell everyday life — farewell 'personality', 'conversation', 'episode', 'experience', 'harmony'. It is once again the incompatibility between the novelistic world and revolution-ary crisis, as the latter indicates the moment when the great superindividual forces, in addition to being 'inevitable', become *irresistible:* heedlessly tearing to shreds all the plots, all the networks that had been so carefully woven.

And not just 'material' plots. Revolutionary crisis undermines everyday life, and its novelistic form, on the plane of perception as well. For the novel is founded on the assumption that social relationships are representable through the filter of *personaliza-tion.*[52] Such is the paradigm of the Bennet family, which reads its social destiny in terms of well-to-do bachelors and matrimonial strategies. But it is also the law of any novel: where there is neither commerce nor aristocracy, but only merchants and nobles — each of them different, each overdetermined and complicated by countless other features.

In other words, personalized. And anything that is personalized is also, in a certain sense, 'humanized': it becomes more balanced, tolerable, resistible.[53] Simplicity — the simplicity of abstraction, both epistemological and ontological — this is what the novel does not want us to see. If it keeps silent before revolutionary rupture, it is because such an event makes visible all too clearly the abstract one-sidedness of the great forces at the heart of every civilization, forces which any novel tries to exorcise through mediation and compromise. Whether, then, it is preferable to weave patiently the veil of compromise, or to slash through it — this is another matter. My purpose here was only to clarify in what way a specific literary genre has encouraged one possible choice to the detriment of the other. Whether the anti-tragic and anti-epic tendency impressed by the novel on Western culture has been a progress or a loss, this is something we must each decide for ourselves.

III

Unlike the usual nineteenth-century novel, in the classical *Bildungsroman* the ending and the aim of narration coincide. The story ends as soon as an intentional design has been realized: a design which involves the protagonist and determines the overall meaning of events. The happy ending, in its highest form, is not a dubious 'success', but this triumph of meaning over time. Hegel: 'The true is the whole. But the whole is nothing else than the essence consummating itself through its development. Of the Absolute, it must be said that it is essentially a *result,* that only in the *end* is it what it truly is ...'[54]

In this famous passage of the *Phenomenology,* the only purpose of time is to lead us to the end, thus enabling the epiphany of an essence: then, having become superfluous, time abandons the stage to the harmonious dance of Truth and the Whole. To use the terminology of the *Theory of the Novel,* of Meaning and Totality: of meaning *as* totality. Meaning is no longer 'assigned' by an *act* both subjective and precarious: it has become an ontological *fact* enclosed within a stable system of relationships. It can only be reached by *belonging* to this system, which is Lukács's concrete and organic totality. It is the final stage of *Bildung,* we have often said: its *definitive* stage. It is the disturbing symbiosis of homeland and prison that the classical *Bildungsroman* shares with every other utopian form of thought; and it leads us to ask how the reader can enjoy a situation where individual self-determination is totally, and forever, erased from the picture.

The answer lies in the symbolic exchange that is the *raison d'être* of the classical *Bildungsroman:* if the hero wishes to enjoy absolute freedom in a specific domain of his existence, in other sectors of social activity there must prevail instead complete *conformity.* Everyday life, we have seen, demands the *stability* of social relationships. If within it everything has to be 'personalized' — outside it it is best that everything be absolutely 'objective'. The omnivorous narcissism of private man has its counterpoint in the

timidity that dominates him as soon as he ventures into the larger
world. Arrogant and shrewd in everyday life, he becomes humble
and weak-willed when faced with the choices that support and
frame his existence: here he will gladly yield to a superindividual
Truth that makes his own intellectual 'personality' useless, or even
harmful. But we shall see all this more clearly in a moment. For
now, let us examine a rhetorical detail central to our view of the
text as a 'totality': the construction of point of view.[55]

The Sociology of Prejudice

As a rule, the classical *Bildungsroman* has the reader perceive the
text through the eyes of the protagonist: which is logical, since the
protagonist is undergoing the experience of formation, and the
reading too is intended to be a formative process.[56] The reader's
vision hinges then on that of the protagonist: he identifies with the
hero, sharing the partiality and individuality of his reactions. But
— at a certain point — he wishes to free himself from this position,
because he discovers that the protagonist's viewpoint, contrary to
his hopes, does not allow him to *see,* or not enough, since it is too
often mistaken. It is a problem that Goethe dealt with in the
opening chapters of *Wilhelm Meister:*

> 'It is a beautiful sensation, dear Mariana,' replied Wilhelm, 'when
> we call back to memory old times and innocent mistakes, especially
> if it occurs when we have reached a height from which we can look
> round and look over the way that lies behind us. It is so pleasant, in
> contentment with oneself to recall to memory many obstacles
> which we often with a painful feeling thought were insurmountable,
> and to compare that which is now explained for us with that which
> then was unexplained. But now I feel unspeakably fortunate, as I
> now at this moment speak with you of the past, because at the same
> time I look forward into the delightful land through which we can
> wander hand in hand.' *(Wilhelm Meister,* I, 3.)

In this ironic miniature of what will be the true conclusion of the
novel, the 'mistakes' are still merely the result of childish
ignorance. As the narration continues, obviously, their content
changes. Jane Austen synthesized it in that famous word:
prejudice.

In chapter thirty-six of *Pride and Prejudice,* Elizabeth Bennet
mercilessly attaches to herself a sequence of attributes — 'blind,
partial, prejudiced' — which concisely indicates the two semantic

fields joined in the term 'prejudice'. The first domain — that of blindness — is gnoseological in nature: prejudice appears here as the opposite of truth, or at least of 'critical conviction'. It coincides with the propensity to judge hastily (pre-judice: to emit a verdict before having had time to think). Not by chance the title of the lost manuscript of *Pride and Prejudice* was *First Impressions.*[57] But hastiness is not everything; or rather, since it does not allow the time for critical examination, judgement will rest on a more immediate foundation, coinciding more or less with personal interests. Goethe:

> All opinion on things appertains to the individual, and we know all too well that conviction depends not on comprehension but on will, that one understands only that which is convenient, and therefore, acceptable. In knowledge as well as in action, prejudice decides all, and prejudice — as its name so well expresses — is judgment before investigation. It is an affirmation or negation of that which does and does not correspond to *our nature:* it is a joyful instinct of our being alive to truth as well as to falsity, to all that we find in harmony with ourselves.[58]

This passage introduces us into the second semantic field, which is in a broad sense sociological, and where prejudice is partisanship, partiality. Here it need no longer be an intellectual lack, an 'error'. In the practical sphere, prejudice can easily be effective, overpowering: its defect is no longer gnoseological weakness, but the disintegrating force of partisanship. And, having said this, our problem would appear to be solved. It is necessary that the protagonist and the reader rid themselves of prejudice since its one-sidedness would preclude a socialization based on the model of organic totality. In an organism the parts must not — cannot — have interests distinct from those of the whole.

Yet things are not so simple. In Goethe and Austen there is nothing that allows us to ascribe the ethico-intellectual 'prejudices' of Wilhelm and Elizabeth to 'vital instincts', to 'personal' interests of any sort. A careful reading of the two novels gives the impression that the intellectual behaviour of the two protagonists is oddly *unfounded;* without a recognizable basis and a reasonable aim — *absurd,* as Elizabeth herself concludes: 'blind, partial, prejudiced, absurd'. And why absurd? *Pride and Prejudice,* chapter eleven:

> 'And *your* defect is a propensity to hate everybody.'
> 'And yours', [Darcy] replied, with a smile, 'is wilfully to misunderstand them.'

And further on Darcy says to Elizabeth:

> 'I have had the pleasure of your acquaintance long enough to know that you find great enjoyment in occasionally professing opinions which in fact are not your own.' (*Pride and Prejudice,* 31.)

'Opinions which in fact are not your own': nothing could be further from the predominance of interest over judgement. Nothing more absurd, one might say; yet this madness too has its logic. Elizabeth chastises herself:

> 'And yet I meant to be uncommonly clever in taking so decided a dislike to him, without any reason. It is such a spur to one's genius, such an opening for wit to have a dislike of that kind. One may be continually abusive without saying any thing just; but one cannot be always laughing at a man without now and then stumbling on something witty.' (*Pride and Prejudice,* 40.)

And earlier:

> 'How despicably have I acted!' she cried. — 'I, who have prided myself on my discernment! I, who have valued myself on my abilities! who have often disdained the generous candour of my sister, and gratified my vanity, in useless or blameable distrust.' (*Pride and Prejudice,* 36.)

Here is the secret of Elizabeth's prejudice. In order to appear 'uncommonly clever', she ends up the prisoner of *distrust,* of a suspicious lack of faith which generates an even more deplorable blindness than that aroused by passion. — But if this is how things are, then the first definition of prejudice has been totally reversed. Elizabeth Bennet does not err due to a lack — but due to an *excess of criticism:* and therefore the sociological interpretation we had to reject in its first formulation is now — in a different register — fully legitimate. The overcoming of prejudice is the narrative mechanism that embodies the critique of the highest cultural expression of bourgeois civil society: *public opinion:* Habermas's *Öffentlichkeit.* When Elizabeth Bennet traces her exercise of wit back to a mere 'gratification of vanity', and fears that in the end it may all turn against her, her thoughts cannot fail to remind us of two of the fiercest enemies of public opinion:

It has been the misfortune (not as these gentlemen think it, the glory) of this age, that every thing is to be discussed, as if the constitution of our country were to be always a subject rather of altercation than enjoyment.[59]

Now, following one's own conviction is, of course, more than giving oneself over to authority; but changing an opinion accepted on authority into an opinion held out of personal conviction, does not necessarily alter the content of the opinion, or replace error with truth. The only difference between being caught up in a system of opinions and prejudices based on personal conviction, and being caught up in one based on the authority of others, lies in the added conceit that is innate in the former position.[60]

Subjectivity is manifested in its most external form as the undermining of the established life of the state by opinion and ratiocination when they endeavour to assert the authority of their own fortuitous character and so bring about their own destruction.[61]

In the end, therefore, 'following one's own conviction' can be both 'more' and 'less' worthwhile than 'giving oneself over to authority'. And the classical *Bildungsroman* has its protagonist partake in both experiences. Modern socialization is not the necessary consequence of an ontological condition, as in traditional societies: it is a *process*. It encourages a dynamic, youthful, subjective moment — with its superiority to immediately given authority — only to later emphasize its irresolute wandering, its innate risk of self-destruction. And yet, to induce the individual to renounce with conviction the path of individuality, his access to it must not be hindered, and its value in no way lowered. By no means must it be suggested that individuality is an ephemeral and unappealing detour — quite the contrary: it is a journey that risks being too long, too rich in attractions, too stimulating. The individual must *grow weary* of his individuality: only thus will his renunciation be a reliable one.

In narrative terms, the protagonist of the classical *Bildungsroman* will be the initiator and protractor of an engaging story: the ruler of *sjuzhet*. Without Wilhelm and Elizabeth, *Wilhelm Meister* and *Pride and Prejudice* could never begin, and their organicist culture would be indistinguishable from traditional utopian dogmatism. Yet if other historical epochs could take delight in what Lotman calls 'classificatory' texts, where nothing ever happens because nothing is supposed to happen — towards the end of the eighteenth century the accelerated pace of history has robbed such constructions of all attractiveness. The totalizing representation of the world can no longer propose a stable and closed system which it is merely a matter of not leaving: it must present us with a point of arrival, a system that is the result of a diachronic process. Even for Hegel the marriage of Truth and the Whole is celebrated *at the end of a story:* otherwise, it would have neither literary fascination nor force of conviction.

Wilhelm and Elizabeth are thus necessary to revitalize, to put back into motion organicist imagination. But if they can generate a story, they are the least likely to *conclude* it: rulers of *sjuzhet,* they have no control over the fabula. Without them the text would never begin — entrusted solely to them, it would run the risk of never *ending.* It would recall too closely the new image of time linked to the French Revolution: a promise without limits, a beginning without end, a perennial uncertainty. To avert this danger, the classical *Bildungsroman* effects a clearcut division of parts. To Wilhelm and Elizabeth *sjuzhet* — to the Tower and Darcy *fabula.* To the former the story, to the latter the ending. Freedom of opinion can indeed fuel the novel of becoming — but if it does not wish to destroy itself, it must willingly renounce itself. It must — 'in conclusion' — acknowledge its own fatuity. The critical and dynamic exercise of *suspicion* must give way to the calm and trusting willingness to *listen.*

Symbol and Interpretation

To be suspicious, to be willing to listen. As Paul Ricoeur has shown in *Freud and Philosophy,* these attitudes embody opposite hermeneutic strategies, linked to opposite images of the world and of the role of the interpreting subject. In the first instance the world is seen as a *conflictual* system, where the meaning of each phenomenon — being the result of clashing forces — is always *composite.* Meaning therefore is not translucent, but must be constructed (whence suspicion) by means of the decomposition and recomposition of material. It is the act of interpretation in a strong sense: by emphasizing the alterity between the subject of knowledge and its object, it retains conflict, and even puts it at the heart of the cognitive process.

In the second instance the world appears instead as the product of an emanation: its meaning can be grasped only by allowing its essence to 'manifest' itself freely. Any attempt at a strong interpretation runs the risk of troubling this epiphany of meaning:

it will be seen as an arbitrary act — as prejudice. Because this second model — which is also the model of the classical *Bildungsroman* — allows for *one* meaning only, one truth: and, obviously, their contrary: error. The truly gross errors committed by Wilhelm and Elizabeth: all resulting from their desire to be, 'without any reason', in alterity with the world. From their refusal — weak but stubborn echo of Enlightenment criticism — to trust in it *a priori,* and from their belief that being part of a world should not imply the individual's total assimilation to the whole.

In the history of aesthetic thought, what Wilhelm and Elizabeth combat — ineptly, since the classical *Bildungsroman* demands their defeat — is called 'symbolic' representation:

> Allegory for Coleridge is an instance of 'mechanic form', of a deliberate yoking together of the heterogeneous, while the symbol is a case of 'organic form' based on the intuitive grasp of natural relationships. The symbol achieves a fusion of subject and object because in the symbol the truth of the subject or perceiver is also the truth of the object, its natural significance ... .
>
> Coleridge's preference for the symbol is an instance of a metaphysics which makes the relation between subject and object its fundamental problem, and seeks ways of achieving fusion, of abolishing alienation within man, between man and the world, between objects or forms and meanings ... .
>
> We have here, in the symbolic and the allegorical, two fundamental tropes or operations, two ways of organizing the attribution of meaning. The symbolic operation sees meaning as something inherent, to be drawn out of the depths of the object itself.[62]

We encounter here — reformulated in terms of poetics, or aesthetic theory — an antithesis which has become familiar. On the side of allegory, the 'mechanic', arbitrary, ever imperfect cohesion typical of the modern State; on the side of the symbol, the flexible and organic bonds of a world where the living sense of authority is still one with everyday life. In one instance knowledge is rigid and abstract; in the other it flows from concrete life and returns there without effort.[63] The sequence of contrasts is, we know, potentially endless: here, let us focus on the analogy between the aesthetics of the symbol and the cultural framework of the classical *Bildungsroman.* Adorno:

> If the notion of the symbol has any meaning whatsoever in aesthetics — and this is far from certain — then it can only be that the individual moments of the work of art point beyond themselves

by virtue of their interrelations, that their totality coalesces into meaning.[64]

To paraphrase, symbolic construction always 'connects' the 'individual moments' of a text with all the others: they are thus 'preserved' in their singularity, while simultaneously made 'meaningful' — they 'point beyond themselves'. And this, if we think about it, is the perfect translation in aesthetic terms of the possible world evoked by the classical *Bildungsroman:* a closely woven totality of 'connections' that allows individuality to preserve itself *as such* while acquiring a *wider significance.* As in Schiller, there are no clear borders between aesthetics and sociology: in fact, their mutual convertibility — art is 'socializing', and society 'harmonious' — is proposed as a model of cultural cohesion.[65]

Contrary to common practice, there is no reason to limit the distinction between symbol and allegory to lyric poetry: it is just as pertinent a contrast for the analysis of the novel, and Lukács's *Theory of the Novel,* revolving around the notion of the 'immanence of meaning' in different epic forms, is a good case in point. When Lukács discusses the novelistic attempt to restore a 'concrete totality', he is thinking precisely of the continuity of particular and universal in symbolic representation. And when he ascribes the 'problematic' nature of such an attempt to the heterogeneity of 'interiority' and 'second nature', he too, like Coleridge, is envisaging a form of social and cultural relationships no longer marked by ruptures between subject and object, thereby permitting the 'abolishment of alienation'.

The abolishment of alienation ... A very enchanting expression, and very vague ... But leaving aside what it could mean when in the future tense, to establish what it means in the case of the classical *Bildungsroman* we must return briefly to the question of point of view. The reader is forced to share that of the protagonist: but this, we have said, does not allow a satisfying 'vision'. In the long run, the reader will inevitably desire the disappearance of those attributes of the protagonist that hinder a clear perception of the text and threaten to have it go on forever. Like Jarno — 'Free your mind, where it is possible, from all suspicion and all anxiety' (*Wilhelm Meister,* VIII, 5) — he wants Wilhelm and Elizabeth to renounce their stubborn critical stance: only if they agree to give up intellectual autonomy can Darcy and the Tower come forward to ascribe a univocal, definitive and totalizing meaning to what has been read.

In this final passage the classical *Bildungsroman* reveals the true essence of the 'epiphany of meaning' and of the 'abolishment of alienation' that should accompany it. Just as commodities do not get to market unassisted, likewise the sense of the whole is not revealed of its own: it needs someone — a person, an institution, or their combination — to put it forward and vouch for it. And so, in the final sections of *Wilhelm Meister* and *Pride and Prejudice*, as in a catechism or a book of etiquette, a single voice — which is also ours — asks all the questions, while another voice, distant yet omnipresent, provides all the answers. Only by confiding in this second voice — the hermeneutics of being willing to listen! — will our doubts be resolved and our reading achieve the certainty of meaning.

But what is 'abolished' in this process is not 'alienation' — rather *interpretation*, this fever which in the sixteenth century rends the religious unity of Western Europe, and from that moment on is the necessary premise for any sort of intellectual autonomy. For any project of *Bildung*, it would seem. But the symbolic totality of the classical *Bildungsroman* does not allow for interpretation. To do so would be to recognize that an alterity continues to exist between the subject and his world, and that it has established its own *culture:* and this must not be. That clash, that social strife which, on the cognitive plane, the act of interpretation keeps open and alive, is sealed by the beautiful harmony of the symbol. Or in other words: meaning, in the classical *Bildungsroman*, has its price. And this price is freedom.

Far from being mankind's coming of age, the ending of the classical *Bildungsroman* is illuminated by a meaning that is *octroyé:* benignly granted to the 'pliant' subject, not forcibly seized and built by the free citizen. And then we recall that *Wilhelm Meister* was written between 1794 and 1796, and that the lost manuscript of *Pride and Prejudice* dates from 1796-7. Once again the French Revolution — the *elusion* of the French Revolution: for the classical *Bildungsroman*, far from being the proud achievement of the Enlightenment, is the final restatement of a different and far more modest eighteenth-century desire. The desire for a mechanism of social advancement able to reconcile, rather than estrange, the two dominant economic classes of the epoch. Thus, in *Wilhelm Meister* and *Pride and Prejudice*, the representatives of the opposing social poles — Wilhelm and Elizabeth on the one hand; Lothario, Jarno and Darcy on the other — undergo a sea-change that softens and renders inoffensive their respective class features. The 'bourgeois' are cured of the mental poison of 'prejudice' — the aristocrats manage to curb the humiliating indifference of their 'pride'.[66] Which is to say that they lose precisely those features — 'ideological giddiness' and 'aristocratic snobism', to use the terms of recent historiography — which produced the split, the cultural 'crisis' that was the Revolution.

In other words, in the classical *Bildungsroman* we find the very opposite of what occurred in the summer of 1789: not a secession, but rather a convergence. If the conclusive marriages are indeed *mésalliances,* this does not indicate — as Lukács put it in *Goethe and His Age* — the generous supremacy of universalistic-democratic ideals over narrow class interests: it indicates a way — the only way, in the world of the novel — to restore harmony within the ruling class. In short: the classical *Bildungsroman* narrates 'how the French Revolution could have been avoided'. Not by chance is it a genre that developed in Germany — where revolution never had any chance of success — and in England — where, concluded over a century earlier, it had opened the way to a social symbiosis that renewed itself with particular effectiveness at the turn of the eighteenth century.[67] In France, the socio-cultural model of the classical *Bildungsroman* would have seemed unreal, and indeed it never took root there. The socialization of youth will not be at the centre of great French narrative until the advent of Stendhal and Balzac: and then, of course, it will be a wholly different story.

Escape from Freedom

The classical *Bildungsroman* narrates how the French Revolution could have been avoided. Which culture would have been attracted to such a fantastic experiment? The instinctive response: the one that saw in the Revolution the sign of an inexorable decline. The culture of the reformist landed aristocracy — of Darcy, of Lothario — who could perceive, in the narrative mechanism of the classical *Bildungsroman,* a still predominantly aristocratic universe. In exchange for a reasonable modernization — psychological (Darcy) or administrative (the 'catharsis of the feudal estate' discovered by Giuliano Baioni in the Society of the Tower)[68] — this class can continue to live in a symbolically compact world, respectful of 'natural' inequalities: avoiding the risks of an open and conflictual society.

The totality of the classical *Bildungsroman,* we have seen it time and again, seeks to show that non-bourgeois organic principles embody a social cohesion unknown to the culture of criticial individual autonomy. Fine — but *for this very reason* its chosen readers must be quite different from Darcy and Lothario. The latter do not doubt the supremacy of their principles: to read a text that confirms them in such an obvious way may indeed have a 'tranquillizing' effect — but it is a very poor notion of culture and consent to reduce them to this. No, that revolution is avoidable need not be shown to its victims — but rather to its potential protagonists. The ideal reader of the classical *Bildungsroman* is, in a broad sense, a bourgeois reader (who has also been, historically, its actual reader). It is for this reason that the text's point of view hinges on Wilhelm and Elizabeth, rather than on their respective deuteragonists. It is the bourgeois who must be 'educated', convinced of the 'absurdity' of his cultural values. It is the bourgeois reader who must be shown the advantages of social reconciliation. It is to him that meaning — the happy belonging to a harmonious totality — is offered in exchange for freedom.

That exchange — the fame of *Wilhelm Meister* and *Pride and Prejudice* leaves no doubt about it — was accepted. And this fact presents the history of culture with a problem too often eluded: what is the true nature and the historical distribution of what, for lack of a better term, we continue to call 'bourgeois values'? If we think about it, the exchange proposed by the classical *Bildungsroman* — the 'sweet and intimate' feeling of belonging to a system that literally 'takes care of everything', as opposed to the possibility of directing one's life 'to one's own risk and danger' — this exchange is familiar from studies of mass culture. We see in it the anti-liberal epilogue of the dialectics of the Enlightenment: the bourgeoisie betrayed by itself. 'Betrayed': because we are convinced that — at some indefinite time and place — this bourgeoisie must have known an heroic phase, inspired by much more pugnacious principles. Well, the classical *Bildungsroman* forces us to reconsider this historical model, and makes us wonder whether this phase ever did exist: whether the 'rational public sphere' has ever been such a widespread ideal among those who could call themselves free individuals. Or, more concretely and precisely: it makes us wonder whether this sphere was the ideal of those individuals *when they picked up a novel.*

This last sentence needs some clarification. We tend to believe that with the French Revolution freedom finally became a possible ideal. The vision of the strongest continental monarchy falling to pieces, the birth of political parties, the astonishing spread and vehemence of propaganda and political discussion, the discovery of the wholly artificial nature of every law: all this still conveys today (imagine what it was like then) the image of a world which, to quote Furet once again, 'opens up all possibilities'.

Possible freedom. Possible? And why not *inevitable?* Why exclude the likelihood that — with the exception of the select group of protagonists of these events — the vast majority of men were literally *overtaken* by freedom as if by a sudden catastrophe? 'Forced' to enjoy it because of the instantaneous destruction of bonds that habit had rendered almost instinctive? Why not recall that liberal thought itself coined a definition of freedom — 'freedom *from*' which points to its privative aspect? In short, why not admit that freedom — in the only social formation that chose it as its highest principle — is first and foremost solitude, and therefore wearisome and painful?

Questions which are far from new, as we know. Counter-revolutionary thought, for example, justified the irrationalist restoration of authority with the notion that the vast majority of mankind feels freedom to be a 'burden' of which it would rather be 'relieved'. A few decades later, Tocqueville and Mill reached similar analytic conclusions (although, naturally, the value judgement was reversed). Towards the end of the century, this same anthropological 'weakness' was to be evoked by the Grand Inquisitor of *The Brothers Karamazov,* and by Nietzsche in the *Genealogy of Morals.*

And so on. Bourgeois freedom is peculiar in that it has generated the unceasing counter-melody of the 'escape' from its harshness. The Frankfurt school — the line of Marxist thought that has reflected most acutely on this problem — defined this ambivalence as a chronological succession: first freedom — then the escape of which Erich Fromm wrote. Yet our analysis of the classical *Bildungsroman* suggests that this sequence ought to be restated in synchronic terms. The dialectic of bourgeois freedom does not unfold as a succession of 'first, then later' — but as the continual co-presence of the two opposing tensions.

Given, as is obvious, that the weight of each of the two components has varied across time, we must realize that the culture of modern individuality has been from the start a combination of the two extremes: unthinkable without the one or the other. It may be compared to the motion of a pendulum: having reached the furthest point in one direction, it changes course and swings back in the opposite one. Which is to say that the essence of modern individuality lies not so much in the opposite — 'pure' — poles of freedom and its contrary, but in the never-ending motion from one extreme to the other, and in the myriad of intermediate positions.

If it is wrong then to interpret all behaviour patterns in bourgeois society as an escape from freedom — it is equally mistaken not to recognize that many of them are just that. This is why, a few pages back, I limited the desire to rid oneself of interpretive freedom (and of the strain that no doubt accompanies it) to the reading of the classical *Bildungsroman*. Each epoch has its 'spirit of the age' — a precariously balanced system of opposing impulses. In the decades that interest us, one of these forces induced people to desire the immanence of meaning in an organic totality. When this need made itself felt — in both the social and individual symbolic systems — the classical *Bildungsroman* was ready to satisfy it: and in a very gratifying way, because it was unavowed. For the modern individual needs occasionally to turn his back on his highest political values: but he is ashamed to do so. He prefers not to admit it: 'not to know' that he is doing it, so to speak. And if this can happen thanks to a system of rhetorical mechanisms to which he abandons himself without a clear awareness of what his heart and mind are doing, what more could be asked for?

Of Necessity, Virtue

We had begun with a specifically 'bourgeois' dilemma: the clash between individual autonomy and social integration. The image of the escape from freedom, which places the desire to 'belong' within the individual psyche itself, is, as it were, its solution. When the logic of social integration has been interiorized, turning into a desire that the individual perceives as his 'own', as his *greatest* desire in fact, to which all others can be subordinated and sacrificed — then socialization is no longer felt as a mere necessity, but as a value choice: it has become *legitimate*.

    The resulting advantages, for the efficient functioning of the social system, are fairly evident — and it is also interesting that this is the first thing we think of. Inevitably, the process of symbolic legitimation of the existing order continues — 'spontaneously' — to appear as a splendid deception. Not deliberate, perhaps, but a deception nonetheless: and able to bind firmly to a given system those who would have every interest in freeing themselves from it.

Adorno once declared himself astonished at how man was able to ascribe value to what should inspire rejection. True — but we should also learn to be astonished by the contrary. To accept the idea that the values dearest to us are mocked by the existing order of things — to accept the idea that the world is not 'made for us' can be truly disheartening.

Disheartening, these epochs of ordinary administration — the chosen epochs of the novelistic genre — for those who perceive a discrepancy between values and reality, and who perceive that there is no change in power relationships on the horizon. Such a vision must be filtered, for in periods like these one of the keenest 'material interests' of the single individual, sooner or later, is the desire to feel himself in syntony with those rules that he must in any case respect. A symbolic animal, man yearns for a symbolic form that may heal the gap between the values 'within' and the world 'without'. From this viewpoint, the illusion of free consent seems to be far more necessary *for the survival of the individual* than for that of the social system. For the latter, in the end, it is merely the software of control: a weapon to be used in times of peace; in times, precisely, of ordinary administration. But if necessary, it can be done without. Even capitalism has burned books, precisely because it too has inscribed somewhere those famous words, *ultima ratio regum.* But the individual does not have this option. For him consent, the feeling that the world is *his* world, is truly a vital necessity.[69]

To the *ultima ratio regum* the instinctive opposition, on the side of the individual, would seem to be the *spes ultima dea*. But while hope looks ahead, towards the future, the valorization of the existing order by the classical *Bildungsroman* prompts hero and reader to look back, towards the past. The refusal to consider the future still 'open', we have seen, is presented as an indication of maturity. *Bildung* is concluded under the sign of memory, of *mémoire voluntaire,* of the rationalization of the accomplished journey. Such is the meaning of the endless stories scattered throughout the final two books of *Wilhelm Meister;* and the same message is conveyed by a brief episode of *Pride and Prejudice.* Chapter forty-three: all communication between the two protagonists has ceased, and Elizabeth visits Pemberley, having learned that Darcy is in London and that she runs no risk of meeting him. But the episode ends instead with their encounter, which very quickly becomes an explicit prelude to marriage. A typical novelistic coincidence, it seems. Certainly. But what is interesting is the *causal sequence* that directs it. Austen could easily have motivated the encounter through a sudden storm, or a swoon of Mrs Gardiner, and instead what causes it is the fact that — twice, once in the house and then in the park — Elizabeth delays her departure by 'turning back' to see once more a portrait of Darcy, and his home.

What makes their meeting possible, in other words, is the 'retracing of one's steps' to reconsider what belongs to the past: Darcy's face on the canvas, 'with such a smile over the face, as she remembered to have sometimes seen, when he looked at her'. It is not a *new* Darcy which makes her pause 'several minutes' in front of the portrait: it is the Darcy she already knows. The facts have not changed, but their *value* in Elizabeth's eyes has: on second reading, the past is permeated with a new meaning, its aim the well-being of the individual. It is the final topic of this chapter: the *valorization of necessity*, the 'positive' side of what appeared above as the purely privative motion of the escape from freedom.[70]

In the third chapter of *The Theory of the Novel* Lukács expounds the constitutive antithesis of the novelistic universe. The quest of the 'soul' is contrasted to the abrupt reality of the 'world of convention': 'Despite its regularity, it is a world that does not offer itself either as meaning to the aim-seeking subject or as matter, in sensuous immediacy, to the active subject. It is a second nature, and, like nature (first nature), it is determinable only as the embodiment of recognized but senseless necessities.'[71]

In a few concise pages Lukács returns several times to the opposition of 'meaning' and 'senseless causal connections', 'interiority' and 'a necessity that is eternal, immutable and beyond the reach of man'. The entire *Theory of the Novel* rests on the opposition of these 'heterogeneous' principles, the diverse combinations of which generate the three fundamental types of novelistic structure. The third type — the classical *Bildungsroman* — Lukács tends to define as an *'attempt* at synthesis' or a 'problematic *compromise'*: but after what has been said here, these definitions appear all too hesitant. We can speak of compromise when conflicting principles have indeed reached an accord, but without having lost their diversity. They remain heterogenous, and the agreement intrinsically precarious. In the temporal rhetoric of the classical *Bildungsroman,* on the other hand, the subjective yearning for 'meaning' is entirely satisfied by, and subsumed under the objective legislation of 'causality'. In fact, it is not an exaggeration to say that 'meaning' is appropriated by the heroes only thanks to those 'causal connections' which according to Lukács ought to hinder their quest. It is only after having reconstructed with legal precision the causal sequence that links Darcy to Bingley, Jane and Wickham,[72] that Elizabeth Bennet can grasp the ultimate meaning of the personality of others and of her own feelings. It is only after he has connected all the principal episodes of his life to the corresponding interventions of the Tower that Wilhelm finally understands the direction of his quest, and 'acknowledges' the aim to which it had tended from the start.

To put it another way: in the classical *Bildungsroman* the 'meaning' of events is always and intimately linked to the solution of a mystery. Such a connection is far from obligatory (nineteenth-century 'realistic' narrative, for example, will usually do without it) and it has provoked endless criticism of *Meister,* from Schiller on. But Goethe's choice is not motivated by the desire for melodramatic 'effect': it is rather a superb combination of rhetorical and cultural strategies. As for the first, a narration founded on a mystery, and concluded by its solution, highlights once again that theoretical pair, *fabula* and *sjuzhet. Fabula:* the organization of narrative material according to rigorous causal criteria; an 'objective' narration, superior to any particular point of view. *Sjuzhet:* 'the introduction of narrative material into the visual field of the reader' (Tomachevski); a 'subjective' narration, because it is founded on the differentiation of points of view within the story itself.

Fabula, in other words, is the story 'as it is': established, unchangeable, independent of enunciation. *Sjuzhet* is a way of *evaluating* the story, dissecting it according to specific viewpoints and values: it is a perceptual schema, an implicit 'comment' projected on to the 'facts'. Well, what happens to these two narrative modes in a mystery text? *During* the narration they are as distant from one another as possible: it is *sjuzhet* and the differentiation of viewpoints that dominate. But at the *end* of the narration they coincide perfectly; or rather, *sjuzhet* must renounce its characteristic features and bow to the superindividual necessity embodied within the reconstruction of the *fabula.* The subjective point of view — that of the protagonist, and of the reader — loses all validity, and with it vanishes the very idea of a subjective establishment of significance. 'Significance' no longer belongs to the domain of 'value': it coincides with the impersonal (*super*-personal) 'meaning'[73] of 'what has actually taken place', and as such it is valid for anyone.

We find here the fusion of 'rational' and 'real', of value judgements and factual observations, that is characteristic of modern literary discourse[74]: a fusion that by nature is anti-tragic, and finds its fullest manifestation in the novel.[75] Through it, values no longer appear to be the result of a risky and precarious individual choice: they are 'grounded' in the nature of things. As we have already seen: in the classical *Bildungsroman* the renunciation of freedom has its recompense in the 'immanence of meaning'. Ultimate symbolic gratification: the world speaks our language.

In the preceding pages I have identified the Lukácsian concept of 'second nature' with the world of 'facts': that is to say, with a world represented as if it were totally extraneous and impervious to any attribution of value. This is not exactly the case. In the third chapter of *The Theory of the Novel* Lukács tends in fact to distinguish 'second nature' not only from 'interiority', but also from 'first' nature, or nature *tout court*:

> Second nature is not dumb, sensuous and yet senseless like the first: it is a complex of senses — meanings — which has become rigid and strange, and which no longer awakens interiority. [In it] man's experience of his self-made environment is a prison instead of a parental home ... . When the soul-content of these constructs can no longer directly become soul, when the constructs no longer appear as the agglomerate and concentrate of interiorities which can at any moment be transformed back into a soul, then they must, in order to subsist, achieve a power which dominates men blindly, without exception or choice.[76]

Let us forget the metaphysics of alienation that electrifies passages like this one (Hegelian nostalgia for the reunification of the extremes; second nature as the mere 'negation' of interiority; which is meaningful not for what it is, but for what it is 'not', or no longer). Let us concentrate instead on that precious insight which the dialectic structure of *The Theory of the Novel* was unfortunately destined to thwart. Second nature is not a world of mere 'facts', or rather, those facts — that 'blind indifferent absolute authority' — are themselves the result of value choices, of *meaningful projects*. They are values that have become reality, 'soul-contents' that have transformed themselves into social conventions. The pertinent contrast is not therefore between a universe wholly intentional and meaningful (interiority) and one that is wholly bereft of these attributes (social reality). It is rather the contrast between two (or more) universes, *equally endowed with meaning,* but inspired by *different* values, and of different *force* in the actual course of the world.

We may say, to sum up, that 'interiority' and 'second nature' could be redefined as socially *professed* values (those which, in fact, shape our inner soul) and values actually *operational* within society (constituting the 'implicit', absent-present meaning of second nature). Now, the point is that these two value systems — the dominant *ethic* and the dominant *praxis* — do *not* as a rule coincide. This is particularly true for bourgeois society: and from this discrepancy springs its peculiar political pugnaciousness, its unceasing dissatisfaction with the way principles are 'realized', its characteristic dynamism. But...

But if what has been said in this chapter is true, then the classical *Bildungsroman* does not aim at promoting that pugnaciousness and that dynamism. Its goal is not to heighten the discrepancy, but to make it disappear. Here the world is truly what it claims to be; what it should be according to the principles of the dominant ethic. The 'education' of Wilhelm and Elizabeth also consists in the acknowledgement that *social superiority and moral superiority are one and the same.*

It is the magic moment of 'improvement': a term that for a few decades manages to join the notion of 'economic modernization' (and ensuing profits), with that of 'moral betterment' (and ensuing virtues).[77] It is the dream of every ideology: the ethical establishment of socialization — the legitimation of the social order in its fullest sense. But then — then we must inevitably ask ourselves why the classical *Bildungsroman* had such a brief life. Why there are only a handful of texts that fully correspond to its principles. Why Austen herself, just a short time after *Pride and Prejudice,* has one of the protagonists of *Mansfield Park* admit that to be 'honest and rich' at the same time has by now become impossible.[78]

Why, in other words, did modern Western civilization discard such a perfect narrative mechanism? And perhaps the answer lies precisely here: it was *too* perfect. It could only be convincing in so far as historical experience continued to make absolute cohesion and totalizing harmony not only a desirable ideal, but a conceivable one too. But the historico-cultural context suited to the 'perfection' of the classical *Bildungsroman* had an unusually brief life. If we think about it, all the principal narrative choices of Goethe and Austen — the social and intellectual physiognomy of the protagonist; the temporary and inadequate centrality of his point of view; the totalizing features of the ending; the predominance of necessity over possibilities; the 'symbolic' structure — these are all different manifestations of a single desire:

that the French Revolution may be 'disavowed' — or, more realistically, that the irreversibility of its effects may be denied.

When it became clear that this was not to be, a world which had opened itself to a ceaseless clash of values and an erratic development with no end in sight could no longer recognize its own features in the bright normality of *Wilhelm Meister,* nor believe in such a total and easily available happiness. 'Today from this place begins a new era in the history of the world, and you may claim to have been there': Goethe, the evening of the battle of Valmy. He was right, and that new era quickly forgot his most ambitious novel.

2

Waterloo Story

Picking up *The Red and the Black* after finishing *Wilhelm Meister*, one is struck by how much the structure of the *Bildungsroman* has changed in little more than thirty years. The 'great world' can no longer be confined to the story's periphery, in hazy revolutions and bloodless wars, but assaults the 'little world', actively forging the interiority of its new heroes. These are no longer sound and pliant, but passionate and unmanageable, 'dark and strange': they will never become 'mature' in the ways suggested by the classical *Bildungsroman*. Formation as a synthesis of variety and harmony; the homogeneity of individual autonomy and socialization; the very notion of the novel as a 'symbolic' and organic form — all these beliefs are now dismissed as so many fairy-tale illusions.

The classical *Bildungsroman* is over. An entirely new narrative form takes its place, daring to face up to the great transformation of the years 1789 to 1815, eluded by the *Bildungsroman* in its search for organic closure. Perhaps it is not suprising that the new novelistic model left England and Germany for France and Russia — the two countries whose clash had decided the fate of Europe; nor that its two greatest craftsmen were Pushkin, the friend of the Decembrists, and Stendhal, who had chosen Napoleon as the 'idol of a youth'. Their heroes will no longer set out 'on journeys' to 'have experiences'. Whether they want to conquer a woman or obtain a position, their life will be a sequence of battles, a sort of personal campaign. Here youth does not find its meaning in creating countless 'connections' with the existing order, but in breaking them. It is not appeased by the happiness of synthesis, but lives, and dies, in the harshness of conflict. And yet...

Yet the field is not clearly divided between the red and the black, despite the lure of that title. If the moment of conflict had not yet come in Goethe and Austen, in Stendhal and Pushkin it has already passed. Napoleon is just a memory in *The Red and the Black*, and in *The Charterhouse of Parma*, Fabrizio will only be in time for Waterloo; as for the Decembrist rising, the book in *Eugene Onegin* that dealt with it was destroyed, and Lermontov alludes to it in half a line. The moment of conflict has passed, and the heroes of these novels are caught between somehow accepting the world of the Restoration, or remaining faithful to those defeated ideals which make them intolerant and uneasy toward compromise. The only echo of the former decades are the duels they will all take part in, but which are no longer the moment of truth when choosing sides becomes easier and clearer: the hero ends up shooting not his enemy, but a harmless poet, or his own lover, in the back.

It is a highly ambiguous atmosphere — equivocal, as is required by that exemplary life that is at the heart of nineteenth-century imagination. General Bonaparte, the soldier of the Revolution, the liberator who puts merit before status and enthusiasm before calculation — but also the Emperor Napoleon, the despot anointed by the Pope, who treats men as tools and silences public opinion. It may be obvious, but without Napoleon literary history too would have been totally different, for we would not have had that dynamic, ambitious, and ambiguous hero who dominates an entire century. His restless ambiguity makes him the natural representative of an age in which existence truly becomes what the *Theory of the Novel* calls 'problematic'. Here, interests conflict with ideals, desire for freedom with aspirations for happiness, love (as Lukács wrote in his studies on *Faust)* with 'career' in the highest sense of the word. Everything divides in two, each value is opposed by one of equal importance.

So, what does it mean to 'grow up' in such a world? How can one feel part of a world which deep down one despises? Finally, what becomes of the experience of reading a *Bildungsroman* as a formative and socializing process in its own right?

Pushkin and Stendhal answer these radical questions by first of all abandoning any idea of synthesis. Instead of toning down the discordances and resolving the dilemmas, their works accentuate the contradictions and even, as we shall see, the absurdity of their subject matter. In an effort which should still amaze us for its intelligence and courage, *The Red and the Black, The Charterhouse of Parma* and *Eugene Onegin* are all strained and at times unhinged by their keen tenacity in pursuing the new and treacherous paths of individual formation. Whether the results of this mercurial enquiry are of lasting value I will not say: but I shall try to show that this was one of the highest moments of bourgeois consciousness.

I

Politics as Destiny?

Despite the famous assertion that 'politics in the middle of imaginary interests are like a pistol-shot in the middle of a concert. The noise is deafening without being emphatic' (*The Red and the Black,* II, 22), one of the major novelties of *The Red and the Black* and of the *Charterhouse* is precisely the coexistence of fictional biography and political history. Yet the novel revolves around individual destinies, while politics move to collective rhythms. Is it possible for the two domains to become homogeneous, so that individual formation will fully develop within the public sphere?

Looking at Stendhal's philosophico-political background, the answer is definitely yes. In *De l'esprit* (III Discourse, ch. XXII), Helvétius sees the greatness of Greece and Rome in 'the ability with which the legislators had linked private and public interests'. In Chapter VII of the same Discourse ('De la supériorité d'esprit des gens passionnés sur les gens sensés'), we are told that the union of the two kinds of interest is revealed by passions ('similar to volcanoes which unexpectedly change the course of a river with their sudden eruptions': we are reminded of Büchner's Saint-Just), and especially by love of glory, whereby individual energy leads directly to the common good. For Helvétius, this passion is embodied in 'great men' who, similar to volcanoes, defeat 'the forces of idleness and inertia' (ch. VIII) and enable the progress of mankind.

Passion, glory, contempt for idleness and prudence, energy concentrated in a great personality: we are already in the midst of the Stendhalian imagination. Yet those values that were consistent and continuous in Helvétius, in Stendhal disintegrate and clash. Thus, as we read in the *Life of Napoleon,* 'the energy needed to move the enormous mass of habit' is indeed the mainspring of human progress; but, as was the case with Napoleon, it can easily go against political and intellectual freedom. 'To say tyrant is to say superior spirit'; and vice versa, of course. And how can we possibly not hope for superior spirits? And how can we possibly live with tyrants?

No, Stendhal does not believe in the necessary evolution of the human species. In '1880' humanity may be freer, bolder, more passionate and critical; but it may instead have adopted the worse traits of American democracy, becoming even more cowardly and mediocre. This two-sided and contradictory historical perspective makes it impossible for the individual's destiny to find its meaning within the political setting. As his novels gradually approach their ending, Stendhal grants less and less narrative weight to political motifs which he nevertheless continues to use. The *ultra* conspiracy of de La Mole, which at first seemed a rather serious undertaking, literally vanishes into thin air in an incidental little paragraph *(The Red and the Black,* II, 25). Not to mention those famous lines:

> Contessa Mosca had strongly approved, at the time, of her husband's return to the Ministry, but she herself had never been willing to consent to set foot again in Ernesto V's dominions. She held her court at Vignano, on the left bank of the Po, and consequently within Austrian territory. In this magnificent palace of Vignano, which the Conte had built for her, she was at home every Thursday to all the best society in Parma, and every day to her own numerous friends. Fabrizio would not have let a day pass without going to Vignano. The Contessa, in short, combined in her life all the outward appearances of happiness, but she lived for a very short time only after Fabrizio, whom she adored, and who spent but one year in his Charterhouse.
> The prisons of Parma were empty. The Conte was immensely rich, and Ernesto V adored by his subjects, who compared his rule to that of the Grand Dukes of Tuscany.

To all appearances the fate of Sanseverina and of Fabrizio is put aside and the political setting has the last word. But the syntactic prominence is all too obvious here: it is an ironic hyperbole which brands the political universe as insignificant. We are reminded of Hamlet's dying words: some sensible political advice to the diligent Horatio, and the rest is silence. Yet the meaning of the play could only reside in that silence which closes Hamlet's life: the trumpets and cannons of Fortinbras, who will certainly be adored by his subjects, may drown it with their roar, but they will never break its seal.

Contrary to the Erfurt dictum, for Stendhal politics is not the destiny of modern man. This discrepancy, on close examination, was already present in the way Helvétius had joined individual biography and collective historical rhythm. The two trajectories only come together in 'great men', and at the moment of their 'victory': thus, in exceptional personalities and circumstances. But these are neither the men nor the moments which the novel chooses to make meaningful. Unlike the epic, it never relates the material and symbolic *foundation* of a civilization, but rather presupposes its already 'normal' functioning. This is an *a priori* condition of the novel as 'symbolic form',[1] without which it would indeed never have been able to represent its most distinctive theme, totally absent in epic and drama: the individual's formation and socialization, a theme that is conceivable only if the hero is not a 'great man', and if social norms, for their part, enjoy a substantial stability.

The novel however is not epos for another reason as well: because the 'freedom of modern men', Benjamin Constant had observed, tends to withdraw from the public sphere towards 'the enjoyments of private independence'. As a consequence, the novel will not attempt to identify the public and private spheres, but rather to investigate their conflictual relationship, and see whether a balance or a compromise can be struck. The classical *Bildungsroman* had found a solution in the world of 'sociability': a system of adaptable and synthetic realms, of mediations which had eliminated the one-sidedness of public and private life. With Stendhal, though, dialectic synthesis falls apart, and his first major works — the *Life of Napoleon* and *On Love* — explore the opposite poles of a wholly public existence and a strictly private passion. We find an analogous discontinuity in Pushkin, always undecided whether to call his hero 'Eugene' or 'Onegin'; and justifiably undecided, since private and public have indeed come apart — yet are both important. This also explains, we may add in passing, why all the protagonists of these novels are men: it is an age that wants to be active in two domains at once, and it cannot feel represented (as had earlier been the case, and will be again in the future) by anyone who is forced against her will into a single dimension.

'The Uniform of my Generation'

Just like Wilhelm Meister, Julien Sorel and Fabrizio del Dongo feel they cannot be what they want. This is the gap between subjective desires and objective possibilities typical of 'open' societies, and which makes modern socialization so very different from archaic initiation, and so intrinsically problematic. Yet, if for Wilhelm the problem arose from having been born in the wrong *class*, for Julien and Fabrizio it consists in having been born in the wrong *era* — a few years too late. This narrative choice confirms Stendhal's paradoxical intention to use political history not in order to deploy and solve within it the individual's formation, but to render that course even more twisted and contradictory. His heroes, tied to the values of a historical period that is over, are faced with two choices: they can remain faithful to those values, thereby accepting their exclusion from the new context — or they can more or less openly betray them, thereby achieving a satisfactory social position. Individual autonomy and social integration are thus no longer the two aspects of a single course, as in the classical *Bildungsroman*, but incompatible choices. Which shall be the more significant for the new *Bildungsroman*?

Let us begin with the first. It expresses the desire for an identity stronger than circumstances, and ready to bear the personal privations that will inevitably follow. We find here the great symbol of the revolutionary imagination: Robespierre, the 'incorruptible' Robespierre who is first and foremost a 'citizen', a political abstraction — not a man of flesh and blood like Danton, his antitype in the same symbolic universe. Stendhal knew more than one man of this nature, and he created them as well: Altamira in *The Red and the Black*, Ferrante Palla in the *Charterhouse*. It is symptomatic, however, that he always places such characters on the story's periphery: they may be admirable, but they are not interesting. To Stendhal's eyes, the double exile they must endure (in time and in space — Altamira flees to France and Ferrante Palla into hiding) weakens their narrative potential instead of increasing it; and their truly incorruptible integrity — which has Altamira talking about the 'principle of utility' even at the ball — already borders on the stolid obsession of 'citizen Régimbart' in *A Sentimental Education*.

The stubbornness of autonomy does not suit Stendhal's heroes, whose novel begins when Julien 'all at once ceased to speak of Napoleon' (*The Red and the Black*, I, 5) and Fabrizio accepts the Neapolitan Jesuits' rules of the game: 'Whoever thought of protesting against the absurdity of the rules of whist?' (*The Charterhouse of Parma*, 6). What makes these heroes interesting and representative is precisely their forsaking of an ideal not due to a change in inner convictions, but in deference to the spirit of the times. With them is born that distinctively modern and 'historical' type of hypocrisy — *opportunism*:

> 'I, a poor peasant from the Jura,' [Julien] kept on repeating, 'I, condemned always to wear this dismal black coat! Alas, twenty years ago, I should have worn a uniform .... In those days a man of my sort was either killed, or *a General at six and thirty.*' The letter, which he kept tightly clasped in his hand, gave him the bearing and pose of a hero. 'Nowadays, it is true, with the said black coat, at the age of forty, a man has emoluments of one hundred thousand francs and the Blue Riband, like the Bishop of Beauvais.
>
> 'Oh, well!' he said to himself, laughing like Mephistopheles, 'I have more sense than they; I know how to choose the uniform of my generation.' (*The Red and the Black*, II, 43.)

In addition to the uniform, however, 'their' generation also forces Stendhal's heroes to betray the progressive values of the Revolutionary and Napoleonic eras. Such is the case with brotherhood during the supper at Valenod's (*The Red and the Black*, I, 22), when the children at the orphanage are forbidden to sing while Julien strengthens his own position by charming the man who misuses their funds. Later on, it is the turn of meritocracy to be betrayed, when Julien confers a certain post on an 'old imbecile' instead of on 'M. Gros, the celebrated geometrician: a noble-hearted man' (and this ' "is nothing," he told himself; "I must be prepared for many other acts of injustice, if I am to succeed, and, what is more, must know how to conceal them, under a cloak of fine sentimental words." ' *The Red and the Black*, II, 37). In the *Charterhouse*, equality before the law is mocked: Sanseverina's first trial of strength with Ernesto IV is when she obtains a pardon for 'a rascal ... on the strength of whose confessions the famous Ferrante Palla had been sentenced to death' (*The Charterhouse of Parma*, 6), thereby sacrificing justice to the most fleeting of personal whims. Julien and Fabrizio's careers, after all, are precisely two unbroken chains of *ancien régime* favours, either spontaneously granted by the Marquis de La Mole and by Count Mosca or — more often — secured for them thanks to the intercessions of Mathilde or Sanseverina.

'Please speak with more respect of the sex that will make your fortune', exclaims the latter from the very beginning of the *Charterhouse*. These words of a perfect courtesan, fully borne out by the facts, indicate a further gap between Stendhal the novelist and his politico-philosophical background. Both Bentham's utilitarianism and the thought of the *ideologues* — the two cornerstones of Stendhal's culture, in which Helvétius' model had

been rewritten in terms of ordinary bourgeois administration —
were based on the notion that personal interest and the public
welfare could and must coincide. Could coincide, that is to say, not
due to the dialectic acrobatics of Invisible Hands or the Ruses of
Reason, but because the collectivity had everything to gain from
the success of merit. The 'careers open to talent' — from their first
and most spectacular instance, the *Grande Armée* — were not by
chance all connected with the State and public administration,
that is to say, with the world of the 'common good'.

Now, although Stendhal never definitively rejects this model,
from the 1820s on he finds it, if not exactly false, at least shaky. The
homogeneity of private interests and the common good is first put
into doubt in parenthetical asides ('Virtue is for me the habit of
doing what is displeasing [to oneself] **and useful to others'**: *On Love*,
part II, ch. 57), and then criticised at length in the 1825 pamphlet
D'un nouveau complot contre les industriels.[2] Despite sarcasm from
his utilitarian milieu, Stendhal retained his doubt — without,
however, being able to develop a different explanatory picture. In
his novels, he takes the conflict between the two spheres for
granted and fervently analyses its consequences, but without in
any way trying to 'explain' it.

Two passages, one from the beginning and the other from the
end of *The Red and the Black*, will help clarify the matter:

> From his earliest boyhood, [Julien] had had moments of
> exaltation. At such times he dreamed with rapture that one day he
> would be introduced to the beautiful ladies of Paris; he would
> manage to attract their attention by some brilliant action. Why
> should he not be loved by one of them, as Bonaparte, when still
> penniless, had been loved by the brilliant Madame de Beauharnais?
> For many years now, perhaps not an hour of Julien's life had
> passed without his reminding himself that Bonaparte, an obscure
> subaltern with no fortune, had made himself master of the world
> with his sword. (*The Red and the Black*, I, 5.)

> That evening, when [Mathilde] informed Julien that he was a
> Lieutenant of Hussars, his joy knew no bounds. We may form an
> idea of it from the ambition that marked his whole life, and from
> the passionate love that he now felt for his child. The change of
> name [Julien is about to become the 'Chevalier de la Vernaye']
> filled him with astonishment.
>   'At last,' he thought, 'the tale of my adventures is finished, and
> the credit is all mine. I have contrived to make myself loved by this
> monster of pride,' he added, looking at Mathilde; 'her father cannot

live without her, nor she without me.' *(The Red and the Black,* II, 34).

Despite the assonances, a fundamental difference exists between the two passages. In the first case, the brilliant action helps to charm the beautiful ladies of Paris, but at the same time it 'legitimizes' this conquest. Napoleon's personal success goes hand in hand with the establishment of a different world order which Julien feels is better and more just for all.[3] In the second case, however, Julien's triumph is not the outcome of a struggle with the existing order, but the result of a murky tangle of favouritism and blackmail, totally in keeping with the ethos of the Restoration. Unrelated and indifferent to collective fate, this success lacks any symbolic legitimacy. It is the offspring of what Jürgen Habermas has called 'interests': '.... I use the term 'interests' for needs that are — to the extent of the withdrawal of legitimation ... — rendered subjective and detached, as it were, from the crystallizations of commonly shared values supported by tradition ...'[4]

'Withdrawal of legitimation': Stendhal's novels help us realize that in democratic-bourgeois civilization, such loss is not restricted to sporadic crises, but becomes a sort of symbolic constant. This is true above all of France (where the major negative themes of social climbing and success originate), and it is paradoxically due to the *excessive* need for legitimation created by the Revolution. By abruptly interrupting historical continuity, the Revolution in fact decrees that a society has the right to exist only in as much as it respects and puts into effect a given set of principles. Abstract, and thus 'pure' and forward-looking, these principles do not valorize reality as it is (the task we usually ascribe to 'ideology'), but ask for a continual modification of reality until it conforms to their dictates. On the basis of the French model, almost all of modern Western societies have abandoned their trust in God and tradition, to entrust the legitimacy of the existing order to an abstract and atemporal Declaration of Rights:[5] whence their ideal tension and political dynamism, and their inherent lack of legitimation as well. The more abstract and perfect the legitimizing principles, the more necessarily *im*perfect their realization: for reality is also pervaded by other interests and other principles, which will force the new order to compromise, or even, as was temporarily the case with the Restoration, will succeed in defeating it. Furthermore, the galaxy itself of new principles is not nearly as harmonious as would be desired: the canonical example, immediately attested to by Napoleon's career and the English Industrial Revolution, is that liberty and equality can enter into violent and painful conflict.

This explains the problematic, or if one prefers, ambiguous nature of bourgeois consciousness. It also explains, to return to our subject, the contradictory reaction of fascinated contempt the idea of 'success' has evoked during the last two hundred years. For success is the product of a brilliantly dynamic, but never entirely 'just' reality: nineteenth-century Europe, the land of large and sudden successes, is also the theatre, especially in France, of such endless political and social conflict, of such a radical variance over the principles of the social pact, that no fortune, however legal, could ever be seen as completely legitimate. Each success appears also, and simultaneously, to entail the defeat of an opposing principle that did not deserve such a fate.

Therefore, more than a 'realistic' interest in the objective relevance of this phenomenon (which was not lacking either), what compels the French novel to treat almost obsessively the theme of success is its symbolic nature: its symbolic contradictions. For success is creativity, tenacity, determination, far-sightedness, the exercise of freedom and the ability to control reality. But it is also the indifferent abandonment of defeated ideals, complicity with the existing order, a heightening of inequalities. Instead of coinciding with the notion of 'progress', as was to be the case in American culture, success appears in France as its sarcastic double: as what is possible only in a world in which most men are condemned not to be successful.

Hence that typical sequence of the nineteenth-century novel, where the protagonist, more or less willingly, betrays his closest friends (and if this is not so for Stendhal's heroes, it is only because they do not have any friends). Hence also the choice of a certain human type: Julien, not the young bishop of Agde; Fabrizio, Mosca or Sanseverina, not Ascanio del Dongo or the public prosecutor Rassi; Rastignac and Lucien de Rubempré, not Nucingen. Success reveals its frightful fascination when it draws into its orbit those who were not 'fit' for it from the start, and it forces them easily to the fatal pass of betrayal. When Maupassant invented Bel-Ami, who had nothing left to betray, perhaps the novel of success became more consonant with reality, but it lost that painful ambiguity which had made it important.

Homo Clausus

Opportunism, as we have said, consists in betraying certain values in order to succeed. But with Stendhal's heroes betrayal only goes halfway; rather than forgetting their political ideals for good, they conceal them. The incredible number of false passports in the *Charterhouse* points to the fact that behind one's 'public' identity there lies another one, hidden and unavowable. Julien's panic at the thought that Napoleon's portrait, hidden under his bed, may be discovered (*The Red and the Black*, I, 9) ironically exemplifies his double life: his hypocrisy, which the narrator points out from the very first pages. Such hypocrisy, however, is as it were turned inside out: the self Julien hides is *better* than the one he reveals, since the former somehow remains faithful to the only values which could legitimize his actions. Banished from history, these values have found refuge in his 'soul'. It is the case with his pride (the opposite of ambition, Madame de Staël had observed), which continually re-surfaces, jeopardizing his plans. Or with his intensity: 'his conversation ... was still perceptibly too serious, too positive ... one felt that he still regarded too many things as important' (*The Red and the Black*, II, 38), notes the narrator in one of those passages that seem to reproach the as yet imperfect cynicism of his hero. Or, finally, with his hatred for privileges and inequality, which already seeps through from time to time in the Hotel de la Mole, before exploding in his final courtroom speech.

Being forced to hide certain values, therefore, does not mean silencing them: their confinement seems in fact to make them more vehement. It is the paradox of *'homo clausus'*, this typical product of modern socialization, whose most intense 'self-perception' lies precisely in the perception of those impulses he is forced to repress: to the point that they 'appear in self-perception as what is hidden from all others, and often as the true self, the core of individuality'.[6]

We are a long way from the hero of the classical *Bildungsroman*. There, the 'core of identity' was quite *visible:* in fact, identity only existed as such in its ability to objectify, and thus disclose itself. Here instead, it has withdrawn to an area not only different from, but hostile to public behaviour. It is the area of *interiority;* what the *Phenomenology of the Spirit* sees as the 'law of the heart', in conflict with the 'way of the world'. Such interiority no longer has anything in common with the thoughtful 'depth' of Wilhelm Meister or Elizabeth Bennet, which enriched and strengthened their outward choices, thereby buttressing the novelistic character, and the idea itself of the individual, with principles of consistency and sociability. With Julien and Fabrizio, or Onegin and Pechorin, the continuity between the inner and outer man is broken, and interiority appears as a principle of contradiction: of unfaithfulness and inconsistency, duplicity and disharmony. Like the 'strange men' discussed by contemporary Russian culture, these heroes conceal within themselves their own opposite: which does not make them 'likeable', as were Wilhelm Meister and Elizabeth Bennet, but *fascinating;*[7] for it is difficult to turn one's glance from that which constantly contradicts itself.

But they are also fascinating in a more technical sense, from the standpoint of narrative structure. For a contradictory character, placed at the centre of a novel as its hero, must of necessity make the story unpredictable and gripping: it is a guarantee of narrativity, of suspense. And Pushkin and Stendhal's heroes truly never stop surprising us: if we gradually 'come to know better' Wilhelm Meister, David Copperfield or Rastignac as we read along, this is not so for Julien Sorel and Eugene Onegin. As we approach the ending, in fact, their bold turnabouts (Onegin who falls in love with Tatiana; Julien who shoots Madam de Rênal and then delivers his Jacobin harangue) prevent us from forming a truly 'conclusive' image of them.

An unstable plot which lacks a convincing conclusion: we shall return to this point more than once, but for now let us note that these structural constants put the *Bildungsroman* in step, so to speak, with the times. The Restoration has repressed the upheavals and the traumas that marked the turn of the century; but it cannot prevent them being seen still as valid possibilities. The memory of those twenty-five years is too near and too strong — and the symbolic legitimation of 1815 too weak, for its part. A false 'ending' was celebrated in Vienna, and the only certainty of the times continues to be uncertainty: for a repressed conflict is by no means a resolved one.

The spirit of contradiction: here lies the historico-cultural truth of these jumpy plots and inconsistent heroes.[8] Goethe said of Byron: 'He is neither classical nor romantic: he is like the present itself.' Neither classical nor romantic, or, not that it changes much, both classical and romantic. Divided between the gloomy perfection of the *style Empire* and the youthful enthusiasm of the *Grande Armée,* one could say the same of Napoleon. And of Julien Sorel, or Onegin who, 'Homer, Theocritus disdaining, / From Adam Smith sought his training', yet keeps on his desk Napoleon's bust and Byron's portrait, and falls in love with Werther's headlong self-destructiveness.

Much more than in 'progress', this age sees in *contradiction* the hidden essence of history. These are the years in which Hegelian dialectics takes its final shape, and in which Goethe, tackling the theme of historic change, decides to use not one, but two protagonists: a choice which allows him to 'save' the 'immortal part' of mankind. But this is not the case in novels contemporaneous with *Faust,* where no heavenly host will come to disentangle Julien's courage from his unscrupulous ambition, or Onegin's lucid intelligence from his destructive indifference. The question, for Pushkin and Stendhal, is not 'how do we separate the angel from the demon?', but rather: 'how do they manage to *live together?'*

Bovarysm, Disavowal, Bad Faith

The answer to this disturbing question lies in 'fixing' the protagonist's dual nature. There shall be no mitigating compromise to balance the respective demands of the values determining the hero's actions, and the opposite ones animating his thoughts: a wall is instead erected between two lives, which are then both lived to their limits. At Valenod's, Julien enchants the profiteers of Verrières with his Latin, and meanwhile suffers inside for the orphans secluded precisely on the other side of the wall; in the last part of the *Charterhouse,* Fabrizio is hailed as a saint, but his sermons are no more than an agonizing plea for Clelia's love.

Such a doubling seems utterly implausible, at first sight, since it contradicts what seems to be a necessary requirement for any existence: psychic wholeness. Even Freudian theory — although it sees the psyche as a space contended for by hostile and heterogeneous forces — had to hypothesize the existence of a component, the Ego, whose task is explicitly connection and compromise. The Ego's centripetal vocation embodies the essence of the hero of the classical *Bildungsroman,* but is completely lacking in the heroes of Stendhal, Pushkin or Lermontov. Is this situation convincing, in 'psychological' terms?

We are of course not asking here whether people such as Julien Sorel or Eugene Onegin did truly exist. When we think about the lives of Stendhal or Pushkin, we have to conclude that such was indeed the case, but this is not the point. We must instead see whether the protean field of psychology has acknowledged the existence of 'double life', and has considered it to be a key to modern personality.

This definitely seems to me to be the case, and I shall try to show why with the help of three distinct works. The first, written before the birth of psychoanalysis, is Jules de Gaultier's *Le Bovarysme*. Bovarysm, which grows 'in accordance with the development of civilization', is 'man's ability to think himself different from what he is'; it thrives on a division, on the 'gap that exists in each individual between the imaginary and the real, between what he is and what he believes himself to be'. It is an 'exasperated idealism'; 'being an attempt to reform collective reality according to the individual's dreams, Bovarysm entails the principle of failure'. Finally, in its most typical and widespread form, Bovarysm is fueled by the 'belief on which our entire Western civilization seems to be founded: man thinks himself free'.[9]

Although Gaultier has Flaubert in mind, this imaginary life — especially the link between idealistic dream and failure, and the pressing need 'to feel free' — is already fully developed in Stendhal's heroes, who are also brought to mind by the second text I shall quote: a text which, unlike *Le Bovarysme, is* strictly Freudian in inspiration:

> It is difficult to see why things become complicated today when it is a question of identifying with a hero. There has been a historic shift a change in the typical personality of the epoch, of the 'basic' personality. This change seems to have come about precisely in the relations of the Ego to the ideal. It is necessary to study the psychology of honour ... . Today the role of the hero lacks in depth (depth is on the side of the Ego); as regards the ideal, it is rather flat like a painting. It is today impossible to get away from this unpleasant alternative: either one believes oneself to be Rodrigue (and is careful not to fall prey to ridiculousness), or one chooses Rodrigue as a part to play, an equally unbearable solution and one which too clearly reveals a megalomaniacal tendency for braggarts. [10]

Gaultier had brought to light the disjunction of the imaginary from the real; Mannoni points out that this parallel life is centered around the 'relations of the Ego to the ideal': if we cannot act like heroes (whether naively or with theatrical detachment), then this role is played out on the secret stage of imaginary life, determining its structure. But to get at the heart of the matter, how is it possible to maintain a sublime image of oneself while leading an existence that constantly contradicts it?

It is possible, Mannoni replies, thanks to the psychic mechanism Freud called *Verleugnung* (disavowal), which subjects experiences to a sort of decompression chamber that rids them of anything inconsistent with the ideal: '*Verleugnung* of itself has nothing in common with repression ... . It can be considered a simple repudiation of reality ... that which is repudiated in the first place is the denial that a reality inflicts upon a belief.'[11]

These words, taken from another of Mannoni's essays *('Je sais bien, mais quand même'),* introduce my third text, which was written to a large extent as a critique of psychoanalysis: the discussion of 'bad faith' in the first part of *Being and Nothingness.* According to Sartre — who illustrates this phenomenon by describing a person who does one thing while simultaneously offering the opposite image of herself through her words — bad faith is 'the art of forming contradictory concepts which unite in themselves both an idea and the negation of an idea.' These constructions

> ... do not constitute new, solidly structured ideas; on the contrary they are formed so as to remain in perpetual disintegration and that we may slide at any time from naturalistic present to transcendence and vice versa.
>
> We can see the use which bad faith can make of these judgments which all aim at establishing that I am not what I am. If I were only what I *am,* I could, for example, seriously consider an adverse criticism which someone makes of me, question myself scrupulously, and perhaps be compelled to recognize the truth in it. But thanks to transcendence, I am not subject to all that I am.

For bad faith, in short, 'human reality must not be necessarily what it is but must be able to be what it is not'.[12] 'I am not what I am': this is the enigmatic motto of modernity entrusted by Shakespeare to Iago. Julien Sorel at his trial:

> 'I have, therefore, deserved death, Gentlemen of the Jury. *But, even were I less guilty,* I see before me men who, without pausing to consider what pity may be due to my youth, will seek to punish in me and to discourage forever that class of young men who, born in an inferior station and in a sense burdened with poverty, have the good fortune to secure a sound education, and the audacity to mingle with what the pride of rich people calls society.
>
> *'That is my crime, Gentlemen...' (The Red and the Black,* II, 71; emphasis mine).

'J'ai donc mérité la mort, Messieurs les jurés. *Mais quand je serais moins coupable':* 'Je sais bien, *mais quand même:'* it is the first step, disavowal: I am *not* what I am. Then, truth as transcendence, revealed as if by a magician's wand: 'Voilà mon crime, Messieurs': this is my *true* crime: I *am* what I am not.

The Age of Ideals

Everything would be much simpler if we could dismiss Julien's words as mere lies. But the truth of the matter is that his crime, in part, is also boldness — and that he himself, in part, is truly different and better than what he is. Imaginary life is not — is not only — a storehouse of gratifying lies about oneself; it is also that very same interiority of the 'homo clausus' that provides refuge for those values that have been repressed in public behaviour: in what 'we are' in the eyes of others. Bad faith, in other words, is a way of living with the clash, which the modern era has greatly intensified, between professed and actual values.

The principles that legitimize democratic-bourgeois order are indeed more universalistic than in the past: therefore more limpid and demanding (even the workers' movement has added very little to the values of 1789): but precisely for this reason more difficult to realize. Yet they *must* be realized, for if the Christian soul can draw comfort from the thought that its virtues 'are not of this world', this is no longer possible in a secularized age. Moral consciousness becomes thus more and more exacting: it is the interiorization of socially professed values that can eventually lead to the 'hyper-morality' of Freud's Super-ego. These values, moreover, must be realized in *this* world, the only one left. But the undertaking soon proves dangerous and difficult since, in the real world, the desire to dominate wins out over the urge towards freedom; privilege over equality; division over solidarity.

A paradoxical situation: to have to believe in certain values while, at the same time, accepting the impossibility of their realization. To help us live with this paradox, Stendhal and Pushkin reshape the theme of the end of youth according to the symbolic needs of their times. If a sense of interior obligation has been created, which must be silenced in order to 'live', the best solution is then to link it to a brief period of life, giving it almost 'biological' limits. Youth becomes with these writers the age of ideals; but youth, sooner or later, *must* end. Better yet: it can be the age of ideals *precisely because* it will not last long.

These novels establish thus an essential paradigm for modern existence: 'maturity' is no longer perceived as an acquisition, but as a loss. We do not become adults by becoming adults, but by ceasing to be young: the process involves primarily a renunciation. But not the renunciation of aggressive and asocial impulses in the name of superior and even 'sublime' social virtues. What are silenced here are the very values society holds dearest: in Freudian terms, the socialization that takes place in youth requires not the sacrifice of the Id, but — symbolically much more disturbing — that of the Super-ego.[13] It is not surprising then that an entire century identified itself in adolescent heroes, and in what Balzac would coldly refer to as their illusions.

This sympathy, however, is not wholly peaceful. Pushkin:

> To your kind hands I render
> The motley chapters gathered here,
> At times amusing, often doleful ...
> Chance harvest of my pastimes dear,
> Of sleepless moods, light inspirations,
> Fruit of my green, my withered years,
> The mind's dispassionate notations,
> The heart's asides, inscribed in tears. (*Eugene Onegin,* Dedication.)

These few verses contain the two semantic fields whose contrast lies at the heart of Pushkin and Stendhal's works. On the one hand, the heart's asides inscribed in tears and the green years of youth: the hero's age and spiritual physiognomy, the level of story and narration. On the other, the mind's dispassionate notations and the withered years: the narrator's age and spiritual physiognomy, the level of discourse and comment.[14] Realistic narrative will contrast these two symmetrical levels as 'illusion' and 'reality' , and already in Stendhal the conflict is emphasized wherever possible:

> [Julien's] unspoken retort was always: 'What monsters!' or 'What fools!' The amusing thing was that, with all his pride, frequently he understood nothing at all of what was being discussed. (*The Red and the Black*, I, 7.)

> [Fabrizio] was still too young. In his moments of leisure, his mind was occupied in rapturous enjoyment of those sensations evoked by the romantic circumstances with which his imagination was always ready to supply him. He was far from employing his time in a patient examination of the actual character of things in order to discover their causes. Reality still seemed to him dull and sordid. I can understand a person's not caring to look it in the face, but then he ought not to argue about it. Above all, he should not manufacture objections out of the various bits and pieces of his ignorance. (*The Charterhouse of Parma*, 8.)

Passages such as these seem to indicate a clear and irreversible course: from youth to maturity, from romantic imagination to the patient observation of reality. Within the story, however, this trajectory will never be completed. For Julien, Fabrizio or Onegin, we cannot speak of 'apprenticeship', be it in the sense it has in the classical *Bildungsroman* (development of personality, awakening of the hero's soul to the rich variety of the world), or in the opposite sense it will have in Balzac ('dernière larme de jeune homme', maturity as the loss of illusions and repudiation of youth). The heroes of Stendhal and Pushkin, on the contrary, never 'grow up': one of the reasons they must die (or be left, as Onegin, 'at a sore pass in his career'), is that they are unable to forgo their youth, and therefore cannot be pictured as adults:

> Blest he who, green in adolescence,
> Matured at the appointed stage,
> Who tasted of life's acrid essence
> And learnt to stomach it with age;
> Who for strange transports never lusted,
> Through worldly slime strode undisgusted,
> At twenty was a fop or blade,
> At thirty a good marriage made,
> At fifty shed by liquidation
> All debts, both private and the rest,
> And issued painlessly possessed
> Of money, rank, and reputation,
> And whom you hear throughout his span
> Referred to as 'an excellent man'! (*Eugene Onegin,* VIII, 10.)

Blest is he. The heroes of Stendhal and Pushkin, for their part, have undeniably lusted for strange transports, and their love lives — one of our civilization's favourite testing-grounds for measuring the individual's 'maturity' — show just how difficult it is for them to wake from what Pushkin calls their 'greenest dreams'. As every love bond brings with it a possible identity, if the novelistic hero is capable of 'growth', he will either learn to break the bond once and for all, or he will just as firmly shape the rest of his life around it. And perhaps detachment is even more revealing than marriage itself, as it indicates the irreversibility of existence: thus Wilhelm Meister's apprenticeship requires him to forget Mariane, and Elizabeth Bennet's to forget Wickham; in Paris, Lucien de Rubempré will learn to forget Madame de Bargeton, and as for Bel-Ami...

Just the opposite in the novels under investigation here. The hero withdraws from his first love affair, initiates others, believes himself totally 'cured' and indifferent — and then, without fail, is ensnared once again: never of course 'at the appointed stage', but only when there is no longer any hope. Julien and Madame de Rênal, Fabrizio and Clelia, Eugene and Tatyana,[15] Pechorin and Vera: the pattern is always the same: 'There's no one' [muses Pechorin] 'so susceptible to the power of the past as I am. Every memory of past joy or sorrow stabs at my heart and strikes the same old chords. It's silly the way I'm made: I forget nothing — absolutely nothing.' (*A Hero of Our Time,* 'Princess Mary'.)

'I forget nothing — absolutely nothing': this unusual curse extends across time the doubling inherent in bad faith, which is in its turn a way of 'not forgetting' what we have renounced being. A chronological short circuit follows, whereby the power of remembrance never lets the past truly become 'past', while simultaneously dismissing the experience of the present as worthless. What disappears is the very notion of experience as put forward by the classical *Bildungsroman:* as formative encounter with reality, assimilation of the new, incessant reorganization of a developing personality. In *Wilhelm Meister* these experiences were so many milestones along the road towards maturity; for Julien, Fabrizio and Onegin they will be aimless detours, 'roles' that no longer hold the meaning of their existence: neither for them nor the reader. No one bothers to ask what happened to Onegin on his long journey after having killed Liensky; even though the journey is one of the most common metaphors for individual maturation, we take it for granted that it has not changed Onegin in the least. And if the narrator of *The Red and the Black* did not remind us from time to time of the colour of his attire, who would remember that Julien is practically a priest?

'That's the way of the world.'

Neither Stendhal nor Pushkin therefore narrate the transition from youthful illusions to adult realism. Could it be that the theme of maturation has moved from the story to discourse? Given the frequency with which the narrator counters the hero's dreams with his own realistic aphorisms, one would think so. And yet, his reason is not quite as dispassionate as it would seem: the famous digression on his beloved's 'little feet' in book I of *Onegin* reveals a narrator just as disconcerted as his hero when faced with memories of love; as for the narrator of *The Red and the Black,* what he most admires in Julien are the very same traits — sense of duty, impulsiveness, pride — which elsewhere he ridicules as harmful chimeras.

To use the language of the 'ages of man', here we do not find adult reason, but ageing illusions: the narrator's 'realism' is not a positive knowledge of reality, but the mixture of cynicism and nostalgia of one who senses the withering away of a vital force ('How I am saddened by your coming, / Oh, time of love, oh, time of bud! / What languid stir you send benumbing / Into my soul, into my blood!': *Eugene Onegin,* VII, 2). Stendhal and Pushkin are not Balzac; they are not interested in explaining the laws of the world with loquacious wisdom — but in using them as the merely negative and (as we shall see) inexplicable principle upon which to dash the hopes of their heroes. Their realism can be summed up in three words: reality never changes. Its illustrious archetype is Mephisto's *Das ist der Lauf der Welt:* that's the way of the world:

> Depart, 'original' enthusiast!
> How would this insight peeve you: whatsoever
> A human being thinks, if dumb or clever,
> Was thought before him in the past.
> In a few years the young man will have changed;
> There is no danger, he may turn out fine:
> Although the must behaves as if deranged,
> Eventually we get a wine.
>
> (To the younger spectators in the orchestra, who do not applaud:)
>
> My words appear to leave you cold;
> You children need no reprimand:
> You see, the devil is quite old —
> Grow old and you will understand. (*Faust* 6807-6818.)

More sceptical than wise, Mephisto's purpose is not to spur Faust (as the Lord claims in the 'Prologue in Heaven'), but to give voice to historical inertia, to the extremely *longue durée* of thoughts and feelings ('Here, too, occurs what long occurred...'). If it is right to see him as a representative of the modern 'reality principle',[16] this is due to a peculiar semantic shift of the term 'reality', which takes place precisely during the period of *Faust* and *The Red and the Black,* and which from that time on has never completely disappeared. Reality is no longer the infinitely perfectible material it was thought to be during the Enlightenment and throughout the Revolution: as Waterloo has shown, history moves not only forward, in harmony with reason, but it can also resist change and bring back the past. Reality then — such is the plain but disturbing discovery of this age — is characterized by mere existence, independent of any symbolic legitimacy. In fact, the more reality is felt to be illegitimate and unjust, the more 'real' it seems: 'When, generations from now, the historian of our times undertakes to describe the assumptions of our culture, he will surely discover that the word *reality* is of central importance in his understanding of us .... Reality, as conceived by us, is whatever is external and hard, gross, unpleasant'.[17]

This notion of 'reality' is one more product of the short circuit of Revolution and Restoration, with its ensuing lack of legitimacy. Hence, too, those expressions so indispensable to us — 'that's life', 'that's the way of the world' — which strike us as brazen tautologies, words without meaning; and are paradoxically important *for this very reason*. Because it is precisely its 'lack of meaning' that defines for us the essence of 'reality', and which also acts as the enigmatic premise for many forms of 'consensus'. But we shall return to this at the end of the chapter. For now, let us enlarge our discussion of 'reality' by examining the relationship between 'reality principle' and narrative 'realism'.

Reality principle, realism, irony

As is known, the 'reality principle' enjoys an overabundance of meanings in the work of Freud. To limit ourselves to the two conceptual extremes, it is either the antagonist of the 'pleasure principle',[18] or else, by 'modifying' and 'extending' it, enables its fulfillment.[19] Aside from isolated remarks in one sense or the other, the second hypothesis definitely seems more in keeping with developments in Freudian research, especially if we consider the affinity between the reality principle and that psychic component — the Ego — whose task is to obtain pleasure in the only way imaginable for Freud, by avoiding unhappiness. 'A poor creature owing service to three masters and consequently menaced by three dangers: from the external world, from the libido of the Id, and from the severity of the Super-ego',[20] the Ego's task is to mitigate the one-sidedness of these conflicting forces. The reality principle is precisely what enables the Ego to succeed in this, and is therefore, not a 'cognitive' principle, but a wholly 'practical' inclination. The reality principle, in other words, has very little to do with *knowledge* of reality, and very much to do with balance and compromise: devices that ensure the coexistence of forces which, left to themselves, would bring disequilibrium.

Disequilibrium: which is to say, 'tension', or 'displeasure', as in Freud all these terms belong to the same semantic sphere. This is why the Ego, and the reality principle that supports its balancing role, cannot be said to be just an 'extension' of the pleasure principle, or its 'civilized' expression, but rather the only way in which it can actually be fulfilled. Contrary to what is often thought, the reality principle is neither especially stern nor especially critical; after all, its goal is to enable the individual to be at ease in the world. And although Freud has always been hesitant on the matter, this conception of the Ego's tasks necessarily leads to some notion of sociological 'normality', and to its cultural expression, 'common opinion': Blest he who for strange transports never lusted, and whom you hear throughout his span referred to as 'an excellent man'....

'Normality' and 'common opinion', for their part, are concepts that return us to literary criticism, and in particular to two parallel notions of 'realism' put forward in recent years by Roland Barthes and Gérard Genette: realism as the relentless intrusiveness of *doxa*, and as the impossibility of breaking loose from prevailing normative codes. Both Barthes and Genette see the canonical example of this realism in the Balzacian narrator: an unrivalled reality principle, due to his persuasive and all-inclusive wisdom; an unequalled pleasure principle, since that wisdom makes for a trusting and comfortable read.[21]

As we shall see in the next chapter, this is not exactly the case in the *Comédie Humaine*, and even less so for the narrator in Stendhal and Pushkin, or the role played by Mephisto in *Faust*. Far from unifying our perception of the text, and thus contributing to the reality principle's centripetal function, they instead split and double our reading, forcing us to react to the text in a more complex, ambiguous and ironic manner. Mephisto's mocking and biased counterpoint; the centrifugal and nostalgic intelligence of the narrator in *Onegin*; certain pages in Stendhal, shaken and almost torn apart by the abrupt shifts from one viewpoint to the next. Whatever form it assumes, the principle holding sway over perception here is tension, imbalance, uncertainty.

Nothing could be further from realism as 'reason and common sense', to echo Freud's description of the Ego: in fact, a theory of narrative realism totally different from the one sketched above has its origins precisely here. Put forward by Bakhtin in his studies on the novel and given a semiological elaboration in Lotman's *The Structure of the Artistic Text*, this theory sees the greatest novelty of a work like *Onegin* in the presence of 'many "points of view" operating simultaneously'. That their discontinuity is stressed instead of their synthesis is precisely what makes *Onegin* 'realistic', since only in this way does 'the artistic model reproduce a very important aspect of reality — the fact that there is no exhaustive, finite interpretation'. The text's 'truth' is thus no longer found in a privileged perspective, but in the reader's ability to master the 'intersection of various subjective positions'.[22]

Based on this 'structural complexity' and on an endless multiplication of perspectives, Lotman's realism is, at bottom, *irony*: 'The equation of different stylistic planes leads to the realization of the relativity of each stylistic system in isolation, and hence to irony. The dominating role of irony in the stylistic unity of *Eugene Onegin* is an obvious fact that has been noted in critical literature on the subject.'[23]

Thus Lotman; and it is known that for Bakhtin the modern novel has its origins almost entirely in ironic genres: Menippean satire, Socratic dialogue, Rabelaisian grotesque. An 'ironic' realism, therefore: a much more appealing creature, to the modern mind, than a 'realistic' realism. Let us examine this a little more closely.

The Automaton's Rights

Formalist 'foregrounding' and 'estrangement', Cambridge School 'ambiguity', theories of the 'open text' and 'dissemination' of meaning, deconstruction: the desire to understand and emphasize the literary modalities of irony is the thread that links many of the great twentieth-century schools of criticism. It has been a fascinating and necessary enterprise, for irony is a fundamental attitude of modern culture and consciousness. It is the voice of a polytheistic world, of a society in progress, of a many-sided, curious, doubtful and dialogic mind. Irony is the language of restlessness and change. It is a corrosive and de-legitimizing intelligence. It is deconstruction, destruction, revolution...

This crescendo, which echoes the dubious 'development' of contemporary criticism, indicates that something is not quite right. Irony does possess the features listed above, and is an essential aspect of the modern spirit: no doubt about this. But how can it be that the most typical rhetorical mode of an entire age does not somehow support the existing order, but rather erodes its legitimacy? If we believe that social formations have the tendency to 'hold themselves together', and that literature is not exempt by divine grace from this function, we seem to be facing a truly unacceptable paradox.

There are ways out, of course. We can say for instance that modern culture is indeed ironic, but not *just* ironic. If irony loosens and makes problematic the symbolic bonds of legitimation, other cultural forms in the last two hundred years have surely contributed to the opposite effect. In other words, we can hypothesize that modern culture calls for a sort of division of labour, a parallelogram of thrusts and counter-thrusts able to satisfy the opposing requirements of stability and innovation, certainty and doubt. After all, Balzac and Stendhal are contemporaries: the historico-cultural significance of the French Restoration novel lies precisely in the *coexistence* of antithetical choices, and not in their mutual exclusion.

This is probably true. However, I should like to pursue here a slightly more risky yet, to my mind, more interesting hypothesis. Rather than looking *outside* irony for the complacent certainty that irony calls into doubt, we may ask whether the necessity of a stable viewpoint is not generated *from within* ironic representation itself: so that irony will appear, we may say, in contradiction with its own premises.

The point is the following. According to Bakhtin and Lotman, who have succeeded better than anyone in linking irony and the novel, the heterogeneous multiplicity of points of view encourages a 'dialogic' and 'experimental' frame of mind, an attitude towards the world that is eager and adaptable, open, empirical, responsible. In a word: 'mature'. I am afraid, however, that this vision is founded on a dream. The implicit reader of Lotman, and of twentieth-century criticism in general, this admirable creature who enjoys the most asymmetrical perspectives, who unerringly detects semantic ambiguities and shifting judgements, who reproduces in his mind the inexhaustible structural complexity of the text: this is a literary critic preparing an especially difficult lecture, not the average reader of novels. The latter's perception (and in fact anyone's, when reading for pleasure and not for work) probably functions in a totally different way. The endless multiplicity of points of view leads more to skepticism and indecision than to a flexible and problematic maturity. The reader moves from one perspective to the next in that crescendo of dizziness, bewilderment and ultimately sheer fatigue generated by Joyce's *Ulysses:* the only example, by the way, of a 'perfectly' ironic novel.

What I am trying to say is that a systematically ambiguous and unreliable perception will not necessarily sublimate itself into a complex and mature cognitive stance. We are automatism as well as spirit, wrote Pascal, who had a certain familiarity with these matters: if the spirit delights in humbling the automaton and making its life impossible (that art should 'deautomatize' perception: here is the only automatic certainty of twentieth-century criticism) — then it only follows that the automaton will require in turn simpler and stabler criteria than usual for explanation and evaluation, more inflexible viewpoints than even Balzacian *doxa*.

Assumptions, assumptions... Even granted that the 'average' reader does exist, no one knows how his brain works. True indeed. But these assumptions are upheld by the works under investigation here. In the last few pages we have examined mainly the level of discourse and comment: which, as Lotman correctly notes, does not favour that stable viewpoint, that sense of identity that every culture (no matter how experimental), and every individual (no matter how problematic), nevertheless needs. If this certainty is not provided at the level of discourse, why should we not move to the other half of these works, and look for it in the story? And here — here we find melodrama indeed. Passionate love and cruel abandonment, heroic fantasies, duels, deaths, sudden reappearances, midnight rendezvous, masked balls... Try to write a summary of *The Red and the Black,* the *Charterhouse, Onegin* and *A Hero of Our Time:* they are already pulp literature. It is probably for this very reason that criticism has always stressed the level of discourse: because it lends variety and irony to a story which, on its own, is perhaps excessively 'automatic'. But since no novelist 'first' writes the story and then complicates it with discourse, nothing prevents the reverse argument: an overly ironic and problematic discourse *needs* a naive and melodramatic story. It can be what it is *only* because the story is founded on opposite principles — and vice versa, obviously.

We are automatism as well as spirit, and so these novels give us a structure composed of opposing and complementary levels. So far we have concentrated on those aspects — bad faith, unwillingness to grow, irony — which make these works masterpieces of indecision. Now we shall see in what way they nevertheless do reach a decision, and then we shall be able to answer a question that we must leave unsettled for the moment: is there a link, and what is it, between ironic consciousness and that meaningless and painful notion of 'reality' we discussed some pages earlier?

II

'A parody, perhaps...'

On one matter Sartre, Mannoni and Gaultier are in total agreement: prone as it is to the heroic and the sublime, more than the risk of tragedy, the imaginary runs that of ridiculousness. 'A strangely bleak and reckless creature, / Issue of Heaven or of Hell, / Proud demon, angel — who can tell?' asks Pushkin of Onegin; and he continues:

> Perhaps he is all imitation,
> An idle phantom or, poor joke,
> A Muscovite in Harold's cloak,
> An alien whim's interpretation,
> Compound of every faddish pose...?
> A parody, perhaps... who knows? (*Eugene Onegin*, VII, 24.)

Is Julien Sorel a parody when, at the final stroke — 'fatal bell' — of ten, he *must* clasp Madame de Rênal's hand 'or I shall go up to my room and blow my brains out' *(The Red and the Black*, I, 9)? And Fabrizio, who on the page before beginning his career as a bishop speaks of 'becoming an American citizen and a soldier of the Republic.' (' "He is a real hero", [his aunt] thought': *The Charterhouse of Parma*, 6)? Is Mathilde a parody in mourning her sixteenth-century Boniface? Is Julien, in dreaming of throwing handfuls of money to the crowd on his way to the gallows? They all are; and so is Stendhal himself, to the critical eye of his *Souvenirs d'égotisme:* 'Above all I want to be true. That would be quite a miracle in this century of comedy...'

The opposite of parody for Stendhal is 'naturalness', and this opposition is usually connected to the two different types of love he describes: 'French' love, *amour-vanité*, on the side of parody: 'Italian' love, *amour-passion*, on the side of naturalness. And yet it is precisely the game of vanity and deceit — 'love was far more a model which they were imitating than a reality' (*The Red and the Black*, II, 46) — which ends up transforming the bond between Julien and Mathilde into that unmanageable 'fever', that 'disease' which is for Stendhal *amour-passion*. On the other hand, the naturalness between Julien and Madame de Rênal (in the first part of the novel, and in the final prison scenes) converts their love into a domestic idyll; to a peaceful and unaffected, but certainly not passionate, middle-class marriage.

Parody kindles and enflames passion — naturalness becomes

prosaic and placid. The explanation for this unforeseen inversion should perhaps be sought not in the 'analysis of the human heart', but in the political symbolism of the era, starting with the antithesis which was to be the source of all others: Terror and Thermidor. In the first, writes Benjamin Constant in 1797, *'interests flow in the footsteps of exalted opinions... Hate, vengeance, greed, ingratitude, brazenly parody the most noble examples ... Patriotism becomes the banal excuse for all crimes. Great sacrifices, devoted deeds, victories obtained through natural penchant by the austere republicanism of Antiquity, serve as a pretext for the unrestrained unleashing of egotistic passions.'*[24]

Here the Jacobin 'parody' of Republican Rome not only disguises egotistical interests, it also spurs them on, transforming them into something excessive and unrestrained — it changes them from interests proper into 'passions'. 'Once the drama is done, the togas and the masks drop. ... the century becomes "positive".'[25] 'Positive': none of the problematics of bad faith at Thermidor — everyone is happy to 'be what he is'. With the beheading of the heroic, emphatic and cruel claims of the 'Ego ideal', the Ego itself is free to unfold all its 'naturalness'. By this time, Furet has written, the revolution '... lost its legitimacy; all it had left was its legality (even when it violated it). ... That new-found freedom was essentially society's revenge on ideology, and so it conveys to the observer an impression of prosaic heaviness that offends the admirers of the Incorruptible.'[26]

This prosaic naturalness, these interests that are more manageable precisely because they are more 'material', obviously extend far beyond Thermidor, permeating practically the entire history of capitalism and democracy. For capitalism, needless to say, the matter is quite controversial. On the one hand, we have the historical outlines of Max Weber (the spirit of capitalism subjects all that is impulsive and feverish in the *auri sacra fames* to rational control), or of Albert Hirschmann: 'Political Arguments for Capitalism before its Triumph' are based on the idea that 'making money is a calm passion', and that, in short, interests are the most reliable counterbalance to the disruptive force of passions.[27] Along these same lines we can find representative pages from Smith to Schumpeter,[28] and they are all convincing, but perhaps refer more to the voluntary ethos of the capitalist as an *individual* than to the objective cultural consequences of capitalism as a *system*. In the latter perspective, which has its *locus classicus* in the section on 'Bourgeoisie and Proletariat' in the *Communist Manifesto*, the spiritual atmosphere is totally different: capitalism is the world of risk and chance, it is a permanent revolution marked by everlasting uncertainty and a profanation of all things sacred...

These two visions are so antithetic, yet both so well-founded in reason and fact, that it is almost impossible to choose between them: Sombart, in the *Quintessence of Capitalism*, symptomatically eludes the choice by doubling his typology into the opposing figures of the 'entrepreneur' ('bold', 'with plenty of nerve, unshrinking') and the 'bourgeois' ('gregarious', 'economical', 'drab').[29] I leave the problem open, therefore, merely observing that it assumes basically the same form in novelistic tradition: on the one hand, the turbulent and impassioned civil society of the *Comédie humaine* — on the other, Stendhal's identification of 'bourgeois' and 'tedious'. Or, as he writes in 1818, in Milan 'when people talk about politics, it is a heroic politics, full of battles and executions... and not of numbers and taxes as in England.'

In Stendhal's Italy, 'politics agrees with music and love'; but not so in the nation of those 'coarse spirits, wholly satisfied by a sense of security and tranquility' (*On Love*), which for Stendhal, even more than England, is America — the America of democracy, more than that of capitalism. These are the years in which Tocqueville's great project ripens, and many of his ideas are already in circulation in French culture.[30] Tocqueville too, of course, talks about the moderating force of bourgeois interests and the resulting 'materialisme honnête'; but he is especially interested in the dynamics of political democracy and in its guiding value, which is for him not liberty, but equality. Within the domain of culture, equality shatters the authority of dogma and tradition, but is far from replacing it with that of 'superior spirits', or restless and critical intellect: it is numbers that prevail, 'public opinion' as a homogeneous mass of wholly indistinguishable individuals. And when we add to it the growing centralization of political power, we are left with the gloomy concluding images of *Democracy in America*:

> In the ages of aristocracy which preceded our own, there were private persons of great power, and a social authority of extreme weakness. ... The principal efforts of the men of those times were required to strengthen, aggrandize, and secure the supreme power; and, on the other hand, to circumscribe individual independence within narrower limits, and to subject private interests to the interests of the public. Other perils and other cares await the men of our age. Amongst the greater part of modern nations, the government, whatever may be its origin, its constitution, or its

name, has become almost omnipotent, and private persons are falling, more and more, into the lowest stage of weakness and dependence.

In olden society, everything was different: unity and uniformity were nowhere to be met with. In modern society, everything threatens to become so much alike, that the peculiar characteristics of each individual will soon be entirely lost in the general aspect of the world.[31]

Twenty years later, in the most animated section — 'On Individuality' — of his essay on liberty, John Stuart Mill echoes Tocqueville's fears almost to the letter:

Strong impulses are but another name for energy. Energy may be turned to bad uses; but more good may always be made of an energetic nature, than of an indolent and impassive one. ... The same strong susceptibilities which make the personal impulses vivid and powerful, are also the source from whence are generated the most passionate love of virtue, and the sternest self-control. ...

There has been a time when the element of spontaneity and individuality was in excess, and the social principle had a hard struggle with it. ... But society has now fairly got the better of individuality; and the danger which threatens human nature is not the excess, but the deficiency, of personal impulses and preferences.[32]

For Tocqueville and Mill, the fading of individuality into a lifeless standard is in itself an enormous regression. But it has at least one equally severe consequence, and of particular relevance for our study: along with individuality vanishes that 'energy' of 'strong impulses' which they see as the mainspring not only of progress, but of historical change itself. *Democracy in America* and *On Liberty* are incessantly raising the spectre of a world evermore complacent and inert: at a standstill. And how can novels be written if history has stopped?

Socialization Rejected

Even though *The Red and the Black* and the *Charterhouse* do not take place in America, the 'fatuous *tyranny* of public opinion' (*The Red and the Black*, I, 1) plays nevertheless a prominent role. Just as vehemently as in the case of privilege, if not more, Stendhal denounces the work of the Restoration for its lifeless mediocrity. It is a world that is predictable, boring, narratively inert: as we have seen, Stendhal's bourgeois universe is not Balzac's inexhaustible, plot-generating prose of the world, but rather a polite and stagnant marsh. To generate a story in so torpid a context, nothing less than the 'Romantic' interpretation of Napoleon is needed, so widespread in the early 1800s. 'This husband of fate, this warring pilgrim,' as we read in a fragment of the tenth chapter of *Onegin*, 'tormented by the punishment of peace...' Peace as punishment: precisely the state of mind that pervades *The Red and the Black*: 'Alas', says Mathilde, 'nowadays civilisation has banished hazard, there is no room for the unexpected' (*The Red and the Black,* II, 44).[33] No room for the unexpected? Lefebvre: 'Nor was it an accident that the Revolution led to the dictatorship of a general. But it also happened that this general was Napoleon Bonaparte, a man whose temperament, even more than his genius, was unable to adapt to peace and moderation. Thus it was an unforeseeable contingency, which tilted the scale in favour of "la guerre éternelle".'[34]

'France', writes Fievée to Napoleon in 1809, 'is sick with restlessness.' Endless war, restlessness — 'a wearying and unnerving tension', reads a record of the Lyons Chamber of Commerce shortly thereafter. Napoleon here is not alarming because he is the Emperor, the despot whose goal is to freeze France under his laws; just the opposite, he is frightening because he is continually risking what he has already conquered. His image — which foreshadows another great novelistic theme, the *cupio dissolvi* of the compulsive gambler — embodies a very strong notion of 'history': *too* strong, in a certain sense. Restlessness, unnerving tension, endless war and countless other similar expressions are all negative definitions: they are the opposite of peace and tranquility. And whereas the latter seem perfectly understandable — 'natural'! — endless war, vice versa, does not seem so at all. Sheer violation, it dismantles all the existing rules, but it does not seem to have any of its own.

And now we can move back to narrative theory. Investigating the origins of plot, Lotman has argued that to replace the cyclic and classificatory world of myth with the unstable and irreversible course of history, there must be devised 'a text-generating mechanism organized in accordance with linear temporal motion and fixing not laws but anomalies. ... The fixing of unique and chance events, crimes, calamities — anything considered the violation of a certain primordial order — was the historical kernel of plot-narration'.[35]

The antithesis of laws and anomalies is where Lotman's

research most reveals its Formalist legacy. By now, however, it is generally agreed that this legacy does not provide a sufficient foundation for a general narrative theory, precisely because it conceives of the story only as exception and negation of a fixed paradigm: as the anomaly of a law, necessarily fortuitous or even inexplicable. As concerns Stendhal and Pushkin though, Lotman's hypothesis is undoubtedly on the mark. Like their heroes, these authors are not in the least interested in the laws of social life, but only in their violation. Stendhal's famous 'etc.'s, and the abrupt sarcasm of the descriptions in *Onegin*, indicate a truly adamantine indifference towards existing norms. Even in the disciplined world of the Besançon seminary — where we are told that in theory just the way of 'eating a boiled egg' can lead to success or ruin (and how often will this happen in the *Comédie Humaine!*) — even there, the rules of social life do not have in fact the slightest narrative significance.

To use a conceptual pair similar to that of law and anomaly, Pushkin and Stendhal are far more interested in 'foreground' than in 'background'.[36] Or rather, they strive to minimize the relationship between these two components of a story. Whereas the classical *Bildungsroman* typically ends with the foreground — the hero's story — which gradually integrates into the collective background until they merge; and whereas Balzac, symmetrically, will animate social laws so that they will be narratively 'active', and will pervade and determine the hero's destiny — Stendhal and Pushkin, instead, pursue the separation of these narrative units. Hence their coming straight to the point: the slow and detailed approach, the delight in overdetermination, so typical of Goethe or Balzac, are abandoned for a narrative rapidity which leads directly to the core of the episode, usually bestowing to it the sense of a day in battle.

We are thus offered an abrupt succession of 'foregrounds', where causal links give way to the discontinuity of violation. Plot becomes a sequence of *arbitrary acts*: precisely what the bourgeois desire for predictability aimed to do away with, and which here appear under the guise of military-chivalrous pride (Julien's countless imaginary challenges), or of amorous passion (the *coup de foudre* of love at first sight scattered throughout all these works). In Pushkin and Stendhal, plot does not aim at 'realistically' portraying the world in its variety and interconnections; it tries instead to draw attention to those characters who reintroduce 'restlessness' into an appeased world. The plot, that is to say, is there to create a 'strong' notion of narrative hero.

The Red and the Black is subtitled *Chronicles of 1830*, but *The Life of Julien Sorel* would have been more exact; and already Balzac had suggested renaming the *Charterhouse: Fabrizio, or the Nineteenth-Century Italian*. As for Pushkin and Lermontov, they indicate the narrative focus from the very title (*Eugene Onegin, A Hero of Our Time*).

A protagonist who tears himself forcibly from an inert and repetitive background: another symptomatic overturning of the classical *Bildungsroman*, the individual's formation is not identified here with the hero's *insertion* within the rules of society, but with his attempt to undermine them: individualization and socialization are no longer complementary processes, they are antithetical. But there is a second change as well. If Wilhelm Meister and Elizabeth Bennet 'act' in a certain way *because* of who they 'are', Julien, Pechorin and Fabrizio often 'act' *in order* to 'be'. As Jean Starobinski has shown, Stendhal's characters are basically 'dynamic' and 'theatrical',[37] but that also means, to return to our subject, that they incline to 'unnaturalness' and 'parody'.

Here is the central paradox of Stendhal's work: in order to be 'himself' the hero must first of all be an emphatic 'Other', a scarcely believable 'ideal'. It is a suspicious and puzzling process of formation: it has its reasons, however, and its merits.

'A certain amount of impudence...'

Why then run the risk of being a parody? To attempt an answer, let us return to that stage of life which is given new symbolic value in these decades, and see what one of its most thorough and enthusiastic interpreters has to say:

> Adolescence is the period during which a young person ... differentiates himself from his culture, though on the culture's terms. It is the age at which, by becoming a person in his own right, he becomes capable of deeply felt relationships to other individuals, perceived clearly as such. It is precisely this sense of individuality which fails to develop, or develops only feebly, in most primitive cultures or among lower-status social groups. A successful initiation leads to group solidarity and a warm sense of belonging; a successful adolescence adds to these a profound sense of self — of one's own personality.
>
> Personalization is the *métier* of adolescence. Of all persons adolescents are the most intensely personal; their intensity is often uncomfortable to adults. As cooperation and group adjustment

become pervasive social norms; as tolerance supersedes passion as the basis for social action; as personalization becomes false-personalization, adolescence becomes more and more difficult.

... Adolescence *is* the conflict [between individual and society] no matter how old the individual is when it occurs. Adolescent conflict is the instrument by which an individual learns the complex, subtle and precious difference between himself and his environment.[38]

For Friedenberg, then, adolescence is conflict, and conflict is what makes individualization possible. Individualization, in its turn, is not simply withdrawing from one's socio-cultural context, or emphasizing personal idiosyncracies: what makes it possible and meaningful (to use Erik Erikson's terminology in *Identity, Youth, and Crisis*) are the 'identifications', or 'ideal models', put forward by civilization, but which are, significantly, 'in conflict' with its actual functioning.

Youth is especially susceptible to these ideal models because — again in Erikson's words — it is a 'psychosocial moratorium' whose meaning lies less in what the young person actually 'is', than in what he *could* or *would like* to be. In this phase of life, as we have seen, the Super-ego asserts itself with unique force and intolerance: thereby already setting the stage for the emergence of parody. If individualization is to succeed, it must be based on clear-cut and vivid ideals: which however, for this very reason, may easily become excessively emphatic. In order not to become a petty bourgeois of Verrières, Julien Sorel has to dream of Napoleon: and his dream is also somewhat foolish.

To this inherent proximity between youth and parody we may add that historical trend that was a persistent thorn in the side of nineteenth-century critical Liberalism: the decline of those 'strong impulses' without which no individuals in the strong sense — independent and able to hold their own against common opinion — can be imagined. This tyranny of peaceful and contented naturalness is the product of a world which — for Stendhal and Tocqueville, Pushkin and Mill — is too hospitable, too inviting. It is a world where the 'objective' causes of conflict no longer seem to apply: there is none of the struggle for survival of Balzac's civil society, and even political struggle is either missing (in *Onegin* and in Lermontov), deliberately toned down (in *The Red and the Black*), or has dwindled to a mere pretext for petty personal rivalries (in the *Charterhouse*). There is no denying it: Julien and Fabrizio and Onegin are accepted into the world of the Restoration, and they themselves often entertain the thought of joining it for good and seeking their 'happiness' there.

If they never wholly succeed, it is because they still retain the image of a different relationship with the world, of a more daring and exacting youth. Having lost its objective foundations, though, this image becomes what Hegel would have called 'mere fancy': a merely subjective aspiration. The relationship between individuality and conflict is thereby overturned. It is no longer the objective existence of conflict which promotes individuality, *forcing* the hero into being an individual ready to accept the burden and risk of his beliefs. Just the opposite: it is the hero who goes in search of conflict, who tries to put himself to the test all the time, *in order* to become an individual. In Mathilde's naive but exact words: 'I can see nothing but a sentence of death that distinguishes a man' *(The Red and the Black,* II, 38). Individualization requires now a sentence: no more those 'spiritual qualities' which have become 'blurred' forever. Conflict does not exist any longer 'in things': it must be aroused with the 'obstinacy' spoken of in *On Love,* in order for the hero to ascertain his identity. It is Julien's notorious sensitivity, which has him see a hidden meaning in every act, keeps him on his guard, challenges him: a nagging 'unnaturalness' which haunts him even on his first night of love:

> But, in the most delicious moments, the victim of a freakish pride ... instead of his paying attention to the transports which he excited and to the remorse that increased their vivacity, the idea of *duty* was continually before his eyes. He feared a terrible remorse, and undying ridicule, should he depart from the ideal plan that he had set himself to follow. In a word, what made Julien a superior being was precisely what prevented him from enjoying the happiness that sprang up at his feet. *(The Red and the Black,* I,15.)

The narrator's comment here is justifiably two-sided. Julien's behaviour is foolish, affected, ridiculous — yet, *at the same time*, it makes him a 'superior being'. The greatness of this model of self-formation lies entirely in its loyalty to an 'idea of duty' which is never quite necessary; in its creation of conflicts which could easily be avoided. What makes it ridiculous is inseparable from what makes it admirable: the fact that it is *unwarranted*. Nothing — absolutely nothing — forces the individual to flee 'naturalness' and eschew 'common opinion'; nothing guarantees that he will not end up, as Helvétius says, exciting the laughter of his contemporaries instead of their admiration. But precisely so: only choices which are neither inevitable nor guaranteed are true choices. It may be an unpleasant thought, but in an appeased world that invites everybody to enjoy the pleasures of the reality principle, running the risk of being a parody is one of the highest examples of courage.

And vice versa. Donning the garb of others *bestows* uncommon courage. In *The Eighteenth Brumaire*, Marx observed that bourgeois revolutions have always disguised themselves, using biblical costumes in England, Roman ones in France. He attributes this to the self-deception typical of the bourgeoisie's 'false' consciousness, and predicts that socialist revolutions will not 'draw their poetry from the past, but only from the future'. But the poetry of the future (especially the distant future) has a bizarre compulsion to reproduce the very distant past; more to the point, the great social democracies have built their cultures on an openly religious symbolism, while Lenin indicated Jacobinism as a model, and Trotsky interpreted the Russian Revolution against the backdrop of the French; and finally, the history of the workers' movement and of the revolutions of the twentieth century is second to none for disguises — and parodies.

I am not interested here in refuting a casual and metaphorical prediction: the point is rather that costumes and parodies seem to be a necessary companion of any great social change. 'Above all I want to be true. That would be quite a miracle, in this century of comedy,' writes Stendhal in *Souvenirs d'égotisme*. But he immediately adds: 'One of the characteristics of the revolutionary era (1789-1832) is that no success can be had without a certain amount of impudence, or even downright charlatanry.'

If I understand correctly, the problem here is not so much that charlatanry thrives 'also' during revolutions — but that without 'a certain amount' of it, revolutions would be *impossible*. More than a degeneration of revolution, charlatanry seems to be its disturbing premise. Disturbing, and yet reasonable, for only the 'impudence' of thinking themselves better than they are can give the protagonists' destructive thrust that *symbolic legitimacy* which their 'reality' never could. Faced with the threat of annihilation, which is always present in major historical ruptures, the Ego, the 'realistic' and 'natural' protagonist of ordinary administration, becomes a silent spectator: it either backs up, or it abdicates in favour of some form of 'Ego ideal', with its train of unyielding certainties, theatrical exaggeration, and poor sense of proportions. It is this mixture of superstition and intelligence, vanity and courage, lies and truth, that constitute Julien Sorel's speech in court. We have already seen bad faith informing its argumentative structure; let us look now at its turbulent emotional genesis:

> The trial was resumed. As the President was summing up, midnight struck. He was obliged to pause: amid the silence of the universal anxiety, the echoing notes of the clock filled the court.
> 'Here begins the last day of my life,' thought Julien. Presently he felt himself inflamed by the idea of duty. He had kept his emotion in check until then, and maintained his determination not to speak; but when the President of the Assizes asked him if he had anything to say, he rose. He saw in front of him the eyes of Madame Derville, which, in the lamplight, seemed to shine with a strange brilliance. 'Can she be crying, by any chance,' he wondered.
> 'Gentlemen of the Jury...'. *(The Red and the Black,* II, 71.)

It is impossible here to separate Julien's political daring from the superstitious idea of destiny that overcomes him (for the third time in the novel) at the striking of the hours; impossible to disentangle his exacting sense of duty from his common complacency at the tears of the women in the courtroom. Stendhal is to be praised indeed for forcing us to see both the nobility and the mediocrity of his hero: for showing us the dark origin behind even the noblest enterprises — and for revealing, on the other hand, how this not only leaves their greatness intact, but is often the only way to make it possible.

It is an unsettling blend (no one likes to mix saints and devils), but it does manage to keep alive the image of a pugnacious and unsettling individuality — 'dissatisfied', as we read in *Faust*, which Goethe was completing at the same time of *The Red and the Black* and *Onegin*. And the combination of individual strife and historical change examined in these novels becomes even more interesting when read together with Faustian *streben*, their sublimated and infinitely more optimistic counterpart.

Streben

Streben, says Mephisto, sweeps Faust 'ever onward' (*Faust*, line 1857): it is that form of striving which, when it achieves its goal, is still not fully satisfied. 'I have no thought of joy!' (*Faust*, 1765), Faust makes clear from the start; 'Geniessen macht gemein' (*Faust*, 10259), enjoyment makes one common, vulgar, prosaic. Yet, even if Faust had no thought of joy, his *streben* — unlike Stendhal's 'idea of duty' — does not *prevent* enjoyment:

> Through all the world I only raced
> Whatever I might crave, I laid my hand on,
> What would not do, I would abandon,
> And what escaped, I would let go.
> I only would desire and attain,
> And wish for more, and thus with might and main
> I stormed through life. (*Faust*, 11433-11439.)

Faust utters these verses in response to Care, in one of the poem's final scenes, in which Goethe contrasts two different principles of movement and narrativity, thereby dispelling the ambiguities that have crystallized around the notion of *streben* in the course of the work. In Care's version, *streben* recalls novelistic reveries ('He whom I have conquered could / Own the world and not feel good'; 11453-4), and the hero is under the spell of indecision and contradiction: 'Should he go, or should he come?', 'he can never finish', '[he] yields, resenting; must, but hates.' For Faust instead, *streben* is a kind of radical version of Goethian 'activity' ('Let [man] survey this life, be resolute, / For to the able this world is not mute'; 11445-6). It is a concrete and active principle, capable of charting a course 'ever onward'. We can hardly agree therefore with Ladislao Mittner when he claims that 'more than activity, or straightforward impulse, *streben* is an uncontrollable, demonic energy, often accompanied by anxiety, or even generated by it'.[39]

The problem, here, is stated incorrectly: the energy of *streben*, in fact, is 'uncontrollable' and 'demonic' precisely *because* it always turns into 'activity' and 'straightforward impulse'. The hellish feature of Faust's journey — exemplified by Gretchen's fate — lies precisely in the ease with which obstacles are overcome and desires are satisfied. Faust's progress is too quick, too straightforward. Here are his feelings, just before the pact:

> A curse on wine that mocks our thirst!
> A curse on love's last consummations!
> A curse on hope! Faith, too, be cursed!
> And cursed above all else be patience! (*Faust*, 1603-6.)

And later, at the climax of the Gretchen episode:

> Am I not fugitive? without a home?
> Inhuman, without aim or rest,
> As like the cataract, from rock to rock I foam,
> Raging with passion, toward the abyss?

... Help, Devil, shorten this time of dread.
What must be done, come let it be.
Let then her fate come shattering on my head,
And let her perish now with me. (*Faust,* 3348-51; 3362-65.)

'What must be done, come let it be': Macbeth's words before killing Duncan. And Mephisto, whom the young Marx correctly saw as an embodiment of money, is the 'civilized' version of the violence that enables time to be shortened and distance abolished. If the novel's world is always overflowing with obstacles, delays and discrepancies, *Faust*'s is instead symbolized by the endless flatland of its final scene.

It is a world that exalts the omnipotence of thought: whence the symbolic fascination of *streben*, for Western culture. *Streben* does in fact join together two equally important modern desires: the satisfaction of achievement, of Faust's fully living out each historical era — and the freedom of always yearning for the new, of Faust's fervid and visionary final monologue. Goethe's genius lies precisely in proclaiming that these two desires are not hostile and irreconcilable, but form a homogenous and complementary whole. Only the man who is always able to achieve happiness can, so to speak, do without it, and refrain from calling out to the fleeting moment those fateful words: 'Verweile doch! Du bist so schön!' — 'Stop, thou art so beautiful.' In this framework, history truly is *progress*, an 'ever onward': each stage is fully lived to its utmost potential — and once this has been achieved, on the other hand, nothing stops man from moving on.

Dissatisfaction can arise only from satisfaction, and it will always be appeased again and again. It is a wonderful image of historical change. But is it plausible? This seems less certain. In a memorable page of *Beyond the Pleasure Principle*, Freud realized that the only way to save *streben* — 'this benevolent illusion' — was to completely reformulate its motives. The mainspring of human progress is not the ease of satisfaction — but rather its *impossibility*. If an innate drive does indeed exist, rather than pushing us 'ever onward', it encourages us to stop, and 'have thoughts of joy': it is the pleasure principle as the principle of inertia and stasis. If he only could, Freudian man would call out all too often, 'Stop, moment'; what prevents him, according to Freud's stern lucidity, is not the most 'spiritual' part of his nature (Faust will be saved because 'Who ever strives with all his power, / We are allowed to save'; 11936-7) — but rather the material harshness of external circumstances, the unavoidability of pain, the fact that, as is stated in *Civilization and Its Discontents*, man's happiness 'is not provided for' in the master plan of creation: 'Sensations of a pleasurable nature have nothing inherently impelling about them, whereas unpleasurable ones have it in the highest degree. The latter impel towards change, towards discharge, and that is why we interpret unpleasure as implying a heightening and pleasure as a lowering of energic cathexis.'[40]

For Freud, change and the freedom that attends it, are *forced* on mankind, which considers them values unworthy of being pursued in themselves, and even desires to be rid of them as quickly as possible to restore the lost equilibrium:

> The present development of human beings requires, as it seems to me, no different explanation from that of animals. What appears in a minority of human individuals as an untiring impulsion towards further perfection can easily be understood as a result of the instinctual repression upon which is based all that is more precious in human civilization. The repressed instinct never ceases to strive for complete satisfaction, which would consist in a repetition of a primary experience of satisfaction. No substitutive or reactive formations and no sublimations will suffice to remove the repressed instinct's persisting tension; and it is the difference in amount between the pleasure of satisfaction which is *demanded* and that which is actually *achieved* that provides the driving factor which will permit of no halting at any position attained but, in the poet's words, 'Ungebändigt immer vorwärts dringt', — presses ever forwards unsubdued.[41]

It is the same image of human progress we find in Stendhal: what is the second half of the *Charterhouse*, if not a series of 'substitutive formations' which Fabrizio turns to because he cannot reunite with Clelia? And here we encounter yet another version of that familiar theme — the bitter ring of *inauthenticity* that never leaves the modern individual, casting the shadow of parody and doubt even on his noblest actions. No longer the historical roles which Faust could live in such a full and natural way, but rather the sense of being always in disguise, always halved, always in bad faith.[42] And — yes — always free, too. But it is no longer the freedom of having an almighty servant at one's command. It is not the freedom born of a happiness that can always be repeated. It is Onegin's dreaded and '*chill* freedom'.

'All ties cast off.'

> 'In *Faust*' — writes Lukács in *Goethe and His Age* — 'there are
> scarcely any scenes of which the function would be the creation of
> transitions or foundations for what is to come. ... What is depicted
> are neither transitions from one stage to another nor views on past
> or future, but exclusively the sensible presence of the given phase.'[43]

In this process, Lukács sees the prevalence of 'dramatic' over
'epic' technique, and he draws an analogy with Hegel's vision of
history. The *Phenomenology*, however, in no way ignores the
transitions from one stage to another, which are in fact discussed
in some of its critical sections, such as that on Master and Slave, or
on the self-estranged spirit. The reasons behind Goethe's choice
probably lie elsewhere, and perhaps precisely in his great but
implausible notion of *streben*. Such a notion is based, as we have
seen, on a metaphysics of identity: Faust wants to move onward
because he has fully lived a given form, and to emphasize the sense
of fullness that marks his journey, Goethe portrays him only when
he is once again totally absorbed in the next form. Like mankind in
a famous passage of Marx, Faust 'confronts only those problems
he is able to solve'; and Goethe, for his part, only lets us see him
after he has in fact already solved them.

Even though he is continually changing roles, Faust is thus
never hesitant or divided; neither does he seem to possess that
'interiority' divergent from actual behaviour which typifies
modern man.[44] Faust 'is what he is' at every given moment: his
magical ability to 'sleep' and forget (while novelistic heroes, as a
rule, suffer from insomnia) transforms the past into a sort of a
dream; his equally magical ability to fulfil his desires does away
with the future as an uncertain potentiality. In *Faust*, therefore, we
do not find a real plot, but rather a series of independent frames
that exclude the representation of becoming: it is the dream of a
mankind always rooted in the present, and always aware and in
control of itself.

Just the opposite happens in the novels of this period. Here *only*
the uncertainty of becoming is portrayed, and we only find scenes
of transition — but never points of departure or arrival.
Everything is a preparation, and a remembrance, an illusion and a
rude awakening, hope and regret, doing and undoing what has
been done. This ceaseless back and forth — this diachronic
transposition of the duplicity of bad faith — makes the endings of
these novels especially problematic. D.A. Miller on Stendhal:

We might describe the Sartrian *tourniquet* in the following way. Desire treats middles as anticipations of the end; and it puts ends back into a middle, by forgetting or revising their status as ends. Ending can be accepted only as prolepsis; when it is met at its proper position (at the end!) the sequence needs to be extended to eclipse its closural finality.[45]

We are reminded of the *besoin d'anxiété* of an epigraph in *The Red and the Black* — of the anxiety which *Being and Nothingness* posits as the origin of bad faith, and which Kierkegaard's classical discussion saw as leading to two opposite results. The first is that of the 'knight of faith': 'solid all the way through', he 'is always in what he does'. He has chosen the path of 'renewal' (or 'repetition'), thus avoiding the deception of 'hope' and 'remembrance', which marks the opposite destiny: '... he who does not grasp that life is a repetition and that this is the beauty of life has pronounced his own verdict and deserves nothing better than what will happen to him anyway — he will perish.'[46]

This destiny, symbolized for Kierkegaard in Napoleon, is 'demonic', 'silent', 'sudden'. Silent and sudden, hostile to repetition, always prey to hopes and remembrances, never firmly rooted in what they do — such are Julien and Fabrizio, Onegin and Pechorin. Unlike Goethe's *streben* their restlessness is truly linked to anxiety and melancholy: no longer the product and premise of happiness, this freedom generated by mobility makes happiness impossible:

> When chance that summer willed our meeting —
> Though conscious in you of a fleeting
> Fondness for me, I would decline
> To yield, to let dear habit sway me:
> Afraid of love lest it betray me
> Of that chill freedom that was mine. ...
> All ties cast off, as in repentance,
> I thought detachment, calm, would pass
> In place of happiness. Alas!
> How wrong I was; how harsh my sentence! (*Eugene Onegin*, VIII,
> Onegin's Letter to Tatyana.)

This antithesis of happiness and freedom is not new in itself; it was already there in the classical *Bildungsroman*. What has changed is the hierarchy of the two values, and the narrative structure that conveys it. In *Wilhelm Meister*, or in *Pride and Prejudice*, freedom 'resolved' itself into happiness: the hero lived his desire for individuality to the full until, tired of its inconclusiveness, he 'exchanged' it for the exemplary socialization of a successful marriage. Freedom was capable of anything except providing an ending worthy of the exclamation, 'Stop, thou art so beautiful': and so the *Bildungsideal*, which requires instead the strong closure of maturity, willingly relinquished it. A generation later, the interest shifts to the opposite side of the paradigm: rather than investigating what permits the establishment of decisive bonds, these heroes muse about the force that incessantly brings about their destruction.

> Is it my sole function in life, I thought, to be the ruin of other people's hopes? Through all my active life fate always seems to have brought me in for the *dénouement* of other people's dramas. As if nobody could die or despair without my help. I've been the indispensable figure of the fifth act, thrust into the pitiful role of executioner or betrayer. What was fate's purpose? Perhaps I was meant to be a writer of domestic tragedies or novels of family life? (*A Hero of Our Time*, 'Princess Mary'.)

As for domestic tragedies, Pechorin sets the stage for three or four of them, and kills a friend in a duel. Onegin separates Liensky from Olga, kills him in a duel, destroys Tatyana's rural peace, and then tries to take her from her husband. Julien Sorel shatters the de Rênal family, antagonizes Mathilde and her father, shoots Madame de Rênal, and causes her death and that of Croisenois. Fabrizio strains the relationship between Mosca and Sanseverina, and between both of them and the court at Parma; he sets Clelia in opposition first to her father and then to her husband, and brings about her death and that of her child.

It is a disturbing sequence, but it would be wrong to see it as a series of crimes. Far from being *maudit* characters, our heroes are usually not driven to their deeds by illicit and thus potentially 'criminal' desires — but rather by an incredibly weak sense of social contract. If they violate the bonds of love, family and friendship, this happens because they see all bonds as unworthy of being maintained, or as unjustified and unbearable constraints.[47] It is the melancholy but violent version of the liberal concept of freedom: freedom *from*. Pechorin: 'I'll make any sacrifice except this one. I'll hazard my life, even my honour, twenty times, but I will not sell my freedom. Why do I value it so much? What does it hold for me? What am I preparing myself for? What do I expect from the future? Absolutely nothing. I have this innate fear, this uncanny premonition.' (*A Hero of Our Time*, 'Princess Mary'.)

What does freedom hold? Nothing. It is the merely negative principle of atomization and dissociation. That it draws back from marriage is only natural, as this free and mutual sacrifice of freedom had become the dominant metaphor for the modern social contract. Onegin:

> If my own character inclined me
> To the familial hearth and house; ...
> ... On finding you, I dare confide,
> I should have sought no other bride. ...
> And been as happy ... as I could!
> By me such bliss will not be tasted,
> My soul is strange to its delight;
> On me your perfect gift is wasted,
> I dare not claim it as my right.
> I know (my conscience be your warrant),
> Our married life would grow abhorrent
> To both of us; however much
> I loved, at habit's chilling touch
> My heart would cool, and all your weeping
> Would not be able to implore
> It back, but just outrage it more. (*Eugene Onegin*, IV, 13-14.)

'The soul,' writes Stendhal at the beginning of *On Love*, 'tires of all that is uniform, even perfect happiness.' Habit, uniformity: this is what makes happiness undesirable. For happiness invites lingering, one wishes it would last forever: 'Stop, thou art so beautiful' ... but if this were the case it would be the end of that image of history as discontinuity and unpredictability which, despite resistances and counterstrokes, had become the highest symbolic value of these very decades.

An undesirable happiness — and yet, especially in Stendhal, still very much desired. It is a contradiction expressed by the emotional paradox of *amour-passion*: the happiness of unhappiness, or also, as Denis de Rougemont has shown, a craving for fate. And fate (by which all these heroes feel haunted — with an intensity unique in the history of the novel), fate, as we know, only metes out death sentences. The pursuit of happiness is thus transformed in the rush towards self-destruction: into the happiness of unfreedom.

Whence the great Stendhalian image of the happy prison. Its most widespread, and surprisingly idyllic interpretation, sees it as the place where Julien and Fabrizio can finally dismiss the world of vanity and 'disguises' to behold their innermost 'truth'.

But this theory, apart from minor inaccuracies, blinds us to the disturbing, and possibly horrible feature of modern life, which Stendhal was lucid enough to disclose: for a culture which has produced an uncompromising desire for freedom, happiness is only conceivable in prison: as imprisonment.[48] The heroes of such a culture can be sure of their heart's 'truth' only *after* external constraints have deprived them of their freedom. Left to themselves, they are capable of neither 'happiness' nor 'truth': they double and disguise themselves — but they do so because, for them, the world of masquerades and bad faith is no longer separable from that of freedom and history.

Unhappy ending

If the ending is perhaps the most problematic aspect of Pushkin's and Stendhal's works, which seem 'interrupted' more than 'concluded', this is because the only truly consistent ending — the *happy* ending — is here inconceivable. What happens in the happy ending is that plot ceases to be a mere chronological succession and becomes an intentional progress, where the story's ending and the hero's aim fully coincide. Time is transfigured by the meaning it has helped to establish, and the latter is in its turn *immanent* to the world we find at the work's end: no longer a doubtful and precarious individual choice, but a world of shared values, most explicit in love's reciprocity. The achievement of happiness, for its part, makes one wish time would stop, and strengthens the ending's sense of closure. — This is precisely what took place in the classical *Bildungsroman*, such as *Wilhelm Meister* and *Pride and Prejudice*; and the amalgam of time, meaning, happiness and closure was especially suited for emphasizing the irreversible move from youthful experiments to mature identity, and for portraying individual formation as inseparable from and — 'in the end' — directly coinciding with social integration.

Nothing of all this is left in Stendhal and Pushkin. Youth is not a teleological course ending in a superior maturity; the meaning immanent to the world as it is can neither be shared by the protagonist nor grant him happiness; the strain towards autonomy clashes with the dictates of socialization. If a truly convincing ending should give us a sense of peace and balance, showing the systematic integration of a text's various elements, here the latter have become so conflictual, divided and heterogeneous as to make this unimaginable. Yet these novels too, like any other, must at some point end. And if a happy ending is not possible — let them end in the opposite way: let them end *un*happily.

Just as the happy ending implies some kind of 'success', which it sublimates into something wider, so the unhappy ending demands the protagonist's death, but it shapes it in a special way. His death must first of all *isolate* the hero: not only from a social order in which he never felt completely at ease, but especially from those collective expectations which he has never wholly betrayed, and to which — within himself — he has perhaps entrusted the ultimate meaning of his existence. Thus Octave, in *Armance*, leaves to fight in Greece, but kills himself upon seeing the shore. Julien dies in 1830, but not during that July rising which reconciled his author with Paris; he is beheaded in a remote square in the provinces, and the reader shall never know whether for his attempted murder or for his speech. Fabrizio survives Waterloo, political imprisonment, and a Carbonari rebellion, only to die a lonely death in the Charterhouse of a God he has never believed in. As for Pechorin, we know neither how nor where he dies: he simply dies.[49]

A solitary death therefore (while, as the final words of the *Charterhouse* remind us, all the worst characters thrive). And an unjust death:

> 'But send a messenger to Odintsova, Anna Sergeyevna, the landowner over there — you know? ... Yevgeny, that is Bazarov, sends his compliments and word that he is dying. You will do that?'
> 'I will ... Only could it possibly be true that you are dying, you Yevgeny?... Judge for yourself! What justice will there be after this?'
> 'I don't know about that; but just send the messenger.'

This splendid dialogue, from Turgenev's *Fathers and Sons*, shows how questionable is Benjamin's thesis according to which the hero's death has the function of ensuring a meaning to the story: 'But the reader of a novel actually does look for human beings from whom he derives the "meaning of life". Therefore he must, no matter what, know in advance that he will share their experience of death: if need be their figurative death — the end of the novel — but preferably their actual one.'[50]

In these novels, at least, the opposite is true: the story must end with the protagonist's death in order that it be *deprived* of meaning.

Irony and irrationality

These last observations bring us back to the notion of 'reality' expressed by Stendhal and Pushkin, and to problems of narrative realism. As we have seen, the reality these authors portray does not need any justification for existing. The identification of real and rational, of legality and legitimacy, so characteristic of the classical *Bildungsroman* and of Hegel's philosophy of history, has fallen apart. Reality's essence lies not in embodying a society's professed values — but in its violent rejection and open derision of anyone who tries to realize them.

This is why realistic narrative does not tolerate happy endings: these portray the harmony of values and events, while the new image of reality is based on their division. There must be no justice in this world: a realistic story must be *meaningless,* 'signifying nothing'. Even though it comes at the end, the unhappy ending proves here to be the rhetorico-ideological *foundation* of nineteenth-century realism: narrative verisimilitude itself is initially sacrificed by the compelling *need* of these novels to finish unhappily. If, from Balzac on, novelists will strive to show that it is wise to lose faith in society's professed values *because* reality works according to different principles, which are meticulously described in the course of the plot — Stendhal, Pushkin, and later Turgenev, all manipulate plot in highly contradictory and improbable ways *in order to* break that faith.

Here again a quick list will suffice. In *Armance,* an impossible muddle of intercepted and forged love letters is responsible for Octave's suicide. In *The Red and the Black,* it is Julien's unexplained homicidal impulse. In the *Charterhouse,* it is again a muddle of false then true illnesses and imprudent moves. In *Onegin,* a dubious Providence thrusts Eugene, who has just disembarked, before Tatyana. In *A Hero of Our Time,* Lermontov does not even bother to explain how it is that Pechorin dies. Finally, in *Fathers and Sons,* Bazarov contracts tetanus because, just to pass the time, he decides to perform an autopsy on a dead farmer.

In each instance, death (or, for Onegin, unhappiness) does not appear as the final effect in a sequence of causal connections, but as a turning point which is both *necessary* and *arbitrary.* Both necessary and arbitrary... We can now at last solve the problem encountered at the end of the first section of this chapter. Every text, we said, must provide the reader with a reasonably unchallenged viewpoint from which to shape his perception and judgement. Since the level of discourse, ironic and shifting, did not offer this viewpoint, we argued that it may be found within the story. And this is where we have found it, as that unchallenged viewpoint is precisely the unhappy ending. But in having solved this problem, we have also raised a much more disturbing one.

Let us unify the two levels of these works: we are confronted with Doctor Jekyll and Mister Hyde. We discover that the system of ironic discourse — devoted to the creation, to an endless creation of meaning — relies on a story that embodies the opposite principle: the denial of meaning. A culture discursively open, critical and democratic seems inseparable from the notion of history as a relentless, irrational and cruel machine. Is this possible?

Yes — in these texts at least. For a culture that pays tribute to multiple viewpoints, doubt, and irony, is also, by necessity, a culture of *indecision.* Irony's most typical feature is its ability to stop time, to question what has already been decided, or to re-examine already finished events in a different light. But it will never suggest what should be done: it can *restrain* action, but not encourage it. Yet to live is to choose, and decision cannot be eradicated from human existence or from history. That is why the paradigm of indecision is forced to resort — along the syntagmatic axis of plot — to its opposite: to *arbitrary decisions.* If rationality is wholly absorbed in accentuating and enjoying the 'complexity' of a text, the inevitable simplification of that system will necessarily be dictated by *irrationality.*[51]

Such is the disturbing tangle that lies at the origins of our culture. And not just at its origins: Henry James and Joseph Conrad will widen the gap between an extremely sophisticated, problematic and intelligent meditation — and a coarse and crude series of often unfathomable and always inexorable events. 'Destiny' — a term which the eighteenth century had effectively banished — recovers its relevance in the century of progress. But before dealing with this, one last digression on the anti-teleological nature of realistic narrative: on its desire to appear as simply 'what took place' — as 'past'.

The Fall of Wisdom

Vorbei! exclaims Mephisto at Faust's death, 'over!', 'past!'.

Past! What a stupid name.

Why past?
Past and pure nothing, it is all the same.
Why have eternally creation,
When all is subject to annihilation?
Now it is past. What meaning can one see?
It is as if it had not come to be. *(Faust, 11596-11601.)*

Mephisto is wrong. The past *has* come to be and is therefore important. But important in what way? Narrative theory, for its part, has advanced various hypotheses. Bakhtin, for instance, considers the past meaningful only in the epic, in which it is a dimension 'inaccessible' to the narrator, who has to accept 'the reverent point of view of a descendant'. Such a past is 'absolute', it is 'a specifically evaluating (hierarchical) category. In the epic world view, "beginning", "first", "founder", "ancestor", "that which occurred earlier" and so forth are not merely temporal categories, but *valorized* temporal categories'.[52]

This is clearly not the image of the past we are looking for; nor do we find it in Bakhtin's novelistic time — the 'present in its inconclusiveness', a 'world-in-the-making' subject to change and open to experiment. We need an 'accessible' past, on the same hierarchical and chronological level with the present, and yet already 'frozen' and hostile to that experiment — the protagonist's life — which should have given it meaning. Could it be the past Barthes offers in *Writing Degree Zero?*

> The Novel and History have been closely related in the very century which witnessed their greatest development. Their link in depth ... is that in both we find the construction of an autarkic world which elaborates its own dimensions and limits, and organizes within these its own Time, its own Space, its population ... And yet narration is not necessarily a law of the form. A whole period could conceive novels in letters for instance; and another can evolve a practice of History by means of analyses. Therefore Narration, as a form common to both the Novel and to History, does remain, in general, the choice or the expression of an historical moment. ...
>
> So that finally the preterite is the expression of an order, and consequently of a euphoria. Thanks to it, reality is neither mysterious nor absurd; it is clear, almost familiar ... . For all the great storytellers of the nineteenth century the world may be full of pathos but it is not derelict, since it is a grouping of coherent relations...[53]

The past here is both 'contemporary', like the worlds of Stendhal and Pushkin for their readers, and 'closed'. Too closed in fact: its orderly, understandable and 'almost familiar' nature contradicts the sudden loss of meaning that we are trying to account for. We are on the right track though, and the solution lies in developing Barthes' reference to the 'preterite' with the help of the linguistic investigations of Emile Benveniste and Harald Weinrich.

In the 1959 essay, 'The Correlations of Tense in the French Verb', Benveniste was the first to put forward the distinction of 'story' and 'discourse' we have often used: 'The tenses of the French verb are not used as members of a single system, they are distributed in *two* distinct and complementary *systems* [which] are the manifestation of two different planes of enunciation, which we will distinguish as that of *story* and that of *discourse*.'[54]

As concerns *histoire* — story for novelists, and history for historians — 'the fundamental tense is the aorist, which is the tense of the event outside the person of the narrator'.[55] Rather than Bakhtin's inaccessible distance, this tense expresses a subjective attitude to the narrated events, whose aim however (and here we depart from Barthes' thesis), is not the construction of an orderly and almost mythically consistent universe. Its secret lies in a further grammatical peculiarity, the strong connection existing between the aorist itself and the 'third person' enunciation. The third person however, as Benveniste had pointed out already in 1946, is qualitatively different from the first and second 'persons' indicated by the 'I'/'you' pair: '... it is in fact the verbal form which has the function of expressing the non-person... it is the "absent" in Arab grammars.'[56] In fully consistent historical narration, '... even the narrator is no longer there. The events are announced as they are produced in their appearance along the horizon of the story. No one speaks: the events seem to tell themselves on their own. The fundamental tense is the aorist, which is the tense of the event outside the person of the narrator.'[57]

The combined use of the aorist and the third person induces us, therefore, to see the world through a symbolic form that no longer has anything in common with discourse, with the 'here and now' of a dialogue between an 'I' and a 'you'. But the domain of discourse, which Weinrich has analysed in a more articulate way than Benveniste, is the domain of comment and judgement, where subjectivity confronts and discusses all it holds to be important for its existence. It is the domain of values, of great symbolic choices, both social and individual. Given this, what has happened here?

What has happened is that with the realistic novel a new attitude towards life and history has been generated — the 'narrative' attitude. And this attitude has severed all links with comment and judgement as ways of assigning meaning. It is a major historical rupture. This is what Benjamin and Weinrich have to say about its consequences:

> ... the nature of every real story ... contains, openly or covertly, something useful. The usefulness may, in one case, consist in a moral; in another, in some practical advice; in a third, in a proverb or maxim. In every case the storyteller is a man who has counsel for his readers. ... The birthplace of the novel is the solitary individual, who is no longer able to express himself by giving examples of his most important concerns, is himself uncounselled, and cannot counsel others.[58]

> [In the Arabian Nights] we can certainly perceive a trace of the function which the narrator exercises in ancient cultures, especially in oriental ones where story-telling constitutes the form through which wisdom matures into decision. Commenting and narrating are not disjointed from one another; rather, one comments while narrating. Wisdom is not a product of a discursive mental process: it is the flower and fruit of narration.[59]

Our discussion of the 'past' has led us once again to the divergence of story and meaning, of factual reality and value judgements. And once again, as was the case with irony, we are confronted with a contradictory situation. On the one hand, a story that does not automatically yield wisdom is a liberating novelty: it means that the authority of tradition has lost its sway. For wisdom is the opposite, not only of thoughtlessness, but also of risk, imagination, the yearning for still unclear possibilities: the adventures of Robinson Crusoe, and of the modern novel, begin when a son no longer heeds his father's wise counsel.

A story interwoven with wisdom *inevitably* presents the 'past' of which it speaks as still relevant, as an ever valid 'eternal yesterday': that is, it presents a world where the difference between factual observations and value judgements does not as yet exist. It is a symbolic form still under the spell of a mythical substratum — and it is precisely myth that Weinrich turns to[60] in his search for a narrative structure where there is no split between story and comment.

Such a split, in other words, is a basic premise of modern culture; should it be 'healed', it would be impossible to have that multiplicity of viewpoints typical of ironic consciousness and of the democratic ethos itself. Yet we must not be blind to the other side of the coin. Much as we approve of the fact that a story does not *automatically* generate wisdom, that it should *never* generate it, on the other hand, should surprise us. But this is precisely what happens when narration is freed from judgement: the irrational arbitrariness of the unhappy ending, which it inevitably turns to, replaces rational reactions with a painful stupefaction. It encourages us to accept and forget, not to understand.

Here too, if we unify the text's two levels, we are confronted with a twofold message, addressed to a human being in contradiction with himself. The level of discourse treats him as an adaptable, critical and intelligent being — too intelligent perhaps; but the story level speaks to him as a helpless, bewildered, and irrational creature.

The Waterloo Paradox

Christopher Lasch and Richard Sennett have re-established, in recent years, the historico-psychological validity of the Marxist thesis on the violent and irrational nature of nineteenth-century capitalistic development. The men of that age saw the domain of economic relationships as an impenetrable machine, both in the benefits it generated and in the wider and wider catastrophes it left in its wake.

This era of incredible material progress thus gave new life to the notion of 'destiny': to what the *Theory of the Novel* calls the 'blind, and indifferent, total power' of 'second nature'. And if a social force is seen as 'destiny' — if the common belief is that it will be forever incomprehensible and uncontrollable — then it is best to get accustomed to its presence, and try to live with it. So, whereas other eras felt the need to portray history (and the course of individual existence within it) as a progress directed towards a goal, as a 'meaningful' process — this one, as we have seen, had to learn to see it as something senseless: not because catastrophe was everyone's fate, obviously, but for the equally disturbing reason that no one, as an individual, could feel themselves safe from it.

Destiny reappears in the modern novel, but it is different from the destiny of antiquity or tragedy. Foretold neither by oracles nor prophecies, as for Oedipus or Macbeth, it is not the *premise* of events. It appears only *ex post*, at the end: Mathilde de la Mole was right after all, only a death sentence can nowadays 'distinguish' a man. And this sentence always holds that element of arbitrariness or chance that originates the thought (inconceivable with tragedy) that things *could have turned out differently.* But it also tells us that things *did* turn out this way, and that the verdict, however unjustified, is final.

This narrative form based on an unhappy ending therefore helped European culture to adjust to the fortuitous-yet-inexorable nature of nineteenth-century capitalism: a combination already foretold in the tangle of great promises and great tragedies of the Revolutionary and Napoleonic years. And it is precisely in the political sphere that the rhetoric of the 'realistic' ending receives a further, and in a certain sense definitive explanation.

I am thinking of the short circuit between politics and culture we have often mentioned, and may call the 'Waterloo paradox': in the world of events a Restoration did occur — in the world of symbolic values, never. The political reality has no culture to legitimize it; the existing principles of legitimation are not strong enough to become reality. This discrepancy, which has since haunted bourgeois consciousness, has resulted in a highly problematic view of 'social integration'. Integration must obviously take place, and thus the reality principle — which is truly and wholly a pleasure principle: trying to secure a normal, regular and 'happy' life — will lead, sooner or later, to the repudiation of those values on which society nonetheless claims to base its legitimacy. It is a *necessary* repudiation: 'one has to live'. But it is also *unjustifiable*: for these are the highest principles of an entire civilization, and no value judgement can ever justify their abandonment.

'To double business bound', a certain type of modern individual *must* therefore rid himself of that which he *cannot* be rid of. And here we find the great creation of the realistic ending: where there *can*, and does occur precisely that which *should not* occur. ' "Only could it be possibly true that you are dying, you Yevgeny? Judge for yourself! What justice will there be after this ...?" '

Let us call to mind the plots of *The Red and the Black* and *Onegin* one last time. If Stendhal and Pushkin had in mind an unhappy, but ethically meaningful ending, they could have opted for the solution we find, for instance, in *Wuthering Heights*: have the hero degenerate and thus explain his death. Significantly enough, both novels set this process in motion — with the Madame de Rênal and Liensky episodes — but then suddenly abandon it, to return to Julien and Onegin's better sides. And it is precisely *at this moment*, when it is no longer ethically necessary, that falls the axe of Trilling's 'reality': narratively implausible, as we have seen, but never mind — it is there, and that is enough.

The Waterloo paradox is thus solved in the only possible way: not by disentangling it, but by fixing it in a double course of existence. The unhappy ending lets the reader continue *believing* in the professed principles of legitimacy, since no 'higher' values have been offered in their stead: they can be 'kept alive' — simultaneously, they can be 'kept from becoming alive', because the story's unchangeable 'reality' shows that they cannot be realized, as the threat of destiny hangs over them. And one does not argue with destiny: it does away with the very idea of responsibility. And although we all have a certain responsibility in our acceptance of the reality/pleasure principle of *doxa* and tranquility, no one likes admitting such things. Better to think we could have lived in a quite different and much bolder way if — at a certain point — an 'external, hard, gross, unpleasant' reality had not forced its 'that's life' upon us.

Hence the modern world's unique valorization of unhappiness, the uncanny familiarity with which we welcome the unhappy ending, the paradoxical sense of security and stability we derive from the contemplation of an unjustly bitter fate. This melancholy helps us balance ourselves between two lives. It is the price we pay for — for bad faith of course: which is not only a theme of the realistic *Bildungsroman* but also its objective result. And even though bad faith can hardly be seen as something to be proud of, in these times when even the memory of so many principles and hopes has faded, one wonders...

3

The World of Prose

I

Parvenir

> Well, would you like to know what a politically minded man finds
> inscribed above the door-way to this nineteenth century of yours?
> In 1793 Frenchmen invented popular sovereignty and it ended up in
> imperial absolutism ... . Napoleon was a Jacobin in 1793; in 1804 he
> donned the Iron Crown. From 1806 onwards the ferocious
> champions of 'Equality or Death' acquiesced in the creation of a
> new nobility, which Louis XVIII was to legitimize. The emigrant
> aristocracy, which lords it today in its Faubourg Saint-Germain,
> behaved worse still ... . In France then, in politics as well as ethics,
> all and sundry reached a goal which gave the lie to their beginnings:
> their opinions belied their behaviour, or else their behaviour belied
> their opinions. Logic went by the board, both with the people in
> power and private individuals. So you no longer have any ethics.
> Today, with you, success is the ruling motive for all the action you
> take of whatever kind. (*Lost Illusions*, 'A lecture on ethics — by a
> disciple of Mendoza'.)

It is Jacques Collin, here as 'Canon Carlos Herrera', who
pronounces the historical judgement on which Balzac's universe is
founded. In *Lost Illusions*, as Lukács observed, the 'age of ideals'
does not end, as in Stendhal, with the explicit victory of its
enemies: it denies and betrays itself by boldly turning each of its
values into its opposite. 'There are no principles, there are only

circumstances': once again Jacques Collin ('Vautrin'), speaking to his first disciple. Principles no longer determine the origins and goals of power; they no longer 'legitimize' it. They are merely means — words — for obtaining power, thereby achieving success: 'That day you came back, with a word written upon your forehead. I knew it, I could read it — *"Parvenir!"* ' (*Old Goriot*, 'An Entrance into the World').

Parvenir! The sudden spread of this metaphor points to a new stage in the history of individual formation. Nothing remains of Stendhalian autonomy, that sensation of being bound, despite lies and compromises, to one's 'laws of the heart'. Lucien de Rubempré is already radar-like, outer-directed: when asked 'Are you a classicist or a romantic?', he promptly replies 'Which is the stronger party?' *(Lost Illusions*, 'The sonnets'). An ideal bond, of any sort, would hinder his 'wonderful ability to adapt', admired by the Marquise D'Espard; it may tarnish the brilliant versatility of the successful journalist. There is no longer any place for the 'idea of duty'; nor for the final happiness of *Wilhelm Meister:* 'Happiness, old man, depends on what lies between the sole of your feet and the crown of your head; and whether it costs a million or a hundred louis, the actual amount of pleasure that you receive rests entirely with you, and it is just exactly the same in any case. ... A man's affections are just as fully satisfied by the smallest circle as they can be by a vast circumference.' (*Old Goriot*, 'An Entrance into the World'.)

Lothario's calm acceptance of limits (' "Here or nowhere is America!" ', *Wilhelm Meister*, VII, 3) can no longer satisfy the restless demands of *parvenir!* The new keyword requires a new idol, and it finds it in social mobility: in social mobility as an *end in itself.*[1] No longer a stepping stone to something else — to a harmonious personality, for instance, which makes the 'bourgeois' Wilhelm Meister yearn to be 'noble'. Nor, as in Julien Sorel's Napoleonic fantasies, the reward and outcome of 'great deeds' — or else something shady and almost shameful.[2] With Balzac all uncertainty ceases, and the desire for success appears for the first time as a wholly 'natural' impulse needing no justification whatsoever — while the social system, for its part, appears legitimated precisely because it makes individual mobility possible. That this mobility heightens inequalities and injustices is by now of minor importance: the new criterion of legitimacy is not characterized by an agreement *over principles*, but by the 'Thermidorian' possibility of satisfying immediate and 'material' interests.

The opposition between formation and socialization, the alterity of 'soul' and 'second nature' of the *Theory of the Novel*: all of this vanishes. Balzac's heroes desire only what *already exists* in the world, and no longer must decide whether or not to accept the rules of the game, but only learn them better than everyone else. In *The Red and the Black*, every change in Julien's social status was put into perspective by the typically Stendhalian episode of Julien's 'return to his room': alone at night, exalted yet doubtful, he mulls over the meaning of what has transpired, and questions the legitimacy of his behaviour. In *Lost Illusions*, the same changes are illuminated by an opposite sort of episode: Lucien's return *into society*, girded by a panoply of status symbols (clothes, horses, carriages, and ladies). It is no longer the closed interiority of the hero that supplies meaning to events, but 'society': which scrutinizes him, discusses him, and takes note of his new position.

Fascinating for the way in which they enrich every social change through countless echoes and reverberations, these episodes are like thermometers scattered throughout the *Comédie Humaine*: they measure the rise of individuals and indeed they tell us that to 'measure' and to 'evaluate' are by now one and the same. It is the birth of Balzacian 'realism': a symbiosis of intellectual penetration and ethical indifference. It is the culture of a world where values and meanings are always and only 'relative', because they are based solely on social relationships of power and threat: unstable, often enigmatic relationships that must be constantly brought into perspective. It is a way of perceiving reality that has lost any ethical depth and finalistic impulse — but it has also been forced to develop an attention to detail, a penetrating acumen, and an ability to foresee, all previously unknown. For the world of social mobility possesses new vices, but also a new greatness: as well as that new catchword, which we shall now examine more fully.

'Parvenir' — fine. But 'where'? Not only are we not told, but it is hinted that the question itself is childish. As with money, the fascination of social mobility is in its boundlessness: it is not a question of reaching 'a' position, no matter how high (Napoleon), but of the possibility to become 'anything.' It is the euphoria of an 'open' society, where everything is relative and changing; hence the somewhat paradoxical need for a catchword as suggestive as it is indefinite. 'Parvenir' indeed — soon joined by its twin, 'success', which also owes its fortune to a slippery and undefinable semantic core.[3] Even grammar is hard-pressed by this word: 'is' someone a success or does one 'have' success? And the problems only multiply when we approach the concept of success. Karl

Mannheim, for instance, states that success is '... objective success. An achievement which influences or changes the life (being) or conduct of men ...'

A few pages later, Mannheim returns to his definition, clarifying its temporal aspect: 'In general, it can be stated that ambition will be directed towards that form of subjective success which appears to afford the best guarantee of permanence and security.'[4]

A profound and lasting achievement: is this what we mean by 'success'? Certainly not. History has known countless changes of that sort long before the need for the term success was felt. Something new must be responsible for its spread; a radically new form of social achievement must have come into being, which must be distinguished from what existed previously.

To clarify the difference, let us look at one of the basic oppositions of *Lost Illusions*: D'Arthez and high literature — Lucien and journalism. D'Arthez's success does in fact call to mind Mannheim's definition: his works will profoundly change the taste and thinking of his Parisian audience. They are not the result of 'talent' — a word of commercial origins, which Lucien inspires in all those around him — but of 'genius'. The latter can break the rules of the game, and change them, because it has a *goal*, as D'Arthez himself tells us (*Lost Illusions*, 'First friendship'): and each time 'the caprice of destiny keeps [it] still far from [that] goal', genius is able to continue its course through 'will-power', 'struggle', and 'patience'.

Yet if the reader of *Lost Illusions* learns something about success, it is not thanks to the story of D'Arthez (which Balzac, in any case, avoids going into at length). The hero of social mobility is instead Lucien, and he uses his talent not to change existing taste, but to satisfy and confirm it: thereby achieving results which are neither profound nor lasting. In recompense, they are immediate: 'For [editors] a book is merely a capital risk. The finer it is, the less chance it has of selling. Every exceptional man rises above the masses, and therefore his success is in direct ratio to the time needed for his work to prove its value. No publisher is willing to wait for that'. (*Lost Illusions*, 'Behind the scenes'.)

No publisher, no Lucien de Rubempré. The goals of a culture of social mobility may be vague, but one thing is not vague at all, they must be achieved quickly. An evening at the theatre, an article, and Lucien *est parvenu*, he has 'made it'. 'Where' we not only do not know, but we no longer even care, nor does he: it is *speed* that counts, and that enchants. But for this same reason it is not true that 'in Paris success is everything; it is the key of power' (*Old Goriot*, 'A Bourgeois Hotel'). On the contrary, success *distances* from power, since the latter requires that lasting and deep-rooted stability which success, with its speed, attempts to do away with. Rastignac, who in a future novel becomes Minister of the Interior, never knows true success; Lucien, who has blinding success, never enters the domains of power.

In short: success — inseparable from any idea of social mobility — is alien and even inversely proportional to power. What social mechanisms, then, is it linked to, and what historical temporality?

In Fashion

Curiously enough, Balzac never explains the 'reasons' behind Lucien's success, and neither do the few articles he reproduces for us. But perhaps this is so because the key to Lucien's career does not lie in the contents of his work, but in its *form*: in that new intellectual activity — cultural journalism — that Balzac describes for dozens of pages, and which, instead of avoiding the emphemeral nature of success, strengthens and perhaps even creates it.

For if success must be had in a day, it can rest only on what will last but a day. More than into the world of 'power', or of 'capitalism' (as Lukács would have it: which is true, but vague), Lucien ushers us into the world of *fashion*. If we do not find the reasons for his success in his articles, this is because fashion, Simmel observes, 'is indifferent in forming its particular contents in relation to meanings'. What results is an 'absolute indifference for life's objective norms', which makes it the ideal medium of an achievement which is as quick as it is transient.

> In the practice of life anything else similarly new and suddenly disseminated is not called fashion, when we are convinced of its continuance and its material justification. If on the other hand, we feel certain that the fact will vanish as rapidly as it came, then we call it fashion. We can discover one of the reasons why in these latter days fashion exercises such a powerful influence on our consciousness in the circumstance that the great, permanent, unquestionable convictions are continually losing strength, as a consequence of which the transitory and vacillating elements of life acquire more room for the display of their activity.[5]

That is why Stendhal, although he is Balzac's contemporary,

dismisses fashion as a boring effort to elude boredom, worthy of some minor nobleman, but alien to his heroes and to the deeper meaning of his work. Stendhal is still a man of the Enlightenment, grappling with the legitimacy of the social contract and baffled by the 'great, permanent, unquestionable convictions [which] are continually losing strength'. Balzac is already bewitched by the aftermath of all this, by the irreversible spread of fashion, by its 'influence on our consciousness'. And fashion, like any symbolic power, asserts itself because it fills a void, and provides an answer to troubling questions:

> ... a series of uninterrupted, sudden, unjustified and ephemeral diffusions, fashion corresponds to the need for change for the sake of change ... it essentially reflects social mobility ... it is in harmony with the fundamental machinery of modern societies and reproduces at a staggering rate that which constitutes the essence of their system ... It is a question of innovating ceaselessly. Now, the risk inherent to progress — its quickening, the uncertain future — generates uneasiness ... Fashion is the training ground for a symbolization whose function it is to accustom us to the new and to discredit the old.[6]

In this light, Lucien de Rubempré can finally be seen for what he is — a fashionable commodity: discovered, put on the market, triumphant, out of style, thrown away. All in a flash, it is a meteoric course typical of urban 'success', and one with profound consequences for the structure of the *Bildungsroman*. To begin with, it is the first time the protagonist fully identifies with the 'spirit of the times'. Wilhelm Meister, who flees the metropolis, and Julien Sorel, who remains defiant towards society, retain a peripheral or hostile stance to the full modernity of their world. But Balzac's heroes plunge in headlong: for Lucien, the only way to form himself is to merge intimately with the 'fundamental machinery' of Balzacian society.

The only way to form — and also the best way to destroy himself. The same flexibility that keeps Lucien always in step with the times, also keeps him from achieving a lasting individuality: it dictates that he can never be 'himself'. Sooner or later, everyone who is close to Lucien realizes that he cannot be trusted. Because he is an egoist? Yes... But above all because, in essence, Lucien does not exist — he is not a *person*. He is a wholly social creature, a 'child of the century', a transparent image that receives all its colour from forces much greater than itself, and which will only need him for a short while: for a brief 'season', no longer. Because fashion — as a *system* — prospers even if its individual components wither away: in fact, it works best the more it heedlessly tosses them aside.

In the public acknowledgement of success, the individual and the world seem, for a moment, to coincide: but it is only a moment, and no use asking it to stop, because the time of individual life and that of the social system have gone definitely out of step. And so, precisely those features of Balzacian 'capitalism' wherein modernity is most brilliant and dynamic, and the promises of social mobility most appealing — precisely those features which seem best suited to the fulfilment of modern individuality, set the stage for its ruin.[7] It is a sudden and disturbing discovery, which radically changes that relationship — between hero and reader — which has always been crucial for the form of the *Bildungsroman*.

I mean that the reader's progress towards 'maturity' no longer — as was the case in the classical *Bildungsroman* — depends on that basic identification which tied him to every step of Wilhelm and Elizabeth's unfolding youth. Nor does it entail that 'dialogue' with Julien Sorel and Eugene Onegin, stimulated by the narrator's polemical comments, ever undecided between scorn and admiration. With Balzac, all links fall apart: Lucien de Rubempré — who succumbs to the frenetic beat of Parisian life without having the least idea of what is happening to him — is, quite simply, a model to be avoided. A negative example, almost a warning — this is what happens to those who plunge headlong into modernity: they lose their youth without ever becoming adults.

Maturity is no longer to be sought in reference to the lives unfolding 'within' the story, but by listening to the narrator who — being *outside* the story — can nonetheless tell it. In fact, story and discourse undergo an inversely proportional relationship: the more unaware and bewildered the hero, the wiser and more far-sighted the narrator. Fine. But just 'who' is the Balzacian narrator?

The Balzacian Narrator (I):
'Nothing is hidden from me.'

He who tells stories, in the *Comédie*, always knows much more than those who live them. But where does he dwell, this thousand-eyed narrator, and how did he acquire his information? The question is valid for any narration — historical as well as literary — and Balzac's originality lies in having combined the two extreme views on the matter. We find the first in *The Philosophy of History*: 'original history', writes Hegel, is undeniably furthered when it is entrusted to figures such as the Cardinal of Retz or Frederick the Great: 'Writers of this order must occupy an elevated position. Only from such a position is it possible to take an extensive view of affairs — to see everything. This is out of the question for him, who from below merely gets a glimpse of the great world through a miserable cranny.'[8]

These last words evoke, by contrast, the opposite position. Bakhtin: 'The quintessentially private life that entered the novel at this time was, by its very nature and as opposed to public life, *closed*. In essence one could only *spy* and *eavesdrop* on it.'

Whence various solutions: the use of 'legal-criminal categories in the novel ... as specific forms for uncovering and making private life public' (a technique which culminates with Dostoevsky and the detective novel); but especially the use of the viewpoint of the *servant* ('eternal "third person" in the private life of his lords, the servant is the most privileged witness to private life'), of the *adventurer* and of the *parvenu*:

> Building a career, accumulating wealth, winning glory (always out of personal interest, 'for themselves'), their roles impel them to study personal life, uncover its hidden workings, spy and eavesdrop on its most intimate secrets. And so they begin their journey 'to the depths' (where they rub shoulders with servants, prostitutes, pimps, and from them learn about life 'as it really is').[9]

Bakhtin is certainly right in maintaining that the novel's sphere of action is the private one of civil society, and not the public-official one of Hegelian history. The dismissive and hasty indifference with which Hegel treats the novel can perhaps be ascribed, more than to an aesthetic diffidence, to a philosophical bias: to his hostility towards the idea that there can be a 'story without the State',[10] and that civil society may achieve so full a self-consciousness as to generate, in addition to the object of narration, the categories with which to organize it as well.

Civil society then: and who, if not Balzac, has been the bard of this protean creature? And yet, precisely in the *Comédie*, where the 'knowledge of private life' assumes an intensity never to be equalled again, Bakhtin's thesis of the 'view from below' does not seem to correspond to the facts, and it is Hegel who appears to be right: 'Only from such an elevated position is it possible to take an extensive view of affairs.' 'To see', for nineteenth-century mentality, is more than ever before a prerogative of power: from the 'personal and moral statistics of the Empire' desired by Napoleon to Bentham's Panopticon, the idea of a 'total inspectionability' (Polanyi) keeps gaining ground. Balzac's motto — 'to compete with the Registry' — is a part of this trend: to narrate is to appropriate the viewpoint of power, or even surpass it.

But which power? We should not be misled by the metaphor of the Registry: the place of omniscience, in the *Comédie*, resembles a bank, not a Ministry. Those who know life 'as it really is' — the social referents of the Balzacian 'narrator' — are characters such as Jacques Collin, 'the banker of convicts', or the usurer Gobseck, a veritable semi-legal financial power:

> '... all human passions, enlarged by the interplay of your social interests, come to parade before me who lives in quietude. ... Do you think it nothing to penetrate thus into the recesses of the human heart, to espouse the lives of others and see them denuded? Ever varied spectacles: hideous sores, mortal misfortunes, love scenes, miseries that the waters of the Seine await, the joys of young men which lead to the scaffold, desperate laughter and sumptuous parties. Yesterday, a tragedy ... Tomorrow, a comedy ... Often a lovelorn girl, an old merchant on the brink of bankruptcy, a mother who tries to hide some guilt of her son's, an artist with no bread, a great man in decline, who, for lack of money, runs the risk of losing the fruit of his labours, have made me tremble with the power of their words. Those sublime actors played for me alone, yet without managing to trick me. My gaze is like God's, I see into hearts. Nothing is hidden from me.' (*Gobseck* , II.)

There is no doubt about it: speaking through Gobseck here, is the 'narrator' of the *Comédie*, who condenses in half a page the melodramatic ups and downs of the Balzacian universe: certain allusions, in fact, are nothing less than one-line summaries of well-known novels. But what is it that gives Gobseck his ominiscience?

> 'My gaze is like God's, I see into hearts. Nothing is hidden from me. One refuses nothing to him who tightens and loosens the purse-strings. ... In Paris, there are about ten of us, all silent and unknown kings, arbiters of your destinies. ... No fortune can lie, we possess the secrets of all families. We have a sort of *black book* in which the most important observations are written...'.*(Gobseck*, II.)

This irresistible and inexorably 'realistic' gaze, born of civil society and dominating it, has no need to 'spy and eavesdrop': it merely has to turn its ear to the chorus of Paris: 'Everyone tells us his neighbour's secrets. Tricked passions, offended vanities, gossip. Vices, disappointments, revenges are the best police agents.' (*Gobseck* , II.)

To learn something, Balzacian police must disguise themselves, roam about, bribe, threaten — Gobseck has only to open a door. The 'system of needs' that is nineteenth-century civil society is not for him — as for the Hegelian State — a mysterious and menacing unruliness: it reveals itself to him in total transparency because, precisely, it needs his money. It needs it to keep on living, to be what it is: which is to say that, without Gobseck, or Jacques Collin, or someone like them, Balzacian *narrative* could not exist. If all the 'silent and unknown kings' were to tighten their purse-strings, farewell *Comédie Humaine.*

The importance of this hidden yet all-powerful reality has, of course, often been pointed out by criticism.[11] But when I said that, without a Gobseck, Balzacian narrative could not exist, I was thinking not so much of his role as userer *within the plot*, but rather of his function as a point of view *on* the plot. About Gobseck, there 'is' not much to say — but he 'has' much to tell. A mediocre character, he is instead an excellent point of observation: in narratological terms, his true world is not the story but discourse, as it should be with any narrator.

But we need not stop here. More than 'viewpoints' on events, Gobseck and Jacques Collin seem to be actual 'transcendental categories' of Balzacian narrative. It is not that they help us see it 'better', but that, without them, we could not see it *at all*. The plot of the *Comédie*, this world that becomes increasingly more complex and ungovernable, where heterogeneous and opposite fates meet and disperse, and all principles are betrayed, and every desire gives way to its opposite — all of this could have remained mere chaos, noise, magmatic confusion. If this is not the case, and we have instead the great narrative network of the *Comédie Humaine*, it is precisely because Balzac positioned his narrator on the shoulders of that social class that seemed to him the only one capable of 'seeing' this new world: of discerning some kind of order, and being able to narrate it. If in other words, starting with Marx, no one has ever withheld admiration for what the nineteenth-century bourgeoisie has been capable of doing, Balzac, somewhat atypically, admires it, and uses it, for what it managed to *see*.

'Nineteenth-century bourgeoisie' — the worst sort, in Balzac: usurers, convicts, 'wolves', 'bloodthirsty hunters' (Adorno).

Together with their 'spiritual mobility', and their perspicacity in 'a knowledge of the weaknesses and disadvantages of one's surroundings', that characterize for Sombart the Faustian figure of the 'entrepreneur',[12] these characters display, as is inevitable, some of the most repugnant features of capitalist society: cynicism, cruelty, heedless indifference to the fate of others, or a predatory promptness to take advantage of it. Balzac, as is well known, not only does not tone down these aspects, he stresses them. Because of Lukács's celebrated 'incorruptible artistic integrity' which is responsible for the equally famous 'triumph of realism'? I doubt it. It appears to me instead the uncanny challenge of one who realizes that certain ideas and deeds, not in spite of their loathesomeness, but *due to it*, have given this new class a power, and with it a *power of vision*, previously unknown. After five hundred years, this contradictory development has once again made possible a *universal narration*: a 'comedy' that dares the analogy with its divine precedent. This new comedy is the vision of a heartless usurer, and we must not forget it; but it is the *Comédie Humaine*, and this too must not be forgotten.

The Balzacian Narrator (II):
'At a time like this it would be a wonderful spectacle...'

A generation goes by, and the demon that had spoken through Balzac reappears. This time, under the name of Jacob Burkhardt:

> The mind must transmute into a possession the remembrance of its passage through the ages of the world. What was once joy and sorrow must now become knowledge, as it must in the life of the individual.
>
> Therewith the saying *Historia vitae magistra* takes on a higher yet humbler sense. We wish experience to make us, not shrewder (for next time), but wiser (for ever).
>
> How far does this result in scepticism? True scepticism has its indisputable place in a world where beginning and end are all unknown, and the middle in constant flux ... .
>
> Of the true kind [of scepticism] there can never be enough.[13]

This passage, which could pass for a commentary on the *Comédie Humaine*, so alike is its inspiration, specifies the new image of 'maturity' implicit in the Balzacian narrator. 'In the life of the individual', as in that of the species, maturity now means one thing only: *knowledge*.

...The ideas of fortune and misfortune inevitably fade. 'Ripeness is all.' Instead of happiness, the able mind will, *nolens volens*, take knowledge as its goal. Nor does that happen from indifference to a wretchedness that may befall us too — whereby we are guarded against all pretence of cool detachment — but because we realize the blindness of our desires, since the desires of people and of individuals neutralize each other.[14]

A splendid affirmation, perhaps more than of scepticism, of modern stoicism; yet there is something that rings hollow — something unhealthy and sick, Nietzsche will maintain in *On the Use and Abuse of History*. The fate of 'the able mind' is knowledge: but knowledge has lost all practical relevance, since the blind mutability of history makes any rational design useless. Knowledge is maturity, and 'ripeness is all': it means being 'wiser (for ever)' instead of 'shrewder (for next time)'. But can this be the goal of the living, immersed in 'the middle in constant flux' where there will most certainly be a 'next time' and where there can never be enough 'scepticism'? What good are a maturity and a knowledge that are 'of no use' to life?

No good at all, the next generation will answer with Nietzsche. But we must first of all understand the genesis of this new paradigm, and then see whether it really is as simple and also as absurd as it seems. As for its genesis, Burkhardt places it at the origins of modernity, in that 'ontological' scepticism inherent in the incessant change of all human institutions: 'And above all, only the fairy-tale equates changelessness with happiness. ... We must admit that permanence means paralysis and death. Only in movement, with all its pain, can life live.'[15]

In turning happiness as 'changelessness' into 'paralysis and death', Burkhardt pitilessly summarizes the passage from the last, radiant page of *Wilhelm Meister* to the closed and mournful world of *Elective Affinities*. From that point on, life is movement, 'with all its pain': all the more painful, we may add, when an individual fate is intimately caught up in the whirlpool of the new century. So it is, we have seen, with Lucien de Rubempré: 'a child of the times', and of their movement, if ever there was one; forced to grow old, and kill himself, without ever having grown up.

As a result, the narrative locus of 'maturity' shifts, sealing what in Stendhal and Pushkin was still a hesitant and contradictory development. Maturity leaves the story, refuses to mingle with life and direct it: those maxims that in *Wilhelm Meister* imparted wisdom to the dialogue *among characters*, in Balzac are found only in the disembodied world of the *narrator*'s discourse. No longer the crowning of growth, nor 'wisdom' generated directly from the story, Balzacian maturity is founded on a rupture: on its *estrangement* from the narrative universe. Just as Lucien will never become an adult, so Jacques Collin and Gobseck can never have been young. There is no bridge or growth between youth and maturity, only antagonism: and so between success and power, illusion and scepticism, passion and realism.

All parallel oppositions: and not by chance do all the first terms refer to the story in the *Comédie*, and the second ones to discourse. The result is the notion that maturity is fullest and strongest the further and more sheltered it is from the seething cauldron of modern existence. Maturity as a *retreat from life*: the paradoxical and disturbing outcome of a historical acceleration that seemed to overflow with promises, and turns out instead to be a menace. We shall come back to this. But here let us see whether this 'wisdom' truly is, as it seems, something 'conclusive': the consequence of an irreversible retreat from history and life. Both Balzac and Burkhardt, of course, encourage such a view — but both then contradict it, and more vividly still. We have already seen as much for Balzac: Gobseck's scepticism, or the narrator's, more than the *outcome* of the story, is its *premise*. It is what makes concretely visible the most extraordinary narrative undertaking of modern times: a starting point, not a terminus. As for Burkhardt, we need only read the conclusive section — 'conclusive' — of the *Meditations*, that passage entitled, 'Idea of the Magnificence of a totally objective Contemplation of our Time,' which may well be the greatest theoretical manifesto of nineteenth-century realism:

> At a time when the illusory peace of thirty years in which we grew up has long since utterly vanished, and a series of fresh wars seems to be imminent;
> when the established political forms of the greatest civilized peoples are tottering or changing;
> when, with the spread of education and communications, the realization and the impatience of suffering is visibly and rapidly growing;
> when social institutions are being shaken to their foundations by world movements, not to speak of all the accumulated crises which have not yet found their issues;
> it would be a wonderful spectacle — though not for contemporary earthly beings — to follow with knowledge the spirit of man as it builds its new house, soaring above, yet closely bound up with all these things. Any man with an inkling of what that meant would completely forget fortune and misfortune, and would spend his life in the quest of that wisdom.[16]

The speaker, here, is not wise. He is a visionary: like Balzac. But to muster the courage to uphold such a 'wholly objective' vision, he needs to think of it as 'wisdom': he needs to support and buttress and even 'smear' it with wisdom, as Barthes will put it in *S/Z*. It is the price modernity exacts from both Balzac and Burkhardt. But the price required to stare it straight on and *see* it, not to elude it.

Stare it straight on to the point of becoming lost in it once again. It is the immense vicious circle of the *Comédie*, where that 'maturity', so very estranged from life, is what allows us to see modern life — to see it as a 'wonderful spectacle' which makes all distance impossible, has us forget all knowledge, all 'wiser (for ever)' in favour of the 'joy' and 'sorrow' of the 'next time', of the next act in the cosmic drama sketched in the final lines of Burkhardt's text. An endless circle, or perhaps a sort of compromise between the demands, equally imperious, of proximity and distance, of passionate participation and reliable knowledge. An endless circle: let us go back then to the core of the Balzacian vision, to the source of that 'painful movement' that shakes the *Comédie Humaine*; and let us try to understand how Balzacian 'capitalism' works.

II

Capitalism and Narration

In *Wilhelm Meister*, everyday life was a spacious domain where the hero was free to discover what the world had to offer, and to leisurely build his 'personality'. In *The Red and the Black*, this space had become a mire, and what could give a meaning to life — *amour-passion*, politics — had become alien and hostile to a stifling and somewhat cowardly everydayness. With Balzac things change once more, and each everyday occurrence — expanding a business or finding a job, but also buying boòts or greeting a passer-by — is suddenly a complex and unpredictable event, full of promises, or threats, or at least surprises. Hegel's prose of the world has become novelistic, and even melodramatic. Why is this? What has happened?

What has happened is that great metamorphosis that Fernand Braudel places precisely in the first half of the nineteenth century: for the first time in the history of mankind the domain of everyday reproduction, perennially closed and given to inertia, has been invaded and shaken by the cosmopolitan and 'brilliant' restlessness of great capitalism.[17] The world, observes another historian of the period, has suddenly become much larger (obviously enough), but above all much smaller, because everything is intertwined, and among all sorts of activities, people and places there is an ever greater and tighter interdependence.[18]

Emblematic locus of this network of relationships is the metropolis — Paris, where the great novels of the *Comédie Humaine* take place: Paris, 'the city of a hundred thousand novels' *(Ferragus)*. Its centre, if it has one, is the nineteenth-century Stock Exchange: 'at once the symbol and the central institution of an economic order founded upon the vagaries of chance'. The 'marriage of capital and chance',[19] which Balzac celebrates here, is as disturbing a union as the one — 'bourgeois respectability founded on chance' — indicated by Richard Sennett. The point being, Sennett continues, that for the first two-thirds of the last century capitalism, while becoming ever more dynamic and intrusive, remained nonetheless 'an economic order which neither victors nor victims understood'.[20]

A narrower world, and also a more turbulent one; more interdependent, but more indecipherable. It is not surprising then if we find here 'the fall of public man'; if 'maturity' withdraws to observe the course of the world, instead of taking part in it. From here there is no escape, Balzac himself seems to say when he discards the very popular and effective narrative theme of the hero's 'flight'. No escape — this closely woven universe is a trap, full of pitfalls and snares, of hunters and preys. All metaphors which show how the Balzacian vision of the new social order is indelibly linked to the sudden *advent* of capitalism, rather than to its 'growth' or, as Lukács would have it, its 'triumph'. That a usurer always gets the better of a foolish *profumier*, or a banker of an indolent intellectual, is obviously not enough to speak of the consolidation of capitalism: Marxist orthodoxy missed the point here, for long-range historical 'perspective' is precisely what is lacking in Balzac, and Adorno is right in observing that his 'realism' '... proceeds in the opposite direction from economic analysis. Like a child, he is mesmerized by the nightmare and madness of the usurer. ... What is seriously reactionary in [Balzac] is not his conservative orientation but his complicity with the legend of the capitalist predator. The indignation about the *auri sacra fames* is part of the inexhaustible supply of bourgeois apologetic.'[21]

An impeccable historical judgement; but Adorno's words also indicate that he is not the person best suited to do full justice to the *Comédie Humaine*. A critic of capitalism's excessive rationality and abstractness, Adorno is of necessity cold and a little sceptical when he sees this system represented as a bloody and passionate chaos. Yet Balzac cannot be relegated to the past quite so easily — because, from time to time, capitalism's 'primitive' features do breathe new life; and because precisely those features enabled Balzac to conceive a narrative rhetoric that is perhaps the most widespread of the last two centuries. They enabled him, in short, to finally write the novel of capitalism. The novel of capitalism... According to countless pages of Marx — but also of Goethe, or Hegel, or many others still — the infernal rhythm of the new social relationships should of necessity generate an equally grandiose narrative, or even epic, culture.[22] Yet, this has not been the case, and in the propagation of capitalism narrative has usually seen an increase of regularity and predictability: a *hindrance* to narrativity and the generation of story. Just think of that emblematic work, *Around the World in Eighty Days*: adventure occurs only where the railway ends and the punctuality which kings have bequeathed to the Englishmen has not yet been imposed; it occurs on the border between an archaic world and the orderliness of the Empire, but no longer within the latter, and even less in its capital.

But the capitalism of the *Comédie* is neither orderly nor predictable yet, and with nearly magical foresight, Balzac isolates in *Lost Illusions* that form of production — fashion — which will long retain, and in fact still does so today, the feverish and anarchic features of early capitalism. Fascination with the new and rejection of the old, enigmatic alternation of success and ruin, colourful battlefield between brilliant and unscrupulous personalities: if one wants to see in capitalism an immense and fascinating narrative system, there is no better way to observe it than from the viewpoint of fashion.[23] On the diachronic plane, in other words, fashion reproduces and intensifies the tempestuous features — the narrativity — of early capitalism. But on the 'spatial' plane, so to speak, fashion acts in the opposite way, and helps restrain the sense of threat which the nineteenth century came to know only too well. By acting as a miniature model of the new social relationships, fashion makes them concretely representable — it makes them *visible*. It reduces the disorientation of this narrow-enormous world; it deprives that Minos of nineteenth-century mentality — the Market — of its remote and enigmatic anonymity. Using fashion as an interpretive grid, Balzac can imagine a sociological totality, where one can once again follow the progress of a commodity, or of a man, from birth to death. The best example of such sociological condensation, the true marketplace or stock exchange of the *Comédie Humaine*, is the Balzacian salon. Bakhtin:

> Political, business, social, literary reputations are made and destroyed, careers are begun and wrecked, here are decided the fates of high politics and high finance as well as the success or failure of a proposed bill, a book, a play, a minister, a courtesan-singer; here in their full array (that is, brought together in one place at one time) are all the gradations of the new social hierarchy.[24]

The verdict of this consensus can, of course, be cruel and fickle: but at least the jury is known. It is a dangerous world, but no longer an unfathomable one. Likewise Balzacian narration, which keeps the reader permanently uneasy, but does not force on him the anxiety — *Angst, anxieté* — so typical of the nineteenth century. The distinctive Balzacian emotion is rather a blend of suspense and surprise: quite different from anxiety, as can be seen with particular clarity in the way these two emotions relate to time.

Anxiety lives each moment as potentially the last: but since what hangs over it is unknown, it has no foresight whatsoever, and is thus bound to a meaningless but perhaps eternal present — or left waiting, defenceless and blind, for an irremediably 'other' future. The feeling I am trying to describe is founded instead on a *rhetoric of far-sightedness*: it is a sort of compulsive fore-vision, which can always discern in the present the germs of the future: which indeed seems to see *only* the outline of the future: as if what is barely discernible, but does not as yet exist, were the only reality worthy of notice.

Here we finally have it, the narrative technique which captured the pace of that famous passage:

> Constant revolutionizing of production, uninterrupted disturbance of all social relations, everlasting uncertainly and agitation, distinguish the bourgeois epoch from all earlier times. All fixed, fast-frozen relationships, with their train of venerable ideas and opinions, are swept away, all new-formed ones become obsolete before they can ossify. All that is solid melts into air, all that is holy is profaned ....[25]

Yes indeed, everlasting uncertainty and agitation distinguish the *Comédie Humaine* from all earlier narratives. If each new episode of the cycle 'sharpens the awareness of the present' (as, for Simmel, does fashion), this is because it reveals its precariousness, its ephemeral nature. The Balzacian episode implacably points to the new, beyond which it already spies the glimmer of something 'newer' still, as if to push not just the present, but the future itself into the past. Think of the first conversation between Lucien, still a poor and unknown newcomer, and Lousteau: a few lines are enough to hint, not just the future triumph of Lucien, but his fall as well.

It is precisely the 'frenzy of disappearance' that the *Phenomenology* ascribes to the modern spirit; and Balzac, being convinced, as Hegel was, that 'happy epochs are the blank pages of history', certainly does not lavish happiness on his heroes. Nor on his readers, to whom he never grants the satisfaction of a well-closed narrative sequence, of a clear and stable meaning: there are always other plots that knock on the door, loose threads everywhere, divergent viewpoints to take into account — it is always difficult, with the *Comédie*, to interrupt one's reading with any reasonable degree of certainty.

This world in which there is nothing certain or solid is, once again, the outcome of Balzacian scepticism: much more convincing in the *Comédie*'s narrative rhetoric than in the narrator's maxims. Convincing? Imperious. If it is difficult to interrupt our reading, this is beause our perception of the text — always attuned to the new, and ready to forsake it for the newer still — ends up resembling, strongly resembling, the perception of the characters that 'live' within the world of fashion and chance. We are no longer observers: we do not enjoy that distance which for Balzac is necessary to generate knowledge. The promise of learning something from the blind adventures of Lucien de Rubempré has not been maintained: nor could it be, for Balzac's plot forces us to rush on with an impetus that makes interpretation impossible, and that after a while is barely distinguishable from the all too unwitting progress of his young hero.

The goal of the *Comédie Humaine* is not 'knowledge': it was not so in the case of the narrator, it is not so in the construction of plot. It is instead a form of perception, which will become firmly rooted in modern culture, sustained by a consuming desire for the new *as such*, regardless of all else. It is an attitude that would have been inconceivable to Goethe and Austen, to Stendhal and Pushkin, and which ushers in a new phase of the European novel. What has come to be is a need for *sheer narration* — without beginning or end, just like the *Comédie Humaine*.

Fifty Thousand Young Men, One Hundred Thousand Novels

A narration 'without beginning or end'. At first, it seems hardly plausible. To have a story, according to contemporary narratology, there must be a kind of event — Weinrich's 'unheard-of', Lotham's 'violation' — capable of disrupting the regular flow of time and 'beginning' an unusual and unpredictable sequence. And in order to 'motivate' such a disruption, there should be a character who, for some reason, is not contained within prevailing norms. Robinson Crusoe's 'rambling thoughts', Wilhelm Meister's multiform interiority, Julien Sorel's mixture of pride and ambition, Tom Jones's rash generosity — these are all examples of a common procedure, which emphasizes the discontinuity between the hero and his world, and is therefore particularly well-suited as a starting point for the *Bildungsroman*.

Like all true beginnings, the ones we have mentioned are fundamentally *arbitrary*: the world was following its usual course when someone decides there should be light, or that this marriage must not take place, or that that eagle above Lake Garda is a sign to go to Waterloo. In this respect, Balzac's great innovation lies in shifting the origin of plot from an *individual volition* to a *superindividual mechanism*: the mechanism of *competition*, which with the unification of the national markets, in the first half of the nineteenth century, ceases to be an exception to become the *norm* of social relations. And this new 'plot' of associated life is especially conspicuous, once again, where the concentration of people is greatest. Paris, in the words of Jacques Collin:

> 'There are fifty thousand young men in your position at this moment, all bent as you are on solving one and the same problem — how to acquire a fortune rapidly. You are but a unit in that aggregate. You can guess, therefore, what efforts you must make, how desperate the struggle is. There are not fifty thousand good positions for you; you must fight and devour one another like spiders in a pot.' (*Old Goriot*, 'An Entrance into the World'.)

Here we are completely outside of Lotman's *neoclassical* framework, discussed in the first two chapters, where the hero is already a modern individual, but the world is still a traditional and 'classified' society. That model could work for *Wilhelm Meister*, and was perfect for *The Red and the Black*, but in Balzac's Paris the paradigm is overturned: here it is not the hero who generates the story, but rather the world, with its many-sided and endless conflict. Narration no longer requires that the rules of the social system be 'violated': it is in fact *objectively inscribed* within them, in an 'ordinary administration' that never generates anything truly 'unheard-of', but in exchange makes *everything* risky and unpredictable.

In Balzac's world, in short, to *desire* a novelistic existence is perfectly superfluous. Once in Paris, all his characters, whatever they do, are very quickly *forced* to lead a novelistic life:[26] to the point that, as we have seen, there is the urge to 'leave' the novel, to escape from a story that is all too gripping. If Balzac has to resort to an arbitrary act therefore, it is not to begin a story — but to *stop* it. The most convincing narrative ending, we know, is one that establishes (or restores) a *stable* classification: a system that draws its fundamental meaning by *remaining what it is*. But the social system of the *Comédie Humaine* has its meaning *in the act of becoming*: in being always inconclusive, in generating narration. On the basis of this uncheckable flow, any conclusion will always be felt to be an arbitrary break, and not by chance do some of Balzac's most famous 'endings' — that of *Père Goriot*, for instance, or that of *Lost Illusions* — refer to another novel: it is the only way to remain faithful to that 'monstrous wonder' that is 'the city of a hundred thousand novels'; a city, precisely, without beginning or end.

On the Genesis of Tolerance

Those young men trapped like spiders in a jar, or the recurrent image of Paris as the 'arena' of struggles to the death, lead us far beyond narratology. They reveal Balzac's interest in that new situation — the struggle for survival — which from Malthus on dominates nineteenth-century thought like few others; and which, before social Darwinism, refers not so much to the struggle between wolf and lamb, but to that between wolf and wolf (or lamb and lamb). *The Origin of the Species*: 'The dependency of one organic being on another, as of a parasite on its prey, lies generally between beings remote in the scale of nature ... .But the struggle almost invariably will be most severe between the individuals of the same species, for they frequent the same districts, require the same food, and are exposed to the same dangers.'[27]

They frequent the same districts, require the same food, and are exposed to the same dangers; the image we think of here, more than of enemies, is that of *friends*. And in effect, Balzac has painted the greatest and most problematic *tableau* of modern friendship, of this feeling that no longer binds together just *two* individuals, in the sign of complementarity, and often with a strong, if disguised erotic undercurrent[28] — but has become a wider and less defined relationship, free and open, as befits an uncertain youth, in search of someone who, like a living mirror, can help it define itself.[29]

Readers of *Lost Illusions* will remember the many pages dedicated to this mutual scrutiny, recognition, and discovery that the two belong 'to the same species'. But the open world of the metropolis, having made this feeling possible, proceeds immediately — 'there are not fifty thousand good positions' — to crush it. The *Cénacle*, reincarnation of the organic harmony of the Society of the Tower, is a vivid and insignificant lie: the truth about friendship and its opposite, in *Lost Illusions*, is revealed in the worlds of theatre and journalism, where creatures that require the same food engage in a struggle to the finish.

In this sense the 'sentimental' theme of friendship turns into the 'political' theme of coexistence. How to survive, and what to do, when faced with the universal clash of competition? What ethos will be most in keeping with the new conflictual society? Where does that crucial new value — 'tolerance' — originate, and what is its nature? But let us start at the beginning:

> Every newspaper is, as Blondet says, a shop which sells to the public whatever shades of opinion it wants. If there were a journal for hunchbacks it would prove night and morning how handsome, how good-natured, now necessary hunchbacks are. A journal is no longer concerned to enlighten, but to flatter public opinion. Consequently, in due course, all journals will be treacherous, hypocritical, infamous, mendacious, murderous: they'll kill ideas, systems and men, and thrive on it. (*Lost Illusions*, 'The supper'.)

According to passages like this, there are two types of journalism. The first — infamous mendacious murderous: a mere mouthpiece for conflicting interests — is that of Lousteau and Blondet, who in two memorable scenes show Lucien how to write both for and against the same book (*Lost Illusions*, 'The battle begins'; 'A study in the art of recantation'). The journalism 'concerned to enlighten public opinion' is embodied instead in D'Arthez who, when Lucien is forced to attack him, and can only muster 'mockery', which 'brings dishonour on a work', decides to write against himself, since 'grave and serious criticism is sometimes praise'. (*Lost Illusions*, 'The fatal week'.)

One would expect D'Arthez's impartial severity to be far better than the hasty and mercenary efforts of the other two — and yet the opposite is true. Lousteau and Blondet's articles appear to Lucien (and probably to every reader) 'full of good sense and just': fiercely polemical, but well thought out. But when D'Arthez's article (which Balzac does not 'transcribe') is read by his best friend, Michel Chrestien (who is unaware that only the signature is Lucien's), he sets out to find Lucien to spit in his face — 'There's an honorarium for your article' — precisely in defence of the idea of journalism as 'a priestly function, respectable and respected', so dear to D'Arthez (*Lost Illusions*, 'The fatal week'). Lucien challenges him to a duel, and from this moment on his fate is sealed.

Of course, it could be just one of the many inconsistencies of the *Comédie Humaine*. But it may also be a very effective way of suggesting that whoever, like D'Arthez, strives to rise above the great mechanism of competition, not only does not succeed, but brings out its purely destructive side; while those who comply with it, even in its baser aspects, as do Lousteau and Blondet, are forced to produce commodities that are intelligent and, all things considered, civil. 'Interest will not lie', Balzac seems to say in agreement with liberal tradition. It is useless to want to 'transcend' the antagonism intrinsic to market society: one should rather accept it as a fact of life, and it will then turn out to be the firmest foundation for any project of 'society' among men.

One must therefore, first of all, learn to 'see' interest, to recognize it in all its manifestations, and not to flinch at the sight. With unshakeable firmness, Balzac forces us to get thoroughly acquainted with the new impulse. He permeates each action with it, each moment. He magnifies it into melodramatic passion. He hardens it in the pitiless cruelty that surrounds old Goriot on his deathbed, when in the space of a hundred lines Restaud, Anastasie, Delphine, and finally Madame Vauquer all come up with very good reasons for denying a last visit to the dying man, or robbing him for the last time. A rather implausible sequence, but precisely for this reason indicative of Balzac's will to impress indelibly upon us not only the force, but also the validity, the 'reasonableness' of selfish interest. To Madame Vauquer's ruthless ejaculation — 'Be fair, Monsieur Eugène: it is my life' — neither Rastignac, nor the narrator, nor I believe the reader, know any longer what to reply.

Given these sociological co-ordinates, the *Comédie Humaine* should be the best example of the novel as it has been theorized by Mikhail Bakhtin. In scattered but crucial passages, Bakhtin does in fact link novelistic 'heteroglossia' to the new relationships established by capitalism, which multiplies the social languages, makes them all potentially equal, and thus forces them to meet and contend with one another: to engage in *dialogue*. And from this incessant and anti-dogmatic exchange originates, according to Bakhtin, the new ethos which the novel introduces into modern life: a spiritual attitude that is curious and open, flexible and experimental.

An attitude, we may conclude, that is *mature* and *democratic*. Although, as far as I can tell, it has gone by unnoticed, Bakhtin in fact reproposes in the domain of literary criticism some of the basic tenets of liberal-democratic thought. His notion of 'dialogue' and 'dialogism' fulfils the same function attributed by the latter to political 'discussion'; and both dialogue and discussion take place in, or better still establish that new domain — *public* and rational — where an atomized and conflicting universe achieves its distinctive self-consciousness, and generates the highest public virtue of the bourgeois world: tolerance. Tolerance as a *double presence*: John Stuart Mill's 'strong impulses' joined to 'the sternest self-control', and an adamantine respect for the laws of coexistence; a firm belief in one's own ideas, and just as ready a willingness to hear opposing arguments. Is this idea of tolerance — very dear, incidentally, to the author of these pages — also corroborated by the greatest novelistic representation of modern civil society?

No. And for various reasons. First of all, according to Balzac a world of conflicting interests and heterogeneous ideologies can indeed generate heteroglossia and dialogue: but these are not necessarily the *main* consequence of such a situation. In the *Comédie*, in fact, the open plurality of capitalistic society manifests itself not so much in *words* as in *actions*. When faced with a possible viewpoint, or a new social 'language', Balzac wants to illustrate first and foremost its *material roots*. He wants to represent it as a force in action, clashing with other forces, and in the clash there is a winner and a loser — and the loser, incidentally, also loses forever his place in the chorus of 'heteroglossia'.

In other words: for Bakhtin, the parallelogram of forces at the core of every novel manifests itself primarily as a *paradigmatic configuration*;[30] for Balzac, as a *syntagmatic sequence*. Plot is not 'subordinated' to the representation of the text's many languages, but rather the opposite: social languages acquire flesh and blood, and are wholly — and ruthlessly — translated into plot. It is, once again, the relentless *narrative* propensity of the Balzacian text: and the result, to return to the matter at hand, is a genealogy of tolerance totally different from the one sketched above.

Or more precisely: the result is a genealogy of *in*tolerance, and what is left of the original virtue is supported by values quite remote from those imagined by liberal thought: fundamentally, it is supported by *indifference* and *opportunism*. It is not tolerance, therefore, that we should be talking about, but *compliance*. Yet there is a logic in this fall, and the new value — however distasteful it may appear — has its irreplaceable symbolic function. If the way of the world becomes — as it does in the *Comédie* — a grandiose and ruthless process, which the single individual can in no way resist, but with which he must nevertheless live — he then has two choices. If one is made of steel, like Jacques Collin, then scepticism is the way: understanding everything and everyone, but forming bonds with nothing and no one. If one is made, like Lucien, of a weaker metal, then this amoral lucidity (which has, of course, nothing to do with tolerance) is unattainable, and in order to coexist with threat one should not sharpen one's vision, but rather dim it. Such is Lucien's third and final lesson in journalism, the one he cannot understand. After having written against and in praise of Nathan, Blondet explains, Lucien should appease his readers with a third article, in which he should 'say nothing': summarize his earlier pieces, pick out here and there some minor defects, add a few inoffensive platitudes and, most of all, *avoid taking a stand.*

Here, the pugnacious maturity of liberal tolerance has become the art of taking the middle course; Bakhtin's open and meaningful 'dialogue' an exchange of stock phrases. Later, and Flaubert will speak of it, there will not even be anything left to hide: the fear of conflict, as Horkheimer and Adorno have written, can easily generate stupidity.[31] Rather than being grounded in the struggle, and drawing strength from it, this torpid 'tolerance' longs to avoid it. It does not produce the 'co-ordination and exposure' of different social languages, but tries to keep them within a dim limbo. It is a negative virtue, a dilution of principles, a weak-spirited scepticism for weak souls...

Yes indeed, tolerance as compliance: a vocation to compromise — accommodation, acceptance of the *fait accompli*, ethico-intellectual confusion. Not an inspiring image — but indicative perhaps of the hidden feature of modern *Weltanschauungen*. Only in extreme instances do these rear up in an irreconcilable alterity of principles: more often, and in fact most of the time, they are induced by the 'ordinariness' of contact and conflict to infect one another — to resemble one another, to draw closer, to mitigate or

corrupt each other in turn. That inert and conciliatory third article
... how many times have we read it, and perhaps even imagined it?

'Narration'

Let us return to Lucien de Rubempré's 'fatal week'. If we were to
reduce it to a series of paradigmatic oppositions, it would read
more or less as follows. Lucien has one true friend, D'Arthez; he
has to treat him as an enemy; the latter answers as a friend,
rewriting the review; but in so doing, D'Arthez's best friend (and
thus, till now, Lucien's too) treats Lucien as an enemy; Lucien
challenges him, is fatally wounded, and forces in fact Coralie to die
for him. On the other hand, insulted by Michel, Lucien turns to
Rastignac and de Marsay; the latter, perhaps his fiercest enemies,
act as though they were his truest and only friends.

Please forgive the lexical monotony: but it does highlight what
Balzac is up to. We are at the decisive turning point of Lucien's life,
his moment of truth: and Lucien — reasonably enough, at first
sight — adopts a 'strong' reading of events, the irreconcilable
opposition between 'friend' and 'enemy'. But this opposition is a
false one, since all characters are both things at once, and any
unilateral reduction betrays their essence. And besides being false,
it is destructive: who knows, perhaps Lucien could save himself
yet, and if he does not it is precisely because he applies to events
too drastic a paradigm.

Through his self-destructive blindness, Lucien shows — a fatal
weakness, in the world of the *Comédie* — that he is not *realistic*.
Like tolerance-compliance, to which it is indeed related, Balzacian
'realism' is founded on the rejection of sharp contrasts. Aware that
the way of the world will never change at any given stage, it sees all
conflict as a necessary and yet transitory passage, which should
never become binding: 'there are no principles, there are only
circumstances'. In structural terms: to be realistic means to deny
the existence of stable and clearly opposed paradigms.

To deny the existence of stable and clearly opposed paradigms.
The theory of realism developed by Lukács in the thirties (in its
historiography: not in its aesthetics, which has really nothing to
say any more) had already reached a similar conclusion, when it
saw the core of nineteenth-century narrative in the defeat,
disillusionment, or corruption that experience inflicts on the
'subjective idealism' of the hero. Lukács's insistence on this
symbolic loss is quite right, and certainly pertinent to the study of

the *Bildungsroman*. But one can go further, and say that the paradigmatic de-stabilization of the *Comédie* also implies a moment that is, so to speak, 'constructive'. Balzac's paradigmatic disillusionment simultaneously produces a new illusion — more precisely: a *syntagmatic fascination*.[32] And this should not surprise us, for the weaker and more unhinged the paradigmatic classification of a narrative universe — the more entirely, and almost obsessively, the text's meaning will rely on the incessant progression of plot.

To clarify matters, let us take an almost identical episode in Balzac and Maupassant (an episode which, focusing on an adultery, also presents a typical case of de-stabilized classification), and see what an analysis of variants can tell us. In *Cousine Bette*, the civil servant Marneffe decides that the quickest way to advance in his career is to barge in, gendarmes close behind, on an adulterous encounter between his wife and his superior Hulot; likewise, thirty years later, Bel-Ami. But the scene has a totally opposite function within the respective plots. In Maupassant, it allows Bel-Ami to obtain a divorce (thereby freeing him for the much more profitable marriage to Suzanne Walter); and to ruin the Foreign Minister, thus increasing his own power. The episode helps therefore to prepare the conclusive classification: it *simplifies* the plot, both in 'spatial' terms (the characters involved are assigned to their definitive niches), and in 'temporal' terms (the protagonist is brought closer to his goal). In Balzac, vice versa, Marneffe's scheme *complicates* the plot: it ensnares Hulot in all sorts of blackmail, forces him to betray friends to win the favour of enemies to involve what were till now secondary characters. In other words: it increases the narrativity of the text and makes any sort of conclusive classification ever more remote, implausible and chaotic.

The same can be said for the 'simplifying' episode *par excellence*, the duel. Bel-Ami's life, which unfolds in the relatively isolated world of his 'career', results in a binary form of competition: there are always two opponents only, and the clash is resolved with the elimination of one or the other. The novel's plot is a long succession of social duels to the death, all the more clear in that the only true duel is a futile and harmless farce. In *Père Goriot, Lost Illusions*, and also *Sentimental Education*, things change. As we have seen, the Balzacian duel is not the climactic confrontation of 'real' enemies, but makes the reasons behind the clash more indefinable still, and obscures the physiognomy of the contending forces: it is dangerous, and cruel, without being noble or clarifying.

This being the case, it is understandable that, in the *Comédie Humaine*, everyone tries to fight their duels by proxy: whether it be Valerie Marneffe, the young and unscrupulous middle-class wife with whom cousin Bette ruins the family that has humiliated her, or Jacques Collin's unidentified friend who, by dragging in half a dozen new characters, will obtain a considerable inheritance for Rastignac. Conflict tends to be as *mediated* as possible, in accordance with the maxim — 'treat people as means' — that echoes in the *Comédie* each time we approach the theme of power.

But where each individual wants to reduce others to his private instruments, someone is inevitably preparing for him an identical fate. In a maze of conflicting perspectives reminiscent of Jacobean tragedy — except that there the social universe is narrow and immobile, and conflict always ends in a bloodbath, while in Balzac it is in continual expansion, and defeat need not result in death — each character of the *Comédie*, whether they want it or not, and whether they know it or not, is always simultaneously cause and effect of an infinitely *polycentric* plot, and which no invisible hand directs towards the common good.[33]

Overdetermination — this is the key to the Balzacian plot. Let us take that well-known overdetermined plot, *Hamlet*: yet there the unfolding of action entails clearing the scene — out with Polonius, out with Rosencrantz and Guildenstern, Ophelia, Laertes, Gertrude, all gone — so that the prince and the usurper can finally meet, face to face. But in *Lost Illusions*, the 'moment' of truth has become a fatal *week*, and 'fate' is not a drastic paradigmatic simplification, but rather its opposite, a sudden overlapping of heterogeneous domains — competition in the workplace (the journalists), lovers' strife (Madame de Bargeton, Lousteau), political struggle (liberals and monarchists), caste hostility (the old aristocracy, the dandies), the crude economic interests of creditors, even the intransigent friendship of the members of the *Cénacle*.

Sequences like this tell us that, in the *Comédie Humaine*, no event is ever 'simple': they are all composed and overdetermined by countless forces acting in accordance with different designs. And since some of these forces are always in movement, every moment of life, even the seemingly most ordinary and 'classified' one, can become a novelistic event. We are at the opposite extreme to the situation described by Schlegel: 'A well-known philosopher was of the opinion that in a truly perfect government (when commerce is totally closed, and travellers' passports contain a full biography and a true-to-life portrait) a novel would be absolutely impossible, since there would be nothing in real life that could offer it a subject, or any likely material.'[34]

If this is the way to make novels impossible, then where commerce is completely open, and passports are not very accurate, *everything* offers material for narration: it is impossible *not* to have novels. And this crucial turning point that Balzac imposed on narrative *construction* inevitably requires a re-examination of narrative *theory*, especially recent theory.

Let us begin with a technical question: Barthes' and Chatman's distinction between 'kernels' (episodes which are indispensable for the progress of action, since they involve a choice between incompatible directions) and 'catalyses', or 'satellites', which merely accompany and enrich the chosen direction. It seems to be an indisputable distinction, and yet the overdetermination of the *Comédie Humaine* weakens it to the point of uselessness: what is a satellite in the plot woven by one character is a kernel in the plot of another. Often, in fact, it is precisely the features of satellites — the 'automatic', and apparently 'insignificant', words and actions that usually follow a particularly important turning point — that betray a character, providing his opponent with valuable clues for use in a kernel to come. Nothing goes by unnoticed, nothing is without reverberations in this polycentric and overpopulated universe. It is an overlapping of asymmetrical and asynchronous perspectives that minimizes the semantic inertia — the 'insignificance' — of each segment of the text, giving the *Comédie Humaine* its enthralling, and almost obsessive, narrative vitality.

The same can be said for Harald Weinrich's opposition between 'foreground' and 'background'. Like kernels, the foreground is 'the reason for which the story is told, that which is recorded in the summary ... that which in substance induces people ... to listen to a story whose world is not their own; in Goethe's words: *the unheard-of fact.*' The background, like satellites, is instead 'that which is not unheard-of, that which by itself would induce no one to lend an ear, that which, however helps the listener to do so by facilitating his orientation in the narrated world.'[35]

A little further on, in a brief excursus on the varying importance of these two forms of 'narrative relief' in different historical moments, Weinrich observes that 'from Balzac onwards, the novel becomes realistic and that means sociological. The authors are no longer content to tell a more or less interesting and moving story, but they aspire more and more to give reliable information at the same time ... . With the *Sentimental Education* ... the relation between the narration's foreground and background is reversed in that now the background becomes the more important of the two, and the foreground, the less important.'[36]

Leaving Flaubert aside for the moment, and having acknowledged that the attempt to use rhetorical conventions to better understand the history of culture makes Weinrich's research much more interesting than most French narratology, we must also add that, in the *Comédie Humaine*, things are somewhat different. Just as it is hard to distinguish between kernels and satellites, so is it difficult to single out the unheard-of event, and to establish when an event belongs to the foreground, and when to the background. And the reason for this is that the great social forces of the Balzacian world are not motionless entities to be seen as the 'background' of an event, but actors directly involved in the plot: they *generate* plot, and what appears to be in its foreground is nothing other than the *result*, often unconscious, of their movement. If therefore, with the *Comédie*, 'the novel becomes sociological', it is not because Balzac 'shows' us countless bankers, publishers or businessmen: here Lukács is right, Balzac does not 'describe', he 'narrates', and in fact he subordinates sociology itself to narration, and uses it as a means for the production of plot.

Hence, a transformation in the very notion of narrative plot, which is no longer a 'violation' of the laws of the world, but their full and irresistible enactment; and a new kind of novelistic hero as well. Lucien de Rubempré is the protagonist of one of the greatest novels of the nineteenth century not because he possesses features which are meaningful in and of themselves — such as Wilhelm Meister's versatility, or Julien Sorel's pride, or David Copperfield's naiveté — but because he possesses none whatsoever, and this emptiness, this transparency allow us to perceive the great game of social 'backgrounds' played out through him. Everyone 'invests' in Lucien, everyone 'bets' on him, or against him: his sister and his mother, journalists and philosophers, dandies and managers, women, old men, saints, scoundrels... His immaculate beauty, his pliant and impressionable intelligence, both ask for a determination from without — a shove, one could say, which thrusts him into the foreground, to enact the drama of success without merit, and of failure without blame.

Lucien's story would not exist without the social network within which he operates: but this does not mean that his adventures are, so to speak, at the service of that sociological background, a mere tool for Weinrich's 'reliable information'. The initial pages on the development of printing techniques, or the long, mocking chapter of the last part — 'A free lecture on dishonoured bills for those unable to meet them' — are acceptable only because they accompany and explain decisive turning points in the relationships between David Séchard and his father, or between Lucien, David and the Cointet brothers. Printing techniques, or banking procedures, are not thrown into relief *as such*: and the reader does not retain what is necessary for an objective knowledge of them, but only that which corresponds to his *narrative* interests.

If, therefore, when reading Balzac we are first struck by the breathtaking broadening of the sociological domain of the novel — the truly revolutionary innovation of the *Comédie* is its subordination of this incredibly vast and full universe *to narrative form*. Even 'descriptions', as Auerbach saw, are condensed stories here; and if no great individual 'pages' can be isolated in Balzac, or no explicitly 'symbolic' scenes (as is instead the norm with the novel), this is precisely because, in the *Comédie Humaine*, the urge to classify — to establish *paradigms* — has given way to the fascination of an uninterrupted and inextricable sequence of *syntagms*.

Thus we return, along a different route, to a point we dealt with earlier: there comes into being, with Balzac, a new attitude, a vision of reality hostile to *analysis*, and literally bewitched by *pure narration*. Try to 'discuss' the novels of the *Comédie*: you will end up merely re-telling them. It is no longer possible to break free from this complex and enthralling narration: instead of being an instrument of knowledge, it has turned against knowledge, throwing a new and disturbing light on that 'historical consciousness' that was the great boast of the last century, and no doubt of Balzac as well. The comparison with Burkhardt had already opened up quite a few problems; here, in anticipation of what we shall see a little later, we may add that the *Comédie Humaine* appears to have taught us to view the way of the world very attentively, with a previously unthinkable involvement: *but without asking any more what it 'means'*.[37] We are concerned only that it keep on changing: only thus do we deem it interesting, and worthy of our attention.

This is not a small change. It is another possible version of what we call 'life', which often seems all the more 'real' and 'alive' if it is jumbled, indecipherable, complex. It is the more fascinating the more it drags us along, incomprehensible and indeed inherently hostile to comprehension. Narration or description, asked Lukács. Narration, without a doubt. But once aroused, where will the demon of narration lead us?

Balzac At His Very Worst

Before answering this question we must first resolve a difficulty. According to a well-established critical trend, Balzac's novels are dominated by the opposite principle to the one just described: by a true fanaticism for *causality*. Each event must become knowledge, as is shown by the incessant explanations, direct or indirect ('This is why'; 'Like all young men newly arrived in Paris...') of the Balzacian narrator.

Causality. In *What is Literature*, Sartre maintains that in narrative such a category 'is appearance and might be called "causality without cause", and it is the finality which is the profound reality'.[38] Twenty years later, Gérard Genette repeats Sartre's distinction: '... the real answer to the eternal *why* of realist criticism is: because I need it ... the *how do you explain it*? allows one to forget the *what is it for* ... . The law of the story ...,' Genette concludes with Machiavellian aplomb, 'is simple and brutal: *the end must justify the means*'.[39]

Given that only the 'end' is important in Balzac's narrative, it is a pity that Genette makes no attempt whatsover to define it; but the end does indeed determine the means, and Genette's end is to defend a poetics of *narrative arbitrariness*:[40] once the masks of realism are taken off, down comes the curtain and the show is over.

If however we remove for a moment the lenses of modernist poetics, one question inevitably arises: why should Balzac have sought out and emphasized narrative arbitrariness? Or in other words: given that the advent of capitalism injects uncertainty and anxiety into modern life, and endows historical progress (and through it spontaneous 'narrative' sensibility) with features that are all too arbitrary and threatening — is it really surprising that 'defensive' narrative conventions should be devised, conventions, I mean, which give the impression that arbitrariness and threat — even though they continue to exist — are in some way under control?[41]

No, it is not surprising, and it is not something to get indignant about. Not everyone is an *esprit fort* like contemporary Parisian professors, always ready to launch into the turbulent waters of history, and never having enough of a literature that intensifies discomfort and restlessness. But literary pleasure, for its part, arises from the opposite process — from the perception of a form that reduces and 'binds' the tensions and disequilibrium of everyday experience. What makes literature symbolically necessary is precisely its capacity to mediate and compromise — to teach us how to 'live with' disturbing phenomena.[42] It does this in ways that change with circumstances; as concerns the *Comédie,* Roland Barthes is certainly right in emphasizing the role played in it by a new and all-inclusive form of *common opinion:* 'If we collect all such knowledge, all such vulgarisms, we create a monster, and this monster is ideology. ... Social truth, the code of institutions — the principle of reality.'[43]

'Reality principle': social truth, the 'code of institutions'? Yes and no. Yes, in that it is *common* opinion, a normalizing belief. But the reality principle is first and foremost an *individual* need. Institutions can function even in its absence: not so the individual who, without it — without an 'Ego' — would be torn apart by those superior forces which, in Freud's view, attack him from within and without.

We are thus brought back to a topic already discussed in the first two chapters: the symbolic apparatus of socialization as a need of the individual, and in a sense a *preliminary* one, as well as of the social system. With this I do not in any way mean to suggest that Balzacian *doxa* is in fact 'better' than it appears to be. No, on the descriptive plane Barthes is right when he brands it 'a nauseating mixture of common opinions, a smothering layer of received ideas';[44] and Genette is right too, when he acutely points out its intimate, and often crudely contradictory nature.[45] Where Barthes and Genette are not right, however, is in the *function* they attribute to *doxa* in the *Comédie:* in maintaining that it is the *hidden goal* of Balzac's work, and that therefore, by extension, the narrator's discourse embodies the final word of the *Comédie* — its social truth.

This is not true. As with the 'scepticism' of the narrator, as with 'realism' and 'tolerance-compliance', the 'common opinion' embodied in the countless maxims of the *Comédie* has nothing 'conclusive' about it: it is not a goal — it is a means. Far from being the finishing touch of the story, it allows us to continually *return* to it: to confront that 'earthquake' which, in Burkhardt's metaphor, shakes modern history, without falling prey to panic, and being blinded to it.

This mediating function of common opinion, needless to say, is not symbolically neutral. But its meaning lies not so much in what it is, as in what it allows and encourages us to do: to leap into the great plot of the *Comédie*. And it is there — in the story, not in the discourse — that Balzac forges his most distinctive reality principle: not in the *doxa* diligently impressed upon us by the narrator. The latter is only a sort of scaffolding, necessary for the construction of the much more imposing edifice of the Balzacian plot. Let us turn therefore one last time to the narrative mechanisms of the *Comédie:* where its social truth appears in ways that pass almost unnoticed, and thereby shape all the more deeply and irresistibly our understanding and judgement.[46]

The World of Prose

Unusually, in the *Comédie Humaine* the moral tends to precede the fable instead of ensuing from it. Characters and situations are often judged, and at times even the essential features of their fate are revealed, prior to the narrative sequence in which they figure as protagonists. And in a certain sense this inversion is valid for the *Comédie Humaine* as a whole: *La Peau de Chagrin,* one of the earliest novels of the cycle, announces with such clarity the meaning of all that is to come that, when faced with enucleating the great themes of Balzac's work, critics almost automatically turn to the story of Raphael de Valentin — against the backdrop of which, in effect, the 'hundred thousand novels' to come seem to be a mere narrative proliferation of a basic situation, already defined and evaluated in its essence.

But why overturn what would seem to be the most logical sequence (first the story, then comment), and which is certainly the most widespread? Precisely because, in the *Comédie,* judgement — both cognitive and normative — is no longer a true conclusion, just as those maxims that are its privileged vehicle have nothing at all 'memorable' about them. *Faust* and *Eugene Onegin* impress on the reader countless phrases of Mephisto or the Pushkinian narrator: but of the innumerable maxims in *Lost Illusions,* who can remember a single one? Not many, I believe, and rightly so, since they do not act to 'fix' indelibly our perception and evaluation of the text, but play a more modest role, almost subservient — or perhaps just less noticeable. By assuring us that each event has an explanation and a meaning, they exempt us from verifying whether they truly do have one, and what it is: they thereby allow us to savour each episode thoughtlessly as if it were a 'pure' event, part of a narrative flow in which we can indulge 'without stopping to think'.

It is the full-blown version of the split Weinrich indicated in modern narrative, and already discussed in the previous chapter: narration becomes independent of, and even inversely proportional to wisdom. The less a story forces us to take a stand, to 'comment', the more it captures our interest. Think of *Lost Illusions* against the backdrop of *The Red and the Black*. To succeed, Julien Sorel and Lucien de Rubempré must both betray certain fundamental values. But while the Stendhalian text draws our attention to the clash between actions and ideals, and the story repeatedly pauses to allow for that three-way 'dialogue' in which narrator and reader weigh the hero's choices, in Balzac the opposite occurs: if Lucien betrays a friend, or joins the monarchists, we never question the legitimacy of his choices, and are only interested in knowing what — in narrative terms — will come of them. The most bitter issues of choice and value are turned into instruments for suspense, and the most shameful about-face does not arouse ethical reactions, but only the value-free and strictly narrative expectation of that vengeance which, sooner or later, has to come.

And perhaps vengeance itself — which at the end of the cycle, in *Cousine Bette,* is magnified into a veritable nightmare — is the most appropriate theme to introduce the hidden meaning of the Balzacian plot. It shows us that in a narrow and competitive universe, every action is like the proverbial snowball: it becomes each time an avalanche, generating a myriad of echoes and replies that can no longer be controlled or opposed. Each action, once performed, can never be undone, cancelled. It is the triumph of *prose* as defined by classical rhetoric: 'Forward oriented discourse [*provorsa*], unlike *versus* ['turn around', 'return'], it knows no regular return of dance, of equal rhythmic cadences.'[47]

'Forward oriented discourse' without hesitation or concessions (Lucien's return home, towards the end of *Lost Illusions,* will result in tragedy), the prose of the *Comédie Humaine* places history, and individual existence, under the sign of the *irrevocable*. That future to which narrative suspense draws our gaze is no longer the time of hopes, or of promises: it is a future we are *forced* into by a past that allows no rest. Much more than the *streben* of *Faust,* Balzacian suspense makes us see the demonic dynamism of the last century as the drive to act of a world which can never catch its breath. It is the idea of progress as *compulsory change* which we also find in the great *tableaux* of Marx and Weber: with the consolidation of the new social relationships, the bourgeois 'ethic' moves from the individual to the system, and is thus transformed from free choice to an inescapable objective imperative.

And who knows: perhaps this compulsion to the future has achieved greater results than more rationalistic and humanitarian versions of progress; and in some ways this history that proceeds by leaps and bounds, but blindly and without goals, has something uncannily fascinating about it. But there comes a point at which it rings hollow: the moment — well-known to all of Balzac's heroes, and all of his readers — in which, without warning, and almost without reason, one is overcome by a fatal weariness.

Lucien de Rubempré who stays in bed until noon, the reader who puts down the book and cannot seem to pick it up again — why? For the countless good reasons that Balzac could rattle off, but in reality for one alone. Because that never-ending and bewitching progression may be fine for a system, for a *society*, but no longer for an individual. The latter must either manage to extricate himself from the flow and reach the shore (which is very difficult though), or he will be prostrated by fatigue. Even Vautrin succumbs, and Nucingen is almost ruined, and Gobseck goes mad: and if this is the fate of the 'invisible and silent kings', we can imagine that of the others. Precisely because he took very seriously the systematic and superindividual nature of contemporary history, Balzac ended up dismantling one of its greatest illusions: that social progress and individual growth could be parallel processes — like those gleaming rails stretching to infinity, pride and glory of the nineteenth century.

It is the great Faustian myth that Balzac brings to its end here. With the *Comédie Humaine,* the idea that mankind can be seen as 'a single man' is dismissed; in fact, this dynamic and vibrant society clearly reveals that it is not designed for the individual. But we should not grieve too much: we saw in *Wilhelm Meister* that a world in which 'man is the measure of all things' imposes a heavy, perhaps intolerable burden on modern consciousness. Balzac can be credited with having shown the price of the opposite model, of a boundlessly open society. It is an antithesis which can be traced in each moment of life, and even in the manner of death: by a sort of suffocation, like Ottilie and Edward in *Elective Affinities,* since in a world that is too perfectly sheltered one finally cannot breathe — or by a stroke, like Goriot, as if to show that the human organism cannot keep the relentless beat of social life.

I have said several times that the 'ending' is the most unhinged aspect of the *Comédie,* both as a whole and in its parts. And the ultimate reason is perhaps this: for social transformations, no ending is conceivable, since there is no goal in sight that would appease them — while for the individual an ending is indeed imaginable, but it now coincides with that event, death, which can hardly be seen as a meaningful goal. Another turning point in the history of the *Bildungsroman:* the narrative of youth is no longer the symbolic form able to 'humanize' the social structure, as in *Wilhelm Meister*, nor, as in *The Red and the Black,* to question its cultural legitimacy. It only acts to magnify the indifferent and inhuman vigour of the modern world, which it reconstructs — as if it were an autopsy — from the wounds inflicted upon the individual.

The society of 'possessive individualism' — as Balzac conceived it, in its 'pure' form — is therefore that in which the individual is exposed to the cruelest of threats: and that fatigue we spoke of, the sudden 'having had enough' of life, or of reading, is perhaps the coded sign, the spontaneous reaction to this situation. A withdrawal from life: the unexpected but perhaps inevitable outcome of an overindulgence in vitality. It is the new dilemma of bourgeois consciousness, which Balzac places at the furthest limits of his work. For Flaubert, it will be the starting-point.

III

Dialectics of Desire

In *Wilhelm Meister,* Wilhelm's experiences begin when he refuses to devote himself to business; and his alter ego Werner, who makes the opposite choice, is condemned by it to a secondary role deprived of any 'growth'. A few decades go by, the *Bildungsroman* moves to French soil, and many things change: but Julien Sorel and Fouqué, Lucien and David Séchard, Frédéric Moreau and Martinon all re-emphasize that 'novels' are the prize only for those characters who, having reached the 'crossroads of life' illustrated by Jacques Collin to Rastignac, decide not to entrust their identity to work.

As was mentioned in the first chapter, this paradigm contradicts, in an increasingly insistent and explicit way, the well-known thesis according to which modern bourgeois culture is fundamentally a work ethic. Given that one of the great novelties of capitalism is to make production independent of the immediate satisfaction of need — so that man no longer is 'the measure of all things', as was the case in precapitalist societies[48] — then it seems inevitable that the legitimation of the new order should crystallize around that abstract labour which has become its only recognizable foundation.

And yet the great European *Bildungsroman* insists on telling us a different story. The more capitalism grows, the more the work ethic is devalued; still vibrant and almost poetic in Werner, with Fouqué and David Séchard there is already something limited about it, and it is relegated to the provinces; with Charles Bovary it drops to simple-mindedness, to which Martinon in *Sentimental Education* will add low intrigue and, when required, blackmail. Closing the sequence is Bel-Ami: and the bishop's blessing which concludes the novel should strike us as a true Black Mass, when we think of the righteous and deeply felt *certitudo salutis* longed for by the Weberian bourgeois.

Let us now switch sides, and approach the question from the stance of the novelistic hero: if Wilhelm and Julien do not actually reject work, although they do not entrust the meaning of their lives to it, Rastignac and Lucien already try to avoid it as much as possible: Frédéric Moreau, for his part, abhors it: at home he immediately knocks down a wall to enlarge his *salon* at the expense of his studio, and is ready to do the same with the Dambreuse home. Here too, each successive step takes us further away from the bourgeois work ethic. And yet, this new novelistic hero — young, male, just arrived in the city, socially mobile — is the typical representative of that middle class, in vertiginous growth, which shapes the public opinion of the metropolis: his spiritual physiognomy must necessarily be linked to the development of 'bourgeois culture'. If this link is not to be found in work, where should we look for it? Where, in other words, does the symbolic legitimation of the new social order lie?

It lies — with a shift already emergent in *Meister,* and definitive in Balzac and Flaubert — in the world of *consumption.* No longer subject to a pre-existent need, for this very reason production soon begins to *increase* needs. It shows them unthought of and bewitching possibilities. It transforms them from 'needs' — a term which evokes the static image of an always identical reproduction — to 'desires': which imply dynamism, change, novelty. This new realm of possibilities does not, evidently, open up for everyone: but it certainly does so for the protagonists described above, and if a historical epoch has chosen them as its representative heroes, this should tell us a good deal about how it saw capitalism, and what it saw 'in' capitalism.

More than a system of production, it saw in capitalism an ever-wider consumer universe. It is the London-Paris antithesis, and it is the reason why 'the capital of the nineteenth century' was not that of the 'workshop of the world', and of the Empire, but Paris. Because in Paris, much more than in London, 'money could buy anything';[49] and the act of buying was first surrounded by that kaleidoscopic display — advertising placards and newspaper campaigns, show-cases and department stores[50] — that changed it from a basically economic activity into a highly emotional enterprise, guided no longer by need but by desire.

Yes, indeed, modern desire is, to a very large extent, a *product* of capitalism, and one of its most typical products at that. In *The Red and the Black,* where the new social relationships are still of little importance, Paris does not change Julien: for better or worse, his identity is already fixed, as are his (conflicting) desires. But Rastignac, Lucien, Frederic all come to Paris not knowing who they are nor what they want: it is Paris itself, that immense show-case of new social wealth, that will teach them what it means to desire — to desire everything, at every moment, starting with the countless 'necessary trifles' that will remain forever mysterious to those they left behind in the provinces.

The darling of the seventies — the 'desiring subject' — is thus the new human type generated by the capitalist metropolis, and who has always remained in syntony with it. His desire is a longing to be admitted into it, and a fury at failure. All the more surprising then that this desire could be interpreted as a force hostile to the social order, de-legitimizing, even subversive. Leo Bersani: 'Desire is a threat to the form of realistic fiction. Desire can subvert social order: it can also disrupt novelistic order .... Realistic fiction seems to give an enormous importance to disruptive desires by embodying them in its heroes .... Realistic fiction admits heroes of desire in order to submit them to ceremonies of expulsion.'[51]

The defeat of the 'heroes of desire' is undeniable: what is mistaken is to see it as the consequence of an *alterity of principles* between 'desire' and 'reality'. In the world of Balzac and Flaubert the hero desires only what the world itself wishes him to desire: and according to the ways it prescribes. 'There is nothing so jesuitical as desire', we read at the outset of the story of Lucien *(Lost Illusions,* 'Catastrophic sequels of provincial love'). And further along: 'After showing Lousteau the deep disgust he felt for this most odious sharing of women [of Florine with old Matifat, who provides for her; and therefore, implicitly, of Coralie with Camusot] he was falling into the same pit and was immersed in lustful desire, carried away by the sophistry of passion' *(Lost Illusions,* 'Coralie'.)

Rastignac says after his long conversation with Jacques Collin: 'The devil! My head is swimming. I do not want to think at all; the heart is a sure guide.' *(Old Goriot*, 'An Entrance into the World'.) Twenty lines after this appeal to the purity of the soul we are told:

> Eugène felt a thrill of pleasure at the thought of appearing before the Vicomtesse, dressed as henceforward he always meant to be. The 'abysses of the human heart', in the moralists' phase, are only insidious thoughts, involuntary promptings of personal interest. The instinct of enjoyment turns the scale; those rapid changes of purpose which have furnished the text for so much rhetoric are calculations prompted by the hope of pleasure. Rastignac, beholding himself well dressed and impeccable as to gloves and boots, forgot his virtuous resolutions. (*Old Goriot*, 'An Entrance into the World'.)

Hypocrisy, sophistry, calculations, personal interest — are these disruptive desires? Here even the duplicity of bad faith has disappeared, and what dwells 'within' the hero of desire is indistinguishable from the Hobbesian impulses that thrive in bourgeois Paris. If therefore the hero meets with ruin, it is not due to his unyielding diversity, but simply, as it should be, to miscalculation. It is not hope that destroys him, but rather illusion, which in Balzac's world means: not knowing the true value of things. So it is with Lucien, who initially sells himself cheap, and afterwards, when it is too late, asks for too high a price.

Let there be no confusion: in doing so Lucien — who comes back from his first walk in Paris crying 'Great God! Gold at all cost!' — is not in contradiction with market society. He is simply unable to understand its laws, as is Balzacian 'passion', which as a rule in no way rejects the mediation of money, but uses it in ways that are economically irrational: by *overvaluing* its object, it continually forces one to pay too high a price for it. Passion is a bad deal, but in the predatory capitalism of the *Comédie*, which has not yet come to appreciate the exchange of equivalents, it is precisely bad deals that keep everything in motion. If illusions were ever truly lost, and desire obliterated, it would mean the end for a system that works solely because of them: and that therefore, far from wanting to expel illusions and desires, arouses them over and over again.

For a 'colder' economic realism, we must turn to Flaubert: and specifically to the first of the great final scenes of *Sentimental Education*, the auction of the Arnoux's possessions. In this unforgettable episode, Flaubert invites us to observe those by now familiar objects (the worktable, the shelves of *Industrial Art,* the two firescreens, the blue rug with camellias ...) through two simultaneous and opposite perspectives. First of all through the eyes of Frédéric, who associates with each of them a memory, an emotion, perhaps still a promise. For him these objects are not things: they are *symbols* — vehicles of meaning, of *the* meaning of his life. They are, in other words, objects which through subjectivity increase in value: to the point of being overrated. But next to Frédéric's, there are the eyes of the countless anonymous buyers: the eyes of the market. For this profane but lucid gaze the Arnoux's possessions have no 'meaning', only a price. They are not symbols, but *commodities* (shoddy ones, like the piano — 'her piano!' — which no one wants). And this, Flaubert suggests, is in the end their truth.

Balzac would never have constructed the scene in this way. He would have had everything secretly purchased by Madame Dambreuse, thereby projecting on the dying illusion the just as passionate vengeance of a further illusion. And Madame Dambreuse is present in Flaubert too, and she does buy (paying too high a price) a jewelry-case: but it is an echo, a homage to the great predecessor, not the primary function of the scene. There is no intent here to retain the symbolic surplus embodied in those objects, shifting it from one character to another — but to dissolve it in the rational calculations of faceless buyers.

The sudden and bitter loss of 'meaning' conveyed by this episode is a new version of that 'realism' we had already encountered in Stendhal: an abrupt and final shift which declares that 'reality', in and of itself, is indifferent to any symbolic investment.[52] With one difference, of course. In *The Red and the Black,* the imposition of the 'way of the world' on the 'law of the heart' still leaves the text open and ambiguous, and the reader restless and uncertain between factual reality and value judgements. In *Sentimental Education* however, the obliteration of illusion at the hands of price has something irremediable about it, since the former had never had the courage to question the law of money. Its defeat may make us sad, but it is wholly legitimate, and there is nothing left to be said.

It is a well-known fact: Flaubert is the most disillusioned of nineteenth-century novelists. But dispelling illusions, here, no longer generates knowledge: this abrupt awakening brings only the certainty that the dream is over (and that it was a mediocre dream at that). Yet dreams, especially mediocre dreams, are one of the most necessary things in life[53] — as Flaubert not only knew, but went so far as to teach us. To dispel the magic of dreams is not, in the end, all that difficult; what is difficult is understanding how they work, why they are inevitable, and what is the price we pay for them. Flaubert's greatness lies much more here than in the pitiless lucidity of his 'conclusions'.

'And in return, what do you hope to take?'

'Suggestion: such is the devil's rhetoric' says Mephisto (*Faust*, 6400). Suggestion, suggestive, evocative — it is the new strategy of surprise by which the unprecedented variety of commodities seizes Parisian collective fancy. If Mephisto must still 'evoke' from nothingness what will ignite Faust's desire, Jacques Collin need only indicate nonchalantly what Paris has to offer; and in *Sentimental Education* no demonic presence at all is needed any more to make the metropolis the highest object of desire. And yet — first problem — if in this world to desire has become all too easy, to choose, on the contrary, has become extremely difficult. And furthermore — second problem — if desire is totally entrusted to the mediation of money, its satisfaction will be haunted by very disturbing and unforeseen circumstances. Let us try then to pursue these problems in the transition from *Faust* to *Sentimental Education*. Faust:

> Do you not hear, I have no thought of joy!
> The reeling whirl I seek, the most painful excess,
> Enamoured hate and quickening distress.
> Cured from the craving to know all, my mind
> Shall not henceforth be closed to any pain,
> And what is portioned out to all mankind,
> I shall enjoy deep in my self, contain
> Within my spirit summit and abyss,
> Pile on my breast their agony and bliss,
> And thus let my own self grow into theirs, unfettered,
> Till as they are, at last I, too, am shattered (*Faust*, 1765–75).

Here Faust's desire reaches its most fervent pitch. But what makes it so intense is not a positively determined thought, so much as a yearning for things that are inherently *contradictory*. And why so? Because 'deep in [his] self', Faust wants to 'enjoy what is portioned out to all mankind': not just this or that aspect of a millenial history, which precisely now is becoming even more dynamic and multiform still, but this history as 'a whole'. Paradoxically, desire is all the more consuming the more it *refuses to choose*. *Omnis determinatio est negatio*, and to choose would destroy the 'unfettered growth of self' that inflames Faust — while leaving his partner rather sceptical:

> Trust one like me, this whole array
> Is for a God ...
> If there were such a man, I'd like to meet him
> As Mr Microcosm I would greet him. (*Faust*, 1780–81, 1801–2.)

His initial aspiration vanished, Faust seems to lose heart:

> Alas, what am I, if I can
> Not reach for mankind's crown which merely mocks
> Our senses craving like a star?
>
> *Mephisto:* You're in the end — just what you are!
> Put wigs on with a million locks
> And put your foot on ell-high socks,
> You still remain just what you are. (*Faust*, 1803–9.)

A memorable reply, and splendidly emphasized in the film *Mephisto* against the backdrop of the rise of Nazism. But Goethe's Mephisto has a second reply as well, in the opposite key, which brings us to our second problem:

> *Faust:* I feel, I gathered up and piled up high
> In vain the treasures of the human mind:
> When I sit down at last, I cannot find
> New strength within — it is all dry.
> My stature has not grown a whit,
> No closer to the Infinite.
>
> *Mephisto:* Well, my good sir, to put it crudely,
> You see matters just as they lie;
> We have to look at them more shrewdly,
> Or all life's pleasures pass us by.
> Your hands and feet — indeed that's trite —
> And head and seat are yours alone;
> Yet all in which I find delight,
> Should they be less my own?
> Suppose I buy myself six steeds:
> I buy their strength: while I recline
> I dash along at whirlwind speeds,

For their two dozen legs are mine.
Come on! Let your reflections rest
And plunge into the world with zest! (*Faust*, 1810–29.)

To an exceptional dialogue, an exceptional comment:

That which exists for me through the medium of *money*, that
which I can pay for, i.e., which money can buy, that *am I*, the
possessor of the money. The stronger the power of my money, the
stronger am I. The properties of money are my, the possessor's,
properties and essential powers. Therefore what I *am* and what I
can do is by no means determined by my individuality. I *am* ugly,
but I can buy the *most beautiful* woman. Which means to say that
I am not *ugly*, for the effect of ugliness, its repelling power, is
destroyed by money. As an individual, I am *lame*, but money
procures me twenty-four legs. Consequently, I am not lame. I am
a wicked, dishonest, unscrupulous individual, but money is
respected, and so also is its owner. ... Through money I can have
anything the human heart desires. Do I not therefore possess all
human abilities? Does not money therefore transform all my
incapacities into their opposite?[54]

Paradoxical and insistent, this passage of the early Marx seems an
echo of Mephisto's 'plunge into the world with zest': it is driven
by an unstoppable curiosity to see just how much money can do,
how many obstacles it can overcome, how many absurdities it can
make acceptable. As a vision of the 'magic' power of money, it is
unforgettable. But is this magic truly without limits, and can it
reshape *ab imis* not only social *relationships* but also the *essence*
(the 'essential powers') of each of their individual components?

Marx has no doubts: 'That which exists for me through the
medium of *money* ... that *am I* ... . I *am* ugly, but I can buy the
most beautiful woman ... which means to say that I am not *ugly*.'
Goethe was more cautious, more elusive: Mephisto's second reply
('Suppose I buy myself six steeds: / I buy their strength') does not
cancel the first ('You are in the end — just what you are! ... You
still remain just what you are') but, so to speak, postpones it.
Contrary to Marx, in other words, Goethe avoids the explicit
assertion that 'having' will fully replace the dimension of 'being'.
He only suggests it: as befits the devil's rhetoric — and the spirit
of the times itself.

Fascinated yet perplexed, nineteenth-century mentality
hesitated a long while at this new crossroads.[55] It did indeed
increasingly entrust the formation of individual identity to the
mediation of money — nor could it do otherwise: from *Wilhelm*

Meister to Balzac and Flaubert, the history of the *Bildungsroman* itself bears witness to the sudden rise of the new social bond. But if 'having' achieves a prominence unimaginable — only two generations earlier — in the Goethian *Bildungsroman,* nineteenth-century culture is still reluctant to entrust to it all the reality of 'being': despite the increasingly lifeless and indefinable features of the latter dimension — from the dynamism and versatility of 'having' something was still missing.

Better yet, it was not a problem of something missing, but rather the reverse: with the growth of the domain of having, the individual ended up being *too many* things at once. A typical modern paradox, already apparent in Rameau's nephew, in Faust, in the 'self-estranged spirit' of the *Phenomenology*. But these figures are still at the beginning of the great adventure, where new promises overshadow doubts, and they are each an abstract microcosm, a miniature of the World Spirit, each able to absorb and enjoy the multiform and the transient (even though Rameau, the most 'concrete' of the three, already borders on madness). But when we reach the end of the century, and start talking in terms of 'individuals' and not abstract entities, the relationship between the two sides of the problem is reversed: '... man has become richer and more overloaded', observes Simmel in 'On the Concept and Tragedy of Culture', *'Cultures omnia habentes, nihil possidentes* (cultures which have everything own nothing).'[56] The reason:

> With the increase in culture these contents [Simmel uses this term to indicate all aspects of social production from objects to ideas] more and more stand under a paradox: they were originally created by subjects and for subjects: but in their immediate form of objectivity, which they take on ... they follow an immanent logic of development. In so doing they estrange themselves from their origin as well as from their purpose.[57]

A highly paradoxical situation is thereby created. On the one hand, the fascination of modernity lies first and foremost in the amazing growth of 'objective culture', and, in the fact that, as money becomes the universal mediation, each individual is potentially able to appropriate some of that objective culture: that is to say, he can — as a solvent consumer — aspire to be 'Mr. Microcosm'. But this aspiration soon becomes an exhausting and hopeless pursuit, in which individual growth fatally runs the risk of remaining at the stage of 'unfolded multiplicity', without ever reaching that 'unfolded *unity*' which is for Simmel — as we saw in Chapter I — the essence of individual culture.[58] And when things reach this point — when we are *omnia habentes*, and *nihil possidentes* — individual identity, besides being problematic, takes on an unreal elusive quality. Trilling:

> The individual who lives in this new circumstance ['the *public*, that human entity which is defined by its urban habitat, its multitudinousness, and its ready accessibility to opinion'] is subject to the constant influence, the literal *in-flowing*, of the mental processes of others, which, in the degree that they stimulate or enlarge his consciousness, make it less his own. He finds it ever more difficult to know what his own self is, and what being true to it consists in.[59]

This individual is Frédéric Moreau, and we shall return to him; but before examining the *consequences* of the progressive subordination of 'being' to 'having', let us pause longer on the *premises* of such a change. One only needs to accept Mephisto's suggestion — 'Suppose I buy myself six steeds: / I buy their strength'. It all seems so easy, so natural! But it only works if one is able to *pay*. Faust: 'And in return, what do you hope to take?'; Mephisto: 'There's so much time — so why insist?' (*Faust*, vv. 1649-50). Here the stipulation of the contract is pushed into the background by the metaphysical 'bet', and by many other things; but if we reread the last line carefully, we can discern a tragedy, or perhaps just a sad farce, which is extremely characteristic of modern life. It is the tragedy of the consumer, and Flaubert was the first to narrate it with *Madame Bovary*.

There is in this novel a narrative detail so absurd, yet also so decisive, that it deserves our attention. Let us say that Emma too has her Mephisto, whose name is Lheureux and who is, as expected, a haberdasher. Lheureux imports 'fashionable' goods from the metropolis and sells them to Emma, who is by far his best client, ensnaring her in such a colossal debt that she is forced into ruin and ends up killing herself. Well, the point is that Emma *has no need* of these fatal objects. Yet she buys them. Why?

It is difficult to say, but perhaps the reason is that, just as the pact with Mephisto lets Faust live a second life ('Congratulations, friend, on your rebirth!', *Faust*, V, 2072) — so is adultery a second life for Emma, and one very different from that of 'Mrs Bovary'. Already inclined to lose herself in each situation, Emma cannot help asking herself how to take control of this new life: in what sense, like Trilling's modern individual, she can still consider it 'her' life. The only reply she manages to come up with is: by *buying* it. As long as I can pay for these objects that make me feel 'far away' from Yonville and Charles, as long as I can sprinkle my love for Leon with extravagant expenses — as long as I can keep doing so, this secret life will be real, mine, inalienable.

As long as ... 'And in return, what do you hope to take?'; 'There's so much time — so why insist?' When set in Emma's story, Mephisto's words betray the sneer of one who sells on credit. In *Faust* the due date was far off, the stakes metaphysical; in Yonville everything becomes prosaic and crude: time is up — payment in cash only. The enormous power with which 'having' endows the individual — to put aside one's 'being' and forge a new one: something that Emma, an avid reader of novels, is prone to from the start — reveals its link, as was in any case part of the terms, to the possession of money. Consumer ethics can do without many things, but not this one: for perhaps money cannot buy existence, but its lack, on the other hand, definitely forces one *not* to be. Or in other words, to die.

Forever Young?

In his discussion on the 'romanticism of disillusionment' in the *Theory of the Novel*, Lukács explains Frédéric Moreau's 'tendency towards passivity', his 'tendency to avoid outside conflicts and struggles', as the result of 'the soul's being wider and larger than the destinies that life has to offer it'. 'Defeat' — being 'crushed by the brute force of reality' — thereby becomes 'the precondition of subjectivity'; of a subjectivity, needless to say, that no longer intends to objectify itself in the external world, since 'when the interiority is like a cosmos, it is self-sufficient, at rest within itself'.[60]

The initial chapters of *Sentimental Education* seem to endorse Lukács's view. If not exactly 'crushed', Frédéric is nonetheless repulsed by a 'world of convention', fraught with delays, misunderstandings, promises not kept. What embitters him most is that nothing decisive ever takes place: in narratological terms, as soon as an event is on the verge of becoming a kernel (univocal, propulsive, irreversible) it lapses once again, for any number of reasons, into a mere satellite in a plot that never takes off. No progress ever seems to be made, especially with Madame Arnoux: and this defeat *sui generis* encourages Frédéric to dream — to transform his interiority into a 'self-sufficient cosmos', one that compensates for the shortcomings of the real cosmos.

But already at the end of the first part of the novel all this suddenly changes: 'He was to inherit!' Frédéric Moreau inherits indeed, and since money, Gobseck had said, 'potentially contains all, and in reality gives all', nothing should hold him back any longer from fulfilling his desires, thereby freeing himself from the substitutive cosmos of his imagination. Yet this, as we know, does not happen. First of all with Madame Arnoux: unlike the long youthful text of 1845 (the so-called *First Sentimental Education*), here the adultery is never 'consummated'. A worn metaphor, but indicative here of a not-so-trivial truth: the real satisfaction of desire is inevitably narrower than its imaginary satisfaction. Any determination is denial, and reality is always determined: amongst its advantages there will never be that *unlimited pliability* of the object of fantasy. If this is what one yearns for, it is better to entrust desire to what Latin grammars describe as the 'hypothetic sentence of impossibility':

> 'Why was it not the will of Heaven? If we had only met— !'
> 'Ah! if I had been younger!' she sighed.
> 'No, but if I had been a little older.'
> And they pictured to themselves a life entirely given up to love... in which the hours would glide away in a continual outpouring of their own emotions ... . (*Sentimental Education*, II, 6.)

This longing for a purely hypothetical counter-world directs every move Frédéric makes. We have said that at the beginning of the novel he is frustrated — as were Julien, Lucien, and Rastignac — by the lack of kernels, of turning points in his life in Paris. Now that he has the money to impose them, however, he takes upon himself the opposite task, and does everything he can to hinder, or at least weaken them. Unlike his predecessors, Frédéric *holds back* plot rather than accelerating it. He is the champion of mediation, of compromise: between the Arnoux, between Arnoux and Dambreuse, between Dambreuse and the revolution of 1848. Each time the simplified but relentless sociology of *Sentimental Education* tends to polarize positions, Frédéric is there to reconcile them; each time a character's life seems over, a loan from Frédéric keeps him going. In both the space and time of the novel, in economic as in sentimental or ideological relations, whenever one must choose and therefore separate and exclude, Frédéric steps in to postpone this moment.

Does he do it because he is 'good', as he is told at various points by each of the Arnoux? I do not think so: Frédéric is not a 'beautiful soul', and there is nothing expressly generous about him. What moves him is an uncontrollable aversion towards all things *definite.*[61] If he therefore 'avoids outside conflicts rather than engaging in them', it is not, as Lukács believes, *because* his soul is 'wider' than the outside world, but rather, and there is quite a difference, *in order to* make it wider. It is a new desire — a desire for 'romanticism' as defined by Carl Schmitt in *Political Romanticism*: 'subjective occasionalism', an ironico-aesthetic appropriation of the existing world, the triumph of 'possibility' over 'reality'.[62] All notions very close to those which Pierre Bourdieu — in a sociological analysis of *Sentimental Education* to which the present study owes much — groups under the heading of 'the imaginary', as the 'com-possibility of all possibles': precisely what holds together Frédéric's spiritual attitude and practical behavior throughout the novel.[63]

Schmitt and Bourdieu sketch such a rich phenomenology, that many other instances could be mentioned here, from Frédéric's dilettantism to the romantic 'unpoliticality' icily emphasized by the chapters on 1848. But rather than offer an inevitably incomplete summary, let us investigate some of the corollaries of Frédéric's 'romanticism'. To begin with, what is it that has made this spirtual inclination *appealing*? What, on the other hand, has made it *possible*? Finally, how has it affected the structure of the *Bildungsroman*?

As for the first question, the answer lies in that growing gap between social development and subjective formation we examined with the help of Simmel. The limitless offer of 'cultural contents' typical of the capitalist metropolis presents the individual with a paradox: to realize a determined identity, thereby fatally renouncing, however, the ever new and varied products of modernity — or to plunge into the great adventure of 'self-estrangement', but at the risk of psychic and spiritual disintegration. One either has to renounce being 'modern', it seems, or renounce being an 'individual'. But thanks to the ironico-aesthetic attitude, the contradiction disappears: on the one hand, the romanticism of fantasy keeps alive all the possibilities of the surrounding world, and even strengthens them beyond measure; on the other hand, since this is an imaginary space and time, which can be reorganized at will, the individual is not forced into that merry-go-round of real identifications which, as was the case with Rameau, would leave him exhausted and in a thousand pieces.[64]

Second question: apart from being desirable or necessary, what has made all this possible? First and foremost, as we have already seen, is the adhesion of modern imagination to the domain of 'having', where money — the *universal* mediator — potentially makes anything available to its possessor. And it is precisely this universality of money that suggests a rejection of Gobseck's formula: money is not important because it 'in reality gives all' — the word 'all' does not have much meaning in reality — but because it 'potentially contains all'. More than to fulfil desires, money enables people to *conceive* them, thereby becoming the paradoxical mainstay of the new idol of interior possibility.

But in order for the latter to assert itself once and for all, in addition to money, something else was needed — youth. The youth of the past hundred years, first portrayed in Frédéric Moreau: *protracted* youth. A fate perhaps inevitable, given the way in which the modern world has shaped this phase of life: for if the individual is granted the shelter of a 'psycho-social moratorium' in which to explore countless possible social roles, and to imagine all the possible future lives open to him — then it is not surprising that, at a certain point, the fascination of experimentation and dreams wins out over that of discovery and choice.

Youth considered as a boundless field of possibility — and this alone is the typical bourgeois idea of youth — paradoxically results in the overturning of its function: rather than a *preparation for something else*, it becomes a *value in itself*, and the individual's greatest desire is to *prolong* it. Rastignac's motto was 'Parvenir!'; Frédéric Moreau's, undoubtedly, is 'Procrastinate!'. If he holds back plot and tries to defuse its kernels, it is precisely to preserve as long as possible that state of *psycho-social indetermination* which, from a training ground for maturity, has become the autonomous and jealously defended *goal* of modern youth.[65]

But if youth only desires to 'be itself', and therefore to preserve itself *as youth*, then there is no longer any real need for the *Bildungsroman*. With its lean and cold lucidity, *Sentimental Education* brings to an end a century of narrative attempts, and its characters who seem so inauthentic, as if they were reciting a role that no longer concerns them; its imitative plot, almost a stitching-together of scraps of previous novels; its dialogues where what was once problematic and alive has become bogged down in the trite certainty of clichés — these are all signs of a literary genre that is dying, of a structure that no longer holds together.

The *Bildungsroman* is over — and it ends, we may add, by returning to its initial problem: to Wilhelm Meister, of whom Frédéric Moreau is none other than a faded avatar. Wilhelm himself, if we think about it, also preferred fantasy to reality, would get caught up in circumstances, held back plot and tried to have everyone take part in it. More than anything, Wilhelm too was a *dilettante*, and in no way wished to *conclude* his 'apprenticeship'. If this is not what happens, it is because the world of *Meister* is not yet truly 'open', and the coercive goodwill of the Society of the Tower forces Wilhelm's 'happiness' on him: a social role, a home, a wife, even a child (which Frédéric too will have with Rosannette, herself a reincarnation of Goethe's Mariane, but who will quickly die, to the ill-disguised relief of his father).

In *Wilhelm Meister*, in other words, there still exists an authority capable of decreeing the end of a youth that would prefer to go on forever. In *Sentimental Education* it seems to have completely vanished, and Frédéric can protract his youth: as always, thanks to money — thanks to the countless drafts that circulate in the novel, demonstrating that by now even *time* can be bought. 'And in return, what do you hope to take?'; 'There's so much time — so why insist?'. So much time, not forever though. The final thirty pages of *Sentimental Education* are all meant to illustrate this simple truth. For at a certain point the bills become due, and the possessions of the Arnoux must be auctioned; in politics the power gap does not last forever, and Sénécal kills Dussardier; Madame Arnoux grows old and her hair, unlike that kept in lockets, turns white, arousing in Frédéric 'disappointment', 'repulsion', and ultimately 'disgust':

> In spite of its ironies and paradoxes, romanticism is in a constant position of dependence ... it unwittingly submits to the nearest and strongest external power. Its supposed superiority over a present that is faced only occasionally is thus subject to a supremely ironic reversal: every form of romanticism is effectively at the mercy of other unromantic tendencies and its supposed sublimity with regard to definitions and decisions is overturned in a servile accompaniment of forces and decisions extraneous to it. [66]

Applied to Frédéric Moreau, the last lines of *Political Romanticism* perhaps ring too harshly, but they nonetheless indicate that interiority can never truly become 'a cosmos that is self-sufficient and at rest within itself'. In the long run its freedom must be paid for with a subjugation more drastic still, since it is unforeseen, to the laws of reality. So it is with Frédéric's long youth: despite all efforts it ends just the same — and it ends in the *worst* possible way, since he arrives defenseless when his time runs out. A rude awakening for which there is no new day, this youth falls headlong into an *old age* fed only by what were once 'hopes', and are now faded 'memories'. The twenty years in between are dismissed in a few famous, and icy lines ('Il voyagea. Il connut la mélancolie des paquebots...'). And yes, the *Bildungsroman* was always hesitant when faced with defining 'maturity': in a certain sense it came into being as a literary genre precisely because the new fascination of youth had blurred that idea, making it hard to put it back into perspective. But it is the first time that maturity appears to be — nothing. A void, an empty hole between a somewhat vile youth and an imbecilic old age.

'Et ce fut tout' (*Sentimental Education*, III, 6.)

4

The Conspiracy of the Innocents

The continental *Bildungsroman* has undoubtedly been a narrative form very sensitive to major historical changes. The French Revolution, the post-Napoleonic Restoration, the apotheosis of capitalism in the metropolis: each of these phenomena radically altered the logic of the novel's structure and forced three generations of writers to begin each time all over again.

Not so in England. If we take a fairly broad historical cross-section of exemplary novels — from *Tom Jones* (1749) to *Great Expectations* (1861) — we are struck by the stability of narrative conventions and basic cultural assumptions.[1] There are, naturally, excellent reasons why this should be so. In politics, the bourgeois revolution had taken place between 1640 and 1688 and England, which had never been touched by Napoleon's forces, was perhaps the only European nation for which 1789 did not seem like year one of modernity. As for the Industrial Revolution, this specifically English transformation could not have, for reasons we have already seen, relevant consequences on the structure of the novel.[2]

Thus stability, and also, to be clear from the start, conformity. But even a culture of stability and conformity has its reasons and its techniques. The reconstruction of the 'possible world' of the English *Bildungsroman* will not, I hope, be devoid of interest.

I

The Confinement of Youth

'I am Born'. This is the title of the first chapter of *David Copperfield*, and in a good four of our six novels (*Tom Jones, Jane Eyre, David Copperfield* and *Great Expectations*), the heroes' childhood, if not always their birth, is granted an emblematic and lasting prominence. It is the first of the many differences between the English *Bildungsroman* and the continental one. Only the Christmas performance in *Meister* generated a similar *incipit*, and of a comparable temporal span, where Wilhelm is an enchanted and curioius spectator, and then an actor, director and author of short dramas. With childhood behind him, he becomes a theatrical financier and manager, and once again an actor and director, then a theoretician. He moves in the countryside and in aristocratic homes among hopes, delusions, uncertainties, meditations, intellectual discoveries. There is no doubt about it, that first performance put on almost by chance has a formative and lasting influence on Wilhelm's life. Formative and lasting, however, because he does not remain faithful to his youthful impressions but is able to break with them. Subject to the modifying impetus of 'experiences', Wilhelm is constantly reconsidering his relationship with the theatre until one day he can entrust it to the memories of the past and turn toward a 'maturity' shaped by wholly different interests.

But the point of *Tom Jones*, for example, is that it is impossible for Tom even to meditate on his love for Sophia — let alone forget her. The young hero's numerous erotic exploits are the very opposite of what we call 'experiences'. They are mere digressions, also in a narrative sense, and they will never shed a different light on, nor force Tom from, the straight and narrow path of asexual love, of *childhood* love. Contrary to *Wilhelm Meister*, in the English novel the most significant experiences are not those that alter but those which *confirm* the choices made by childhood 'innocence'. Rather than novels of 'initiation' one feels they should be called novels of 'preservation'. In Tom's case, it is the preservation of a chosen way of life; in David's case, the preservation of what could be called a hermeneutic choice:

> ... I believe the power of observation in numbers of very young children to be quite wonderful for its closeness and accuracy.

Indeed, I think that most grown men who are remarkable in this respect, may with greater propriety be said not to have lost the faculty, than to have acquired it. (*David Copperfield*, 3.)

David may doubt that he will 'turn out to be the hero of my own life' (*David Copperfield*, 1), but he is without a doubt the ethical-cognitive compass of the novel. Upon his first encounter with every other character (an encounter which as a rule takes place in childhood), he unfailingly reacts in such a way that the 'experience' of the adult reader proves to be absolutely superfluous, and it has to give way to the child's naive perception. Aunt Betsey's true wisdom, for instance, lies in her learning to see things through little David's eyes; and Allworthy, for all his experience as a Justice of the Peace, will eventually be forced to regret not having believed in Tom's naive sincerity.

If then, as with Steerforth, innocence proves to be mistaken — too bad for experience. What has been learned will be disavowed and forgotten, rather than revise that initial judgement. The last image David wishes to remember his friend by (*wishes* to: 'let me think of him so again') is the tender and harmless one of a boy sleeping with his head resting on his arm, 'as I had often seen him sleep at school' (*David Copperfield*, 29). David has just learned about the seduction of Emily, but instead of questioning Steerforth's behavior, his only impulse is to create a retroactive and purely hypothetical scenario: '... I thought more of all that was brilliant in him, I softened more towards all that was good in him, I did more justice to the qualities that might have made him a man of a noble nature and a great name ...' (*David Copperfield*, 32).

The antithesis with Uriah Heep will later on provide us with a sociological reason for the 'rescuing' of Steerforth. Dickens, however, is interested most of all in the salvation via Steerforth of David himself,[3] and of the *truth* of the childlike clairvoyance — 'quite wonderful for its clearness and accuracy' — that serves as the ethical-hermeneutic foundation of the entire novel. Not surprisingly, we find the same narrative decision elsewhere. With time Blifil could become a little less of a scoundrel and Mrs Reed, on her death bed, could forget for a moment her frenzied sadism. That would only be logical, but then, inevitably, childhood judgements would have to be revised, and the entire system of moral and intellectual certainties of the English *Bildungsroman* would crumble with them.

An inverse confirmation of this state of affairs is provided by the only relevant character David encounters *after* childhood, as a young man: Dora. This is the *only* time David's judgement is so far off the mark that, were it not for a slightly mysterious death, his life would risk becoming bogged down for good. But if this is true, then perhaps in the idealization of childhood insight — and in the way adult wisdom latches onto it — we can discern something else: a drastic *devaluation of youth*. That romantic-novelistic 'possibility', which nourished European youth, withers away here into the possibility (or, rather the certainty) of error: Tom's errors, in his flight towards London, and Waverley's on the Scottish Highlands; David's errors ('Blind, blind, blind!') and also, or almost, the immaculate Jane Eyre's.

And Pip's errors: plentiful and worse, rightly enough, since he more than anyone else entertains 'great expectations' concerning his own youth. Well-provided for financially and set up in London, Pip is placed in conditions which are analogous to those of his 'Parisian' confrères. Money and the metropolis, however, only succeed in turning him into an unappealing and inept snob. After an empty life of leisure, Pip only desires to return to his first love, as did Tom and David; but since, unlike them, he had joyfully grasped at the chance to break away from the world of his childhood, Biddy will be denied him. The greater the expectations that give youth a special significance, the lesser the happiness and the self-realization the protagonist will be able to experience as an adult. The marriage of Biddy and Joe — that adult who had never ceased being a child — seals in exemplary fashion the encirclement of youth by the other stages of life.

This message is confirmed by an entirely different sort of ritual which casts its shadow over roughly two centuries of English scholastic history: flogging. Philippe Ariés: '[If, in the nineteenth century] the birch was retained, it was no longer simply as a punishment but above all as an instrument of education, an opportunity for the boy being flogged to exercise self-control, the first duty of an English gentleman.'[4]

These boys who prove they have 'grown up' by undergoing in silence the chastisement of their youthful restlessness, these children dressed up in black like the oldest of adults — here is a truly vivid portrait of youth downgraded and undermined. Undermined, first of all, thanks to a very early institutionalization. Channeled into places and activities tightly secluded from the rest of the world (boarding schools, and that major nineteenth-century invention — sport), English youth could not possibly identify with those symbolic values — indefiniteness, social and spiritual mobility, 'giddiness of freedom' — which were its essence on the Continent.

There is, however, a second reason for this symbolic void that transcends the 'real' history of youth. We have seen it in the first three chapters: the more a society is and perceives itself as a system still unstable and precariously legitimized, the fuller and stronger the image of youth. Youth acts as a sort of *symbolic concentrate* of the uncertainties and tensions of an entire cultural system, and the hero's growth becomes the narrative convention or *fictio* that permits the exploration of conflicting values.

But English society in the eighteenth and nineteenth centuries, despite the Industrial Revolution and Chartism, is by far the most stable in Europe, and proud to be so. Its value-system is decidedly stable, and stability itself is seen as a value, and as one of the strongest ones at that. In this framework, the notion of social mobility cannot evoke the certainly ambiguous but fascinating and vital figures of Julien Sorel, Rastignac, or Bel-Ami. It has rather the bestial and slimy face of Uriah Heep, the feeble and snobbish behavior of Pip. And as for ideological conflict, when the Jacobin William Godwin needs to 'motivate' in narrative terms the persecution of Caleb Williams, he does not for a moment think of a possible 'political' origin, and turns automatically to the judicial format so common in English narrative.

Here is a solid world, sure of itself and at ease in a continuity that fuses together 'tradition' and 'progress'. It is a world that cannot and does not want to identify with the spirit of adventure of modern youth. Young Europeans, in the first part of the nineteenth century, had two idols: one was the French emperor and the other — the other was an Englishman, but an Englishman in exile.

The White and the Black

Can you picture a child reading *Wilhelm Meister, The Red and the Black, Lost Illusions*? Impossible. But *Waverley* and *Jane Eyre, David Copperfield* and *Great Expectations*: here we have the 'great tradition' of children's literature (and our era, less intimidated by sex, can easily add *Tom Jones*). Yet, how could this change in the age of readership have taken place? Could it be that the 'novelistic' appearance of these works is upheld in each of its parts by an older sort of framework, one more suited to, and easily recognized by childhood? Could it in fact be that, deep down, these novels are fairy tales?

'The fairy tale begins with the hero at the mercy of those who think little of him and his abilities, who mistreat him and even threaten his life ...'[5] This is the basic predicament (if not always the starting point) of every protagonist of the English *Bildungsroman*: in *Jane Eyre*, the *incipit* is actually duplicated when the adult Jane flees Thornfield and finds herself hungry, feverish, alone and penniless in an unending rain. Such a situation of extreme duress announces, as is obvious, equally extreme paradigmatic oppositions:

> Ambiguities must wait until a relatively firm personality has been established ... . The figures in fairy tales are not ambivalent — not good and bad at the same time, as we all are in reality. But since polarization dominates the child's mind, it also dominates fairy tales. ... One brother is stupid, the other is clever. One sister is virtuous and industrious, the others are vile and lazy. ... One parent is all good, the other evil.[6]

We will return later to parents. As regards 'siblings', or other comparable characters, it is symptomatic how often — Blifil, Fergus, Steerforth and Uriah, the three Reeds — they magnetically attract the negative values of the narrative universe, thereby rendering inevitable a drastic emotional polarization: 'As the parent in the fairy tale becomes separated into two figures, representative of the opposite feeling of love and rejecting, so the child externalizes and projects onto a "somebody" all the bad things which are too scary to be recognized as part of oneself.'[7]

If the initial syntagm of the hero at the mercy of his enemies encouraged a particularly sharp paradigmatic perception, the latter in its turn requires an unusually definitive and taxonomic final syntagm, one that dissipates any residual ambiguity and irreversibly separates the hero and his alter ego: Blifil virtually in exile, Fergus beheaded, Steerforth drowned, Heep in prison, the Reeds having committed suicide or become nuns, or wicked spinsters.[8] Granted, the happy end is not all here, but the unbridgeable separation of 'good' and 'evil' is without a doubt an essential requirement for it:

> Tolkien, addressing himself to the question of 'Is it true?' remarks that 'It is not one to be rashly or idly answered.' He adds that of much more real concern to the child is the question: 'Was he good? Was he wicked?' That is, [the child] is more concerned to get the Right side and the Wrong side clear. 'Fairy stories,' he continues,

are 'plainly not primarily concerned with possibility, but with desirability.' This the child clearly recognizes, since nothing is more 'true' to him than what he desires.[9]

Let there be no misunderstanding. Establishing 'the Right side and the Wrong side', in itself, has nothing childlike about it. Childlike, and fairy-tale-like, is the belief that such a judgement can be made *always* and *everywhere*; that it is, in the end, the *only* meaningful type of judgement. When this happens — as it does in these fairy-tale novels — the standards of common morality invade every page and every action: the world has meaning *only if* it is relentlessly divided into good and evil.

And vice versa, which is perhaps even worse. If the oppositional paradigm, for whatever reason, loses its clarity, the result is an out and out *paralysis of judgement*, making it impossible to deal with those ambiguous situations or questionable behaviors which, in adult life and in the ordinary course of events, are by far the most prevalent. So it is with Steerforth, as we know: one must not 'understand', but forget. And, in *Great Expectations*, when Pip finds himself with a fortune without any particular moral merit, the only solution is to take it away from him, down to the last penny, via the usual legal witchcraft. Moreover, since the limits between good and evil characters in the same work are a little too blurred, not only is a 'happy end' impossible but so is any ending whatsoever, and Dickens has to write two of them and does not know himself which one to choose.

The perfect instance of this impasse, however, is *Jane Eyre*, where the utmost moral severity and self-complacency co-exist with the utmost irrational escapism when faced with the problematic side of existence. Although often praised for its 'adult' dimension, Charlotte Brontë's novel is strewn with fairy-tale ingredients. Besides those we have already seen, there is a very active animism consisting in admonitory storms (23), messages from the beyond (27), nocturnal voices that travel across space (35, 37) not to mention forewarning pictures and dreams (just about everywhere). Rochester sees in Jane his 'good genius' (15) and promises to reveal his secrets to her 'when we have been married a year and a day' (25). When they are on the verge of getting married, Jane admits that 'to imagine such a lot befalling me is a fairy-tale — a daydream' (24). A few pages later, Rochester explains to Adèle: 'I am to take mademoiselle to the moon ... mademoiselle is a fairy' (24).

Furthermore, what is the reason for those so very insistent

dialogues (20, 23), in which Rochester tortures Jane listing the good qualities of Blanche Ingram, the woman everyone says he is soon to marry? Male sadism along with class insolence? Of course, but above all the construction of a cut and dried alternative — the lady and the governess, one strikingly beautiful and the other quite plain, one rich and the other poor (to strengthen the point, Blanche is the exact copy of Georgiana Reed, one of Jane's childhood enemies). It is an all or nothing logic, without gradations between total happiness and absolute misery, typical of fairy-tales. In order that the message be perfectly clear and reciprocal, Jane behaves in exactly the same fashion when she returns to Rochester (37), leading him to believe that she might be on the verge of marrying St John Rivers, who is everything that Rochester no longer is.

But to return one must first leave — and just why is it that Jane abandons Rochester? Because when the couple is in front of the altar, and the minister has just finished the ritual question as to whether there are any reasons they may not be married (in fairy-tales only the culminating moments are significant, but then there is no fooling around), we discover that Rochester is already married, and that his wife Bertha is alive, incurably mad, and shut up in the attic of the house at Thornfield. The inhuman moral baseness of a world, which nonetheless claimed morality as its loftiest achievement, is indelibly brought to light in the portrayal of Bertha Mason. We shall let that be, however. Let us instead ask ourselves: why does Jane flee? Why does she not remain with Rochester? Why does it *never* occur to her that perhaps this is just the situation in which her celebrated humanity could really prove its worth?

The answer is very simple. To stay would mean becoming an *adulteress*, and a world intoxicated with ethical dichotomies cannot tolerate the thought of an *ambiguous* situation, suspended between two value-systems, two persons, two lives. Every great narrative tradition has dealt with the theme of adultery, in France and in Germany, in America and in Russia. In England, nothing — absolutely nothing. Any *Bildungsroman* worthy of the name would have had Jane remain among the needles of Thornfield. But this would have meant facing the imperfect, debatable, and perhaps incorrect nature of each fundamental ethical choice. Better to begin all over again, and as the first tale did not work, start afresh with a new one, with the orphan brought to the brink of death but then taken in and warmed by two good fairies; let them have a cruel brother, who almost devours Jane, but then grant her an inheritance from a rich and distant uncle and meanwhile have Bertha Mason perish in a fire. Finally, let Jane go back to Rochester, who has gone blind but regains his sight after she marries him.

> 'Is it true?'
> Well, ..
> 'Is it right?'
> What!
> 'Is it desirable?'
> If it is this you desire...

Very Common Persons

Since the prescriptive vocation of the fairy-tale novel is already totally entrusted to its structure — in the clearcut opposition between 'good' and 'bad' characters, and in the ending that deals out rewards and punishments — there is really not much left for the protagonist of the English *Bildungsroman* to do. He is certainly not expected to establish a moral universe that already exists, eternal and unchangeable, and even less to question that universe. His most typical function lies rather in making that world *recognizable* for any and all readers. The more the hero himself is an 'anybody', better yet with a nondescript name such as 'Tom Jones', the more easily will this process of identification take place. One last quote from Bettelheim:

> Myths and fairy tales have much in common. But in myths, much more than in fairy stories, the culture hero is presented to the listener as a figure he ought to emulate in his own life, as far as possible. ...
> Much as we, the mortals, may strive to be like these heroes, we will remain always and obviously inferior to them. ...
> The fairy tale is presented in a simple, homely way; no demands are made on the listener. This prevents even the smallest child from feeling compelled to act in specific ways, and he is never made to feel inferior. Far from making demands, the fairy tale reassures ...[10]

The mythical hero is, in other words, a model, a *normative* character: the fairy-tale hero, a *normal* one. Samuel Richardson was already aware of this in 1750, when he complained about

> the good Reception the Character of the weak, the insipid, the Run-away, the Inn-frequenting Sophia has met with. In that, as in the

> Character of her illegitimate Tom, there is nothing that very
> Common Persons may not attain to; nothing that will reproach the
> Conduct or Actions of very ordinary Capacities, and very free
> Livers: while Clarissa's Character, as it might appear unattainable
> by them, might be supposed ...a silent Reproach to themselves.

All rancour aside, Richardson is right. The incorrigible Pip
confirms as much upon returning from his first meeting with
Estella, stating 'that she had said I was common, and that I knew I
was common, and that I wished I was not common' (*Great
Expectations*, 9). 'Common' is a term with a long and complex
history dominated — since a famous exchange in *Hamlet* — [12] by
the overlapping of the semantic sphere of 'widespread', 'ordinary',
'normal' and that of 'not worthy of notice', 'banal', 'vulgar', even
'contemptible'. Sensitive as he is to class distinctions, and anxious
to make his mark, Pip automatically reads the pejorative meaning
into the term and tries to free himself from it. In doing so, however,
he alienates himself from the genealogy of the English novelistic
hero, which instead privileges, and rewards, the other semantic
sphere: the socially 'neutral' and thus potentially universalistic
one. To those *very Common Persons* Tom and Sophia, one can
easily add Jane Eyre, who everyone insists on defining as 'plain' (a
term with semantic oscillations very much like those of
'common'), until she ends up writing the word herself ('Portrait of
a Governess, disconnected, poor, and plain', *Jane Eyre*, 16) under
her self-portrait. And there is also Walter Scott who, in an
anonymous review of himself published in 1817 in the *Quarterly
Review*, observes that 'every hero in poetry, in fictitious narrative,
ought to come forth and do or say something or other which no
other person could have done or said', but then melancholically
concludes that 'Another leading fault in these novels [i.e. his own]
is the total want of interest which the reader attaches to the
character of the hero. Waverley, Brown, or Bertram in *Guy
Mannering*, and Lovel in the *Antiquary*, are all brethren of a family;
very amiable and very insipid sort of young men. ... His chief
characters are never actors, but always acted upon the by the spur
of circumstances.'[13]
Consciously or not, the last sentence is an almost exact copy of
Wilhelm Meister's thoughts on the novelistic hero, and of
Schiller's remarks on Goethe's novel, which we have already
discussed in the first chapter. The terminological similarity
conceals, however, a very substantial difference. Wilhelm, or
Lucien de Rubempré, see in being 'acted upon by the spur of

circumstances' the *opportunity* to shape their own identity; the English heroes, on the contrary, experience the same situation as a betrayal of their true identity. They perceive it as a process tearing them from their 'common' existence, and they only hope it will end as soon as possible.

This is further evidence of the devaluation of youth to a sort of undesirable interlude, but something else is also at stake. Such fidelity to a 'common' nature qualifies these heroes as ideal representatives of that 'middle' class which, in the European novel, was the 'sociological' equivalent of youth: unsettled, mobile, enterprising, alive. But as Perry Anderson has observed, the English 'middle class' has 'never produced institutions and culture of anything like a comparable distinctiveness and density to those of the "upper", or for that matter, working class'.[14]

More than a 'middle' class — restless and undefined, exposed to grand hopes and crushing disappointments alike — these English heroes represent a class 'in the middle': between Steerforth and Heep, Prince Charles and King George. It is not the galvanizing combination of social and cultural extremes: it is *neither* the one *nor* the other: a double negation, a universal negation, in fact, which withstands any process of particularization. Rastignac, Vautrin explains, is no different than 'fifty thousand other young men'. It is the narrative of *Père Goriot* that distinguishes him, and creates, for better or for worse, a destiny that is *his* and no-one else's. But if the English hero wants to have a destiny, he must preserve precisely those 'common' qualities — anonymous, ordinary and widespread — that characterize him right from the start: by repudiating them, Pip sees his fortune go up in smoke.

The 'common' hero is a structural requisite of the fairy-tale novel, and also as the representative of a 'middle class' endowed with little daring and a dim self-consciousness. One more point remains to be made: this hero is an essential component of a *democratic* culture. If there is a notion that has never turned up, in the analysis of the continental *Bildungsroman*, it is precisely the notion — democratic par excellence — of *equality*; that very common person, the English hero, is able to convey it. To identify oneself with Julien Sorel or Rastignac or Bel Ami is exacting, risky, partly unpleasant: but Tom's or David's fate could happen to everyone — and everyone, more or less, could react just like them.

Is this a dull and colorless message, 'common' in the negative sense? Perhaps so, but democracy — as de Tocqueville, John Stuart Mill and Burkhardt realized early on — does not aim at furthering great individualities. These latter are able to look after themselves, and in any case, capitalism (which is not the same as democracy) offers them a new and immense field of application. For its part, democracy is rather antiheroic; it thrives on universalistic and standardized values, around which it has to create the widest possible consensus: and no widespread consensus can come to light if a culture is too demanding, or too steeped in partiality, inequality, uniqueness.

Am I suggesting that David Copperfield and Jane Eyre are the inevitable offsprings of a democratic culture? Not exactly, one could do better, but certainly the symbolic texture that holds together democratic culture has more affinities with David Copperfield than with Julien Sorel. We may not like it, and we certainly do not like it when we are reading a novel. *But democracy is not interested in the production of good novels.* If anything, it aims at limiting the domain of the novelistic, at counterbalancing the destabilizing tendencies of modernity. It aims at reducing the rate of 'adventure' in our lives while expanding the jurisdiction — so inert in narrative terms — of 'security'.

The culture of the English novel was the first to confront this state of affairs. It did so in a naive and moralistic way which was also, as we shall see, very incomplete and too imbued with a caste spirit. However, it is fair to point out that all these faults arise from the attempt — of unique interest for the history of culture — to combine 'democratic' and 'narrative' values: 'protagonism' and 'antiheroism'. It may well be an impossible enterprise, like mixing oil and water, but it is without a doubt the backbone of a narrative tradition that was to be crowned by the modernist triumph of *Ulysses.*

Anthropological Garden

As if to make the slightly colorless universalism of the 'common' hero stand out, and to balance it with an entirely different value system, the English novel surrounds the protagonist with a dense array of peculiar, maniacal and unmistakable characters incarnating the opposite principle. Orwell: 'Dickens sees human beings with the most intense vividness, but he sees them always in private life, as "characters", not as functional members of society; that is to say, he sees them statically ... always in a single unchangeable attitude, like pictures or pieces of furniture.'[15]

Thus Dickens, but also, in more articulated forms, Fielding and

Scott, and of course Sterne. It is a device that makes us see society like a gigantic Foucaultian *tableau*, where an implacably detailed and yet conspicuous taxonomy confines every individual to his slot for life. It is a decidedly pre-modern vision, 'a seemingly "feudal" hierarchy of orders and ranks ... the projective image of society naturally held and propagated by a landowning class ... expression and instrument of the hegemony of an (ancestrally agrarian) aristocracy'.[16]

It is an intellectual framework already manifest in Burke, who attacked the French revolutionaries who 'have attempted to confound all sorts of citizens, as well as they could, into one homogeneous mass', praising instead the wisdom of the 'legislators who framed the ancient republics'. This wisdom (emulated only by the English) pursued 'the many diversities amongst men' and their 'peculiar habits', finally consolidating them, to use Burke's words, in a 'second nature'.[17] The term 'second nature' is just what we need — for isn't an English plot a sort of visit to the zoo, where countless and amazing human exemplars are offered to our eyes, each one tightly locked in his cage? Raymond Williams observes that Dickens carries out a 'reduction of people to caricatures'; but then he adds: 'Dickens was creating, openly and deliberately, a world in which people had been deprived of any customary identity and yet in which, paradoxically, the deprivation was a kind of liberation, in which the most fantastic and idiosyncratic kinds of growth could come about. People had to define themselves and their position in the world.'[18]

A kind of liberation? Shouldn't we rather say that Dickens succeeds in keeping alive the taxonomical rigidity of 'traditional-feudal' thought even *after* the erosion of its material bases, still fairly evident in Fielding's and Sterne's humour? What marks the vast majority of Dickensian characters is, after all, the very same impossibility to 'escape from oneself' which in *Tom Jones* was the result of one's 'trade', and in Dickens, who is writing about a socially more fluid world, is connected to something strictly personal. However, the difference in motivation is less important than the identity of the result: almost all of humanity is encaged once and for all by an inflexible 'second nature', whether it be social or personal.

Here — in this accentuated rigidity, which Bergson was to call 'automatism' — lies the origin of the comic dominant to which the English novel owes such a great deal of its popularity. But if meticulous and unwavering classification is the ideal for the comic, it is not at all so for the generation of a narrative plot. The latter, being a *dynamic* system of relationships, requires precisely those changes of position, modifying interactions and mutual hybridizations that a taxonomic order, for its part, seeks to exclude. From this impasse stems the universally deplored, but nonetheless imperative necessity of narrative *coincidences*.[19] Even with coincidences, however, one cannot do too much. The double stasis of an ordinary and undemanding protagonist, and of a world too solidly classified makes us feel that at the origin of the English plot there must be something, if not extra-social, at least socially *unnatural*: a monstrosity. We shall come to it; right now, let us pause on the consequences that a taxonomic imagination implies for novelistic *language*. Bakhtin:

> The so-called comic novel ['an encylopedia of all strata and forms of literary language'] makes available a form for appropriating and organizing heteroglossia that is both externally very vivid and at the same time historically profound: its classic representatives in England were Fielding, Smollett, Sterne, Dickens, Thackeray and others. ... Against the backdrop of the 'common language', of the impersonal, going opinion, one can isolate in the comic novel those parodic stylizations of generic, professional and other languages.[20]

Quite true, and true also for works which are not comic in the strict sense, as are Scott's. But as we all know, Bakhtin's theory of the novel does not stop here, and it maintains that 'heteroglossia' necessarily generates 'dialogism' — a ceaseless interaction and reciprocal modification among different 'languages'. It is this conclusion — so often taken for granted — that I wish to challenge: and the English novel is perhaps the best case in point. Here, the more numerous and heterogeneous the languages in the text, the less possible the dialogue between them, and the less meaningful their influence on the ever common and 'basic' language of the hero. Heteroglossia and dialogism, in other words, are *inversely proportional*: if people don't speak the same language, after all, how is dialogue ever going to be possible? It shouldn't then be surprising that in these masterpieces of heteroglossia the dominant linguistic exchange — quite frequent in Fielding and Dickens, and truly ubiquitous in Sterne and Scott — is *misunderstanding*, which is the opposite of communication and the collapse of all dialogue.

'If people don't speak the same language': my expression was a little forced. Still, the point is that heteroglossia, as such, embodies a principle *hostile* to dialogue, and not only for linguistic reasons.

Its most typical habitat is, symptomatically, traditional societies, 'status' societies — those rigidly classified worlds that generate all sorts of local and professional jargons, of almost sumptuary distinctions and nuances, of expressive idiosyncracies and arcana of communications (the *latinorum* of Manzoni's *Betrothed*). Heteroglossia here flourishes because such worlds do not tolerate dialogue, which by nature is *anti*classificatory, as it implies equality, spiritual mobility, interchangeability of positions. It is significant that, in England, we really find dialogue only in Austen and Eliot, the only two novelists in whose work the taxonomic project is largely overcome by the attention devoted to social mobility, 'improvement', 'reform', and the reciprocal coming to terms of different individuals, social classes and cultures. 'To speak to one another', and even to merely 'converse', thereby becomes at once instrument and metaphor of a broader understanding. But precisely because people talk to one another and understand one another, heteroglossia tends to disappear, and instead we find an 'average' linguistic tone potentially accessible to all.

Together with dialogue, finally what withers away behind the taxonomic bars of the English novel is language itself, which degenerates from a system of 'signs' to a collection of 'symbols'.[21] As its function is not to 'communicate', but to 'express' and confirm the 'peculiar habits' of social second nature, language becomes little more than a parading of idiosyncratic monologues where speaking has lost contact with listening. From Square to Thwackum to Partridge, from Uncle Toby to Cosmo Comyne Bradwardine to Micawber: the great English comic characters are always terribly deaf and irrepressibly talkative. The reason is that they do not speak but rather, so to say, *secrete* language: their words are not 'signs', abstract entities potentially available to everyone, but 'symbols', as integral a part of their nature as their physical features, their trade, their hobby horse. This endless flow of words is — 'in short', as Micawber would say, as if to indicate its semantic irrelevance — a status symbol, a caste indicator. 'Tell me how you speak and I shall tell you who you are': this disturbing proverb is the most appropriate motto of the realm of 'heteroglossia'.

'In this enlighted age...'

The 'common' hero, we have said, is the product of democratic-universalistic values; comic taxonomy, on the other hand, is a symptom of unyielding social inequalities. At the core of the English novel, we find the same ideological doubling that pervades eighteenth and nineteenth-century England: tendential universalism in the legal-political domain, and a subservience to principles of status within civil society. However, when two such antithetical value systems manage to coexist in the same text (and in the same world), they must be provided with a sort of 'mitigating' mechanism to make them compatible. By existing side by side for a long time, furthermore, these two systems will adulterate each other more and more, until — conceivably — they shall merge into something partly new.

We have already talked about fairy-tale novel and comic novel. Let us see if genre theory can help us in this instance too. Once again, Bakhtin:

> The primary source of language usage in the comic novel is a highly specific treatment of 'common language'. This 'common language' — usually the average norm of spoken and written language for a given social group — is taken by the author precisely as the *common view*, as the verbal approach to people and things normal for a given sphere of society, as the *going point of view* and the going *value*. To one degree or another, the author distances himself from this common language, he steps back and objectifies it, forcing his own intentions to refract and diffuse themselves through the medium of this common view that has become embodied in language (a view that is always superficial and frequently hypocritical) .... One of the most basic tasks for the novel will become the laying-bare of any sort of conventionality, the exposure of all that is vulgar and falsely stereotyped in human relationships.[22]

The laying-bare of any sort of conventionality: this passage seems to refer more to *satire* than to the comic novel, and Bakhtin, as we know, maintains the genetic and cultural *continuity* of these two literary genres. But if we take the eighteenth century, for example, and compare English narrative culture with its French counterpart, satire and the novel give every sign of being inversely proportional rather than homogeneous. In the France of Montesquieu, Voltaire and Diderot, the vigour of satiric wit undermines the consolidation of novelistic structure, which will only take place well into the nineteenth century, and after the decline of the great satire. In the England of the rise of the novel, on the other hand, satire is confined to one masterpiece only, written in the first quarter of the century, and by an avowedly conservative intellectual.

The ultimate reason for this asymmetry lies quite naturally in the contrasting political predicament of the two countries: but this shows precisely that satire and the novel embody opposite symbolic functions. Satire strives to delegitimize the existing state of affairs, which it proclaims to be stupid and unreformable. It holds up to 'all that is vulgar and falsely stereotyped in human relationships' a repressed and polemical 'naturalness', longing for its unfettered development. It separates 'good sense' from the much more widespread 'common sense', which it spurns as cowardly or opportunistic prejudice. It is, in short, polemical and destabilizing: a genre bent on destruction.[23]

If we now move to the English comic novel, the structural premises change one by one. Its hero is not natural in the hypothetical-polemical guise of the Persian, or the Huron, or Candide, but in a way that is suggestive of something already widespread and usual — *normality.* As for the world in which the hero operates it is indeed full of abuses, but precisely, of *ab*uses: it is not a question of 'laying-bare' its everyday conventions, but of taking to task anything which departs from and subverts them. To do this, there is no reason why 'good sense' should be severed from 'common sense': if anything, the common root of these two terms must be stressed — it must be demonstrated how good common sense really is, and how widespread the former is.

This stand is not exactly hostile towards the Enlightenment, but declares it superfluous on English soil, where it has supposedly already materialized, already merged with 'life'. Burke at his most impudent and witty:

> You see, Sir, that in this enlightened age I am bold enough to confess, that we are generally men of untaught feelings; that instead of casting away all our old prejudices, we cherish them to a very considerable degree, and, to take more shame to ourselves, we cherish them because they are prejudices; and the longer they have lasted, and the more generally they have prevailed, the more we cherish them. ... Many of our men of speculation, instead of exploding general prejudices, employ their sagacity to discover the latent wisdom which prevails in them. If they find what they seek, and they seldom fail, they think it more wise to continue the prejudice, with the reason involved, than to cast away the coat of prejudice, and to leave nothing but the naked reason.[24]

This coolness towards the critical spirit of the Enlightenment should not surprise us too much: in England, after all, the constitutional revolution was already a century old. It is no longer the time for the struggle among principles, Burke writes elsewhere, but for agreement and adjustment — 'we compensate, we reconcile, we balance'.[25] A goal that does not exclude 'reformism', in which Mario Praz, a critic definitely not suspect of hyper-politicism, saw the mainstream of the English novel from Fielding to Dickens.[26]

Nevertheless — as we already saw in the case of French narrative — political revolution, however much excluded from novelistic representation, bequeathes to the latter a set of problems and attitudes — a sort of 'primal scene' that the novel will never be able to forget. Its specific components and structure will be discussed in the next section; here, let us dwell a little longer on what lies outside it — on what today's readers would perceive as a 'shortcoming' of the English Revolution. Perry Anderson:

> The ideological legacy of the Revolution was almost nil. Its most militant creed, radical Puritanism, was the great loser from the Restoration Settlement ... . Because of its 'primitive', pre-Englightenment character, the ideology of the Revolution founded no significant tradition, and left no major after-effects. Never was a major revolutionary ideology neutralized and absorbed so completely.[27]

To stick to our original point: a Revolution not inspired by 'naked reason', and which does not lay down a Declaration of abstract rights, must by necessity generate a decidedly weak ethico-political universalism. And if the period of the clash of principles was short and quickly forgotten, it's difficult to extricate 'good' sense from 'common' sense: all the more so in that a revolution has nevertheless taken place, and common sense has changed and improved.

We are left with a web, so to say, of weak principles and strong factual results (institutional practices, economic organization, everyday attitudes). The 'normality' of the novelistic hero — where the ideological appraisal is lukewarm and hesitant, but the factual statement explicit and firm — is the most conspicuous and lasting result of this state of affairs. It is a wholly empirical adjustment, to be sure: neither demanding nor contentious, normality does not challenge the existing social order in the name of principles it does not possess. All it asks is to be left alone, and there is no doubt that, in the long run, it will prevail. This is why it can coexist so effortlessly with the rigid socio-cultural taxonomy that surrounds it on all sides: the destiny of others is none of its concern, and besides, mankind is a dubious abstraction, and nothing changes overnight. We should not be surprised if en route — from Tom, let us say, to David — good sense, generosity and naturalness wilt into common sense, conformity and emotional miserliness.

But the watering-down process also works in the opposite direction, by softening the harshness of status classification and transforming it into a fundamentally comic *dispositif.* And although laughter always has a punitive side to it, here it is far from being what Dupréel called 'laughter of exclusion'. Who is excluding whom, after all, when the comic spirit implicates the whole of society, and society as a whole is willing to laugh? The comic dominant thus moderates and counterbalances the taxonomic ideology, injecting into it a dose of that universalism and tolerance which are alien to taxonomy, but indispensable for the tendentially democratic component of English culture. Just as classificatory rigidity weakens the hero's common humanity, but without seriously hindering its course, so this humanity, although unable to do away with the taxonomic cage, manages nevertheless not to take it too seriously. It isn't a world of strong ideal tensions, but of empirical stratagems, steering a middle course between possible extremes. Burke is right: 'we compensate, we reconcile, we balance'.

II

The Devil's Party

If we move on from the 'statics' to the 'dynamics' of the English *Bildungsroman,* we are immediately struck by yet another difference with its continental counterpart. In Germany, in France, in Russia, the plot is the product of a disequilibrium between the spiritual physiognomy of the protagonist and the values implicit in the way society functions. The ultimate source of the plot may lie in the hero, as in Stendhal, in the world, as in Balzac, or midway between, as in *Meister*: but the story's two magnetic poles are, however, always the same, and it is symptomatic that the narrative theories of Lukács, Lotman and Weinrich retain, for all their diversity, an essentially binary foundation. Just as symptomatic is the fact that none of these theories have ever generated a convincing analysis of the English novelistic tradition: for in England, between the insipid normality of the hero, and a stable and a thoroughly classified world, no spark will ever flash. We have to look for another element.

Or perhaps for The Other. For the Enemy who brings Death into even the best of worlds: Iago, Satan. Later on, more prosaically, Blifil, Lovelace, Falkland, Fergus, Murdstone, Steerforth, Heep, the Reeds, Bertha Mason — but also Heathcliff, Kurtz, Dorian Grey, Hyde ... Frankenstein, Dracula, Moriarty ...

So many 'monsters' in English fiction — libertine or educational, realistic, gothic, popular ... . With time, of course, their features change, and in *David Copperfield* (a small summa of teratology, with Murdstone, Creakle, Steerforth, Heep and Maldon), the avid and subtle upstart has become more horrifying than the brilliantly cruel aristocrat (although a rough estimate of the dead and missing tells us that Steerforth is far more efficient than Heep). But apart from this predictable sociological rotation, the essential point is that the threat always comes from above or from below: never from the 'middle', never from that social position to which the hero basically belongs.

It is one more instance of the peculiarly 'innocent' way of seeing and presenting itself so typical of the English middle class. Whereas in France, or in Dostoevsky, this class identifies itself with *mobility*, even to the point of transgression or crime, in England it is the champion of the opposite values: security, stability, transparency. The highest virtue of the English novelistic hero — sincerity: certainly not Julien, Lucien or Bel-Ami's best quality — also acquires its true significance in this historico-cultural framework. Lionel Trilling:

> If we undertake to explain in Hegelian terms the English trait [sincerity] to which Emerson responded so warmly, we must ascribe it to the archaic intractability of the English social organization: the English sincerity depends upon the English class structure. And plainly this was the implicit belief of the English novelists of the nineteenth century. They would all of them appear to be in agreement that the person who accepts his class situation, whatever it may be, as a given and necessary condition of his life will be sincere beyond question.[28]

Opposing this sincerity, an equally adamant *lie*: the language of the villain. His language and his weapon, for the villain (as Hegel's *Phenomenology* makes clear) stands for social mobility in a world that does not acknowledge its right of citizenship: it must therefore protect and disguise itself. And it must do so not only for obvious personal profit, but for a sort of ontological reason, since whoever yearns for a change of status in a rigidly classified universe is perceived by the latter as a taxonomic anomaly: a freak, a 'monster'.

A monster — and an archaic intractability: a system that would be unyielding. A monster *inside* an unyielding system. Here, finally, narrative becomes possible: or rather — alas — unavoidable. For with the villain's every action anomalies multiply, and with them disequilibrium, suspense, unpredictability. The villain, in fact, generates plot merely by existing: from his point of view, after all, it is the only way to achieve what he wants. He needs plot, the 'story' is his element and also (as we will see) his trade. But if this is true, then the opposite is true for the hero and his allies: the plot affects them as a merely 'negative' force. Plot is violence and coercion, and they only agree to take part in it to avert the total disappearance of the violated order: to prevent the consummation of the *unnatural* marriages between Blifil and Sophia, or Uriah and Agnes.

The essential elements of the English plot are all right here: in the double and mirror-like sequence of a violated and restored order which has not helped us to understand the narrative of *modernity*, but applies very well indeed to a more 'restrained' culture. Claude Lévi-Strauss has written that 'there is a sort of fundamental antipathy between history and systems of classification':[29] the English novel is a case in point. If the villain did not 'force' it to generate stories, it would rather do without them: the 'awful Victorian plot', unanimously ridiculed by critics, is the logical product of this novel's *reluctance* to engage in narrative proper. In this English tradition, plot — and historical transformations, of which plot is a metaphor — is far from being the most significant aspect of the novelistic form (and of modernity as well). It is the product of lies, a negative force, a nonentity: which sentences to non-being, as we shall see shortly, the hero himself.

But first, let us consider another structural peculiarity of these novels: the uncompromisingly asymmetrical distribution of the specifically *narrative* function of generating events (usually carried out by the villain), and the *evaluative* function, usually carried out instead by the hero (who in Godwin, Brontë and Dickens is also the narrator), or by characters close to him. Blifil slanders Tom just as Falkland slanders Caleb Williams; the Reeds torment Jane, and Bertha prevents her from marrying Rochester; Steerforth seduces Emily and Uriah entraps Wickfield: but we invariably see all this through the eyes of Tom, Caleb, Jane and David. In the actions of their antagonists, what automatically strikes us is therefore the affront to the established morality, not the reasons for a different way of behaving (and perhaps a worse one, but that is not the point). It would be like focalizing *The Red and the Black* around Madame de Rênal, or *Lost Illusions* around Lucien's sister; like having *Eugene Onegin* narrated by Tatiana's nurse (which is basically what happens in *Wuthering Heights*). And since point of view has its own logic — which compels the reader to appropriate the point of view that makes the text readable to him — when it coincides with a violated order, he inevitably desires the anomalies to cease, and order to be reestablished.

The Hero in Exile

The monster's violation, albeit a constant of English narrative, does not always take the same form. In *Wuthering Heights, Frankenstein,* and *Heart of Darkness,* to take three rather diverse instances, the threat pervades the fictional world as a whole, which tends in fact (be it Yorkshire, Switzerland or the Congo) to take on the universal and self-sufficient features of a true microcosm. But in the *Bildungsroman* (and even in *Waverley),* the threat always focuses on one element only: the protagonist. The universal connotations weaken, and we are left with so many embryos of detective novels, of *cases* —'The Case of the Defamed Bastard', 'The Case of the Inquisitive Secretary', 'The Case of the Missing Governess' ...[30]

As in every detective novel, we need a victim and some sort of crime, and if the victim is the protagonist, the crime is usually an unjust accusation — if not indictment proper — levelled against him, or her. This is the turning point in the lives of Caleb Williams and Waverley; the spectre that haunts Tom Jones from birth until the final London chapters.[31] But the same is true for David, in the sections dominated by the Murdstones and Creakle's school, and Jane, in the Reeds, and Lowood episodes; with some modifications, it also applies to the rest of their lives. Let us then follow this lead: a normal and innocent protagonist is unjustly accused and, for one reason or another, is not able to defend himself. What happens next?

What happens is that he is sentenced to exile (Tom, Waverley) or forced to flee (Caleb, Jane, David). It is the English version of the most common narrative metaphor for youth — *the journey*. But unlike Wilhelm Meister, Lucien de Rubempré or Frédéric Moreau, who are quite happy to leave their childhood homes, or Julien Sorel and Fabrizio del Dongo, who are forced to leave because they have deliberately defied their world — the English heroes always leave against their will, and without having in any way deserved such a fate.[32]

The journey, and the mobility that goes with it, cannot therefore be seen by them as the ideal opportunity to *try out new identities*. It is just the opposite, a long and bewildering detour in which the roles they play in the course of time are merely disguises — unnatural, and sometimes repugnant — dictated by necessity. Whether framed in a comedy of errors, in a chivalrous epic or in a legal nightmare, the transformations of the hero during his journey are in each case alien and hostile to his nature. The farther he strays from his point of departure, the stronger the anxiety at 'no longer being himself'. He finds himself forced into the ever more theatrical disguises of Caleb Williams in his flight toward London, or is caught up in that crescendo of self-estrangement that leads Jane to use a false name, to learn a remote and disagreeable language like Hindu, and to be on the verge of committing herself to a fatal journey across the ocean.

Thus, for his part, Waverley, on the eve of his first battle: 'It was at that instant, that, looking around him, he saw the wild dress and appearance of his Highland associates, heard their whispers in an uncouth and unknown language, looked upon his own dress, so unlike that which he had worn from his infancy, and wished to awake from what seemed at the moment a dream, strange, horrible, and unnatural.' (*Waverley*, 46.)

Waverley and Jane aside, the place where strange, horrible, and unnatural dreams reach their maximum intensity is, predictably, London — the metropolis, the theater of fluctuating and changing identities. It is here that Tom Jones ends up proposing to a woman who is not Sophia, and coming extremely close to the gallows; that Caleb Williams, running into a street-singer who has rewritten his life according to the worst criminal stereotypes, realizes that he is now surrounded by 'a million of men, in arms against me'; that Pip burns the bridges with his too 'common' past, only to wake up (after a long and painful illness studded with nightmares) and discover that his life is ruined beyond repair. It is in London, finally, that David Copperfield undergoes the most traumatic of his childhood experiences (his job in the bottle factory), and it is again in London that he meets and marries Dora — an episode he at first describes as a 'dream' (*David Copperfield*, 43), but which turns very soon into a nightmare.[33]

The English journey, to sum up, is eerie, confusing, sterile, dangerous; but it nonetheless remains a metaphor for youth, upon which it conveys all its negative attributes. The syntagmatic unfolding of the text fully corroborates the devaluation of youth already manifest in its paradigmatic order. Youth is a haphazard and dangerous interlude: since it is unfortunately impossible to avoid it, the only hope left is that, like Tom's meteoric journey, it will pass by as swiftly and harmlessly as possible. Youth's lessons will be 'negative' ones too, therefore: they will not teach what one could be, but always and only what one is not, does not want to be, and should not be.[34] It is a narrative convention that Bakhtin has described perfectly ... but speaking of works written two thousand years earlier, the 'Greek romance' or 'adventure novel of ordeal':

> In the type of time [of these novels], an individual can be nothing other than completely *passive*, completely *unchanging* ... all the character's actions in Greek romance are reduced to *enforced movement through space* ...
>
> At the end of the novel that initial equilibrium that had been destroyed by chance is restored once again. Everything returns to its source, everything returns to its own place. ... And yet people and things have gone *through* something, something that did not, indeed, change them but that did (in a manner of speaking) affirm what they, and precisely they, were as individuals, something that did verify and establish their identity, their durability and continuity. ... Thus is constituted the artistic and ideological meaning of the Greek romance...
>
> In the majority of these novels legal procedures play a critical role: they serve to sum up the adventures of the heroes and provide a legal and judicial affirmation of their identity, especially in its most crucial aspect — the lovers' fidelity to each other.[35]

With these last few sentences we have already touched upon our next topic. If the state of exile or flight is forced upon the hero by an unjust indictment followed by an undeserved sentence, the latter is not, however, final. More exactly, it will not be final if youth has remained an empty segment, 'an extratemporal hiatus between two moments of biographical time'.[36] If the hero has remained 'completely passive, completely unchanging', if he hasn't contracted any binding ties — Dora! — then he can go back and enjoy, as Bakhtin says, 'the *reversibility* of moments in a temporal sequence'.[37] He can thus be finally recognized for what he has always been.

Ur-Novel

> It is true that Pip rises through class lines, but to equate him ... with
> young men like Julien Sorel, who drive upward on nerve and talent
> is quite misleading. The word 'expectations' is explicit and
> appropriate; in the circle of gentility where Pip has been placed one
> waits for one's destiny and accepts it. Money is what counts, but
> making money is vulgar; a genteel young man must have wealth to
> begin with or acquire it passively. This is one reason for the
> recurrent fables in eighteenth- and nineteenth-century fiction of
> discovered identities and suppressed wills — one gets the
> inheritance, but actually one had it all along.[38]

It is true, the recognition-inheritance pattern, virtually non-existent in European narrative, is instead the most typical form of the English happy end. Through it, the bourgeois theme of social mobility is given explicitly *aristocratic* features: for its goal, often enough, but above all for the *form* imparted to the entire process. Although the bourgeoisie has always taken excellent care of its wills and inheritances, the idea that wealth par excellence is something to be passed on from generation to generation, rather than being produced *ex novo*, is certainly far more typical of the landed aristocracy. This is why the hero is given rather faded bourgeois features: the more neutral his social identity, the easier will he 'fill' the role which awaits him, and which takes him back to his birth — one more reason to slight whatever can be accomplished during youth.

All this is true: but there is more. To begin with these inheritances are not gifts offered by saintly cardinals or repented sinners as in *The Betrothed*. They are something which Tom, Waverley and Jane *have a right to*. And this 'something' is not only a vast rural estate, or a nice sum of money, or a title: it is their very identity — better yet, their identity as *people endowed with rights*. They had been deprived, we could say, of the right to have rights: restoring it to them is nothing more than an act of justice.

Fairy-tale justice, of course, worthy of the 'family romances' we dream of in childhood: our parents are not our true ones, they are wicked impostors who have intercepted what is rightfully ours and want to cheat us out of it.[39] Hence the unfailing clash between absent, dead, or cruel parental figures, and the host of 'uncles' and 'aunts' (Allworthy, Everard Waverley, Betsey Trotwood, Joe, John Eyre) who, novel after novel, set things right. And why always and only uncles and aunts? Because in this way the principle of family inheritance is simultaneously respected and 'adapted', avoiding conflict with justice.

And now we come to the point. If English narrative is so fond of the 'family romance' structure, it is because of its uncanny similarity to one of the 'myths' that prepared and justified the English Revolution. Christopher Hill:

> [Edward Coke] gave Englishmen an historical myth of the English constitution parallel to Foxe's myth of English religion. In primitive times Englishmen had had good laws (as they had had a pure Church): the continuous enjoyment of those laws had been broken by William the Conqueror (with the support of the Pope) and by many of his successors. But Englishmen had fought back, as the heretics had fought back, and with greater success.[40]

This proper Ur-Novel of origins lost and rights restored may well have strengthened — as Hill suggests — the revolutionary spirit. What is certain, in any case, is that it gave it a very peculiar drift, to the point of paradoxically encouraging a *conservative* interpretation of the revolution itself. Burke: 'The very idea of the fabrication of a new government, is enough to fill us with disgust and horror. We wished at the period of the Revolution, and do now wish, to derive all we possess as *an inheritance from our forefathers.*'

And a few lines later, after stating that Coke was the first to have shown 'the pedigree of our liberties': 'In the famous law of the 3d of Charles I called the *Petition of Right*, the parliament says to the king, "your subjects have *inherited* this freedom", claiming their franchises not on abstract principles "as the rights of men", but as the rights of Englishmen, and as a patrimony derived from their forefathers.'[41]

We have here one of the great symbolic oppositions of the modern world. On the one hand, the French revolution, legitimized by its forcing the future open: whence the boundless historical vista which animates its dynamic enthusiasm, but which is also haunted by the pangs of uncertainty, of opportunism, of betrayal. On the other hand, the English revolution, with contrary symbolic vices and virtues: a weak political universalism, a reluctance to embrace modernity, a cult of origins and traditions — but also a commendable obstinacy in advocating the respect, and even the sanctity, of laws and contracts. As with narrative plot, it is a 'defensive' attitude to historical events: it would be best if nothing happened, but if a villain tries to. cheat, of course, 'Englishmen fight back'. It is as if the term 'revolution' were still chained to its etymon (which is quite plausible, in a century so fascinated by astronomy): a return back, 'full circle', to the original spot. The politico-institutional break is not legitimated *as a break* — but as the supreme act of legal *continuity*, and of respect for the rules of the game.[42]

A revolution that appeals to a 'pedigree' of privileges, while disregarding normative and universal principles! Which does not want to change the rules of the game, but punish those who have violated them! Which aims at the revival of the 'original contract', and has no interest in future utopias! 1789 truly is year zero — and the attitude of the English revolutionaries so remote as to seem almost unfathomable. It is quite reasonable to see precisely here — as Perry Anderson and Tom Nairn have done — the 'origin of the present crisis', the fatal immaturity that has nipped in the bud the full modernity of English political institutions and culture, and which has gradually emasculated the hegemonic potential of the industrial bourgeoisie and the cultural autonomy of the workers' movement.

In at least one domain, however, this immature revolution had truly long-lasting symbolic consequences. *Precisely because* it was immature, and could not establish its legitimacy on the politico-institutional, national or social contents of later revolutions, it was pressed into a very heavy symbolic investment in the least 'modern' and least 'bourgeois' of domains — the domain, as we have seen, of the law.[43] Not the law in its technical aspects (where the model will be the *Code Napoléon*, while English jurisprudence will remain abstrusely unintelligible for a long time), but the law as 'justice', in the broadest sense.

To see the revolution as a 'legal' act implied an inevitable weakening of its 'revolutionary' aspects. But it encouraged the more peaceful yet firm growth of a culture of justice, of a pride in the intangibility of one's rights, and in the guarantees they provide against the abuses of political power. In the course of time, this has become an essential feature of modern democratic culture, and *this* legacy is one which the more pulsating and plastic continental Europe (and certainly Italy) can only envy dusty old England.

The Great Tribunal of the World

This culture of justice must be by now such an obvious aspect of the English scene, that at times it goes unnoticed. In the fierce polemic over the role of the Revolution in English history that took place in the mid-sixties between Anderson, Nairn and

Thompson — a dispute that evoked Cardinal Newman and the Bath civilization, the realistic novel and utilitarianism — not a single line was devoted to it. Then ten years went by and — as in every good English novel — Edward Thompson stepped in to reestablish the truth, and wrote those memorable pages of cultural history that conclude *Whigs and Hunters*:

> What we have observed is something more than the law as a pliant medium to be twisted this way and that by whichever interests already possess effective power. Eighteenth-century law was more substantial than that. Over and above its pliant, instrumental functions it existed in its own right, as ideology; as an ideology which not only served, in most respects, but also legitimized class power. The hegemony of the eighteenth-century gentry and aristocracy was expressed, above all, not in military force, not in the mystifications of a priesthood or of the press, not even in economic coercion, but in the rituals of the study of the Justices of Peace, in the quarter-sessions, in the pomp of the Assizes and in the theatre of Tyburn. ... The rhetoric of eighteenth-century England is saturated with the notion of the law ... immense efforts were made ... to project the image of a ruling class which was itself subject to the rule of law, and whose legitimacy rested upon the equity and universality of those legal forms.[44]

The legitimacy of a ruling class and through it of an entire social order: whatever its domain (the 'aesthetic' dimension of everyday life in *Meister*, politics in Stendhal, market economy in Balzac and Flaubert), this is always the distinctive framework of the *Bildungsroman*. No socialization of the individual will ever be convincing if it lacks a symbolic legitimation: if it cannot justify itself with values held to be fundamental such as those which — as Thompson has pointed out — in eighteenth-century England converged around the idea and practice of the law.

A rapid glance at our novels offers ample evidence of this. *Caleb Williams* is a succession of legal actions embedded one in the other and sewn together by the unending investigation into Falkland's original crime. The London section of *Great Expectations* takes place entirely in the realm of the law and ends with the legal confiscation of Pip's assets. David Copperfield's first job is at the Commons, and the book's climax is the trial — although an informal one — of Uriah Heep, whom we will later find in prison. *Tom Jones* ends just short of the gallows, after a whirl of false and true testimonies; *Waverley*, with two parallel proceedings, resulting in the pardon of the protagonist and the execution of

Fergus. Moreover, the legal ritual outgrows its specific territory to pervade almost the whole of society. If Micawber finds himself playing the part of the Prosecution, in *Caleb Williams* the convicts themselves organize a 'mock tribunal' in the prison courtyard, and so do the highwaymen in their hideout. In *Tom Jones*, it is the gypsies who demonstrate juridicial passion and expertise; in *Jane Eyre*, the schoolmistresses.

Although the presence of the law in a strict sense is far from negligible in these novels, its diffusion into civil society and everyday life is certainly their most interesting aspect. If we take, for example, their dialogues, and compare them to their continental equivalents, the incredibly high frequency of interrogative sentences reveals that these are not dialogues, but rather *interrogations* — as is especially evident between Rochester and Jane. And when we read *Tom Jones*, it doesn't take long to realize that almost every episode, even a quarrel between little boys, is structured like a court case in miniature: it begins with a description of the 'crime', we listen to the indictment, the defendant is questioned and finally, in a crescendo of legal terminology, we have the sentence and the punishment.[45]

Given the centrality of the law in the English symbolic universe, its conquest of everyday life may have been inevitable; but it elicits nevertheless a certain amount of surprise and, in myself at least, of resistance. After all, the history of the European novel (but also, with Defoe, the origins of the English tradition) was inspired by a totally different principle, perfectly summarized by Locke in his *Second Treatise*:

> *Freedom of Men under Government* is ... a Liberty to follow my own Will in all things where the Rule prescribes not.[46]

This is where the narrative tradition we have examined in the first three chapters draws its inspiration, in its attempt to show that the domain where Rule prescribes not is — for precisely this reason — the most significant for modern individual existence. The most significant because it enhances freedom, obviously enough, but above all because it confronts the individual with the truly modern problem of *choosing*. The absence of 'Rule' in no way leaves this space 'empty': on the contrary, it generates all sorts of values, tastes, interests, options. Every behaviour becomes subjective, transitory, questionable: there arises the problem of how to assess it — there arises, in fictional rhetoric, the varied phenomenology of the relationships between story and discourse, narration and comment.

The English *Bildungsroman* seems, however, to stop short of these problems: combining constraint and consolation, it implies that Rule prescribes everywhere. Any type of conflict or diversity — whether of interests, ideas, ethical options, or erotic preferences — is removed from the realm of the questionable and translated into the fairy-tale-juridical opposition of 'right' and 'wrong'.[47] Once this path has been taken, evaluation and comment become superfluous because, just like in court, one need only ascertain the truth and judgement comes naturally. As an English juridical commonplace puts it: 'Justice is as simple as truth.'[48]

'Justice is as simple as truth.' The essence and common feature of truth and justice is that they are 'simple', and what is simple is opposed to what is 'intricate', 'complicated'. It is a paradigm that will return in a famous conceptual pair of formalist theory: *fabula* and *sujet*. The latter is dilatory, incomplete, arbitrary, discontinuous and deceptive — as artificial and 'complicated' as the movement of the knight in chess. The former instead is logical, complete, chronologically consequential, objective — in a word, 'simple'.[49]

Or rather, it would be simple if not for the distortions imposed by the *sujet*, to which the villain imparts a concrete reality, resulting in the deception not only of the reader (as is the case in detective fiction), but of all the various judges present *in* the text as well — Allworthy, Forester, King George and so on. The *sujet*, here, is not merely a literary device, but a true counter-*fabula*, the unjust but powerful version of things aimed at crushing forever the original truth. The only chance to thwart this plan is once more the all-pervading spatio-temporal dispositif of reversal: the return *back*, to a place, a time, a character or an event which enables the restoration of the truth about oneself and one's life.

Hence the story of Uriah Heep's swindles, which we perceived in bits and pieces, and always from incomplete viewpoints. Hence the explanation of the misunderstandings and intrigues that drove Waverley into the Highlands, under suspicion of treason. Hence the full account of the murder committed by Falkland, which explains and ends the persecution of Caleb Williams. Hence the illustration of Blifil's frauds, and of the countless misunderstandings arising therefrom. And all these twice-told stories — why, they are so many *fabulae*, so many forerunners of those indisputable realignments of facts that will be made famous and repeated *ad infinitum* by Sherlock Holmes and Hercule Poirot.

This rhetorical choice may seem neutral and innocent, but in fact it shapes narration in a very special way. In other novelistic traditions, the *fabula* remains 'hidden' in the story; in the English novel, its 'discovery' is instead a narrative episode, and the conclusive, definitive one at that. When a plot has been erected on lies and misunderstandings, once the truth has been re-established, nothing more need be said, of course. But one doubt lingers: this unproblematic countering of lie and truth, this unshakable belief in totally neutral and objective narratives — are these the cultural assumptions to which the novelistic form owes its historical significance? Or isn't something else needed to explain them?

'Narratio' versus Novel

'We are now arrived at the last stage of our long journey', writes Fielding in the opening chapter of the last book of *Tom Jones*: 'Now it is well known, that all jokes and raillery are at this time laid aside; whatever characters any of the passengers have for the jest-sake personated on the road, are now thrown off, and the conversation is usually plain and serious.

'In the same manner ... in this last book ... all will be plain narrative only.' (*Tom Jones*, XVIII. 1)

This excellent miniature of the English opposition of *fabula* and *sujet* proves that the latter is always, from a structural point of view, no more than an *interlude*: it may be enormous — like *Tom Jones*'s plot — but it nonetheless dissolves with the appearance of the *fabula*. The *fabula*, for its part, is 'plain', like Jane Eyre's face, without a trace of make-up, clean, natural. It is an *oratio recta*, or better yet, an *ordo naturalis*: 'The normal expressive state of thoughts and words is called *ordo naturalis*; it is found, for example, in the succession of events of the *narratio*, which corresponds to the historical unfolding of the events themselves.'[50]

'Narratio'. Graeco-Roman culture crumbles, but at a certain moment this term reappears. In the literary domain? No, in the courts:

> Pleading began when the defendant appeared at the bar of the court and the plaintiff stated his complaint. In the royal courts the complaint was made in French in a *counte* (*narratio* in Latin), meaning a tale or a story. ... Before the middle of the thirteenth century a new profession of countors or narrators had emerged, whose business was to compose *countes* ... . Numerous written collections of precedents of *narrationes* were produced in the thirteenth and fourteenth centuries.

> In the earliest times, pleading began and ended with the *counte*.
> The defendant had merely to deny ('defend') everything in the
> *counte*, and then the proof was awarded.[51]

Here the threads of this chapter begin to join together. The false
testimonies of the villain and the sincere confessions of the hero;
the cult of innocence and the all-pervasive opposition of 'right'
and 'wrong'; the firm belief that it is possible to tell a story in an
entirely 'natural' and unquestionable fashion, that in so doing the
meaning of events will automatically reveal itself, and that its
evaluation will as a matter of course be unanimous .... This is not a
novel — it is a trial. It is the popular view of how a trial should
melodramatically emphasize the 'simplicity' of justice.[52]

Well beyond 'contents', the cooperation of literature and law in
the symbolic legitimation of the existing order is inscribed and
articulated in the very *rhetorical structure* of the *Bildungsroman*.
The *Bildungsroman*, in fact, seems to justify itself as a form in so far
as it duplicates the proceedings of a trial. It is for this reason that in
the last book of *Tom Jones*, Fielding informs us that there will be
no more room for 'entertainment' (*Tom Jones*, XVIII.1): the
moment has come to serve a more 'serious' purpose than the
pleasure of the text:

> It is inherent in the special character of law, as a body of rules and
> procedures, that it shall apply logical criteria with reference to
> standards of universality and equity. It is true that certain
> categories of persons may be excluded from this logic (as children
> or slaves), that other categories may be debarred from access to
> parts of the logic (as women or, for many forms of eighteenth
> century law, those without certain kinds of property), and that the
> poor may often be excluded, through penury, from the law's costly
> procedures. All this, and more, is true. But if too much of this is
> true, then the consequences are mainly counterproductive. Most
> men have a strong sense of justice, at least with regard to their own
> interests. If the law is evidently partial and unjust, then it will mask
> nothing, legitimize nothing, contribute nothing to any class's
> hegemony. The essential precondition for the effectiveness of law,
> in its function as ideology, is that it shall display an independence
> from gross manipulation and shall seem to be just. It cannot seem
> to be so without upholding its own logic and criteria of equity;
> indeed, on occasion, by actually *being* just. And furthermore it is
> not often the case that a ruling ideology can be dismissed as a mere
> hypocrisy; even rulers find a need to legitimize their power, to
> moralize their functions, to feel themselves to be useful and
> just.[53]

The novels we talked about constitute the large and informal *corpus* that backs up this ideology of justice, introduces it into all aspects of life, and above all strives to prove, in explicitly egalitarian fashion, that *everyone* — bastard child, woman, drunk, fugitive, pauper — has the right to tell her/his side of the story, to be listened to, and to receive justice. More exactly: these novels do not simply state that everyone 'has a right' to justice; they maintain instead that everyone, in fact, *receives* justice. This difference emphasizes their incurably *fairy-tale-like* quality, which not even Godwin was able to do without when he rewrote the ending of *Caleb Williams* and transformed the novel, from a description of 'things as they are' (as we find in the subtitle), into an omen of 'things as they should be'.

And at this point — at this point every reader must decide from which viewpoint to observe the English *Bildungsroman* from Fielding to Dickens. If one adopts the viewpoint of the literary critic — well, there is little to be said, we have but one long fairy-tale with a happy ending, far more elementary and limited than its continental counterparts. But if one adopts the viewpoint of the historian of culture, and of 'political' culture in a broad sense, matters change. What we see is a tradition that has absorbed and propagated one of the most basic expectations of liberal-democratic civilization: the desire that the realm of the law be certain, universalistic, and provided with mechanisms for correction and control.[54]

We may ask ourselves, of course, whether it was truly inevitable for these aspirations to be embodied in *fairy-tales*, rather than in more 'adult' symbolic forms. Who knows, perhaps it was not inevitable, and the course of events was dictated by reasons still beyond our grasp. Nonetheless, they *were* embodied in fairy-tales: we might as well take note of it. And also add that perhaps a truly *widespread* culture of justice must necessarily cherish certainties, prohibitions, punishments and rewards; it must necessarily see things in black and white, as the never ending story of innocents and criminals. If this is the case — and I am not certain, but there is enough evidence for a hypothesis at least — if this is the case, then the fairy-tale may well be the most appropriate narrative genre for the task, and childhood (or its lingering residues) the stage of life most suited for absorbing such a clearcut and unquestionable value structure.[55]

This is not to deny that the English *Bildungsroman* leaves us, so to speak, with an empty stomach. One enjoys oneself, without ever being carried away; one finds plenty of certainties, but no way of addressing problems. True, but a trial is less enthralling than a duel, and a jury cannot pass sentence in a problematic manner. The juridical frame of mind is moreover, as Max Weber observed, the most remote from the narrative one — if, as I believe, narrative is related to history. The law desires the firm certainty of rules — not the pulsating doubts of change and transformation. Its universe is not interested in analyzing ways of behaviour, but in judging them and prohibiting them. And so forth. Let us therefore say that, due to a unique historical conjunction, the novel was born in England precisely when the ideology of the law reigned supreme. The result was the worst novel of the West, and the boldest culture of justice. *Unicuique suum.*

III

George Eliot ... and everything changes. Together with Jane Austen, she was the only novelist to dismiss the judicial-fairy-tale model and deal with the issues characteristic of the continental *Bildungsroman*: going so far, in fact, as to bring this genre to its natural conclusion. But before dealing with that aspect, let us examine her inscription within the English narrative tradition, and the many fundamental modifications she brought about.

The first thing to change is the protagonist's intellectual physiognomy, in that now, thank God, they have one. Neither 'innocent' nor 'insipid', Felix and Dorothea, Lydgate and Deronda (but also Harold Transome, Will Ladislaw, Bulstrode, Gwendolen Harleth), all have a forceful and marked personality, which their world perceives as unusual, and perhaps even disturbing. Felix Holt's resolution — 'I shall never marry' (*Felix Holt*, 5) — which is echoed more or less explicitly in Dorothea, Gwendolen, Lydgate, Will and Deronda, is the sign of an exacting nature, aware of its own worth and devoted to a solitary dream which, in one way or another, will make it hard to come to terms with reality.

This dream — the notion that one's identity is to be created, and not 'inherited' — brings us back to the beginning of our investigation: to the ideal of *Bildung* which Eliot, with her excellent knowledge of *Meister* and German culture, reformulates as 'vocation'. A vocation which may be political,.religious, social, scientific, artistic; but which embodies in every case the synthesis of individual expression and collective benefit. The more one is

able to be 'oneself', the greater the objective results — the progress
— that will take place in all fields.

Or rather: this is what the ideal of vocation professes. But the
goal is very ambitious — more so, for instance, than the
complementarity of free individual development and happy social
integration of the classical *Bildungsroman*. That correlation
needed to repress the fully *historical* nature of the novelistic world,
and imagine, as we have seen, that the eighteenth century could
have a different ending than the French revolution. For George
Eliot, though — just think of her favourite keyword: *reform* — the
synthesis of the highly motivated individual and of social structure
can occur *only if* history moves forward: only through progress,
and as progress. A demanding conviction, and one destined to
measure itself against the harsh facts of nineteenth-century
history: symptomatically, her work bifurcates on this very point —
on the one hand *Middlemarch*, on the other *Felix Holt* and *Daniel
Deronda*.

Before coming to this, however, a further difference between
Eliot and her predecessors must be stressed. Once the hero is no
longer an innocent child, but a young adult fighting for values not
yet socially accepted, the plot can finally dispense with its fairy-
tale-judicial framework. When Dickens's ghost bestows on Esther
and Will Ladislaw the usual princely inheritance, they simply
reject it; *Daniel Deronda*, for its part, turns the sociological vector
of the 'family romance' towards the lower classes. No more hidden
antagonists, no more hellish conspiracies: Eliot's heroes always
choose freely those characters who will most harm them —
Dorothea and Casaubon, Lydgate and Rosamond, Gwendolen
and Grandcourt, and, if we extend the concept somehow, Felix
Holt and the rioting mob. Finally, no more misunderstandings
and persecutions from which to emerge perfectly immaculate:
Felix is condemned (almost) unjustly, but the easy antithesis of lies
and simple truth has been replaced by the investigation of the
consequences, perhaps unjustly painful, of an act that was
important precisely because questionable and open to different
evaluations.

The new plot also affects the background characters; although
still to a large extent comic and unalterable, they are no longer a
colorful picture gallery to be gazed at from a distance, but are
active forces which must be interacted with in the plot itself.
Active, that is to say, as expressions of that socio-cultural *inertia*
which places them, through complex mediations, in conflict with
the protagonists: just as, in the *Theory of the Novel*, the 'second

nature' of social structure opposes the strength of its 'mere existence' to the yearning of the hero's 'soul'. But since this is true above all for *Middlemarch*, and since the analogies among the three novels we are interested in end here, the time has come for a separate discussion of Eliot's two models of the *Bildungsroman*.

'To alter the world a little'

Besides being by far the finest nineteenth-century English novel, *Middlemarch* is also the only one which dares to deal with the major theme of the European *Bildungsroman*: failure. In our case, the failure of one's 'vocation', illustrated by Eliot's inventive and rich phenomenology: the inexcusable amateurishness of Brooke's political adventure, the bitter parable of Casaubon's lack of talent, the still barbaric violence of Bulstrode's sense of being one of the chosen — and, naturally, the stories of Will, Dorothea and Lydgate. Stories which reproduce the antithesis, already there in Goethe, between the *objective historical demands* of the idea of vocation, and that which is instead *significant for novelistic narration*. Alan Mintz:

> It is possible to distinguish within the novel's larger concern with character two distinct lines of valuation. According to the vocational line, an individual is judged on the basis of his contributions to society, culture, and history, in other words, on the basis of works that stand on their own. The other line of value — what may be called the unhistorical or novelistic line — judges an individual by his contribution to the personal moral life of those closest to him (in proximity, not in sentiment), as measured by renunciations of self-interest. ... These two lines of judgment, in their essential configurations of value, roughly correspond to Weber's types of traditional and antitraditional economic ethics. The novelistic standard stresses the older values of family and community and views work as a means of maintaining the physical basis of these institutions. The vocational standard, on the other hand, stresses the improvement of one's own estate, regardless of older ties; and requires that a man be judged on the basis of his worldly achievements.[56]

To this first opposition we may add the truly classical one — also present in Goethe — between *Beruf* and

... idols whose cult today occupies a broad place on all street corners and in all periodicals. These idols are 'personality' and 'personal experience' [Erlebnis]. ...

Ladies and gentlemen. In the field of science only he who is devoted *solely* to the work at hand has 'personality'. And this holds not only for the field of science; we know of no great artist who has ever done anything but serve his work and only his work. ... In the field of science, however, the man who ... seeks to legitimate himself through 'experience', ... is no 'personality'. ... Instead of this, an inner devotion to the task, and that alone, should lift the scientist to the height and dignity of the subject he pretends to serve.[57]

What is crucial for Weber, here as in many other similar passages, is to throw light on the 'tragic' split that the modern world has produced between 'life' and 'profession' (science, politics, economics, art: it makes no difference). In the latter field, rationalization and specialization have gone so far that whoever engages in it must accept the biblical sacrifice of his subjective yearnings to its unyielding laws. It is the very same dilemma of *Wilhelm Meister*, which Goethe had solved by creating the aesthetic harmony of everyday life: an environment where the two conflicting drives could be reconciled. But a century has gone by, and synthesis is no longer possible. This is the secret message entrusted to Will Ladislaw, this potential but finally impossible protagonist of *Middlemarch*, who is a true reincarnation — even in his name — of Goethe's Wilhelm. Unwilling — just like his German predecessor — to devote his life to a profession, because its 'one-sidedness' will thwart his desire for 'self-culture' (*Middlemarch*, 21 and 46), Will however no longer occupies the centre of the novel: the representative of aesthetic harmony has moved to the periphery, to a sub-plot which becomes significant only when linked to Dorothea's story. Synthesis is no longer possible, and that sort of androgyny so typical of Wilhelm, and even more marked in Will, splits up — as if to emphasize, with the help of 'nature', the break between the two 'halves' of existence mentioned in the last sentence of the novel — into Dorothea's 'feminine' destiny and Lydgate's 'masculine' counterpart.

Dorothea's 'theoretic mind', as we know, yearns for 'some lofty conception of the world': but such as — and not even a comma is there to mark a discontinuity — 'might frankly include the parish of Tipton and her own rule of conduct there'. (*Middlemarch*, 1.) Even though her relations hold her to be too 'abstract', Dorothea's true vocation seems to lie rather in the realm of the 'concrete', and she can only conceive of 'reforms' immediately at one with everyday life: 'I should like to make life beautiful — I mean everybody's life. And then all this immense expense of art [Dorothea is in Rome], that seems somehow to lie outside life and make it no better for the world, pains one.' (*Middlemarch*, 22.)

What transcends direct personal experiences does not interest Dorothea *because* it transcends them, but in so far as it can be restored to everyday life. Her most emphatic vocational pronouncement comes to her lips, symptomatically enough, at the thought of marriage: 'There would be nothing trivial about our lives. Everyday-things with us would mean the greatest things. It would be like marrying Pascal.' (*Middlemarch*, 3.)

Dorothea's error, as the text will make clear, does not lie so much in constraining the vocational ethic within domestic walls: does not lie in her desire to '*marry* Pascal', but in having married *Casaubon*, i.e. chosen the wrong husband. When she marries Will, her contribution to the 'growing good of the world' will be limited but undisputable. The last paragraph of the novel:

> Her full nature, like that river of which Cyrus broke the strength, spent itself in channels which had no great name on the earth. But the effect of her being on those around her was incalculably diffusive: for the growing good of the world is partly dependent on unhistoric acts; and that things are not so ill with you and me as they might have been, is half owing to the number who lived faithfully a hidden life, and rest in unvisited tombs. (*Middlemarch*, 'Finale')

It would be foolish to dismiss these words as mere hyperbolic consolation, and just as foolish to underestimate the sphere in which Dorothea is truly superior to her world — the ethical sphere of 'the effect of her being on those around her': Casaubon, Lydgate, Rosamond, Will. The point lies elsewhere. The 'unhistoric acts' praised in this passage may be of the highest worth, but they nevertheless indicate that the standpoint of vocation has been abandoned. For better or for worse, vocation is depersonalized, objective, hostile to 'personal experience': to suggest that it can be fulfilled within everyday personal relationships implies a perversion of its meaning. It also implies a repression of the 'other half' of the novel: of the splendid and sorrowful account — short was the happy life of Tertius Lydgate — of the *conflict* between vocation and everyday life.

Why has this young biologist — a man who has studied 'at London, Edinburgh and Paris' (*Middlemarch*, 15), and dreams of epoch-making discoveries — why has he come to Middlemarch? His scientific background, his culture, his personality — including the notorious 'spots of commonness' and his lack of sensitivity for interpersonal dynamics — mark him out as the one truly urban character in the novel. But the medical profession, in London, has degenerated into 'intrigues, jealousies, and social truckling' (*Middlemarch*, 15), and so he finds himself in Middlemarch: not so much for what Middlemarch is, but for what it enables him to avoid.

And this is the problem: Lydgate, unlike Dorothea, simply cannot bring himself to take Middlemarch seriously; nor can he believe, even after Farebrother's friendly warning, that this little town peopled with mediocrities might obstruct his professional plans. Thus, with total nonchalance he starts frequenting the local 'society', and given that 'our young men here cannot cope with you' (*Middlemarch*, 31), he ends up having 'the prettiest girl in town' (*Middlemarch*, 63) fall in love with him.

The quintessence of Middlemarch mentality, as is proper for the town *belle*, Rosamond Vincy, is the lively and strong-willed reincarnation of Dickens's Dora. Her narrative task lies in carrying off the slow and almost imperceptible, but tenacious, process which is for Eliot the worst threat to youthful vocations:

> In the multitude of middle-aged men who go about their vocations in a daily course determined for them much in the same way as the tie of their cravats, there is always a good number who once meant to shape their own deeds and alter the world a little. The story of their coming to be shapen after the average and fit to be packed by the gross, is hardly ever told even in their consciousness. ... Nothing in the world more subtle than the process of their gradual change! In the beginning they inhaled it unknowingly; you and I may have sent some of our breath towards infecting them, when we uttered our conforming falsities or drew our silly conclusions: or perhaps it came with the vibrations from a woman's glance. (*Middlemarch*, 15.)

And in another passage, also devoted to Lydgate: 'Will felt inexpressibly mournful, and said nothing ... it seemed to him as if he were beholding in a magic panorama a future where he himself was sliding into that pleasureless yielding to the small solicitations of circumstance, which is a commoner history of perdition than any single momentous bargain.' (*Middlemarch*, 79)

'A commoner history of perdition than any single momentous bargain': in the apparent denial of the *Teufelspakt*, Eliot does in fact confirm its essence. From Faust to Weber's 'demon' to Adrian Leverkühn, the success of vocation always demands the sacrifice of 'life' — of love, of Gretchen's, of Nepomuk's. Here victory moves to the other side of the paradigm, but the paradigm itself is left unaltered: Lydgate's generous impulse at the sight of Rosamond's tears — 'the vibrations from a woman's glance' — subjects him to life, and buries his vocation alive. If Faust's perdition and curse was summarized in the murder of others so that he will fulfil himself in his vocation, Lydgate's is perfectly specular: he murders his aspirations, and with them himself, in restoring Rosamond's youth to her. In each instance, life and vocation are at war: whether one is bewitched by the garrulous beckoning of a devil or by the silent entreaties of an angel does not seem to make any difference.

Where a difference should be emphasized, however, is in the way Lydgate's destiny reshapes the novelistic theme of failure and disillusionment. In the full metropolitan world of the *Comédie* — to take the clearest example — social relationships are a system of impersonal, and even mechanical, forces. These forces fight each other incessantly, introduce countless catastrophes into everyday life, and force the hero into the worst pacts with the devil; then, after having pushed him to the foreground, they banish him forever from the world of power. In the provincial world of *Middlemarch*, on the other hand, social relationships are still inextricable from personal ties. The social world is a great living organism — Eliot's celebrated 'web' — where individuals, like so many organs, have no right to autonomy. And when this organism comes into contact with an alien body — with a Lydgate — it ensnares him, it slowly sucks up all his vitality, and finally it swallows him.

In other words: the French novel outlines modernity's *internal* contradictions. George Eliot — in writing the greatest English novel of her century — surveys instead the conflict *between modernity and tradition*: urban culture and provincial life, *Gesellschaft* and *Gemeinschaft*, abstract vocation and everyday viscosity. Having nursed for a long time a strong disappointment that *Middlemarch* takes place where it does, and not in London, the reality principle has finally convinced me that Eliot's choice struck a *punctum dolens* of nineteenth-century English culture. Due to the social peculiarity of the national ruling class, and of its values, urban culture never became dominant in England, nor did the new magnetism of the metropolis ever replace the gravitational pull of the countryside.

Middlemarch's subtitle mentions 'provincial life'. But this is not the French novelistic provinces (Verrières, Angoulême, Yonville), that pathetic puppet show where a remote capital is aped to no avail. Middlemarch is no *Ersatz*: it is — it *still* is — the symbolic apex of an entire social formation.[58] The story of Tertius Lydgate — the man who in deference to the wishes of Middlemarch's beauty does indeed become 'what is called a successful man', and yet 'always regarded himself as a failure: he had not done what he once meant to do' — this story is the bitter tribute to the lasting power of 'provincial life'.

Eliot's Narrator: Maturity as Humour

'The fruits of Lydgate's life's work will be a treatise on gout. But the narrator has produced the novel itself, whose palpable reality signifies that the vocational claims of at least one aspirant have been made good.'[59]

Very true, and this happens because the narrator — unlike the characters, and especially Lydgate — has never hoped 'to alter the world a little', but has accomplished the opposite task of giving voice to the disenchanted interiorization of the harshness of reality: an achievement which allows Eliot to replace the traditional English polarization of pathetic and comic with that 'synthetic' attitude which, in the final pages of *Jokes and their relation to the unconscious*, Freud defines as 'humour': 'Humour can be regarded as the highest of defensive processes. It scorns to withdraw the ideational content bearing the distressing affect from conscious attention as repression does, and thus surmounts the automatism of defence.'[60]

This fortitude in confronting the distressing affect, Freud continues, reveals humour's connection with 'maturity': 'The exaltation of [the adult's] ego, to which the humorous displacement bears witness, and of which the translation would no doubt be "I am too big (too fine) to be distressed by these things", might well be derived from his comparing his present ego with his childish one.'[61]

This comparison with one's childish self is the more significant in that the ensuing 'exaltation' is not the easy and unchallenged superiority which the reader enjoyed with the countless child-adults in Fielding, Scott, or Dickens. Humorous maturity is not as simple as that, and it doesn't define itself as a definitive and unalterable closure, but rather as an unending process of self-improvement, in which the adult subject will have to play over and over again the part of the 'child': 'It is even conceivable that once again it may be a connection with the infantile that puts the means for achieving [the transformation of unpleasure into pleasure] at humour's disposal. Only in childhood have there been distressing affects at which the adult would smile today — just as he laughs, as a humourist, at his present distressing affects.'[62]

Freud's text was written in 1905. About a half century later, it is unknowingly echoed in F.R. Leavis's encomium of George Eliot's *'mature* genius'. Although this maturity is nowhere explicitly defined, it seems however to imply 'complexity and completeness, fullness of vision and response ... inclusiveness — an adequacy to the complexities of the real in its inclusiveness'.[63]

It is a maturity, in other words, with both a cognitive and an ethical side to it. The former is the 'fullness of vision': thanks to it, as a very Burkean statement has it, 'George Eliot sees too much and has too strong a sense of the real ... to be a satirist.' The latter is the 'fullness of response' which, once the Scylla of satire is avoided, allows to steer clear of the Charybdis of aestheticism as well.[64] Whether cognitive or ethical, maturity always implies a broadening of consciousness: the key word is 'fullness', or better still, 'inclusiveness'. It is the very word which, in the twenties dominated by T.S. Eliot and I.A. Richards, had epitomized the new criterion of aesthetic judgment. Leavis extends its field of application: in his version, 'inclusiveness' strengthens its intellectual and moral overtones, and becomes the standard, not just for 'art', but for 'life'.

Is this extension plausible, however? Let us recall what was implicit from the very beginning of this discussion: in Eliot's novels the representative of humour and maturity is — the narrator. A character *sui generis* who reiterates the rupture we had already noticed in Balzac: maturity is no longer achieved within the story, but only in the disembodied universe of discourse. And the relationship between the two levels of the text is inversely proportional: the more devastating the characters' failure, the more impressive the narrator's self-mastery. It is the discontinuity between maturity and life that is stressed here, not their amalgam.[65]

But once maturity is no longer entrusted to 'actions', but only to the awareness of their meaning, then a wholly new paradigm has been created: the paradigm which will later be developed by Henry James and T.S. Eliot, and which places the broadening of consciousness above all other values. We are all familiar with the superb achievements of this cultural trend; but we should not forget that its emphasis on self-awareness is bound to encourage meditation at the expense of active and practical concerns. *Pace* Leavis, Freud had already observed that 'the small contributions of humour that we produce ourselves are as a rule made at the cost of anger — instead of getting angry'.[66] Getting angry is possibly not a very mature behaviour, but it is undoubtedly very active, and perhaps the highly civilized attitude of *Middlemarch's* narrator discourages it a little too much. Perhaps. What is certain, instead, is that immediately following *Middlemarch* — spurred by what Lukács would have called 'incorruptible aesthetic integrity' — Eliot put her ideal of maturity to the test. And she did so in the most exacting and reliable of circumstances: by returning it from the discourse to the story, and by entrusting it to a character, so to say, of flesh and blood. We do not know whether she was aware of her choice, but it is as if Eliot wanted to verify whether the maturity *of Middlemarch* could truly be interwoven with 'life'. The results were to be *Daniel Deronda,* and Daniel Deronda: the most unreal of her novels, the most oppressive of her heroes.

End of a Genre

Felix Holt, The Radical and *Daniel Deronda* — the two novels where, contrary to *Middlemarch,* the protagonist doesn't betray his vocation and, at the end, seems destined to fulfil it — share a virtually identical sociological and actantial structure. The stage is sharply divided between an aristocratic pole (the Transomes, Grandcourt and Gwendolen) and its social opposite: a world in between artisans and industrial workers (Felix), or the Jewish lower classes (Mordecai and Mirah). In between, their parents unknown, Esther and Daniel, who could go one way or the other, by marrying the most important representative of either class. After having learned their true identity, thanks to coincidences incredible even for Victorian times, they both opt for the socially inferior world.

Given these analogies, and since after *Middlemarch* any of Eliot's novels is in anticlimax, we may discuss either work indifferently: there is even a universal consensus, which I fully share, according to which both novels are split into a beautiful and interesting part (the Transomes; Gwendolen) and a grimly didactic one (Felix; Daniel, Mordecai and Mirah). Here, in any case, I will deal mainly with *Daniel Deronda,* as its hero combines narrative functions and features which in *Felix Holt* are distributed between Esther (indecision regarding two conflicting choices; a sudden and perturbing discovery regarding her past), and Felix (the 'positive' pole of the story; the representative of the vocational ethic).

Daniel has 'the stamp of rarity' — we are told in chapter 16 — in his 'subdued fervour of sympathy, an activity of imagination on behalf of others'. Daniel's gifts, as I had anticipated, are the same ones that marked the narrator in *Middlemarch*. In a further passage, where these qualities are again under observation, Eliot draws our attention to those 'practical' consequences which, irrelevant in the narrator's case, can no longer go unmentioned when dealing with a 'real' character:

> His early-wakened sensibility and reflectiveness had developed into a many-sided sympathy, which threatened to hinder any persistent course of action. ... His imagination had so wrought itself to the habit of seeing things as they probably appeared to others, that a strong partisanship, unless it were against an immediate oppression, had become an insincerity for him. ... A too reflective and diffusive sympathy was in danger of paralysing in him that indignation against wrong and that selectness of fellowship which are the conditions of moral force. (*Daniel Deronda*, 32)

Having gotten used to seeing 'too many sides to every question', John Stuart Mill had written in his Diary in 1854, 'scarcely anyone, in the more educated classes, seems to have any opinions, or to place any real faith in those which he professes to have'.[68] At various points in the first half of the novel, we have the feeling that *Daniel Deronda* could in fact become a 'case study' on the ethical-intellectual indecisiveness of the upper classes, and that Daniel himself could turn out to be a member of the same family as the Beautiful Soul and Frédéric Moreau, social parasitism included:

> Not that he was in a sentimental stage; but he was in another sort of contemplative mood perhaps more common in the young men of our day — that of questioning whether it were worth while to take part in the battle of the world: I mean, of course, the young men in whom the unproductive labour of questioning is sustained by three of five per cent on capital which somebody else has battled for.. (*Daniel Deronda*, 17)

The novel sketched in these lines would perhaps be more interesting than *Daniel Deronda*: but it would cast too harsh a light on the 'material base' from which many of the narrator's virtues have sprung up. And so — while Daniel is rowing on the Thames, 'occupied chiefly with uncertainties about his own course' and 'indulging himself in the solemn passivity' of the twilight hour — Eliot shifts literary genres. From the rescue of Mirah to the meeting with Mordecai; from the enigmatic question of a stranger in the Frankfurt Synagogue ('what is your parentage — your mother's family — her maiden name') to the conversation with his hitherto unknown mother, Deronda becomes the hero of a melodramatic fairy-tale. Its last act — the discovery that he is Jewish — enables him simultaneously to achieve happiness with Mirah (who would refuse to marry outside of her religion) and to fulfil his vocation by firmly rooting himself in Jewish culture.

This culture is opposed to that of English high society — or of England *tout court*, given that the novel's morally admirable characters are all foreigners — as *Gemeinschaft* is opposed to *Gesellschaft*: a sense of identity and belonging, an ethnic continuity that transcends the individual versus inauthenticity, conflict, agreements which may well be unfair, possessive individualism. In the latter case we have the marriage of Grandcourt and Gwendolen, 'a contract where all ostensible advantages were on her side' (*Daniel Deronda*, 54); a contract which terminates only when Grandcourt drowns, and Gwendolen does not stir for that brief moment which — perhaps — could have saved him. In the former, the bond between Daniel and Mirah, which begins precisely with the opposite episode, and is sealed in the embrace of the dying Mordecai ('Have I not breathed my soul into you? We shall live together,' *Daniel Deronda*, 70): a symbol of that 'stronger Something' which has restored Daniel to his race frustrating his mother's plan for 'assimilation'.

This revulsion from *Gesellschaft* is already apparent in the — splendid — opening scene of the novel: Gwendolen at the roulette table, who initially wins a lot but then loses everything, while Deronda watches her (and, incidentally, brings her bad luck). Some time later, when they meet again, Deronda explains to Gwendolen why he thought it 'wrong' that she should gamble:

> There is something revolting to me in raking a heap of money together, and internally chuckling over it, when others are feeling the loss of it. I should even call it base, if it were more than an exceptional lapse. There are enough inevitable turns of fortune which force us to see that our gain is another's loss: — that is one of the ugly aspects of life. One would like to reduce it as much as one could, not get amusement out of exaggerating it. (*Daniel Deronda*, 29)[69].

There is really no need for comment: let us just say that the only other character who enjoys gambling is Mirah's father, the assimilated Jew who has abducted his daughter and tried to make a prostitute of her. Against this destiny inscribed in the gaming table, *Daniel Deronda* posits the values of *Gemeinschaft* — illustrated at length by Mordecai in the philosophical discussion of chapter 42[70] — which Eliot quite clearly considers vastly superior. Superior, of course, from the point of view of a *possible* society, since in real society they are despised and even repressed; as, for that matter, are the very similar values of Felix Holt. Have we, with all this, come back to the predicament of vocation as 'reform'?

Not really, because with Daniel and Felix vocation no longer has anything universalistic about it: it originates from an ethnic or social partiality which it tries to *preserve and even accentuate as such*. Hence the rejection of assimilation in *Daniel Deronda*, and Felix's anti-Chartist speeches against the extension of the franchise: Daniel and Felix are not interested in the public sphere, with its polyphony and its conflicts, but in the erection of barriers, and in the 'purification' of small enclaves. In other words, they entrench themselves within *sub-cultures* totally impervious to the dynamics of the 'great world', and therefore still endowed with old 'communal' features: 'Where great things can't happen, I care for very small things, such as will never be known beyond a few garrets and workshops.' (*Felix Holt*, 45.)

Felix's final pronouncement will be echoed, as we know, in the last words of *Middlemarch*: in the latter, however, Dorothea's distance from the public sphere was acknowledged, although reluctantly — while here, as in *Daniel Deronda* it is disguised by vague and grandiose prophetic intimations. While waiting for them to occur, Felix's and Daniel's enchanted enclaves — complete with their beloved, pleasing work and many good books — will shelter them from the bewitching temptations which, from Julien Sorel on, had shown the precarious and dangerous dialectics of many firm resolutions.

Yes indeed, terrible novels. But symptomatic, in a way that parallels Flaubert's case, that the historical and cultural configuration which had made the *Bildungsroman* possible and necessary had come to an end. In *Sentimental Education*, this symbolic form was being undermined by the unreal and stupefied hypertrophy of individual personality; by the cowardly and indifferent remoteness of the individual from collective destiny. Swollen and isolated beyond recognition, the very idea of 'the individual' ended up negating the bold and proud autonomy that had endeared it to such a large part of nineteenth-century culture.

In *Felix Holt* and *Daniel Deronda*, the contrary historical process becomes legible: the *sacrifice* of individuality typical of the 'age of the masses' — of the age of the great social and national movements which we can read in the *Gemeinschaft* of Eliot's two novels. And even if the sacrifice is willingly accepted — 'Felix' — and compensated by fairy-tale rewards, a sacrifice it is. Just think of Felix's and Daniel's personalities: they are so perfectly suited to the task at hand, that in Eliot's heroes we no longer see two men dedicated to their ideals, but the first *functionaries* of abstract beliefs. No wonder their vocation doesn't demand the painful self-repression described by Weber: there is nothing left to renounce. The rich variety of life's domains, the great lure and torment of the classical *Bildungsroman*, has collapsed like a house of cards. The conflict with the world — individuality as risk, burden, and perhaps parody — has been abolished by organic culture. The giddiness of mobility, of being swept by history's flow across the whole of society, has been anaesthetized by the superstitious expectation of monumental palingeneses. Youth, for its part, relapses into 'apprenticeship' in the narrowest sense, or into *school*, complete with teachers and homework.

And finally: when we are dealing with the author of *Middlemarch*, it's not lack of talent that can explain such disaster. If anything, it was precisely because Eliot had enough and to spare that she was tempted by the impossible, and tried to capture the essence of a new historical phase with the most significant symbolic form of the previous age. It was impossible for her to succeed, and she did not succeed: by 'reading' the age of the masses through the lense of the *Bildungsroman*, she saw in it only a new, fairylike refuge for individuality, and finally missed the historical essence of both phenomena. But this is not important, novelists are not prophets, and if *Felix Holt* and *Daniel Deronda* do not help us to understand the genesis of our world, we should not be too dismayed.

What they do enable us to understand is that the 'central' symbolic form of this new world could no longer be the *Bildungsroman* which, in all its diverse manifestations, had always held fast to the notion that *the biography of a young individual was the most meaningful viewpoint for the understanding and the evaluation of history*. This may well have been the highest artistic convention ever produced by modern Western society — it was certainly the most typical. But no convention outlives the fall of its foundations. And when the new psychology started to dismantle the unified image of the individual; when the social sciences turned to 'synchrony' and 'classification', thereby shattering the synthetic perception of history; when youth betrayed itself in its narcissistic desire to last forever; when in ideology after ideology the individual figured simply as a part of the whole — then the century of the *Bildungsroman* was truly at an end.

Appendix
'A Useless Longing for Myself':
The Crisis of the European
Bildungsroman, 1898–1914

Youth, by Joseph Conrad, in 1898. *Tonio Kröger*, by Thomas Mann, in 1903. *The Perplexities of Young Törless*, by Robert Musil, in 1906. *Jakob von Gunten*, by Robert Walser, in 1909. *The Notebooks of Malte Laurids Brigge*, by Rainer Maria Rilke, in 1910. *A Portrait of the Artist as a Young Man*, by James Joyce, written between 1904 and 1914. *Amerika* (or *The Lost One*), by Franz Kafka, written between 1911 and 1914.

That such an unusual concentration of wonders should not open a new phase in the history of the European *Bildungsroman*, but bring it to a sudden close, is at first glance an enigma. Then one notices the year Joyce completed, and Kafka abandoned, their novels: 1914. 'No one shall come out of this war', wrote a German volunteer, 'if not as a different person.' And indeed, as Fussell and Leed have shown, the initial feeling of European youth was that of being on the verge of a collective, immense initiation ritual. Rather than fulfilling the archetype, though, the war was to shatter it, because, unlike rites of passage, the war killed — and its only mystery didn't decree the renewal of individual existence, but its insignificance. If one wonders about the disappearance of the novel of youth, then, the youth of 1919 — maimed, shocked, speechless, decimated — provide quite a clear answer. We tend to see social and political history as a creative influence on literary evolution, yet its destructive role may be just as relevant. If history can make cultural forms necessary, it can make them impossible as well, and this is what the war did to the *Bildungsroman*. More precisely, perhaps, the war was the final act in a longer process — the cosmic coup de grâce to a genre that, at the turn of the century, was already doomed. Before discussing the interrelated tendencies that had undermined the form of the *Bildungsroman*, however, I will briefly recapitulate the reasons for its previous significance.

In the course of the nineteenth century, the *Bildungsroman* had performed three great symbolic tasks. It had contained the unpredictability of social change, representing it through the fiction of youth: a turbulent segment of life, no doubt, but with a clear beginning, and an unmistakable end. At a micro-narrative level, furthermore, the structure of the novelistic episode had established the flexible, anti-tragic modality of modern experience. Finally, the novel's many-sided, unheroic hero had embodied a new kind of subjectivity: everyday, worldly, pliant — 'normal'. A smaller, more peaceful history; within it, a fuller experience; and a weaker, but more versatile Ego: a perfect compound for the Great Socialization of the European middle classes. But problems change, and old solutions stop working. Let us then turn to our group of novels — which, for lack of anything better, I shall call the late *Bildungsroman* — and see what the new problems were.

Whereas previous novels tended to personalize social relations, presenting them as relations among individuals, in the late *Bildungsroman* social institutions began to appear as such: the business bureaucracy of *Amerika*, the Church of *Portrait*, and above all the School of Mann and Musil, of Walser and Joyce. The growth of institutions was a massive historical fact, of course, which a realistic narrative could hardly ignore: acknowledging it, though, proved just as difficult. 'One is not supposed to say so,' complains Törless, 'but of all we are doing all day long here at school, what does have a meaning? What do we get out of it? For ourselves, I mean. ... We know we have learned this and that ... but inside, we are as empty as before.' But inside ... this is the trouble with the school: it teaches this and that, stressing the objective side of socialization — functional integration of individuals *in* the social system. But in so doing it neglects the subjective side of the process: the legitimation *of* the social system inside the mind of individuals, which had been a great achievement of the *Bildungsroman*. What the school deals with are means, not ends; techniques, not values. A pupil must know his lesson, but he doesn't have to believe in its truth. Convincing the subject that what he must do is also symbolically right is, however, exactly what modern socialization is all about. If this does not happen, and shared values are replaced by sheer coercion (how many arbitrary and unfair punishments in these novels!), the individual will hardly feel at home in his world, and socialization will not be fully accomplished. When Tonio Kröger returns to the home of his childhood, he finds in its place a public library; and think of Karl Rossmann, the lost one, banished by his parents across the ocean; of Törless's enforced exile ('A small station on the line to Russia. Four parallel rails run straight, out of sight, in opposite directions'), and of Stephen's deliberate one. 'The time has come', writes Malte Laurids Brigge, 'when all things are leaving the houses. ...' No wonder that in 1916, writing *The Theory of the Novel*, Lukács should define the novel as the genre of 'transcendental homelessness': a questionable statement for the nineteenth century — but quite true for the late *Bildungsroman*, with its rootless heroes and inhospitable environments. Malte's anxious loneliness, Jakob's abject submission, Karl's blank passivity, Stephen's contemptuous isolation: here are some versions of Lukács's homelessness. But the most uncanny result of a merely functional socialization, and of its disregard for a shared symbolic universe, is Törless's nonchalant violence, which flatly rejects all notion of a common humanity: 'One last question. What do you feel now? Pain? Mere pain, which you would wish to stop? Just this, with no complications?' And that the best pupil of a 'renowned boarding school' should announce the brown shirts — what a setback for the civilizing machinery of liberal Europe!

Lothar and Jarno in *Meister*, de la Mole and Mosca in Stendhal, Jacques Collin in the *Comédie Humaine*, Austen's and Eliot's narrator: in the nineteenth century, the wisdom of adults had been a constant, critical counterpoint to the hero's adventures. But from Mann onwards countless stolid professors will suggest that, as soon as they become professional teachers, adults have nothing left to teach. Youth begins to despise maturity, and to define itself in revulsion from it. Encouraged by the internal logic of the school — where the outside world disappears, while grades overdevelop the sense of the slightest age difference — youth looks now for its meaning within itself: gravitating further and further away from adult age, and more and more toward adolescence, or preadolescence, or beyond.[1] If twentieth-century heroes are as a rule younger than their predecessors, this is so because, historically, the relevant symbolic process is no longer growth but regression. The adult world refuses to be a hospitable home for the subject? Then let childhood be it — the Lost Kingdom, the 'Domaine mystérieux' of Alain-Fournier's

Meaulnes. Hence Malte's longing for his mother, or Jakob's anguished final cry ('Ah, to be a small child — to be that only, and forever!'); or, in a more militant vein, Törless's devastating sense of omnipotence: that most regressive of features, out of which will arise — through *Le grand Meaulnes* (1913), *Le Diable au corps* (1923), and *Lord of the Flies* (1954) — a veritable tradition of counter-*Bildungsroman.* 'What is the matter,' asks the hero of *Meaulnes*, 'are children in charge here?' They are, and readers of Golding know the end of this story, where childhood may well be the biological trope for the new phenomenon of mass behaviour. The regression from youth to adolescence and childhood would thus be the narrative form for what liberal Europe saw as an anthropological reversal from the individual as an autonomous entity to the individual as mere member of a mass. Given this framework, the postwar political scenario could hardly encourage a rebirth of the *Bildungsroman*: that mass movements may be constitutive of individual identity — and not just destructive of it — was to remain an unexplored possibility of Western narrative.

Homeless, narcissistic, regressive: the metamorphosis of the image of youth in our century is by now a familiar fact. Less familiar is its rapidity: only fifteen years before the war, Marlow's and Kröger's destiny had been quite a different one. However problematical, their subjectivity had been free to unfold in a world not yet enclosed and dominated by institutions. 'The school was over,' reads the first page of *Tonio Kröger*, in perfect contrast to *Törless*: 'Through the paved courtyard, and out of the iron gate, flowed the liberated troops.' In *Youth*, for its part, Marlow's ship — this British Trinity of School, Army, and Factory all in one — is conveniently burned and sunk so that the young second mate may enjoy the independence of 'seeing the East first as a commander of a small boat'. Yes, institutions still have limited power here, and Marlow and Kröger will be among the last novelistic heroes to grow up and achieve maturity. Which is to say that Conrad's and Mann's *Bildungsromane* are morphologically closer to Goethe's than, say, to Kafka's or Joyce's: or also, turning the matter around, that there were more structural novelties in a decade than in an entire century. Surprising? Maybe — if one sees literature as a restless, self-questioning discourse engaged in a sort of permanent revolution. Not really, if one accepts the idea that inertia rules literature just as many other things, and that the rhythm of literary evolution is thus necessarily uneven: long periods of stability 'punctuated', as Gould and Eldredge would say, by bursts of sudden change like the one I am trying to describe. Why change should occur at all, and how, is something I shall return to after a short technical parenthesis.

Following Barthes and Chatman, contemporary narratology usually groups narrative episodes in two basic classes: 'kernels', abrupt, irreversible choices among widely different options, and 'satellites', slower, subordinate events that qualify and enrich the chosen course. In tune with their respective functions, satellites belong to the narrative 'background' (to use Harald Weinrich's terms), embodying social regularity, whereas the 'foreground' is occupied by kernels, which are typically the hero's doing, and have therefore enjoyed a structural centrality in most narrative forms, from epos to tragedies and short stories. From the eighteenth century onwards, though, at one with the growing regularity and interdependence of social life, novels started to bridge the gap between background and foreground, and in the narrative slowdown that followed, the role of kernels started to decline, and that of satellites to grow. The *Bildungsroman* happened to come into being at the very moment when the new trend and the old conventions were balancing each other, and out of this unique historical conjuncture arose a narrative episode of unprecedented flexibility. An episode organized as an *opportunity*: as a satellite, hence with nothing frightening about it — yet a satellite so rich in potentialities that the hero may well want to transform it into a kernel. An opportunity in which the social background offers a choice to the hero: the ideal medium for a story of socialization and growth — of socialization *as* subjective growth. And also a beautiful way to rescue one of the key words of modernity — 'experience' — from its metaphysical captivity, offering a visible form to its sense of discovery free from danger, of renewal without revolution, of homogeneity between the individual and his world. Would experience be such an important word for us, had not the novelistic episode taught us to recognize its features?

Growth, then, and experience. But the world of the late *Bildungsroman* has solidified into impersonal institutions, while youth has become more vulnerable, and reluctant to grow. With a shift in narrative agency, opportunities turn into accidents: kernels are no longer produced *by* the hero as turning points of his free growth — but *against* him, by a world that is thoroughly indifferent to his personal development. In the abstract and often uselessly painful tests enforced by the school, the individualized socialization of Western modernity seems to collapse back into archaic initiation rituals; more informally, seemingly harmless episodes turn out to be, most strikingly in Kafka, all-encompassing trials.[2] Or, as we also say, 'traumas': a metaphor which, according to the *OED*, crystallized in 1916. At the polar opposite from experience, in a trauma the external world proves too strong for the subject — too violent: and institutions (whether run by Irish Jesuits, Austro-Hungarian bureaucrats, or American managers) tend of course to be careless and shattering in their violence. And as the whole process of socialization becomes more violent, regression inevitably acquires its symbolic prominence: faced with an increasing probability of being wounded, it is quite reasonable for the subject to try and make himself, so to speak, smaller and smaller. Under artillery fire, the favourite position of World War I infantrymen was the fetal one.

This centrality of traumas — and hence of kernels, which are their narrative equivalents — helps to throw some light on a feature of literary evolution that is often misunderstood. In most historical accounts, literature is taken to change not only at a constant rhythm, rather than in punctuated fashion, but also along a sort of straight line: one step after another, one genre after another. At first sight, the early twentieth century seems to support this view, suggesting a continuity between the *Bildungsroman*, its 'late' version, and modernism. After all, don't we have the biographical evidence of Musil and Rilke and Kafka and Joyce, who all inherited the *Bildungsroman*, developed it, and then proceeded 'from' it 'to' modernism? Well, not quite. If the internal structure of the novelistic episode is a good test for literary evolution, and I think it is, then we have three data with which to work: first, the nineteenth-century episode, where the functions of a kernel and those of a satellite balance each other; second, the late *Bildungsroman* episode, which is undoubtedly closer to a kernel; third, the modernist episode, best exemplified by *Ulysses*, which is an overgrown satellite and nothing else. Do these three forms constitute a continuum, with the late *Bildungsroman* acting as the transitional form between the nineteenth century and modernism? Obviously not. We need a different geometrical pattern here — not a straight line but a tree, with plenty of bifurcations for genres to branch off from each other. What really happened when the nineteenth-century episode fell apart, then, was that narratives could concentrate *either* on kernels *or* on satellites: the late *Bildungsroman* chose the former, and modernism the latter. From their common starting point they proceeded in opposite directions: there isn't the least morphological continuity here, biographical data notwithstanding.

In fact, one is tempted to claim that — in its commitment to traumatic narratives — the late *Bildungsroman*, far from preparing modernism, did, if anything, *delay* it. But of this, more at the end.

The prevalence of traumas and kernels also created a taxonomic paradox, since they were making it difficult for the late *Bildungsroman* to be a novel at all. To use the terms of *Soul and Forms*, which Lukács was writing in those very years, 'isolated events' and 'fateful moments' characterize the short story, or the novella, making it a more 'rigorous' form than the novel, but also preventing it from representing 'the evolution of an entire life' — the *Bildung* — that is the novel's prerogative. But the *Zeitgeist* must have been on the side of the short story, and in stark contrast to Goethe and Austen, to Stendhal and Eliot, and even to Balzac and Flaubert, who had shown little or no interest for short narratives, all the authors of the late *Bildungsroman* were superb writers of short stories. So much so, in fact, that they even attempted an alchemic experiment — the '*Bildungsnovelle*', so to speak, best represented by *Youth* and *Tonio Kröger* (and, in a less consistent way, by *Jakob von Gunten* and *Törless*). Interestingly enough, in order to blend novella and novel together, Conrad and Mann both had recourse to the same device of 'variation': the repeated shipwrecks of *Youth* or the emotional frustrations of *Tonio Kröger*. Combining the symbolic clarity of the short story's 'fateful moment' and the empirical variety of the novel's 'entire life', a story constructed on the principle of variation seems indeed to embody the best of both forms: except that it isn't really a story, as its parts are not held together by chronological relations, but only by the semantic affinity perceived by the unifying gaze of conscious memory — by the adult wisdom of Conrad's 'strong bond of the sea', or Mann's haut-bourgeois composure. And here, of course, was the rub: because this retrospective maturity, so close to the spirit of the classical *Bildungsroman*, was unappealing, and even incomprehensible, to the younger generation of writers. As early as 1904 Joyce had rejected precisely the all-encompassing voice that had made *Youth* and *Tonio Kröger* possible: 'So capricious are we,' he wrote in the very first sketch for *Portrait*, 'that we cannot or will not conceive the past in any other than its iron memorial aspect. Yet the past assuredly implies a fluid succession of presents.'

A fluid succession of presents: 'Yesterday Basini was still the same, just as Törless himself; but a trapdoor had opened, and Basini had precipitated.' *Törless* is a veritable collection of such traumatic discoveries — imaginary numbers and moral duplicity, the infinity of the universe, homosexuality, the hero's 'second sight'. The novel's meaning is thus no longer to be found in the narrative, diachronic relation *between* events, but rather *within* each single 'present', taken as a self-contained, discontinuous entity. Törless's adolescence is less a story than a string of lyrical moments; after all, his keenest perplexity has to do with finding the right words — better, the right *tropes* for his discoveries. After the *Bildungsnovelle*, then, the crisis of the novelistic episode was generating another hybrid: the lyric novel. Unusual as it is for a great lyric poet to write a good novel, in these years Rainer Maria Rilke did it (he did it twice, if one considers the shorter text of 1898, *Ewald Tragy*), and in *Malte* he posed a kind of symbolic problem that only the later poetry of the *Elegies* would solve. As for Joyce, in *Stephen Hero* he had already mentioned Dante's *Vita Nuova* — where the story is literally a pre-text for the lyrics — as a possible model; later on, his hero's theory of epiphanies was another attempt to subordinate the narrative line to punctual poetic vision. Lyric novel then. But what are those privileged moments that set poetry in motion?

Predictably, they are traumas again — traumatic discoveries of sexual desires that are as a rule both socially illicit and psychically irresistible. After the collapse of Youth and Experience, this new, alien force (the Es, the Id) pulverizes the only remaining cornerstone of the *Bildungsroman*: the unity of the Ego. Yet its disruptive violence also brings to light the hidden worlds and unexpected possibilities out of which will arise the 'poetry' thematized in the late *Bildungsroman*. What Tonio learns from his secret, unreciprocated love for Hans Hansen proves 'more important than what he was forced to learn at school'. It is in the bedroom of a prostitute that Törless has a first glimpse of that 'second sight' that will be his major intellectual discovery. It is while approaching a prostitute that Stephen 'awakes from a slumber of centuries' and feels the 'dark presence' of his future poetry. All these episodes (which have no equivalent in the tradition of the *Bildungsroman*) are announcing that new reality — the unconscious, taken in a broad sense — which will play a crucial role in the constitution of twentieth-century subjects, and in their socialization, which will consist more and more in an attempt to address and colonize, in a variety of ways, their prelogical, submerged selves. (Modernism, in fact, may well be seen as the aesthetic protagonist of this new pattern of Western socialization, in which unconscious psychic materials are no longer obstacles but instruments of social integration.) But in our novels such long-term developments are not in sight yet; we have the problem, not the solution, and the unconscious is still the spellbinding discovery of an unforgettable page by Rilke, in which Malte, still a child, finds himself trapped in alien clothes, and in front of a mirror: 'For a moment I felt an undescribable, painful, and useless longing for myself: then there was "he" alone, *der Unbekannte*, the Unknown; there was nothing but him. ... He was the stronger of the two, and I was the mirror.' A child facing a mirror, and trying on some new clothes, like so many young novelistic heroes. Two archetypal scenes in the construction of Western identity: but the emergence of the unconscious-unknown reverses their meaning, and they appear now as the destructive trauma described in *Beyond the Pleasure Principle*, against which, writes Freud, 'all possible means of defense will be mobilized.' 'God, all these thoughts, these strange desires, this looking for and groping after a meaning! To be able to dream, to be able to sleep! And what is to come — let it come.' Thus Jakob von Gunten; and Törless: ' "You used to be so gentle to me ..." "Shut up! It wasn't me! ... It was a dream ... A whim." ' — It wasn't me! Törless's disavowal of his emotions sums up the strategy of the genre as a whole: having always dealt with the growth of self-consciousness, it was inevitable for the *Bildungsroman* to recoil in front of an alien, unconscious reality. As is often the case in history, the very conditions of its previous supremacy prevented the *Bildungsroman* from playing a central role in the new phase of Western socialization.

'I am in between two worlds, at home in neither, and as a consequence everything is a bit difficult for me.' Although Tonio Kröger's last letter to his Russian friend seems to announce the emotional fissures to come, his story suggests that the acclaimed artist and impeccable bourgeois is in fact at home in *both* worlds. 'But what had there been, in all that time in which he had become what he now was? Waste; desert; chill; and spirit! And art!' Waste — and art! The secret of Mann's narrative lies in the simultaneity of the two: the humiliations inflicted on the young Tonio always reshaped by the beautiful words of the mature Kröger. This isn't just a *story* of traumas overcome: it is Mann's very style that is anti-traumatic. To borrow another expression from *Beyond the Pleasure Principle*, it is a style that unfailingly brings those shocks 'to the level of consciousness', ordering as 'lived experiences' within conscious memory those traumas that, for the younger generation, will aimlessly follow each other as so many unrelated presents. This is even truer of *Youth*, where Marlow defuses traumas by transforming them, so to speak, into instant memories:

> We pumped watch and watch, for dear life, and it seemed to last for months, for years, for all eternity, as though we had been dead and gone to a hell for sailors. ... And there was something in me that thought, By Jove! This is the deuce of an adventure — something you read about; and it is my first voyage as second mate — and I am only twenty — and here I am. ... I was pleased. I would not have given up the experience for worlds.

How remote is this 'something' from Malte's *'Unbekannte'*! It is a reflexive, friendly support to personal identity, not a threat to it: and whereas Rilke's hero will feel 'a useless longing' for himself, Marlow still cries aloud his confident 'here I am!'

Rilke on traumas: 'If words did indeed exist for that event, I was still too much of a child to find them.' In Benjamin's famous essay, traumas force Baudelaire's poet to cry out in pain; in Musil, they are encircled by a labyrinth of dubious tropes; in Kafka, hidden by a haze of qualifying clauses. In all these instances, the clearest sign that a trauma has occurred is the fact that language no longer works well: that it is impossible to find adequate words for the reality of war, as millions of veterans will put it. In Conrad and Mann, on the contrary, the proper words are always at hand. As Marlow's ship blows up, nearly killing him, 'the sky and the serenity of the sea were distinctly surprising. I suppose I expected to see them convulsed with horror.' In a single sentence Conrad combines here hyperbole and scepticism, danger and distance, youth and maturity: the trauma has been overcome because it has been *stylized*. And the style is, of course, irony: 'Yet, on the other hand, Tonio himself could feel that the writing of verses was something excessive, something definitely unbecoming, and, to a certain extent, he had to concur with all those people who considered it a surprising occupation. Except that ...' Tonio's poetic vocation has arisen out of a sequence of traumas, and its discovery was itself a trauma: but the words of 'all those people' — the prosaic words of common opinion — are there, and are capable of counterbalancing all that. It is the antiradicalism of irony, which so much delighted the young Mann: irony as mediation, as the diplomatic device to keep crises under control. Irony as the style of good breeding, and of bourgeois decorum:

'As an artist, Lisaweta, one is already enough of an adventurer in his heart. Outwardly, one has to wear proper clothes, for God's sake, and behave like a respectable person!' And also, why not, write in a sensible, civilized style.

And behave like a respectable person. According to Norbert Elias, this would imply first of all holding in check one's animal drives. This is why table manners are such a basic test of urbanity, and also why dinners have had such relevance in civilized and civilizing novels. But *Portrait* opens with a dinner's violent disruption, and *Amerika*'s first turning point is announced — at dinner again — by the violation of all bodily and linguistic etiquette. The hour of *Dinnerdämmerung* has come, and it is not (only) a joke, because dinners embody a vital social need — the need for *neutralized spaces*: for areas where people may meet without fear under the protection of clear, unchallenged rules. (The rules themselves, of course, cannot be socially neutral, but they apply impartially to everybody.) Moreover, when a world enjoys a Hundred Years' Peace (as Polanyi defined European history between 1815 and 1914) neutralized spaces tend inevitably to increase in number, and to occupy a growing portion of social existence: the *Bildungsroman*, for instance, took place almost entirely within their boundaries — and understandably so, because in such areas individual growth is sheltered, and easier, and less painful. When Mr. Green's behaviour at dinner makes Karl Rossmann feel that 'their inevitable social and worldly relations were to bring total victory or total defeat to one of them', what Kafka implies is that the neutralized space par excellence has reverted to the state of a battlefield; so that, even from this side, the subject is no longer shielded from traumatic encounters.

Free, equal, homogeneous enclaves — within societies that are emphatically not so. There is something so unreal about neutralized spaces that their disruption, however threatening, has nonetheless a liberating quality. As in the tragic paradigm, the pain of trauma is the price for truth: for the discovery of a violent power behind the facade of an impartial civilization: for the epiphany of 'Class relations', as Jean-Marie Straub retitled his lucid, pitiless version of *Amerika*. But something is missing from these social epiphanies: *claritas*, as Stephen would say. The moment of revelation turns out to be also the moment of maximum ambiguity — most notably in *Amerika*, where hesitant and contradictory formulations are the puzzling echoes of all narrative turning points (so much so that Straub, in order to establish his reading of the text, erased from it almost all of the dialogue). Despite Stephen's peroration on 'radiance', then, the striking fact about epiphanies, in the late *Bildungsroman*, is that they are indeed signs — but signs belonging to an unknown language, 'a language we cannot hear', as Törless puts it. 'He was thinking of ancient paintings he had seen in museums without understanding them well. He was waiting for something, just as he always had when in front of those paintings — but nothing ever happened. What would it be? ... Something extraordinary, never seen before ... words could not say it.' 'My life here', writes Jakob von Gunten, 'strikes me at times as an incomprehensible dream.' And Malte: 'If words did indeed exist for that event, I was still too much of a child to find them. ... I obscurely foresaw that life would be full of strange things, meant for *one* only, and unspeakable.'

What promised to be a painful knowledge turns out to be a painful enigma. Rilke again:

> What did that old woman want from me, creeping out of that hole? ... I understood that the old pencil was a sign, a sign for the initiated; a sign that drop-outs know well. ... This was two weeks ago. But now not a single day goes by without one of these encounters. Not only at sunset, but at midday, in the most crowded streets, all of a sudden a short man appears, or an old woman, and they beckon, they show me something, and then they vanish.

We are so used to grieving for the meaninglessness of life that, at first, it may be hard to realize that Malte's complaint, here, is that the world is too meaning*ful*; there are too many signs, and signs are threats, because in them lurks *der Unbekannte*, the Unknown. ('All / Is not itself', as the *Elegies* will say.) This veritable semiotic anxiety will then produce its own form of regression: the yearning for a world freed from the plurality, and hence the uncertainties, of signification: for a world of Un-signs, as it were. It is Tonio Kröger's longing for what is 'irrelevant and simple'. It is Kafka's impossible hope — so well described by Sartre — for a stretch of flat meaningless nature. It is Jakob's compulsive drive to hide all personal signs under a uniform. But the most revealing figure is Rilke's 'mother': the *Erklärer*, the 'light-thrower' of *Malte* and the *Elegies*, who turns signs into things; who de-semiotizes, so to say, what is 'nightly-suspect', restoring in its place the solid reality of 'those dear, usual objects which stay there, *ohne Hintersinn*, with no hidden meaning, good, simple, unequivocal'.

> Till that moment he had not known how beautiful and peaceful life could be. The green square of paper pinned round the lamp cast down a tender shade. On the dresser was a plate of sausages and white pudding and on the shelf there were eggs. They would be for the breakfast in the morning after the communion in the college chapel. White pudding and eggs and sausages and cups of tea. How simple and beautiful was life after all!

It is the most obedient evening in Stephen's life, and his words echo Malte's delight in the lack of hidden meaning of good simple objects. But it is only a passing moment: in the struggle among signs and Un-signs *Portrait* sides resolutely with the former. 'Many in our day', reads the 1904 sketch, 'cannot avoid a choice between sensitiveness and dullness.' Simplicity may be a form of dullness, after all: sensitiveness, the capacity to perceive and confront Rilke's unknown — to see 'a winged form flying above the waves and slowly climbing the air'. As *Portrait*'s great epiphanic passage begins, Stephen faces the same question — 'What did it mean?' — that paralysed his predecessors. But in his case the enigmatic meaningfulness of 'a girl gazing out to sea' is 'an instant of ecstasy', and his prompt mention of medieval illuminations — signs growing out of signs — shows that he is perfectly at home in the labyrinth of endless semiosis. In a Rimbaud-like episode of initiation and rebirth — a perfect kernel, in all possible respects — epiphany redeems the meaninglessness of the past, revealing that Stephen's youth had always had a secret aim — the discovery of an artist's 'soul' — and that it has finally achieved it. One could not wish for a better closure for Joyce's ambitious *Künstlerroman*.

Except that, of course, *Portrait* goes on, and the following chapter, compared to all previous ones, is strikingly blank and pointless. Neither visions nor rebirths here, but idle conversations to kill the time; no menacing institutions, but a banal everydayness; the seer has turned into a young pedant, for whom epiphany is just a tricky philological riddle. In every respect, this last chapter seems to have one possible function only: the merely negative one of invalidating what, up to then, had been constructed as the meaning of the novel. And here, of course, one may claim that all texts play this trick upon themselves, plunging happily into unreadability, with which the case is dismissed. But I happen to think that literature is not produced to multiply symbolic tensions out of control, but rather to reduce and contain them: and as the ending of *Portrait* seems to contradict this thesis, I have to provide an explanation for it. Why this slowdown, this anticlimax? Why should Joyce undo the meaningful irreversibility of chapter four? Indeed, why did Joyce write the fifth chapter at all?

Perhaps the last question is stupid, period. Or perhaps it would be stupid if novels were perfect beings, thoroughly inspired by one unitary design: in which case all that is there *has* to be there, and the idea of a useless element is simply inconceivable. Like most things human, however, novels may be closer to *bricolage* than to engineering: and in this case images, episodes, or whole chapters would be highly contingent products, which may, or may not, be where they are; and may, or may not, work well in the overall structure. Writers make literature, as the saying goes, but cannot chose the conditions, nor the materials with which they make it.

Let us think of Joyce as *bricoleur*, then, musing upon the materials put at his disposal by literary tradition. First of all, reasonably enough, the debris of the *Bildungsroman* itself: Flaubert's flat prose of the world, where the very notions of experience and growth had disappeared. 'It would be easier', wrote Pound in 1917, 'to compare *Portrait* with *L'éducation sentimentale* than with anything else': true, but to revitalize the form of the *Bildungsroman* Joyce also needed an antidote to Flaubert's insignificant everydayness. And what better choice than the poetry of traumatic intensity originating in Baudelaire, and developed by Rimbaud, who was, after all, the archetypal 'artist as a young man' of the late nineteenth century? In a somewhat similar vein to Benjamin's Baudelaire, Joyce's use of epiphany may thus be seen as a bold attempt to confront traumas and their linguistic turbulence: to master and 'use' them as means for self-revelation, and growth (and even socialization: they point the road to adult work).

Flaubert and Rimbaud: a plausible matrix for *Portrait*'s well-known oscillation between 'dullness' and 'sensitiveness', between a meaningless everyday (preferably at the beginning of chapters), and meaningful revelations (preferably at the end). Flaubert and Rimbaud ... Flaubert *or* Rimbaud, we should rather say. Their versions of experience were so utterly incompatible that, 'in the end', no reconciliation or compromise was possible: Joyce had to choose between them. But what should be the criterion for his final choice? What made more sense in terms of the regeneration of the *Bildungsroman* was clear enough: Rimbaud, kernels, epiphany, chapter four. But just as clear was what made more sense within the wider historical trend of Western narrative: Flaubert, satellites, prosaic dullness, chapter five. Joyce's double choice was, then, the sign of a double bind: of a contradiction that even the most scrupulous *bricoleur* in the world (which Joyce certainly was) could not hope to solve. The merit of *Portrait* lies precisely in not having solved its problem. Or in plainer words: the merit of *Portrait* lies in its being an unmistakable failure.

Portrait as *bricolage*; as *bricolage manqué*: as a structural failure. And fortunately so. Had it been otherwise — had *Portrait* been, say, as good as *Tonio Kröger* — we would have no *Ulysses*. Thomas Mann's *bricolage* — his essayistic mediation between the realistic novel and German tragic thought — proved so successful that he preserved its formula for half a century, thereby introducing no great novelty in the evolution of narrative. Inertia is the dominant force, even in the realm of literature, and as long as a form works well there is no reason to modify it: *it is only when it fails that the need for change arises*. Think of the internal articulation of the late *Bildungsroman*: at one pole the smooth formal achievements of *Youth* and *Tonio Kröger*; at the opposite one, the increasingly unstable-unfinished mosaics of *Malte*, *Portrait*, and *Amerika* (with *Törless* and *Jakob von Gunten* somewhere in between). In terms of historical evolution: on one side a well-functioning *Bildungsroman*, and the Long Nineteenth Century of Conrad and Mann; on the opposite side, erratic and unsteady structures, and the modernism-to-come of Rilke, Kafka, and Joyce. Doesn't this suggest that the latter trio was literally *forced* into modernism by its failure with the previous form? Without failures, I insist, we would have no literary evolution, because we would have no *need* for it. Perhaps, then, we should stop pretending that failures are really masterpieces in disguise, and should learn to accept them as failures, appreciating their unique historical role.

To the inevitable question, 'Would you mind explaining what exactly *is* a literary failure?' I would reply, although sketchily, that it is the sort of thing that occurs when a form deals with problems it is unable to solve. This definition presupposes in its turn the idea that symbolic forms are fundamentally problem-solving devices: that they are the means through which the cultural tensions and paradoxes produced by social conflict and historical change are disentangled (or at least reduced). Here lies the so-called social function of literature, with its so-called aesthetic pleasure: solving problems is useful and sweet. So much for my personal convictions, which I have tried to justify more at length elsewhere, and which are of course thoroughly questionable. But if they strike you as plausible, then a form that addresses problems it cannot solve is indeed a failure, socially and aesthetically. For the late *Bildungsroman* — this most painfully intelligent and strangely short-lived episode of modern literature — this insoluble problem was the trauma. The trauma introduced discontinuity within novelistic temporality, generating centrifugal tendencies toward the short story and the lyric; it disrupted the unity of the Ego, putting the language of self-consciousness out of work; it dismantled neutralized spaces, originating a regressive semiotic anxiety. In the end, nothing was left of the form of the *Bildungsroman*: a phase of Western socialization had come to an end, a phase the *Bildungsroman* had both represented and contributed to. The strength of its pattern — the stubbornness, in a sense — can be seen nowhere as clearly as in Joyce, who devoted a first novel to Stephen Dedalus, and then a second novel, and then the beginning of a third novel. But the nineteenth-century individual — Stephen Hero — could hardly survive in the new context, and in an epoch-making change the decentered subjectivity of Leopold Bloom — this more adaptable, more 'developed' form of bourgeois identity — set the pattern for twentieth-century socialization.

Just one final remark, on *Portrait* again. As we saw, we have here a Flaubertian field of repetition, satellites, and meaninglessness — and a Rimbaudian one of epiphanies, kernels, and meaningfulness. Joyce's first representation of epiphany, however, had been more complicated than that. *Stephen Hero*, chapter 25:

> He was passing through Eccles St one evening, one misty evening, with all these thoughts dancing the dance of unrest in his brain when a trivial incident set him composing some ardent verses which he entitled a 'Villanelle of the Temptress'. A young lady was standing on the steps of one of those brown brick houses which seem the very incarnation of Irish paralysis. A young gentleman was leaning on the rusty railings of the area. Stephen as he passed on his quest heard the following fragment of colloquy out of which he received an impression keen enough to afflict his sensitiveness very severely.

The Young Lady — (drawing discreetly) ... O, yes ... I was ... at the ... cha ... pel ...

The Young Gentleman — (inaudibly) ... I ... (again inaudibly) ... I ...

The Young Lady — (softly) ... O ... but you're ... ve ... ry ... wick ... ed ...

This triviality made him think of collecting many such moments together in a book of epiphanies. By epiphany he meant a sudden spiritual manifestation, whether in the vulgarity of speech or of gesture or in a memorable phase of the mind itself. He believed that it was for the man of letters to record these epiphanies with extreme care, seeing that they themselves are the most delicate and evanescent of moments.

Triviality, vulgarity, the commonplaces uttered by the Young Lady ... The significance of what is insignificant: this was the pathbreaking discovery made by Stephen Dedalus as he was walking, of all places, through Eccles St: *Ulysses*. But the encounter had taken place too early, and the oxymoron of a meaningful meaninglessness was still too elusive: and so, in that same page of *Stephen Hero*, Joyce hid his discovery under a stratum of symbolist *topoi* — ardent, extreme care, delicate, evanescent — that make it almost unrecognizable. Inertia again; the resistance to change; the new that can manifest itself only in disguise, as a compromise formation. And an ephemeral compromise: after *Stephen Hero*, Joyce soon veered away from 'superficial' epiphanies, soon to replace them with the 'deeply deep' ones of *Portrait*. Yet that early page had been written, and since Stanislaus Joyce was nice enough not to throw it away, it may teach us that literary change does not occur as a straight growth (*Stephen Hero*, then *Portrait*, then *Ulysses*), but as a branching process (*Stephen Hero*, and then either *Portrait* or *Ulysses*). Joyce chose the *Portrait* way, as we know, but it led nowhere. Far from preparing *Ulysses*, *Portrait* delayed it, and in order to invent Bloom, Joyce had to forget his *Künstlerroman* and retrace his steps all the way back to that initial bifurcation near Eccles St. It is an arabesque that may be taken as a miniature for the late *Bildungsroman* as a whole: every tree has its dead branches, and this, alas, was one of them.

Notes

Preface

1. 'After two years of terror, the ruling classes of continental Europe regrouped, determined to defend themselves as much against the revolt of their sons as against a proletarian revolution. During the second half of the century, in the most advanced countries of the continent, the combined mechanisms of obligatory education and military service would ensure social discipline, more than compensating for the potential disorder deriving from the granting of universal suffrage. The schools were modelled on the barracks: the literature of the period abounds in reports of arbitrary punishments inflicted on young students by teachers who were stricter than any sergeant.' Sergio Luzzatto, 'Young Rebels and Revolutionaries 1789–1917', in Giovanni Levi and Jean-Claude Schmitt, eds, *History of Youth*, Harvard University Press 1997 [orig. 1994], vol. II, p. 176.

2. Georg Wilhelm Friedrich Hegel, *Aesthetics*, Oxford University Press 1975 [1823–29], p. 162.

3. Ibid., p. 169 (translation slightly modified).

4. 'The *Bildungsroman* and its Significance in the History of Realism', 1936–38, in *Speech Genres and Other Late Essays*, Texas University Press, Austin 1986, pp. 23–4.

5. If the relationship between the two bourgeoisies plays almost no role in the *Bildungsroman*, it is on the other hand a very significant theme in the parallel (and very German) genre of the *Künstlerroman*, or artist's novel, on which Herbert Marcuse wrote his dissertation in 1922.

6. In other words: although the difference between the bourgeoisie and the old ruling class is quite clear in the sphere of work, in the sphere of 'free time' it becomes by contrast hardly visible. 'Bourgeois sociability' (as Agulhon calls it), just like the 'everyday familiarity' described in this book, don't therefore embody new and 'bourgeois' types of behaviour, but are simply the democratization of activities which, within aristocratic circles, still preserved an exclusive character (conversation, for instance). Whence my disagreement with Wolfgang Kaschuba's otherwise very engaging essay on *Bürgerlichkeit*, which maintains that bourgeois identity is most recognizable precisely in the sphere of culture. (See Wolfgang Kaschuba, 'German *Bürgerlichkeit* after 1800. Culture as symbolic Practice', in Jürgen Kocka and Allan Mitchell, eds, *Bourgeois Society in Nineteenth-century Europe*, Berg, Oxford 1993 [1988].)

7. Difficult; not impossible. There is a distinct female *Bildungsroman*, for instance (the Austen–Eliot thread; Charlotte Brontë), although basically limited to English literature. An interesting parallel case is that of genres functioning as 'proxies' for the *Bildungsroman* — like the novel of adultery, which offers middle-class wives a freedom they had never enjoyed before (whence the '*nouvelle puberté*' that Rudolphe arouses in Emma Bovary, or the 'awakening' described by Kate Chopin). As for non-European cultures, certain stories of supernatural metamorphosis (Mário de Andrade's *Macunaíma*; Amos Tutuola's *My Life in the Bush of Ghosts*) seem to lie at the meeting point between rites of passage, mythic narratives, and the *Bildungsroman*.

8. Michelle Perrot, 'Worker Youth: from the Workshop to the Factory', in

Giovanni Levi and Jean-Claude Schmitt, eds, *History of Youth*, vol. II, p. 67.

As for young women, another historian of youth has reached, via a different route, the same general conclusions: 'Personal independence can only emerge where there is the opportunity to make choices and decisions... Furthermore, the opportunity to confront new ideas... is a question of mobility. The greater the mobility in adolescence, the greater the likelihood of an independent personality developing. ... Here again there were differences between males and females. *For reasons of morality, girls always had far less scope.*' (Michael Mitterauer, *A History of Youth*, Blackwell, Oxford 1992 [1986], pp. 28–9; emphasis added.)

9. Perrot, p. 74.

10. I was completely unprepared for this discovery, as is perfectly visible — almost a geological trace of my initial project — at the ending of the *Meister* chapter, and the beginning of the Stendhal one. One senses here the desire to establish an *immediate* link between the history of literature and the history of ideology (and especially of political ideology): a hypothesis which is in itself perfectly plausible, but happens to be wrong — and thus requires all sorts of ad hoc theoretical contortions.

11. The essay, entitled 'On Literary Evolution', was published in the second edition of *Signs Taken for Wonders*, in 1988. Only after reading Darwin (and Gould) did I realize that literary theory had actually already worked on morphological imperfection in the magic years of Russian Formalism (especially Viktor Sklovsky, in his studies of *Don Quixote* and *War and Peace*). But this aspect of formalist theory is so foreign to the normative (and panglossian) vocation of literary criticism that it has been universally ignored.

Introduction

1. For reasons given in the first chapter, I shall use the term 'classical *Bildungsroman*', when necessary, to distinguish the narrative model created by Goethe and Austen from the *Bildungsroman* genre as a whole. 'Novel of formation' or perhaps the more precise 'novel of socialization' are other possible generic labels, which have not been used however to avoid unnecessary confusion.

Let me also justify, in passing, a double exclusion that would not have displeased General De Gaulle: that of the Russian novel (represented here only by authors closely linked to the Western European tradition, such as Pushkin and Turgenev), and the American novel (missing completely). As for Russia, this is due to the persistence of a marked religious dimension (be it the 'politico-national' version of *War and Peace*, or Dostoevsky's ethico-metaphysical one), which attaches meaning to individual existence in ways unthinkable in the fully secularized universe of the Western European *Bildungsroman*. The same is true for American narrative, where, in addition, 'nature' retains a symbolic value alien to the essentially urban thematics of the European novel; and where the hero's decisive experience, unlike in Europe, is not an encounter with the 'unknown,' but with an 'alien' — usually an Indian or a Black.

2. Karl Mannheim, 'The Problem of Generations', in *Essays on the Sociology of Knowledge* (ed. Paul Kecskemeti), London 1952, p.300 (footnote 2).

3. Especially striking has been the constant antipathy between School and the Novel: School condemns novel reading as having bad effects on students — and the novel, for its part, requires its hero to leave his studies early on, and treats school as a useless interlude that can be done without.

This opposition indicates the dual nature of modern socialization: an objective-specialistic process aimed at 'functional integration' *into* the social order, which is the task of institutionalized education — and a subjective-generic process aimed at the 'symbolic legitimation' *of* the social order, which is the task of literature. In other words: institutions such as schools act to socialize behavior, regardless of individual belief (one must *know* one's lesson — not believe in its truth). Institutions such as the novel aim at socializing what *The Theory of the Novel* calls our 'soul': they see to that more or less conscious 'consent' that guarantees continuity between individual existence and social structure. The enigmatic success of the *Teufelspakt* in modern culture — which surely has no fear of hell — is a sort of allegory of this second process: not only does modern man have a soul, but he can sell it, and there are always bidders.

4. Erwin Panofsky, 'Die Perspektive als "Symbolische Form",' *Vorträge der Bibliothek Warburg*, Leipzig — Berlin 1927.

5. This also explains the *Bildungsroman*'s fondness for middle-class heroes: while the limits of the social spectrum usually remain relatively stable (conditions of extreme wealth and extreme poverty tend to change slowly), 'in the middle' anything can happen — each individual can 'make it' or 'be broken' on his own, and life starts to resemble a novel. What makes the middle class an ideal sounding-board of modernity is thus the *co-presence* of hope and disillusion: the very opposite of the Anglo-Saxon 'middle-class theory of the novel', which explains the link between the novel and the middle class in terms of the 'rise' and social consolidation of the latter. When this actually does take place — with the great bureaucratization of the past hundred years — it means the end of the Western novel in its original form: its two prime subverters, Kafka and Joyce, have very vividly portrayed, among other things, the metamorphis of the middle class in this century.

6. On the thematic level we see this process of 'regularization' in the novelistic hero's socialization. A young, intelligent, single male newly arrived in the city, this socially mobile and undefined hero embodies modernity's most tempestuous aspects: that is why it is precisely him, and not his more faded companions, who must be given 'form' — even if it means, as is often the case, weakening his more lively features.

7. The four principal types of *Bildungsroman* highlight different problematic aspects of the formation of the Ego. The English *Bildungsroman* typically emphasizes the preliminary fear of the outside world as a menace for individual identity, while the Goethian ideal of harmony as a delicate compromise of heterogeneous commitments focuses on the Ego's internal dynamics. The French novelists take a more indirect course, which downplays the Ego proper and emphasizes the dangers of an excessively forceful Super-Ego or Id, embodied in Stendhalian 'idea of duty' and Balzacian 'passion'. In the latter instances — where, at the 'story' level, the Ego is much weaker than in the former — the 'discourse' level symptomatically becomes more important, and the narrator's *doxa* restores that equilibrium which the hero no longer possesses.

8. 'Everyday life', 'ordinary administration', 'anthropocentrism', 'personality', 'experience', 'opportunity': each of these terms will be discussed at length in the first chapter, since we find them most fully and coherently expressed in the classical *Bildungsroman*. Although much remains to be done here, I have nonetheless plunged forward, hoping to have contributed somewhat to an area of study extremely interesting and rich in possibilities.

9. Dostoevsky, *precisely because* he is a novelist of final truths and of tragic and exceptional circumstances — as Bakhtin himself has noted more than

once — never wrote a *Bildungsroman*. And Adorno, who has always insisted on art's vocation to truth, has never shown much interest in the *Bildungsroman*, or in the novel in general.

10.   We should not be surprised then if, in tracing the various narrative rhetorics of nineteenth-century historiography in *Metahistory*, Hayden White mentions comedy, romance, satire and tragedy — but never the novel. Although the novel and historiography flourish during the same period, the former creates in fact — with 'everyday life' and 'ordinary administration' — a sort of *parallel temporality* which nineteenth-century historiography does not perceive as truly historical The history of mentality and of the *longue durée* has of course changed all that, so that the object, and at times even the categories, of much contemporary historiography reveal strong similarities to those of the novel.

Chapter 1

1.   Wilhelm Dilthey, *Esperienza vissuta e poesia* (*Das Erlebnis und die Dichtung*, 1905), Milan 1947, pp.198–9.

2.   Ibid., p.259.

3.   Goethe started to write the *Theatralische Sendung* in 1777, and interrupted it in 1785.

4.   *Pride and Prejudice* can be summarized along nearly identical lines: Elizabeth finally finds herself when she recognizes Darcy's 'superiority' — and Darcy, for his part, reveals his nobility by using his money and private information (power and omniscience link him to the Tower) not to humiliate Elizabeth, but to allow her to happily conclude her youth. On the 'socializing' features of love in Austen, thus Lionel Trilling. '[As an anonymous reviewer wrote in the *North British Review* in 1870] Jane Austen was 'saturated' with a 'Platonic idea' — she was committed to the idea of 'intelligent love', according to which the deepest and truest relationship that can exist between human beings is pedagogic. This relationship consists in the giving and receiving of knowledge about right conduct, in the formation of one person's character by another, the acceptance of another's guidance in one's own growth' (*Sincerity and Authenticity*, Oxford 1972, p.82).

5.   The expression is used by H.S. Maine in *Ancient Law*, 1861, and quoted by Tony Tanner in *Adultery in the Novel: Contract and Transgression*, Johns Hopkin University Press 1979, p.5.

6.   'Between the individual and the world.' Marriages, no doubt, are contracted between just two individuals: but for Wilhelm and Elizabeth (and the rhetorical structure of the two novels forces the reader to share their point of view) something much wider is at stake, since marriage summarizes and stabilizes all of their social relationships. Natalie (through her ties with the Tower) and Darcy are in fact perfect representatives of the power system typical of the classical *Bildungsroman*.

7.   François Furet, 'The French Revolution is over', in *Interpreting the French Revolution*, Cambridge and Paris, 1981, pp.46, 3.

8.   On this see Harald Weinrich's 'Retorica della felicità' in *Retorica e critica letteraria*, eds. Lea Ritter and Ezio Raimondi, Bologna 1978.

9.   In Hegel too the family is seen as the first step towards overcoming 'ungesellige Geselligkeit', the anti-social sociability of the modern economic sphere: 'The arbitrariness of a single owner's particular needs is one moment in property taken abstractly; but this moment, together with the selfishness of desire, is [in the family] transformed into something ethical, into labour and care for a common possession.' ('The Philosophy of Right' (1821) in *The Philosophy*

of Right and The Philosophy of History, Chicago 1952, section 170, p.60).

Similar considerations in Richard Sennett (*The Fall of Public Man*, Cambridge 1976, p.91): in the family only 'measured appetites' find expression, desires that are circumscribed *a priori* — indicative therefore of the possibility of a 'functional unity of the human species' based on a network of 'natural "sympathies"'.

10. After having declared that the life of the housewife offers the highest example of the self-realization of mankind — because of its internal harmony, 'mastery over the means to our ends', and possibility of developing happiness in oneself and in others — Lothario does not hesitate to suggest it as a model 'for the State' (*Wilhelm Meister*, VII, 6). That it is precisely Lothario who says as much — the most adventurous and extroverted of the characters of *Meister*, and also the most devoted to any sort of public activity — makes the process of 'irradiation' I am trying to describe all the more meaningful.

11. Yuri Lotham, *The Structure of the Artistic Text*, 1970, trans. M. Suino (Ann Arbor: University of Michigan Press 1977), p.241.

12. Agnes Heller, *Everyday Life*, London 1984, pp.4–5, italics mine.

13. 'Man is born for a limited condition; objects which are single, new and definite he is able to look into, and he accustoms himself to make use of such means as are at hand, but when he enters upon a wider sphere he does not know what he wants to do, nor what he should do ...' (*Wilhelm Meister*, VI, 'The Confessions of a Beautiful Soul'). These words are spoken by the uncle of the beautiful soul, who is the source of the Society of the Tower, and therefore of the entire socio-cultural project of the *Years of Apprenticeship*: shortly thereafter, he also launches into a long eulogy of the countryside, which he declares to be immensely superior to the city from the point of view of human self-realization.

14. 'We are moved by the story of a good deed and by the sight of every harmonious object; we then feel that we are not quite in a strange country; we fondly imagine that we are nearer a home, towards which what is best and most inward within us is striving.' (*Wilhelm Meister*, VII, 1.)

15. It is through work that one can cure, at least temporarily, the madness of the Harpist: 'I find the means of curing insanity very simple. They are the same by which you prevent healthy people from becoming insane. Their activity has to be aroused, accustom them to order... An active life brings with it so many incidents that he must feel how true it is that every kind of doubt can be removed by activity.' (*Wilhelm Meister*, V, 16.)

16. Wilhelm von Humboldt, *The Sphere and Duties of Government*, trans. J. Coulthard, London 1854, pp.27–28.

17. Friedrich Schiller, *On the Aesthetic Education of Man*, trans. R. Snell, New Haven 1954, letter 6, pp.44–45.

18. Ibid., letter 27, p.138.

19. Werner Sombart, *The Quintessence of Capitalism*, trans. H. Fertig, New York 1967, p.13.

20. Henri Lefebvre, *Critica della vita quotidiana*, Italian trans. Bari 1977, 1:113–14; originally published as *Critique de la vie quotidienne* (Paris 1958).

21. Karel Kosik, 'Metaphysics of Everyday Life,' in *Dialectics of the Concrete*, trans K. Kovanda and J. Schmidt, Dordrecht 1976, p.43; originally published in Czech (Prague 1963).

22. Heller, *op.cit.*, p.20.

23. Ibid, p.16.

24. Georg Hegel, 'Introduction: Reason in History', in *Lectures on the Philosophy of World History*, trans. H. B. Nisbet, Cambridge 1975, p.85.

25. Ibid.

26. 'Our comparison of novel and drama shows that the novel's manner of portrayal is *closer* to life, or rather to the normal appearance of life, than that of drama'; György Lukács, *The Historical Novel*, trans. H. and S. Mitchell, London 1962, p.138. That this affirmation refers to the *historical* novel renders it, in my opinion, more meaningful still.

27. Heller, *op.cit.*, p.22.

28. Ibid., p.251.

29. Ibid., p.252.

30. Abraham Moles, *Le Kitsch: L'Art du bonheur*, Paris 1971, pp.21, 28, 37.

31. I have discussed the fate of the aesthetic dimension in twentieth-century life in 'From the Waste Land to the Artificial Paradise,' in *Signs Taken for Wonders*, London 1983.

32. Philippe Ariès, *Centuries of Childhood*, Harmondsworth 1979, pp.235–6.

33. Richard Sennett, op. cit.

34. Georg Simmel, 'On the Concept and Tragedy of Culture', in *The Conflict in Modern Culture and Other Essays*, trans. K. P. Etzkorn, New York 1968, pp.27–46, esp. 28–29.

35. György Lukács, *The Theory of the Novel*, trans. A. Bostock, Cambridge, Mass. 1971, pp.133–34, 137–38.

36. The novelistic protagonist can no longer be presented as the hero of the classical epic — shrewd Odysseus, fleet-footed Achilles, wise Nestor. One's Christian name must be, and is, enough — 'Wilhelm', 'Elizabeth'. Such a manner of naming denotes a great familiarity and thus suggests a complete and almost 'natural' knowledge of the person in question, but simultaneously gives to our knowledge, as it were, the utmost liberty, neither constraining it in a precise direction, nor binding it to a clearly defined subject. It is a 'knowledge' that combines a maximum of certainty with a minimum of commitment. It is so open and inexhaustible that it can never truly be put to a test. What happens with novelistic heroes is what happens with our friends and relatives: we know them perfectly, and we do not know who they are.

37. One of the more recent forms of the critique of everyday life has been the critique of the *real* via the *surreal*. Surrealism, in departing from the everyday toward the extraordinary and the surprising... rendered the prosaic unbearable.' Furthermore: 'Under the sign of the Supernatural, the literature of the nineteenth century launched an attack against everyday life that has not lost any of its force'; Lefebvre, *Critica*, pp.34 and 122.

38. Kosik, 'Metaphysics of Everyday Life,' p.43.

39. 'A complete scheme of rites of passage theoretically includes *preliminal* rites (rites of separation); *liminal* rites (rites of transition), and *postliminal* rites (rites of incorporation)', thus Arnold Van Gennep in his classic analysis of primitive initiation, *The Rites of Passage*, trans. M. Vizedom and G. Caffee, Chicago 1960, p.11. The 'transition' space, often associated with youth, is narrow, severely regulated, and merely functional to the passage from the infantile incorporation to the adult one. Once this passage is complete, the transition space loses all value. The pattern is still fully valid for *The Magic Flute*, but its hierarchy is unequivocally overturned in *Meister*. Here the transition of youth is vastly expanded; one lives in it in complete liberty, and, above all, it is transformed into the *most meaningful* part of one's existence, precisely that one which 'deserves being told'. We find an analogous overturning in the relationship between that typical period of transition known as

engagement, and marriage. In archaic societies, courtship and engagement chronologically precede marriage but, from a logical standpoint, are a consequence of it: one must get married, and therefore one must first get engaged, but the value of courtship and engagement ends here; they are purely instrumental. In the modern world, and in the novel, the opposite is true. Marriage is the consequence of a satisfying courtship and engagement, and if therefore the *Bildungsroman ends* with marriages, it nevertheless narrates courtships. The emotive and intellectual centre of gravity has decidedly changed.

40.   Thus Wilhelm to the 'gentleman from C.', who is about to leave for war (*Theatrical Mission*, IV, 11): 'Oh, how fortunate you are to be lead by destiny to where a true man can call upon his best powers, where all that he has become in life, all that he has learned is changed in a moment's time into action and appears in its utmost splendour!' Needless to say, the gentleman from C. sees it in a totally different way, and his answer chills Wilhelm's epic enthusiasms.

41.   This dialectic of meaning and episode is the basis of the novelistic *chapter*. An extraordinary mechanism of self-segmentation of a text, the chapter balances our satisfaction with what we have learned (the meaning that has been attributed to an event) and our curiosity for what we still do not know (that meaning is as a rule always incomplete). We can thus continue our reading (giving in to our curiosity) or interrupt it (declaring ourselves satisfied). The narrative structure authorizes both choices and thereby renders symbolically plausible the irregular rhythm of interruptions and resumptions to which the reader is in any case constrained by the size of a novel.

Thanks to this true miracle of self-regulation that is the chapter, the novel imparts to literary enjoyment a totally unique character, which Poe in his *Philosophy of Composition* found self-destructive: 'If any work is too long to be read at one sitting, we must be content to dispense with the immensely important effect derivable from unity of impression — for, if two sittings be required, the affairs of the world interfere, and everything like totality is at once destroyed' (in *Selected Writings of Edgar Allan Poe*, ed. David Galloway, Harmondsworth 1967, p.482.) What Poe did not see is that the novel quite simply *wants* the affairs of the world to interfere. Unlike the short story, or the lyric poem, it does not see everyday life as heterogeneous to its own conventions but as its chosen object, with which it must also 'materially' mix itself — via the patient rhythm of interruptions and resumptions — in order to give it a form and a meaning.

We have here the two major paths — one diurnal and domestic, the other lunar and estranging — of modern literature. And not only of literature: if many cinematographical effects find a surprising anticipation in Poe's theoretical writings, radio and television, on the contrary, pursue with other means the colonialization of everyday existence begun by the novelistic genre. (It is a parallel that could go on forever: to enjoy cinema one must leave the home — radio and television bring the world into a room... At the movies a three-minute delay is a tragedy — we move constantly to and from the television with utter peace of mind... At the movies all must be dark except the screen — we watch television with at least one light on, as if to remind ourselves at all costs of our domestic context...) As long as we are on the subject: the principal novelty of Wim Wenders' films consists precisely in his having 'weakened' the cinematographic episode and the narrative concatenation of plot, thereby bringing both of these closer to novelistic composition. Coincidence or not, Wenders' second film was a remake of *Wilhelm Meister*.

42.   See once again Ariès, *Centuries of Childhood*, especially the second part.

43. 'During most of the ceremonies which have been discussed, and especially during the transition periods, a special language is employed which in some cases includes an entire vocabulary unknown or unusual in the society as a whole, and in others consists simply of a prohibition against using certain words in the common tongue'; Van Gennep, *Rites of Passage*, p.169. We will see how in the *Bildungsroman* it is instead the *obligation* to use the common language that seems to hold.

44. Conversation is thus totally different from Bakhtin's 'heteroglossia'. The *Bildungsroman*'s socializing vocation brings with it the *reduction* of the plurality of social languages to a 'middle of the road' convention with which they may all easily participate.

45. On this point see the fourth chapter of Sennett, *Fall of Public Man*, and especially Jürgen Habermas, *Strukturwandel der Öffentlichkeit*, Neuwied 1962.

46. Peter Brooks, *The Novel of Worldliness*, Princeton 1969, p.54.

47. Heller, *Sociologia*, p.106. On the implications of everyday life, anthropomorphic thought, and artistic production, see also the first chapters of Lukács's *Aesthetics*.

48. Kosik, 'Metaphysics of Everyday Life', p.46

49. Ever since Defoe's *Robinson Crusoe*, whose protagonist, 'born in the city of York in the year 1632', remains in England until 1650. But on the civil war that, after all, permits him to be a merchant in peace and quiet, there is not a word.

50. See Reinhardt Koselleck, *Kritik und Krise. Ein Beitrag zur Pathogenese der bürgerlichen Welt*, Freiburg-München: Verlag Karl Alber 1959.

51. Alexis de Tocqueville, *The Ancièn Régime and the French Revolution*, Manchester 1966, p.164. This passage too is from the chapter cited further above.

52. This hypothesis was advanced some time ago by Francis Mulhern in 'Ideology and Literary Form — A comment', *New Left Review*, 91, 1975, pp.86–7.

53. This is why the novel (even the 'historical' novel) always exiles 'world-historical personalities' to the margins of the narration. Our culture finds such personalities fascinating because it sees in them the embodiment of great social forces in all of their violent one-sidedness: to depict them within the domain of everyday life would be to lower the novel to gossip.

54. G.W.F. Hegel, *Phenomenology of Spirit*, Oxford 1979, p.11.

55. I use the term 'point of view' in accordance with the restrictive definition proposed by Seymour Chatman in *Story and Discourse*, Cornell 1968, ch. 4.

56. This parallelism between the story narrated, and the process of reading it, was noticed by Karl Morgenstern already in the early 1820s: 'It will justly bear the name *Bildungsroman* firstly and primarily on account of its thematic material, because it portrays the *Bildung* of the hero in its beginnings and growth to a certain stage of completeness; and also secondly because it is by virtue of this portrayal that it furthers the reader's *Bildung* to a much greater extent than any other kind of novel' (quoted by Martin Swales in *The German Bildungsroman from Wieland to Hesse*, Princeton 1978, p. 12).

57. On this, see Tony Tanner's introduction to the Penguin edition of *Pride and Prejudice*.

58. Goethe, *Werke*, Stuttgart — Berlin: Jubiläumsausgabe, T.G. Cotta, 1902–1907, v. 21, p.238.

59. Edmund Burke, *Reflections on the Revolution in France*, 1790, Harmondsworth 1981, p. 188.

60. G.W.F. Hegel, *Phenomenology of Spirit, cit.*, p.50.

61. G.W.F. Hegel, *The Philosophy of Right, cit.*, section 320, p.106.

62. Jonathan Culler, 'Literary History, Allegory, and Semiology', *New Literary History*, VII, 2, 1976, p.263. In recent American criticism, the seminal essay on symbol and allegory was Paul De Man's 'The Rhetoric of Temporality', now in *Blindness and Insight*, 2nd edn, revised, Minneapolis 1983.

63. In a famous Goethian reflection:
'There is a great difference between a poet looking for the particular in view of the general, and seeing the general in the particular. The first manner breeds allegory, where the particular is valid only as an example of the general; the second is instead precisely the nature of poetry: it states a particular without thinking of and indicating the general from the outset. But he who captures this particular profoundly comprehends the general with it, yet without realizing it — or realizing it only later' (*Werke, cit.*, vol. 38, p.261).

64. T. W. Adorno, 'Notes on Kafka' in *Prisms*, Cambridge, Mass., 1981, p.245.

65. An analogous similarity with the deep structure of the classical *Bildungsroman* applies to a slightly different version of the concept of the symbol, summarized by Todorov (*Theories of the Symbol*, Oxford 1982, p.181) as follows: 'the ideal relation ... is the one in which an element is both part and image of the whole, in which it "participates" without ceasing for all that to "resemble".'
Wilhelm thus on the one hand 'participates' in the overall project of the Tower — he is a part, a function of it; on the other hand, he 'reflects' it in its entirety in the many-sided harmony of his individual personality. (This being alternatively the part of a whole and its concentrated image is also to be found in one of the greatest musical achievements of the turn of the eighteenth century: the concerto for single instrument and orchestra.)

66. Unlike *Wilhelm Meister* — the son of a merchant — Elizabeth Bennet does not belong to the bourgeoisie, but to the lower village gentry. It is however likely that the extreme modesty of the Bennet income was seen in a broad sense as a 'bourgeois' feature, especially since it is contrasted with the enormous landed wealth of Darcy. Furthermore, Elizabeth's true companions and 'helpers' in the novel are not her parents but the Gardiners, who are indeed bourgeois (from Cheapside even): a sociological detail that becomes meaningful only in the context of the hypothesis proposed here.

67. 'Nothing was of greater importance to the English system at the time of the French Revolution than the relatively easy recruitment of the class of gentlemen. It made England unique among European nations ... Emma's snobbery, then, is nothing less than a contravention of the best — and safest — tendency of English social life' (Lionel Trilling, 'Emma and the Legend of Jane Austen', in *Beyond Culture*, 1955, London, 1966, pp.41–2). 'No "compromise" or "alliance" — the usual terms employed — was, in fact, possible as between contrasting civilizations. No conscious tactical arrangement, no deal lasting for a season, was conceivable between social forces [agrarian and industrial capitalism] of this complexity and magnitude. Amalgamation was the only real possibility, a fusion of different classes and their diverse cultures into one social order capable of guaranteeing social stability and keeping the proletariat in its place' (Tom Nairn, 'The British Political Elite', *New Left Review*, 23, 1964, p.20). This thesis receives a rich analytic development in Raymond Williams' *The English Novel from Dickens to Lawrence*, London 1973, p.21ff.

68. Giuliano Baioni, *Classicismo e rivoluzione. Goethe e la rivoluzione*

francese, Napoli 1969; especially chapter five. Baioni's text however deserves to be read in its entirety.

69.   In Marxist thought, the theses I feel most akin to in this respect are those of Louis Althusser, in his interpretation of ideology as a *necessary illusion* (anticipated, one may add, by a philosophical tradition that goes back at least as far as Spinoza's *Ethics*). I am not convinced however by Althusser's further thesis (accepted by Althusserian critics such as Macherey and Eagleton) according to which art and literature 'de-naturalize', or 'displace', or 'unmask' ideological production. I find the very opposite to be true, and have tried to prove as much in 'The Soul and the Harpy', in *Signs Taken For Wonders, cit.*

70.   The composition of the seventeenth-eighteenth-century reading public strengthens this hypothesis. While in our century the typical reader of novels is an adolescent, in whose reading it is reasonable to see a sort of 'preparation for the future', in those times the percentage of adult readers was far greater (in addition to the fact that 'adulthood' began much earlier than it does now), and, quite plausibly, the novel functioned as a 'rereading of the past', a pleasurable confirmation that the choices which in any case had to be made were truly the best ones possible.

71.   *The Theory of the Novel, cit.*, p.62.

72.   Darcy's letter to Elizabeth (*Pride and Prejudice*, 35) takes the form of a legal deposition: 'Your feelings, I know, will bestow attention unwillingly; but I demand it of your justice'; 'two offences of a very different nature … you last night laid to my charge'; 'for the truth of everything here related, I can appeal more particularly to the testimony of Col. Fitzwilliam.' As in a trial, it must be ascertained *what happened*: when this is done, moral judgement automatically results.

73.   For the distinction between 'significance' as 'value', and 'significance' as 'meaning', see Gottlob Frege's classic essay *Über Sinn und Bedeutung*. The questions dealt with in these pages will become even more apparent in the dominant trend of the English *Bildungsroman*: I will return to them at length in chapter four.

74.   On this see Giulio Preti, *Retorica e logica*, Torino 1968, especially Chapter IV.

75.   Renaissance tragedy consists precisely in the sudden and incomprehensible severing of the world of facts — the dramatic *fabula* — from the value system that should comment on and legitimate it. (I have expounded this thesis at length in 'The Great Eclipse: Tragic Form as the Deconsecration of Sovereignty', in *Signs Taken for Wonders, cit.*) The novel — especially the classical *Bildungsroman* — inherits the tragic split: but it works at healing it. On this, see Erich Heller's splendid essay on Goethe's elusion of tragedy, in *The Disinherited Mind*, London 1952.

76.   *The Theory of the Novel, cit.*, pp.64–5.

77.   See Raymond Williams' *The English Novel from Dickens to Lawrence, cit.*, p.22, and the entry 'Improve', in *Keywords*, Glasgow 1976.

78.   To Edmund's anxious question — 'How may my honesty at least rise to any distinction?' (*Mansfield Park*, 21) — Mary Crawford answers evasively. But Austen, for her part, has no doubts: Edmund and Fanny Price remain 'honest' to the end, but find themselves, therefore, if not exactly poor, not nearly as rich as could have been expected.

Chapter 2

1.   In his most important critical work, *Racine and Shakespeare*, Stendhal

advocates a literature capable of representing great political crises; but when he starts writing his own novels, some years later, he immediately gives up the idea.

2. On the relationship between this work and Stendhal's novels, see Fernand Rudé, *Stendhal et la pensée sociale de son temps*, Paris 1967, pp.115–180; and Geneviève Mouilland, 'Sociologie des romans de Stendhal', in *Sociologie de la création littéraire*, Unesco, 1968.

3. As Mannheim observes in his 1930 essay, 'On the Nature of Economic Ambition and Its Significance for the Social Education of Man', 'one cannot properly speak of "career" in Napoleon's case, since his success was the product of struggle: rather than following the already given paths to success, Napoleon autonomously created by his own efforts his place and role in the world.'

4. Jürgen Habermas, *Legitimation Crisis*, London 1976, pp.113–4.

5. This antithesis between Tradition and Reason explains why the novel, unlike ancient epos, never became the centre of our cultural system. If a social order is legitimized by tradition, its fundamental 'document' will be the *story* of its origins, which is indeed epos. But if its legitimacy lies in a timeless rational paradigm, narration will not be the fundamental, 'original' discourse. This is why the novel cannot deal with revolutions, and has to concentrate on their problematic consequence, which is the discrepancy between 'soul' and 'second nature,' professed values and actual ones.

6. Norbert Elias, *The Civilizing Process: The History of Manners*, Oxford 1978, p.258. Elias's impulses, to be sure, are similar to the drives examined by Freud in *Civilization and Its Discontents*: elementary physical needs or aggressive impulses; whereas in Stendhal, it is an abstract and rationalized political credo that has to be repressed. What seems essential here, however, is not the nature of what is repressed, but the fact that repression makes it the individual's 'core of identity'. Julien's ideals, in fact, are more likely to become one with his 'experience of self' precisely because they are more abstract. Moreover, the episode of Napoleon's portrait (which Madame de Rênal believes to be that of Julien's lover) shows us the *naiveté* of identifying 'interiority' and 'intimacy'.

7. Pushkin is particularly explicit in identifying contradiction as the essence and fascination of the new novelistic hero: 'His features fascinate me, / His bent for dreamy meditation, / His strangeness, free of affectation, / His frigidly dissecting mind.' (*Eugene Onegin*, I, 45).

Further along (III, 10–11), we are told that Eugene is neither the 'noble hero' Grandison, nor Polidori's cursed Vampire. Neither does he lie halfway between the two: 'There is no middle way for you,' says the Abbé Pirard to Julien (*The Red and the Black*, II, 31). He is, if anything, both of them at once, a union of extremes: 'A strangely bleak and reckless creature, / Issue of Heaven or of Hell, / Proud demon, angel — who can tell?' (*Eugene Onegin*, VIII, 24).

8. In what appears to be a unique occurrence in the history of the novel, Julien, Fabrizio, Onegin and Pechorin all take part in the political strife of the era, and all on the same side. Defeated, they nevertheless manage to survive, keeping alive that restlessness which a pacified Europe would rather forget.

9. Jules de Gaultier, *La Bovarysme*, Paris: Societé de Mercure de France, 1902, pp.66–7, 13, 16, 32, 157. An earlier, shorter version of the work had appeared in 1892.

10. Octave Mannoni, *Clefs pour l'Imaginaire ou l'Autre Scène*, Paris 1969, p.172.

11. Ibid, pp. 10–11.

12. Jean Paul Sartre, *Being and Nothingness*, London 1957, pp.56, 57, 58.

13.   I deal more extensively with this, and other similar problems in this section, in 'Kindergarten', now in *Signs Taken for Wonders, cit.*

14.   On the distinction of 'story' and 'discourse', which originates with Emile Benveniste, see Seymour Chatman, *Story and Discourse*, cit.; and Harald Weinrich, *Tempus*, Stuttgart 1964, It. transl. Bolonga 1978.

15.   Particularly instructive in this instance is a comparison of Onegin with Faust. Both being men of the 'great world', they have girls belonging, and almost doomed to the 'little world', fall in love with them. Faust seduces Gretchen, driving her to murder, insanity and death: but when he wakes up in the poem's second part, 'life's pulses awaken' (*Faust*, 4679), and Gretchen is totally forgotten. Onegin, by refusing to seduce Tatyana, in his own way 'saves' her: he then falls in love with her again, risking his own perdition.

16.   See, for instance, Franco Fortini's 'Introduction' to his Italian translation of *Faust*, Milan 1980, especially pp.XXVIII–XXXX.

17.   Lionel Trilling, *Manners, Morals, and the Novel*, 1947, in *The Liberal Imagination*, London 1951, p.215. Concerning Balzacian 'realism', which we shall discuss more fully in Chapter 3, Fredric Jameson writes: 'The Real is thus — virtually by definition in the fallen world of capitalism — that which resists desire, that bedrock against which the desiring subject knows the breakup of hope' ('Realism and Desire: Balzac and the Problem of the Subject,' in *The Political Unconscious*, London 1981, pp.183–4).

18.   'The Ego seeks to bring the influence of the external world to bear upon the Id and its tendencies, and endeavours to substitute the reality principle for the pleasure principle which reigns unrestrictedly in the Id. For the Ego, perception plays the part which in the Id falls to instinct. The Ego represents what may be called reason and common sense, in contrast to the Id, which contains the passions.' (*The Ego and the Id*, The Standard Edition, London 1961, vol.19, p.25).

19.   'The pleasure principle (and its modification, the reality principle)': *Beyond the Pleasure Principle*, The Standard Edition, London 1955, vol. 18, p.35.

Paul Ricoeur comments: 'Man is man only if he postpones satisfaction, abandons possibilities of enjoyment, and temporarily tolerates a certain degree of unpleasure on the long indirect road to pleasure ... the admission of unpleasure into any human behaviour may be regarded as the roundabout path the pleasure principle takes in order to gain ultimate dominance.' (*Freud and Philosophy: An Essay on Interpretation*, New Haven 1970, pp.283–4).

20.   *The Ego and the Id, cit.*, p.83.

21.   See in particular Roland Barthes, *S/Z*, London 1975, and Gérard Genette, 'Vraisemblance et motivation' in *Figures II*, Paris, 1969.

22.   Yuri M. Lotham, *The Structure of the Artistic Text, cit.*, pp.269, 277.

23.   Ibid., p.274.

24.   *Des effets de la Terreur*, cited in Jean Starobinsky, 1789: *Les Emblemes de la raison*, Paris 1979, p.47.

25.   Ibid., p.47.

26.   François Furet, *op.cit.*, p.74.

27.   Albert O. Hirschmann, *The Passions and the Interests. Political Arguments for Capitalism before its Triumph*, Princeton 1977.

28.   *The Theory of Moral Sentiments*, 1759, Part VI, Section I, 'Of the Character of the individual so far as it affects his own Happiness; or of Prudence': 'Security is the first and principal object of prudence. It is averse to expose our health, our fortune, our rank, or reputation, to any sort of hazard. It

is rather cautious than enterprising, and more anxious to preserve the advantages which we already possess than forward to prompt us to the acquisition of still greater advantages ... if [the prudent man] enters into any new projects or enterprises, they are likely to be well concerted and well prepared. He can never be hurried or driven into them by any necessity, but has always time and leisure to deliberate soberly and coolly concerning what are likely to be their consequences.' (London 1853, pp.311 and 315.)

Thus for his part Schumpeter: 'Capitalist civilization is rationalistic and "anti-heroic". The two go together of course. Success in industry and commerce requires a lot of stamina, yet industrial and commercial activity is essentially unheroic in the knight's sense — no flourishing of swords about it, not much physical prowess, no chance to gallop the armoured horse into the enemy, preferably a heretic or heathen — and the ideology that glorifies the idea of fighting for fighting's sake and of victory for victory's sake understandably withers in the office among all the columns of figures ... . Not sharing or even disliking warrior ideology that conflicts with its "rational" utilitarianism, the industrial and commercial bourgeoisie is fundamentally pacifist and inclined to insist on the application of the moral precepts of private life to international relations.' (Joseph A. Schumpeter, *Capitalism, Socialism, and Democracy*, 1942, New York 1947, pp.127–8).

29.   Sombart, *cit.*, pp.203, 205, 206.

30.   See Fernanad Rudé, *Stendhal et la pensée sociale de son temps*, *cit.*, pp.195–209.

31.   Alexis de Tocqueville, *Democracy in America*, Part II, Book IV, Ch. VI: 'What Sort of Despotism Democratic Nations Have To Fear.'

32.   John Stuart Mill, *On Liberty*, 1859, in *Utilitarianism*, London 1978, pp.189–90.

33.   Although I am no expert on the subject, it seems to me that Benjamin Franklin owes his fame to symbolic more than technical reasons. His much acclaimed lightning rod protects the prudent bourgeois from the unknown *par excellence*: it is only right that it should have replaced the cross on our rooftops.

34.   Georges Lefebvre, *Napoleon From 18th Brumaire to Tilsit 1799–1807*, London 1969, vol. 1, p.60.

35.   Yuri M Lotman, 'The Origin of Plot in the Light of Typology', 1973, *Poetics Today*, 1–2, 1979, p.163.

36.   Cf. *Tempus*, Chapter IV and V in particular.

37.   Jean Starobinsky, 'Stendhal Pseudonyme' in *L'Oeil vivant: essai*, Paris 1961.

38.   Edgar Z. Friedenberg, *The Vanishing Adolescent*, 1959, New York 1970, pp.29 and 34.

39.   *Storia della letteratura tedesca, 1700–1820*, Turin 1964, p.544.

40.   *The Ego and the Id*, *cit.*, p.33.

41.   *Beyond the Pleasure Principle*, *cit.*, p.42.

42.   If the novelistic hero is never 'himself' in the various roles he must assume, Faust, on the other hand, always is: 'His wholeness', Cesare Cases tells us, 'is due to that everpresent "streben"; the latter is embodied time and again in different enterprises and passions, which Faust, unlike his gloomy companion, fully indulges in ... each stage is thoroughly complete in itself, and appears in the next as a fleeting memory at most.' ('Introduction' to the Italian trans. of *Faust*, Turin 1965, p.LIII.)

43.   György Lukács, *Goethe and His Age*, 1949, New York 1969, p.235.

44.   The only exception is the Gretchen episode, which, not surprisingly, is

the most 'novelistic' of the poem, as well as that in which the union of 'streben' and historical change is weakest.

45. David A. Miller, *Narrative and Its Discontents*, Princeton 1981, p.211.

46. Søren Kierkegaard, *Fear and Trembling: Repitition*, Princeton 1983, pp.38–9, 132.

47. A good example is Onegin's behaviour at the ball (*Eugene Onegin*, V.29–VI.2). He seduces Olga not because he desires her, but to 'pay the score' with Liensky who, having brought him to the ball, has forced him to see Tatyana again.

48. In this sense, Julien's attempted murder of Madame de Rênal appears as a sort of Black Mass wedding, which, tellingly, takes place in church, and on a Sunday. Julien's act is the expression of a savagely unrestrained freedom, and, at the same time, its ultimate self-suppression.

49. The only attempt contrary to this pattern (Chapter X of *Onegin*, in which Eugene takes part in the Decembrist rising) was destroyed by Pushkin because he feared censorship: an act which paradoxically confirms the paradigm of isolation. Censorship establishes through force what is 'conceivable' and what is not. If Stendhal and later Lermontov had 'interiorized' the inconceivability of a politically meaningful destiny, Pushkin was instead forced to do so by external constraints. But whether by 'civilized' means or not, the spirit of the times in each case managed to avoid the undesired ending.

50. Walter Benjamin, 'The Story Teller: Reflections on the Works of Nikolai Leskov' in Hannah Arendt, ed., *Illuminations*, London 1973, p.101.

51. This accounts for the necessity of inexplicable and irrational episodes such as the attempted murder of Madame de Rênal and, more in general, for the importance all these texts ascribe to love: the latter allows the story to take decisive turns without any need for rational motivation, and even postulates *a priori* their irrational nature.

52. Mikhail Bakhtin, 'Epic and Novel,' 1938, in *The Dialogic Imagination*, ed. M. Holquist, trans. C. Emerson and M. Holquist, Texas 1981, pp.13 and 15.

53. Roland Barthes, *Writing Degree Zero & Elements of Semiology*, London, 1984, pp.26, 27, 28.

54. In Émile Benveniste, 'Les relations de temps dans le verbe français' in *Problèmes de linguistique générale*, Paris 1966, p.238.

55. Ibid., p.241.

56. Benveniste, 'Structures des relations de personne dans le verbe' in *op.cit.*, p.228.

57. Benveniste, 'Les relations de temps dans le verbe français,' *cit.*, p.287.

58. Benjamin, *op.cit.*, pp.86–87.

59. Weinrich, *Tempus*, *cit.*, p.183.

60. Weinrich, 'Structures narratives du myth', *Poétique*, vol.1, 1970.

Chapter 3

1. To quote one of the first to have studied the phenomenon (Pitirim Sorokin, *Social Mobility*, New York-London: Harper and Brothers, 1927, p.516): 'If on the one hand social mobility broadens the mind and makes mental life more intensive, on the other hand it facilitates superficiality …. We are driven to versatility and short cuts at some expense to truth and depth.' It is the portrait of Lucien de Rubempré.

2. Julien achieves 'fame' only after his attempted murder of Madame de Rênal; and Fabrizio when, wasted from desire for Clelia, he upsets all of Parma with his mystical and desperate sermons. These situations tell us, in an extreme

way, that in Stendhal the moment of 'success' is that in which the hero is most *estranged* from himself and his public role: an antithesis between subjective desire and objective outcome inconceivable in the Balzacian universe.

3. 'Success' was originally synonymous with 'succession', to an office or the like; it was later used (a shift still perceptible in German *Erfolg*) to indicate the outcome of an action, and not necessarily a favourable one ('good' or 'ill success'); and finally, in the nineteenth century, although the first such examples date back three centuries earlier, it was established in its current meaning, which is by far the least precise.

4. Karl Mannheim, 'On the Nature of Economic Ambition and Its Significance for the Social Education of Man', in *op. cit.*, pp.237, 214.

5. Georg Simmel, 'Fashion' (1904), in *On Individuality and Social Forms: Selected Writings* (ed. Donald N. Levine), Chicago 1971, pp.297, 303.

6. Marc-Alain Descamps, *Psychosociologie de la mode*, Paris 1979, pp.15, 16, 207, 208.

7. At this point, something must be said about *Bel-Ami*, where individual success does not lead to ruin, but obtains rather the full approval of society. Just think of the ending, when the unscrupulous social climber, marrying the girl whose mother he seduced for sport, receives the bishop's blessing in the Madeleine — 'You, sir, whose genius lifts you above others, you who write, who teach, who advise, you have a fine mission to fulfil, a fine example to offer...' Or reread that brief episode, almost an allegory, in which the Walter family discovers the amazing likeness of Bel-Ami to the Christ of a famous painting: a Christ who walks on water — who 'arrives' (*parvient*) where no-one would have thought possible, with that same supernatural ease with which Georges Duroi ascends the social pyramid...

There is no doubt about it, here success meets with a different fate than in Balzac: and this is so because the social universe of *Bel-Ami* is different. In the *Comédie Humaine* the world is an 'arena', where thousands of men and women engage in simultaneous combat for a myriad of disparate reasons; in *Bel-Ami* it is a *ladder*, where rivals are encountered one at a time, and moreover are few in number and lacking in strength. In Balzac, success comes and goes in enormous and erratic leaps and bounds; in Maupassant it is gradual, predictable, almost rationed out in advance. In Balzac, fortunes are made by inventing something new, even if it is a fraud; in Maupassant one achieves success, more modestly, because already existing posts become free — newspaper editor, husband of Madame Forestier, newspaper owner, husband of Suzanne Walter.

In short: the world of *Bel-Ami* is, at bottom, the world of *bureaucracy*; success, a *career*. The salient features of this novel can be found one by one in Mannheim's analysis of bureaucratic career: only so, on the other hand, is it possible to understand how a work that quite frankly is mediocre, and sloppily implausible, managed to grip the imagination of nineteenth-century France. A career in government was notoriously the most widespread form of social mobility in the last century, but it never became an important narrative theme: by clothing it with eros and adventure Maupassant bestowed a dark allure to an itinerary that in reality had nothing at all fascinating about it.

8. G. W. F. Hegel, *The Philosophy of World History*, New York 1902, p.46.

9. Mikhail Bakhtin, 'Forms of Time and Chronotope in the Novel', 1937–8, in *The Dialogic Imagination*, *cit.*, pp.123–6.

10. Throughout the *Philosophy of World History* Hegel insists that only the state enables men to produce, perceive, and record history in its fullest sense.

11.   A particularly incisive example: 'The effort at significant representation is thematically presented, again and again, as the preoccupation with hidden machinery, with the thing behind, the forms of its manifestation and the extent of its revelation .... The conspiracies that move history, the power of those who are powerful precisely because their action remain invisible ... such are the model of life controlled, manipulated, given its true explanation and significance from behind, most often in a secret and conspiratiorial realm' (Peter Brooks, *The Melodramatic Imagination*, Clinton, Mass. and London: Yale University Press 1976, pp.119–20).

12.   That Balzac's 'entrepreneurs' are usually 'bankers', 'usurers' and the like is, in all likelihood, the obvious consequence of the predominance of finance capital in early French capitalism. But this sociologically obligatory choice has the very important symbolic consequence of centring narration on the most 'mobile' and 'skeptical' — the most *realistic* — cultural form of economic power: of a power, adds Sombart, that can remain such only if it has 'the capacity for forming judgments about the world and men'. When Jacques Collin singles out Rastignac, or Lucien, and decides to wager on their success, his is a small-scale enactment of high-risk speculative investment: not by chance does he begin by lending his proteges large sums of money.

13.   Jacob Burkhardt, *Reflections on History*, London 1943 (written in 1872–3), p.20.

14.   Ibid., pp.218–19.

15.   Ibid., pp.211–12

16.   Ibid., p.219.

17.   Fernand Braudel, *Afterthoughts on Material Civilization and Capitalism*, Johns Hopkins UP 1977.

18.   Eric J. Hobsbawn, *The Age of Revolution. Europe 1789–1848*, London 1977, and *The Age of Capital. 1848–1875*, London: Weidenfeld and Nicolson 1975.

19.   Christopher Prendergast, *Balzac. Fiction and Melodrama*, London: Edward Arnold 1978, pp.50–2.

20.   Richard Sennett, *The Fall of Public Man, cit.*, pp.138–9 and 19.

21.   Theodor W. Adorno, 'Balzac-Lektüre', in *Noten zur Literatur*, Frankfurt am Main 1974, pp.149, 153.

22.   For an excellent reconstruction of the 'narrative' potential capitalism brought to nineteenth-century mentality, see Marshall Berman's *All That Is Solid Melts Into Air. The Experience of Modernity*, New York: Simon and Schuster 1982.

23.   From Harold Robbins to *Dallas*, the most popular narrative forms of the past twenty years have all taken up this aspect of Balzac's work. Personified and nasty, capitalism is once again unpredictable, and it restores the syncopated pace of fashion, when it is not fashion itself or barely distinguishable from it — like the film industry in Robbins's trilogy, a veritable *Lost Illusions, absit iniuria verbis*, of contemporary narrative. Even the never-ending progression of television serials was already foreshadowed by the polycentric and continually expanding structure of the *Comédie Humaine*.

24.   'Forms of Time and Chronotope in the Novel', *cit.*, p.247.

25.   Karl Marx and Friedrich Engels, *The Communist Manifesto*, 1848: I reproduce here Samuel Moore's translation (London, 1888), also used by Marshall Berman in his splendid philological and conceptual analysis of this passage, *op. cit.*, pp.87–129.

26.   I have discussed the narrative function of the metropolis in Balzac more

in depth in 'Homo Palpitans. Balzac's Novels and Urban Personality', in *Signs Taken for Wonders, cit.*

27. Charles Darwin, *The Origin of Species,* 1859, Harmondsworth: Penguin, 1982, p.126. It is a point which Darwin comes back to again and again.

28. The homosexual component of friendship, usually quite openly expressed in classical culture, reappears here with such a slight and uniform shift that it can hardly be the result of chance: Werner marries Wilhelm's sister, and Wilhelm marries Lothario's sister; Darcy and Bingley marry two sisters, and so perhaps would have Arkady and Bazarov (if Bazarov had not died), and Lenski and Onegin (if Onegin had not killed him after having 'seduced' his fiancée); duel aside, this situation is echoed somewhat with David Copperfield and Steerforth. In *Lost Illusions* David Sechard marries Lucien's sister, but the true drama of friendship will be consummated in Paris.

29. For Hegel friendship is born '... when individuals still live in actual relationships which are indefinite on both sides ...' (*Aesthetics: Lectures on Fine Art,* Oxford 1975, vol. I, p.568). Tönnies places it in the domain of urban *Gesellschaft,* where the weakening of family and traditional ties encourages the creation of different bonds, founded on 'similarity of ... intellectual attitude' and on 'crafts or callings ... of similar nature' (*Communities and Society,* New York 1963, p.43).

30. 'The plot itself is subordinated to the task of coordinating and exposing languages to each other. The novelistic plot must organize the exposure of social languages and ideologies, the exhibiting and experiencing of such languages' ('Discourse in the Novel', 1934–5, in *The Dialogic Imagination, cit.,* p.365).

31. Max Horkheimer and Theodor W. Adorno, 'The Genesis of Stupidity', in *Dialectic of Enlightenment,* London 1979.

32. This yielding of realistic 'disillusionment' to a fascination with narration is analyzed at length in D.A. Miller's essay 'Balzac's Illusions Lost and Found', *Yale French Studies,* 67, 1984.

33. Jacques Collin's favorite remark — 'I assume the role of Providence': uttered both in *Père Goriot* and *Lost Illusions* — condemns him to never succeed. Where everyone is out to take care of themselves, there is no room for Providence; and when, in *A Harlot High and Low,* Balzac builds the narration on two conflicting 'providences' only, reviving the basic pattern of the duel, the result is a boring novel, coming to life only when it contradicts its own premises. We are again reminded of Jacobean theater, which delighted in the metaphor of chess, but only achieved greatness when the 'players' disappeared and the pieces moved of their own accord; when instead the metaphor was taken seriously (as in Middleton's *Game at Chesse*), the result was tedious indeed.

34. The passage — whose original source I was unable to locate — is quoted and commented on by Vittorio Strada in his 'Introduction' to Lukács, Bakhtin and others, *Problemi di teoria del romanzo,* Italian trans., Torino: Einaudi 1976, p.XXX.

35. *Tempus, cit.,* p.129.

36. Ibid., pp.135–6

37. In *S/Z* Roland Barthes maintains that Balzacian 'realism' is founded on the manifestation of a univocal and conclusive 'meaning'. That may be true for *Sarrasine,* which is a mystery tale, but it is definitely not true for most of the *Comédie Humaine.* I must confess I have never understood why Barthes chose to build a theory of narrative realism on such an atypical text.

38. Jean-Paul Sartre, *What is Literature?,* New York 1965, p.49.

39.   Gérard Genette, *op. cit.*, pp.88, 90, 91.
40.   Ibid., p.85: 'Determination [in Balzac] is almost always pseudo-determination ... we believe its suspect abundance does nothing more than ultimately underline that which it would mask: *the arbitrariness of the story.*'
41.   Hints in this direction in Seymour Chatman, *Story and Discourse, cit.*, chs. 2 and 5.
42.   I have examined more in depth this and other related questions in 'The Soul and the Harpy', in *Signs Taken for Wonders, cit.*
43.   Barthes, *S/Z. cit.*, pp.97, 185.
44.   Ibid., p.206.
45.   Genette, *op. cit.*, p.85.
46.   If this devaluation of discourse and of the narrator as the bearers of Balzacian ideology seems too abrupt, just think of how the various genres of mass literature work. In this boundless domain of the ideologization of reality, which takes shape — wholly by coincidence? — in the decades of the *Comédie*, the function of the narrator is practically nil, and the meaning of the text is entrusted entirely to the organization of plot.
47.   Heinrich Lausberg, *Elemente der literarischen Rhetorik*, München 1967, par.249.
48.   Sombart, *op. cit.*, p.13.
49.   Eric J. Hobsbawn, *The Age of Revolution, cit.*, p.226.
50.   See Richard Sennett, *The Fall of Public Man, cit.*, chapters 7 and 8; and Eric J. Hobsbawn, *The Age of Revolution, cit.*, ch.10. In his parody of the *Bildungsroman — Confessions of Felix Krull, Confidence Man*, Thomas Mann highlights this new phenomenon: 'Now observe this youth in ragged clothes, alone, friendless, and lost in the crowd, wandering through this bright and alien world. He has no money with which to take any real part in the joys of civilization. ... But his senses are lively, his mind attentive and alert; he sees, he enjoys, he assimilates ... . And what a happy institution the shop window is! How lucky that stores, bazaars, salons, that market places and emporia of luxury do not stingily hide their treasures indoors, but shower them forth in glittering profusion, in inexhaustible variety, spreading them out like a splendid offering behind shining plate glass.'
      Krull, of course, will be able to break any and all windows; but not Frédéric Moreau, who seems to illustrate the mix of imaginative mobility and real immobility that fatally grips us before this happy institution.
51.   Leo Bersani, 'Realism and the Fear of Desire', in *A Future for Astyanax*, London: Marion Boyars, 1978, pp.66–7.
52.   In his first semiological analysis of realistic conventions ('L'Effet de Réel', *Communications*, 11, 1968), Roland Barthes sees the 'effet de réel' precisely in those elements of the text that demonstrate 'a resistance to meaning: a resistance that confirms the great mythical contrast of the lived (or the living) and the intelligible'. My only objection to this splendid article is that it gives an 'interstitial' version of realism ('realism is always something partial, sporadic, confined to "details"'), whereas I believe that the ideology and rhetoric of realism must be located in the macrostructures of plot, point of view, and ending.
53.   'Yes! Very funny this terrible thing is. A man that is born falls into a dream like a man who falls into the sea. If he tries to climb out into the air as inexperienced people endeavour to do, he drowns — *nicht wahr?*' (Joseph Conrad, *Lord Jim*, ch. 20).
54.   Karl Marx, 'Money', *Third Manuscript* in *Early Writings*, Harmondsworth and London 1975, p.377.

55. Cfr. Lionel Trilling, *Sincerity and Authenticity, cit.*, pp.122–5.

56. Georg Simmel, 'On the Concept of Tragedy in Culture', in *The Conflict in Modern Culture and Other Essays*, New York 1968, p.44.

57. Ibid., p.42. Later on Simmel emphasizes that cultural works, '... in their development, have a logic of their own ... they turn away from the direction by which they could join the personal development of human souls. ... Man becomes the mere carrier of the force by which this logic dominates their development and leads them on as if in the tangent of the course through which they would return to the cultural development of living human beings ...' (ibid., p.43).

58. Besides the observations quoted in the text, see Simmel's remarks in 'The Metropolis and Mental Life', in *On Individuality and Social Forms, cit.*: 'The deepest problems of modern life flow from the attempt of the individual to maintain the independence and individuality of his existence against the sovereign powers of society, against the weight of the historical heritage and the external culture and technique of life' (p.324). And later on: 'The development of modern culture is characterised by the predominance of what one can call the objective spirit over the subjective ... the daily growth of the "objective" culture is followed only imperfectly and with ever greater lag by the intellectual development of the individual' (p.337).

59. Lionel Trilling, *Sincerity and Authenticity, cit.*, p.61.

60. György Lukács, *Theory of the Novel, cit.*, pp.112–17.

61. With great perspicacity Flaubert sets the magic moment of his hero in the first months of 1848, when the power void, and the stunned equilibrium between the different classes and opinions, requires 'representatives' just like Frédéric: who would certainly be elected to Parliament as a candidate of compromise between the divergent factions if, as usual, he did not hesitate so much.

62. Carl Schmitt, *Politische Romantik*, München 1925.

63. Pierre Bourdieu, 'L'invention de la vie d'artiste', *Actes de la recherche en sciences sociales*, 2, 1975.

64. I should emphasize that this, shall we say, spiritual device, has nothing bizarre or eccentric about it: just as Frédéric, in essence, is a quite average character, so his inner adventure is in no way exceptional. Even more than appealing, as I have defined it above, daydreaming is 'necessary' for modern man — it is the only way he can avoid the 'dilemma of the consumer' — and thus quickly becomes a part of his everyday life. The situation receives its ultimate expression fifty years after Flaubert, with *Ulysses*: there the complex fantasizing of stream of consciousness (with its hidden links to advertising techniques) has become universal, spontaneous, unnoticed, even banal — a perfect counterbalance to a life in which the category of *real* possibility no longer has any place. (I have discussed these developments in more detail in 'The Long Goodbye. *Ulysses* and the End of Liberal Capitalism', in *Signs Taken for Wonders, cit.*, and 'The Spell of Indecision', forthcoming.)

65. The closing-in of youth upon itself is pitilessly hammered home in the last page of *Sentimental Education*. Frédéric and Deslauriers, now old, remember an episode from their early adolescence, the visit to the bordello of the Turk: 'what with the great heat, the fear of the unknown, and even the very pleasure of seeing at one glance so many women placed at his disposal, [Frédéric] ran away; and, as Frédéric had the money, Deslauriers was obliged to follow him.' (*Sentimental Education*, III, 6.)

Already here, we may add, money is no longer the 'common whore of mankind' of Shakespeare's *Timon of Athens*, and of Marxian comment: rather than compelling us to *fulfil* desire, it pushes in the opposite direction (how to choose between 'so many women placed at his disposal'?; moreover, *why* choose?). But most important of all is Frédéric's remark concerning the episode: 'That was the best time we ever had.' These words, with which the novel ends, indicate, in their nostalgia for an experience that did *not take place*, the advent of a notion of youth — 'cowardly', Flaubert wrote to George Sand — in which the challenge of novelty has become 'fear of the unknown'. Thus there is no longer any room for growth as an irreversible break from the sheltered world of the first years of life: Frédéric, among other things, is the only protagonist of a *Bildungsroman* who returns to settle down in the home of his childhood.

    66.   Schmitt, *op. cit.*, p.228.

Chapter 4

    1.   This does not apply to George Eliot, whom I will deal with separately in the third section of the chapter. In the first two parts, I will examine the two major models of the English *Bildungsroman* (*Tom Jones* and *David Copperfield*), their 'public' and 'intimate' variants (*Waverley* and *Jane Eyre*), as well as the perverse and obstinate counter-model *Great Expectations*. I will also refer, but less often, to *Caleb Williams*, which — such is the power of conventions — is less different from the novels just mentioned than its author, in all likelihood, would have fancied.

    2.   It is symptomatic that Raymond Williams discusses the 'industrial novel' in *Culture and Society*, where he deals with the history of ideas, and neglects it in *The English Novel from Dickens to Lawrence*, which at first glance would seem the more appropriate place. His choice is totally justified, however, by the opacity with which the novel has always surrounded the world of work, and which it extended to that immediately 'collective' event — closely linked to the industrial revolution itself — which was the birth of the workers movement. I shall return to this topic at the end of the chapter.

    3.   Steerforth's death is strewn with highly implausible details (his curly hair and red cap still visible even in the middle of the storm, his joyous and foolish greeting gestures, and finally his corpse tossed upon the shore 'with his head upon his arm, as I had often seen him lie at school': *David Copperfield*, 55), but extremely effective in inducing the reader to take leave of Steerforth with the same image of him that David has refused to question. In addition, while minor and even microscopic characters in *Copperfield* have a tendency to reappear and meet with David again, the same is never granted to Mr Mell, the first victim of Steerforth's destructive arrogance. To spare David unpleasant memories, Dickens sends Mell straight to Australia, which is a very nice trip indeed.

    4.   Ariès, *op. cit.*, p.254.

    5.   Bruno Bettelheim, *The Uses of Enchantment: The Meaning and Importance of Fairy Tales*, Harmondsworth 1978, p.127.

    6.   Ibid., p.9

    7.   Ibid., p.70

    8.   On this point George Eliot's aversion for her predecessors was to be quite explicit: 'Far from being really moral is the so-called moral *dénouement*, in which rewards and punishments are distributed according to those notions of justice on which the novel-writer would have recommended that the world should be governed if he had been consulted at the creation. The emotion of satisfaction which a reader feels when the villain of the book dies of some hideous disease [Falkland, Mrs Reed, Bertha Mason], or is crushed by a railway

train [Carker in *Dombey and Son*], is no more essentially moral than the satisfaction which used to be felt in whipping culprits at the cart-tail.' ('The Morality of Wilhelm Meister', 1855, in *Essays of George Eliot*, ed. Thomas Pinney, London: Routledge and Kegan Paul 1963, p.145.)

9. Bettelheim, *op. cit.*, p.117.

10. Ibid., p.26.

11. Samuel Richardson, letter of 22-1-1750, in *Henry Fielding. The Critical Heritage*, eds. Ronald Paulson and Thomas Lockwood, London: Routledge and Kegan Paul 1969, p.215.

12. 'Thou know'st 'tis common — all that live must die'; 'Ay, madam, it is common' (*Hamlet*, I.2.72–4). On the semantic history of 'common', cfr. Raymond Williams, *Keywords*, *cit.*

13. Quoted in Alexander Welsh, *The Hero of the Waverley Novels*, New Haven and London: Yale UP 1963, pp.49–50. 'Hero', of course, besides 'doer of great deeds', can also mean the 'protagonist' of a literary work, and the word play on the 'non-heroic hero' is quite common. Think, for instance, of the first sentence of *David Copperfield*: 'Whether I shall turn out to be the hero of my own life, or whether that station will be held by anybody else... .' On this matter see Mario Praz, *The Hero in Eclipse in Victorian Fiction*, London 1956.

14. Perry Anderson, 'Origins of the Present Crisis', *New Left Review*, 23, 1964, p.33.

15. George Orwell, 'Charles Dickens', 1939, in *Collected Essays, Journalism and Letters*, eds. Sonia Orwell and Ian Angus, Harmondsworth: Penguin 1969, vol. I, pp.485, 500.

16. Perry Anderson, *Origins of the Present Crisis*, *cit.*, pp.39–40.

17. Edmund Burke, *Reflections on the Revolution in France*, *cit.*, pp.299–300.

18. Raymond Williams, *The English Novel from Dickens to Lawrence*, London: Chatto and Windus 1973, p.53.

19. Goldsmith's vicar, a candid but consequential soul, sees in coincidences the providential web without which even everyday life may fall apart: 'Nor can I go on without a reflection on those accidental meetings, which though they happen every day, seldom excite our surprise but upon some extraordinary occasion. To what a fortuitous concurrence do we not owe every pleasure and convenience of our lives! How many seeming accidents must unite before we can be clothed or fed! The peasant must be disposed to labour, the shower must fall, the wind fill the merchant's sail... .' (Oliver Goldsmith, *The Vicar of Wakefield*, 1776, London: Dent 1979, p.207.)

20. Mikhail Bakhtin, 'Discourse in the Novel', 1934–35, in *The Dialogic Imagination*, pp.301–2.

21. On this distinction see Richard Sennett, *The Fall of Public Man*, *cit.*, pp.79–82.

22. Mikhail Bakhtin, 'Discourse in the Novel' and 'Forms of Time and Chronotope in the Novel', in *The Dialogic Imagination*, *cit.*, pp.301–2 and 162.

23. Thus Burke the Implacable: 'Your legislators seem to have taken their opinions of all professions, ranks, and offices, from the declamations and buffooneries of satirists ... . By listening only to these, your leaders regard all things only on the side of their vices and faults ... but in general, those who are habitually employed in finding and displaying faults, are unqualified for the work of reformation... .' (*Reflections*, *cit.*, pp.282–3.)

24. Ibid., p.183. This passage also provides further historico-cultural reasons for the submission of 'adult' to 'childhood' wisdom, which is so typical

of the English *Bildungsroman*. In early childhood, when the competence for critical analysis has not yet reached full autonomy, all one can assimilate are prejudices. With youth — as with Kant's Enlightenment — one reaches maturity: it's the beginning of the age of reason. However, interjects Burke, the highest and ultimate reason is the rediscovery of those original prejudices. Like youth, reason is an interlude, or a bridge which leads from an unconscious to a fully aware acceptance of prejudices.

25. Ibid., p.281.

26. Mario Praz, *op. cit.*, p.19.

27. Perry Anderson, *Origins of the Present Crisis*, cit., pp.28 and 30.

28. Lionel Trilling, *Sincerity and Authenticity*, cit., pp.114–15. On the moralistic sociology implicit in the term 'villain' see pp.16, 37–8.

29. Claude Lévi-Strauss, *The Savage Mind*, London 1962, p.232.

30. The detective novel could come into its own only in England, as an extreme development of the rhetorical procedures which we are describing — fairy-tale Manichaeism, threatened 'normality', a rigidly classified social universe, the identification of 'story' and crime, a total lack of interest for the 'point of view' of the author of the violation.

31. If it were up to Captain Blifil, Tom would never reach his second birthday. He only survives because Allworthy objects that 'however guilty the parents might be, the children were certainly innocent' (*Tom Jones*, II. 2).

32. As always, *Great Expectations* overturns the dominant paradigm, replacing the undeserved punishment with an equally undeserved reward. Pip's departure for London is thus far from sorrowful, and it's noteworthy that the only character which is happy about moving is also the only one whose fate will be unhappiness.

A forced departure inspired one of Manzoni's most famous pages — the 'Addio, monti...' sequence: 'Farewell, you mountains which rise straight out of the water ... With what a melancholy tread any man must leave you who has grown up in your midst! ... Who, swept away from their most cherished habits, frustrated in their dearest hopes, have to leave the hills, to go and seek out unknown people whom they have never felt any desire to meet, without even being able to guess at a possible time for their return! Farewell, my mother's house...' (*The Betrothed*).

The number of structural analogies between the English narrative model and Manzoni's *Betrothed* is astonishing: unfortunately, I will have to limit myself here to a few brief comments in passing.

33. Dora's case exemplifies another constant of the English plot: the notion that the hero — who during his journey 'is not himself' — would do well not to bind himself to those whom fate throws in his path during his youth. This lesson is most explicit in the theme of the erotic 'double choice': Sophia/Lady Bellaston, Rosa/Flora, Rochester/St John Rivers, Agnes/Dora, Biddy/Estella. In each case the 'right' partner is always met first; then, as the plot gradually develops, the hero meets the wrong one, to whom he, or she, risks being tied for life (like Pip, as usual).

More generally, a journey on which the hero must interact as little as possible with the people he meets, turns him into a *spectator* rather than an actor in the theater of the world. In perfect agreement with a classificatory culture, learning to 'know' society means developing one's own taxonomical skills, which must work at first glance; but this 'education' has nothing to do with getting involved in meaningful interactions. The journey of youth thus degenerates into social *tourism*, all the more so in that people and places are 'spontaneously' introduced in the form of sketches or snapshots. Orwell noticed that Player's cigarette company printed several series of figurines of Dicken's characters; Scott's characters all have their own niche in the Edinburgh mausoleum, and something like that was done in a Milanese palace for the characters of *The Betrothed*.

34.   This is how Renzo Tramaglino, on the last page of *The Betrothed*, recapitulates the significance of his many travels: "'I've learned not to get mixed up in riots ... . I've learned not to preach at street corners; I've learned not to raise my elbow too often. I've learned not to hold door knockers in my hand too long when there are people around who jump to conclusions; I've learned not to tie bells on my ankles without thinking what it might lead to.'" (Manzoni, *op. cit.*, p.720.)

If only Renzo had learned *to do* something, in addition to 'not' doing. For Manzoni too, by the way, the place where one is least 'himself' and comes closest to ruin is the metropolis, Milan.

35.   Mikhail Bakhtin, 'Forms of Time and Chronotope in the Novel', in *The Dialogic Imagination*, *cit.*, pp.252, 254, 256.

36.   Ibid., p.90.

37.   Ibid., p.100.

38.   Ross H. Dabney, *Love and Property in the Novels of Dickens*, Berkeley and Los Angeles: University of California Press 1967, pp.137–8.

39.   See Freud's famous article *The Family Romance of Neurotics*, written in 1908.

40.   Christopher Hill, *Intellectual Origins of the English Revolution*, 1965, London: Panther 1966, p.257.

41.   Burke, *Reflections*, *cit.*, pp.117–18.

42.   This contractualistic principle, which was already at work in the proceedings against Charles I, became even more explicit in the Act which forced, *de facto*, James II to abdicate: 'That King James the second, having endeavoured to *subvert the constitution* of the kingdom, by breaking the *original contract* between king and people, and by the advice of jesuits, and other wicked persons, having violated the *fundamental laws*, and *having withdrawn himself out of the kingdom*, hath *abdicated* the government, and the throne is thereby *vacant*' (quoted from Burke's *Reflections*, p.122 n.).

I wouldn't want to go too far, but forcing a king to abdicate, and replacing him with another king, is not very different from disowning a father in favour of an uncle. In both instances one bows to a markedly hierarchical authority, but retains the 'constitutional' right to oust villains and evil-doers.

43.   Between 1640 and 1660 religious faith was clearly far more important; but already by 1688 'contract' had become the political keyword, and as time went by the *forma mentis* of revolutionary puritanism became increasingly remote, while natural right philosophy became a sort of national ideology. We should therefore say that the juridical legitimation of the revolution was more the work of its heirs than of its protagonists: a specification which does not invalidate our analysis of eighteenth and nineteenth-century culture. The law is also, tendentially at least, much more universalistic and egalitarian than protestant predestination, and this must have influenced the opposite historical fortune of these two ideologies.

44.   Edward P. Thompson, *Whigs and Hunters, 1975*, Harmondsworth 1977 pp.262–3.

45.   See *Tom Jones*, I.6–7, II.6, III.4, and so on until XVIII.12: "'I think, Mr Jones," said she, "I may almost depend on your own justice, and leave it to

yourself to pass sentence on your conduct." — "Alas! madam," answered he, "it is mercy, and not justice, which I implore at your hands. Justice I know must condemn me…".'

46. John Locke, *The Second Treatise*, 1689, in *Two Treatises on Government*, ed. Peter Laslett, New York and London: Signet 1965, par. 22.

47. It cannot be by chance that in English these two terms join together logical evidence, legal definition and moral duty in a much more conspicuous way than in any other language.

48. S.F.C. Milsom, *Historical Foundations of the Common Law*, London: Butterworths 1981, p.89.

49. Developments in narrative theory have shown that the *fabula/sujet* distinction, as it defines the latter only through negation (as a 'deviation' from the first), or tautology (the *sujet* is the narrative arrangement of events actualized by the text) does not command the theoretical solidity ascribed to it by the Formalists, and especially by Sklovski. I do believe however that the distinction retains a 'local' validity for those narrative cultures which are prone to contrast 'artificial' and 'natural', 'appearance' and 'reality', 'lies' and 'truth'. This is not the case, as we have seen, with the French novel — but it is definitely so with English narrative, which enjoys an otherwise inexplicable centrality in Sklovski's theoretical writings. The instances in which the *fabula/sujet* distinction becomes particularly evident are, on the one hand, detective fiction (to which he devotes two long essays of his *Theory of Prose*, focusing on Dickens and Doyle), and on the other that novel with nothing but *sujet* which is *Tristram Shandy*. (Sterne's novel — Sklovski's dearest hobby horse — could have arisen only in a narrative culture obsessed with the pre-eminence of the *fabula*; someday, it will be fascinating to read it as the mirror-image of the English *Bildungsroman*.)

50. Lausberg, *op. cit.*, pp.27–8 (paragraph 47). Lausberg continues: 'The *ordo naturalis* has the effect of medium clarity and medium credibility, but it risks creating uniformity and boredom.'

To this *fabula ante litteram* classical rhetoric contrasts, *nihil sub sole novum*, the artistic mutation of the normal condition which is called *ordo artificialis* or *figura*: 'Figures are, for example, the succession of events which does not correspond to the historic unfolding of events.' (Blifil, if one thinks about it, is simply putting this precept into practice all the time.)

51. J.H. Baker, *An Introduction to English Legal History*, London: Butterworths 1979, p.67.

52. This desire for justice pervades even the 'happy ending', when the innocent hero, at first mercilessly sentenced, is granted the right to have time stop and turn back on itself, so that the consequences of the initial error may be annulled, and he may receive the compensation due to him. The hero is in short granted the right to that *court of appeal* to which the last book of *Tom Jones* is almost entirely devoted. 'People have come to regard the "right to appeal"' — writes Baker — 'as an essential requirement of natural justice, and as long ago as 1723 it was said to be "the glory and happiness of our excellent constitution, that to prevent any injustice no man is concluded by the first judgment; but if he apprehends himself to be aggrieved he has another court to which he can resort for relief".' (*An Introduction to English Legal History*, cit., p.116.) The establishment of the right to appeal followed a very uneven course, but it took place in England much earlier than elsewhere and, for all that a layman can make of it, with much more satisfactory (or less unsatisfactory) results.

53. Edward P. Thompson, *Whigs and Hunters*, *cit.*, pp.262–3. All of Caleb Williams's misadventures arise from his being literally possessed by the sense of justice described by Thompson, which overrides even his will and forces him ('I could not stop myself') into all sorts of imprudent acts, and even minor offences, so that a case 'closed' many years earlier will be re-opened and settled in accordance with justice.

54. Here *The Betrothed* follows a totally different path. In an Italy ringing with *grida* and proclamations, but without laws, and where lawyers speak in Latin, for justice to triumph in a matter not very different from the one narrated in *Tom Jones*, we need a war, a plague, a holocaust, and a miraculous conversion. The work of Providence, not of the State, these events may appeal to religious beliefs, not to our faith in earthly justice.

55. Fairy-tale-like structures are actually often central in the genesis of modern national cultures: melodrama and *feuilleton* in France, opera in Italy, much of the frontier literature in America, actual fairy-tales in Germany. The peculiarity of the English development lies rather in its unsuccessful polarization into 'high' and 'low' literature, testified by the abundance of 'synthetic' figures such as Defoe, Richardson, Fielding, Scott and Dickens, and by the extreme weakness of 'decadent', and later avant-garde culture in England. The main reason for this anomaly is probably to be found once again in the precocious stability of the English socio-political order, which made for a much more gradual growth of the reading public than elsewhere: never exposed to sudden shocks, the narrative 'canon' managed to incorporate little by little new symbolic demands within its tried and tested structures.

56. Alan Mintz, *George Eliot and the Novel of Vocation*, Cambridge, Mass. and London: Harvard UP 1978, p.114.

57. Max Weber, 'Science as a Vocation', in *From Max Weber: Essays in Sociology* (eds. H. H. Gerth and C. Wright Mills), London 1948, p.137.

58. 'The country house, as the image of true civilization and social cultivation, has sunk deeply into the national soul. The modern British town is merely the obverse of this, in its meaninglessness. Culturally, as an artefact of real civilization, it has never existed, because civilization went on elsewhere, in the residences of the territorial aristocracy and gentry.' (Tom Nairn, 'The British Political Elite', *New Left Review*, 23, 1964, p.22.)

59. Alan Mintz, *George Eliot and the Novel of Vocation*, *cit.*, p.101.

60. Sigmund Freud, *Jokes and their relation to the unconscious*, 1905, The Standard Edition, The Hogarth Press, London 1960, vol. VIII, p.233.

61. Ibid., p.234.

62. Ibid., p.233.

63. Frank R. Leavis, *The Great Tradition*, 1948, London: Chatto and Windus 1962, p.91.

64. 'There is nothing sentimental in George Eliot's vision of human mediocrity and "platitude", but she sees in them matters for compassion, and her dealings with them are assertions of human dignity. To be able to assert human dignity in this way is greatness: the contrast with Flaubert is worth pondering' (*ivi*, p.60).

65. 'Whereas the idiom of the novelist in Jane Austen was quite closely connected with the idiom of the characters, in George Eliot a disconnection is the most evident fact.' (Raymond Williams, *The English Novel from Dickens to Lawrence*, *cit.*, p.79.)

66. *Jokes and their relation to the unconscious*, *cit.*, p.231.

67. Gwendolen Harleth, without knowing exactly why, acts as if Daniel

should be the 'narrator' of her life: she tells him everything (including those details which the 'official' narrator had omitted), and continually asks him to comment on her behaviour.

68. Cited by Walter E. Houghton in *The Victorian Frame of Mind*, New Haven: Yale UP 1957, p.18.

69. Incidentally: the marriage of Daniel and Mirah implies a painful loss (of Mirah herself) for Hans Meyrick, who loves her, and who is Daniel's best, or rather only friend. But since Mirah would never marry anyone who was not Jewish, and Hans' feelings (so Daniel says) are superficial and ephemeral, this turn of fortune has nothing ugly about it.

70. 'Where else is there a nation of whom it may be as truly said that their religion and law and moral life mingled as the stream of blood in the heart and made one growth? ... Community was felt before it was called good.'

Appendix

1. The idea that youth would 'naturally' develop into adulthood had apparently become so unconvincing that Joyce inverted Goethe's trajectory, abandoning the *Bildungsroman* for the earlier form of the *Künstlerroman* (the artist's novel), where growth and independence are the prerogatives of an exceptionally gifted minority. As a consequence, the idea of 'vocation', which the nineteenth century had brought down to bourgeois earth, reacquires the metaphysical halo of Stephen's final words ('Welcome, O life! I go to encounter for the millionth time the reality of experience, and to forge in the smithy of my soul the uncreated conscience of my race').

2. Karl accepts an invitation to dinner from his uncle's best friend. At midnight, a letter reaches him: 'Beloved nephew! You have resolved tonight, against my will, to leave me: be therefore constant in your resolution all life long. Only thus yours will be a manly, mature decision.' As a consequence, Karl is once more banished from his family.

Index

Adorno, T. W., 12n, 61–2, 68, 138, 143–4, 152
Aeschylus, 3, 125
Alain-Fournier, Henri, 231
Althusser, Louis, 68
Anderson, Perry, 191, 193n, 198, 207
Arendt, Hannah, 119n
Ariès, Philippe, 38, 46n, 184
Auerbach, Erich, 15, 158
Austen, Jane, vi, 12, 22–3, 26–7, 37–8, 42, 45–7, 49, 51, 53–4, 56–7, 59–65, 68–70, 72, 76, 85–6, 92, 106, 115, 118, 135, 146, 149n, 195, 214, 231, 235

Baioni, Giuliano, 64n
Baker, J.H., 212
Bakhtin, Mikhail, vii, xiii, 12n, 15, 49n, 96–8, 122–3, 136, 145n, 150–2, 194, 196, 204.
Balzac, Honoré de, vi, viii, x–xii, 7–9, 11n, 35, 64, 84, 86, 91–2, 94, 95n, 96, 98–9, 102, 104–7, 120, 129–69, 175, 177, 185, 190–1, 199, 200, 208, 220, 222, 235
Barthes, Roland, 96, 122–3, 142, 156, 158n, 160, 168n, 233
Baudelaire, Charles, 238, 242
Baudrillard, Jean, 41
Benjamin, Walter, 6, 119, 124, 238, 242
Bentham, Jeremy, 81, 137
Benveniste, Emile, 91n, 123
Bergson, Henri, 193
Berman, Marshall, 144n, 145n
Bersani, Leo, 166
Bettelheim, Bruno, 186, 187n, 189
Blumenberg, Hans, xiii
Bourdieu, Pierre, 176
Braudel, Fernand, 142, 143n
Brontë, Charlotte, 11, 181n, 182–90, 192, 200–3, 205, 209, 211
Brontë, Emily, 126, 202
Brooks, Peter, 49n, 138n
Büchner, Georg, 77
Burke, Edmund, 59n, 193, 197–9, 206, 207n
Burkhardt, Jakob, 139–42, 158, 160, 191
Byron, George Gordon, 86, 100

Cases, Cesare, 113n

Cassirer, Ernst, 5
Chatman, Seymour, 56n, 91n, 156, 159n, 233
Christie, Agatha, 210
Coke, Edward, 206
Coleridge, S.T., 61–2
Conan Doyle, A., 200, 210
Conrad, Joseph, 121, 169n, 202, 229, 232, 235, 238, 243
Constant, Benjamin, viii, 79, 101
Culler, Jonathan, 61n

Dabney, Ross H., 205
Dante, Alighieri, 3, 236
Danton, Georges Jacques, 80
Darwin, Charles, 10, 148
Defoe, Daniel, 26, 52n, 124, 147, 209, 213n
della Volpe, xi
De Maistre, Joseph, 6
Descamps, Marc-Alain, 134n
Dickens, Charles, viii, x, 9, 11, 86, 149n, 157, 181–4, 186, 190–5, 198–204, 208–9, 213, 221
Diderot, Denis, 172, 176, 196
Dilthey, Wilhelm, 15, 18
Dostoevsky, Fyodor, 3n, 12n, 66, 136, 200
Dupréel, 199

Eagleton, Terry, 68
Elias, Norbert, 85n, 239
Eliot, George, vi, viii, x, 7–9, 11–2, 38, 181n, 186n, 195, 214–28, 235
Eliot, T. S., 222
Engels, Friedrich, 145n
Erikson, Erik, 107

Fielding, Henry, 147, 181–6, 189–90, 192–5, 198–204, 208–13, 221
Fievée, 104
Flaubert, Gustave, viii, 7–9, 11–2, 23, 80, 88, 152, 154, 156–7, 164–9, 172–9, 208, 220, 224–5, 235, 242
Fontane, Theodor, 23
Fortini, Franco, 94n
Foucault, Michel, 193
Franklin, Benjamin, 104n
Frege, Gottlob, 70n

Printed in the United States
by Baker & Taylor Publisher Services